Doing Cultural Theory

Doing Cultural Theory

David Walton

Los Angeles | London | New Delhi
Singapore | Washington DC

First published 2012

Figure 3.1 © Panzani Freres
Figure 3.2 © Lagardère
Figure 14.1 © Hans Haacke/Artists Rights Society
Figure 14.2 © Hans Haacke/Artists Rights Society
Figure 15.1 © Bas Beentjes/Greenpeace

This book has been written as part of a research project sponsored by the Fundación Séneca (number 15397/PHCS/10).

SAGE Publications Ltd
1 Oliver's Yard
55 City Road
London EC1Y 1SP

SAGE Publications Inc.
2455 Teller Road
Thousand Oaks, California 91320

SAGE Publications India Pvt Ltd
B 1/I 1 Mohan Cooperative Industrial Area
Mathura Road
New Delhi 110 044

SAGE Publications Asia-Pacific Pte Ltd
3 Chruch Street
#10–04 Samsung Hub
Singapore 049483

Library of Congress Control Number: 2011935160

British Library Cataloguing in Publication data

A catalogue record for this book is available from the British Library

ISBN 978-0-85702-484-8
ISBN 978-0-85702-485-5 (pbk)

Typeset by C&M (P) Ltd, Chennai, India
Printed and bound by CPI Group (UK) Ltd, Croydon, CR0 4YY
Printed on paper from sustainable resources

Contents

Contents

Contents

Contents

Contents

List of Figures and Table

Acknowledgements

While this book carries my name, books are always, in varying degrees, collaborative efforts and I would like to offer my thanks to a number of colleagues and friends.

Thanks go to Patricia Bickers from *Art Monthly* for contacting Hans Haacke on my behalf and to Hans Haacke himself for giving me permission to use his photos of his 'MetroMobilitan' installation (Figures 14.1 and 14.2). Also, thanks go to Bas Beentjes for permission to use his E$$O photo (Figure 15.1) and to John Harris who was very generous in terms of sending me valuable feedback on the photo he took of Lesley Boulton at the 'Battle of Orgreave'.

I would also like to thank the anonymous readers at SAGE for their valuable comments. I did not always agree with the points they made but they undoubtedly helped me to refine my ideas and reconsider a number of features. Thanks must go to Elizabeth Ezra who generously offered to read the opening chapters at a very early stage. Her comments, advice and encouragement have been very important in terms of giving me the energy to complete the book. Nuria Urzaiz not only gave me encouragement but kindly offered to give very detailed feedback on the first drafts of a number of chapters from the point of view of the kind of reader I was aiming at. Many thanks, too, to Verónica Morales who offered me her support by reading some of the later drafts of the final chapters. My biggest debt is to Mila Steele, my editor at SAGE, for her very constructive criticism, encouragement, support and advice. Mila helped me to perfect the overall structure and content, and has been there at every stage of the book's development. I would also like to thank Sarah-Jayne Boyd (Mila's assistant) for her advice and help and efficiency, especially in the final stages of completing the book.

Finally, I would like to recognize the support and encouragement of my family and my many friends and colleagues who have helped in a million small (and not so small) ways – sometimes without knowing it. Special thanks go to Cathy Staveley, Liz Murphy, María Reyes, Juan Antonio Suárez, María González, Asensio López, Raquel González and Andy Sotiriou and, last but not least, Dan Walter. Without them the writing of this book would have been a much more arduous task. As it is, the process has been thoroughly enjoyable. Finally, thanks must go to my students who have often helped me to refine my ideas by showing what works and, often, what does not.

Introduction

How to Use this Book

Who is this book written for?

You may have come across terms like semiological systems, signification, the problematic, symptomatic reading, deconstruction, logocentrism, the big Other, anti-essentialism and the postmodern subject, but not have been sure about what they mean or how they might be used in practice. If this is the case this book should be able to help you. This book, then, is aimed at readers who already have some knowledge of cultural studies but who want to get a firmer grasp of the way cultural theory relates to practice. However, those who have little or no knowledge of cultural analysis, but who feel they have the academic experience and confidence to tackle cultural theory and practice at a higher level, will also find it useful. With this in mind, the first chapter is designed to take account of different possible readerships. On the one hand, it helps to show how the theories and ideas explained and illustrated in this book fit into a larger historical picture. On the other hand, it can serve as valuable revision for those readers who are already familiar with the area or a basic introduction for those with no previous knowledge.

General aims and approach of this book

This book can be seen as akin to the viaduct – a conduit which carries something or someone from one place to another (a kind of 'theory-duct'). One aim of this book is to describe the different theories, however complex, in an accessible style. However, I have not avoided the use of complex terms and have tried to describe them as clearly as possible in relation to how they relate to various forms of cultural analysis. This raises the problem of up to what point a technical vocabulary is necessary. As Lawrence Grossberg has said, while scientists who describe the physical world are expected 'to use languages not available to most people', those who explore social reality are often expected to write so that anyone can understand. Yet 'human reality' is not necessarily any less complex than the world of subatomic particles. Thus, 'sometimes we need complex and nonobvious explanations of what's going on' (1992: 30–31). We can try to explain quantum mechanics or computer science in ordinary terms but to get to the finer subtleties it is more often than not necessary to learn specific concepts and ways of thinking.

The specialized vocabulary introduced in this book, then, is not an elitist attempt to put ourselves above others but part of an effort to immerse ourselves in the language of a particular discipline. The understanding of theory is constantly explained with an eye to how it may function in practice. In this way its application is a little like a voyage of discovery, where the world is experienced in new and perhaps surprising ways through the assimilation, adaptation and refinement of concepts previously unknown (or vague) to us. The general approach adopted in this book assumes that interpretation and analysis are always a product of, and dependent on, very particular shaping strategies, something which makes the critic a maker or 'fashioner'. One of the other main aims of the book, then, is to help the reader to become articulate in these theoretical 'languages'.

I would describe most of the theories introduced in this book as 'radical' in the sense that most of them have been used to challenge fixed ideas and have often been used in efforts to change the world for the better. Marx's point that philosophers 'have only interpreted the world, in various ways' but the point is 'to change it' (Marx, 1845/1976: 65) can be seen as one of the most important ethical tenets underpinning much cultural studies. I have tried to reflect something of this ethical concern (and utopian project) in the various theories I have introduced, regardless of how they have been labelled. Finally, this book has been written in the belief that learning to understand theory (and putting it into practice) may be challenging but it does not have to be a chore and that cultural studies can be a bold, stimulating and even exciting enterprise.

Strategies for using this book

As indicated above, the opening chapter will familiarize the reader with something of the history of the cultural studies tradition and reflect on key movements, definitions and strategies. Readers who are already familiar with definitions of culture and the (mainly British) cultural studies tradition (including the work of Matthew Arnold, the Leavises, the Frankfurt School, the 'culturalist' writers like Hoggart, Thompson and Williams, and the early work of the Birmingham Centre for Contemporary Cultural Studies) can skim (or even skip) this chapter. Readers who want to begin experimenting with concepts without any preamble can start with the chapters dedicated to structuralism. Ideally, the chapters should be read chronologically because I introduce important concepts in the early chapters which I develop and refine later on in the book. Readers who read systematically will realize that a number of different thematic threads are developed which provide narrative strands which weave in and out of particular chapters to provide multiple points of comparison, cohesion and a sense of continuity and development. Of course, this does not preclude more creative approaches where readers can dip into the chapters that most interest them.

What can I realistically expect from a careful reading of this book?

A careful reading of this book should help to provide a detailed knowledge of some of the key theoretical trends that have shaped much thinking and interpretation within cultural studies. It should also help readers to develop their interpretive skills and knowledge because many of the concepts are not only described and explained but illustrated with practical examples. Where possible, advice has been given on further practice to aid interpretive independence – the main idea of the book being to help readers get to that 'other place' of the specialist.

What are the chief pedagogical features of this book?

- Each chapter begins with an explanation of its content, the main learning goals and a list of the key concepts that will be explained and illustrated.
- All key concepts are introduced in bold type to help readers navigate through the chapters.
- Regular help files, practice sections and summaries are introduced to consolidate learning and aid practice.
- Ideas are often clarified with reference to examples drawn from the world of popular culture (although not exclusively) and there are some playful, creative sections designed to aid further understanding of complex ideas (for example, in one chapter the idea of postmodernism is expressed in both the form and the content of the section).
- The chapters progress in terms of difficulty so readers can build on their knowledge of previous examples.
- Theories and individual concepts are always related to the ways they may help to elucidate various forms of culture.
- Each chapter is concluded with a brief summary of the main points and followed by sections on further reading.
- There is a full glossary of key terms at the end of the book to help in the assimilation of the material.

The organization of chapters and basic content

Following a brief introduction to (British) cultural studies the content can be described as going from structuralism and poststructuralism to postmodernism and beyond. This strategy encompasses the major theorists and includes approaches which have been, and continue to be, of interest to cultural studies scholars concerned with questions of things like gender, class, sexuality, race/ethnicity, ideology, identity politics, post-colonialism, discourse, popular culture, history, media, consumerism, commodification, globalization, new social movements and neoliberalism.

The 'beyond' mentioned above describes the content of the last two chapters which consider ways that cultural analysis can complement or supersede approaches focused on the dominant themes developed within structuralism, poststructuralism and postmodernism. In fact, one of the ways this book attempts to depart from most books dedicated to theory and practice in cultural studies is in the way it helps readers to map out their place within the multinational, corporate world of late capitalism. As stated above, Chapter 1 will go into more detail about the structure of the book and how it relates to general trends within (mainly British) cultural studies.

1

Introducing Cultural Studies

A Brief Contextual History

Learning goals

- To understand the difficulty of defining the term 'culture' and appreciate the multi-disciplinary and complex character of cultural studies.
- To get a sense of the way cultural studies (using the British context) has been developed and consolidated in relation to the themes established by what have become a number of key writers and approaches.
- To see the way the different theories introduced and illustrated in this book reflect developing interests within cultural studies.

Concepts

The key concepts introduced in this chapter are: cultural studies, culture, the culture and civilization tradition, minority culture, mass culture, popular culture, the Frankfurt School, the culture industry, 'culturalism', the uses of literacy, the making of the English working class, culture as a whole way of life, youth subcultures, hegemony and organic intellectuals.

Introduction

These opening sections reflect on how the book fits into the (mainly British) cultural studies tradition, providing a brief 'refresher course' for readers who are familiar with cultural studies and some vital contextualization (or a 'kick start') for those who are relatively new to the area. In very general terms I shall show how contemporary cultural analysis has grown out of (and beyond) approaches which tended to privilege 'high' culture over 'popular' or mass forms and indicate how the writers and theories relate to the general structure of the present book.

Cultural studies?

I want to begin this chapter with a number of questions. One, having sat down to write a book about theory and practice in cultural studies, can I say, beyond all doubt, that I know what culture is? Two, am I so sure about what cultural studies is that I can just start using it, without needing to reflect on it in any way? The answer to these questions is 'yes and no'. The term 'culture' can be made to have specific, intelligible meanings and there are departments of cultural studies with common ways of understanding and analysing 'culture', so where are the problems?

The problems reside in the fact that the practitioners who think of them-selves as working in cultural studies are not necessarily in agreement about the precise definition of culture or about exactly what constitutes the area in which they are working. I have just referred to cultural studies as 'an area'; however (as I have suggested elsewhere, Walton, 2008: 291), it might be more effective to see it as a contested *space* in which a very diverse set of analyti-cal practices take place. Cultural studies exists within educational institutions in many parts of the world and this means that what it 'is' is a product of a constant negotiation that takes place in the lecture room, in conference halls and publications. This means that books recommended for cultural studies will often be aimed at other areas like English Studies, Geography, Sociology, Social Studies, Communication, Film and Media Studies (and vice versa). This is because these areas share both thematic and theoretical legacies and these are all areas in which the meanings of culture are negotiated and deployed.

As Grossberg, Nelson and Treichler have observed, cultural studies has no particular methodology and 'draws from whatever fields are necessary to produce the knowledge required for a particular project' and is sometimes 'agressively anti-disciplinary'. Furthermore, it is 'pragmatic, strategic and self-reflexive' (1992: 2). These factors complicate the identity of cultural studies, even while they create certain dominant ways of thinking about and under-standing culture and producing knowledge about it. This is why John Frow has argued that even though cultural studies exists 'in a state of productive uncer-tainty about its status as a discipline' there has been sufficient institutional consolidation of the area for practitioners to identify themselves with one another (1995: 7). To sum this up we might say that cultural studies did not pre-exist theory and practice – it is a product of them (and one of the inten-tions of this book is to offer an idea of what some of the key theories entail).

Despite the consolidation that Frow mentions, no book can place itself outside national borders and this volume cannot escape its geographical location or its social and intellectual allegiances (written by someone brought up in Britain, but who lives and works in Spain, and has been influenced by North American and other English-speaking cultures, but also by theories developed in other parts of the world). This means that this book comes from a broadly British cultural studies' perspective, and this needs to be kept in mind. As Graeme Turner (a key figure in Australian cultural studies) has observed, alternative traditions of cultural studies tend to have to announce themselves as such, something which suggests a certain Anglo-centric tendency in English/British cultural studies (Turner, 1992: 642).

However, while accepting Turner's point I would argue that there is a certain dialectical tension between the local and the general. For example, when John Frow and Meagan Morris wrote their introduction to *Australian Cultural Studies* (1993) they carefully defined culture within the context of the country in which they were writing. They claimed, for example, that 'culture' can be thought of as not only intimately connected to work and its organization but 'with relations of power and gender in the workplace and the home; with the pleasures and the pressures of consumption; with the complex relations of class and kith and kin through which a sense of self is formed; and with the fantasies and desires through which social relations are carried and actively shaped'. Drawing on the work of Raymond Williams (see below), Frow and Morris suggest that 'culture' is a term that can define the 'whole way of life' of a social group as it is structured by forms of representation and power. Thus, it is not associated with efforts to claim for oneself social distinction and 'good' taste (see the section 'The Culture and Civilization Tradition' below). Within cultural studies it is 'a network of representations – texts, images, talk, codes of behaviour, and the narrative structures organizing these – which shapes every aspect of social life' (viii).

However, within this carefully localized definition something very interesting happens because this may be seen as a very good starting point for understanding cultural studies in a more general way. Thus, while we have to attend to the particularities of local cultures and recognize that what counts as cultural studies may differ from one geographical location to the next (and even be the object of differences within the same country or institution), there are (as Frow suggested) common (even dominant) approaches which enable some meaningful dialogue to take place between practitioners operating in different parts of the world.

It is important, then, to stress that the contextualizing material in this chapter is drawn (mainly) from the narrow, if highly influential, British cultural studies tradition. This narrative strategy has been adopted as a kind of shorthand to give *an idea* of how different theories have developed in relation to one another. But (to practise the self-reflexivity mentioned above) this shorthand has to be treated in a self-conscious and critical way. As Andrew Tudor has written, just like tribal societies, emergent disciplines are drawn to myths of origin, where stories 'stabilize otherwise recalcitrant histories by identifying founding figures' (1999: 19). Thus, the thumbnail sketch I offer below (with its founding and 'semi-founding' figures) must not be mistaken for some kind of seamless, trouble-free history of cultural studies: it is a convenience to give a *sense* of the area. It is partial and self-consciously metonymic: it is a part that stands for the whole but it is offered with the proviso that we should not confuse England with Britain, or British cultural studies with cultural studies as it is practised in the rest of the world (see Morley, 1992: 2–3; Turner, 1992: 640f.; Jordan, 2002: 147f.).

Having said this, the theories discussed in this and the following chapters have been drawn from different critics from many parts of the world and no one tradition of cultural studies can lay special claim to them. The theories I introduce and demonstrate make up the components of a kind of all-purpose toolbox, to be used, questioned, refined or discarded according to the work they are being required to perform. Furthermore, all the approaches I discuss have had a particularly important influence in cultural studies as a whole and I would argue that familiarity with them is to make oneself a member of a cultural studies 'interpretive community' (Fish, 1980). The hope is that this book will help toward realizing that goal.

Of course, like any writer, I have had to take decisions about what aspects of an approach to include or exclude, what to emphasize or leave in the margins, and make choices about how to structure and interpret the concepts and approaches. Even my thumbnail sketch of founding figures in the British cultural studies tradition may be questioned. Chris Jenks has pointed out that there are many neglected antecedents to British cultural studies in the shape of writers like Charles Dickens, George Orwell and Jack London (to name only a few) (Jenks, 1993: 156–157). Many more names might be added, particularly women writers who could be said to be 'founding mothers' like Mary Wollstonecraft, George Eliot and, as I have argued elsewhere (Walton, 2008), Virginia Woolf (to choose only three women from three centuries of possibilities).

Culture?

If this book cannot hope to encompass the full extent of cultural studies, then neither can it exhaust the possibilities for the definition of **culture**, which are enormous – many books having been written about the institutional fortunes of the concept (see particularly Jenks, 1993; Tudor; 1999; Barker, 2000; Hartley, 2003; Turner, 2003). Approaches associated with fully institutionalized cultural studies do not start with a *particular* or narrow definition of culture but are generally interested in an exceptionally broad range of cultural products and practices. If, as will be seen below, this has not always been the case, there is now wide agreement with Raymond Williams's observation that culture 'is one of the two or three most complicated words in the English language'. Despite this complexity, Williams helped his readers get some kind of grip on the word by tracing its etymology back to the idea of cultivating crops or rearing animals. This provided the basis for its metaphorical use from around the sixteenth century to signify 'a process of human development', including the cultivation of refined behaviour, the mind and society in general (1983a: 87f.). This is often the starting point for modern definitions.

The basic notion of culture that commonly informs dictionary definitions reflects this etymology and often draws on Edward Burnett Tylor's anthropological view of culture as 'that complex whole which includes knowledge, belief, art, morals, law, custom, and any other capabilities and habits' acquired by members of a given society (Tylor, 1871/1958: 1). This complex whole (so important to Williams's approach) also includes ideas, values and the shared traditions that comprise the common bases of social (inter)action which are transmitted, reinforced, refined or replaced by members of a group. However, while these lists of possibilities are very useful at a more general and abstract level, any attempt to limit the definition at the level of particular objects of analysis is futile because as the world changes new possibilities (or domains of interest) for the understanding of cultures are constantly appearing.

For example, when Grossberg, Nelson and Treichler compiled a cultural studies' reader in 1992 they mapped the area by listing some of its major categories, which included: gender, sexuality, nationhood and national identity, colonialism and post-colonialism, race and ethnicity, popular culture, identity politics, cultural institutions and global culture. They concluded by saying that cultural studies 'can only partially and uneasily be identified by such domains of interest, since no list can constrain the topics cultural studies may address in the future' (Grossberg et al., 1992: 1). Of course, since 1992 much has changed and the domains of interest have expanded greatly and new areas of interest present a challenge to contemporary ways of defining and thinking about culture. Not only this, but new theories are constantly being developed and tested to try to do justice to these new phenomena.

This means that cultural analysis has to keep itself open to new possibilities and approaches. In order to show one of the ways in which cultural studies has worked towards this position I shall now review a series of writers who comprise some of the key figures of Tudor's founding myth of cultural studies. I shall begin with the idea of culture wedded to the notion of civilization in order to understand how cultural studies (at least in the British context) could be said to have been born out of an antagonistic struggle against certain narrow ways of conceiving the cultural terrain. The first approach I will discuss is what is known as the 'culture and civilization tradition'.

The culture and civilization tradition: Matthew Arnold and the Leavises

The **culture and civilization tradition** can be seen to be reflected by the Victorian writer Matthew Arnold, and later by F. R. and Queenie Leavis (who began to have an influence on English Studies in the years between the First and Second World Wars). What tends to unite them (despite the historical distance that separated them) is their writing against what they believed were the worst excesses of the Industrial Revolution and their belief that great cultural traditions could, at least to some degree, counterbalance these effects and provide a way forward for society. The title of one of Arnold's most important books, *Culture and Anarchy* (1869/1970), is illustrative of this approach. In this book Arnold pitted his idea of culture against those anarchistic forces that threatened what he believed were the very bases of civilized life.

Arnold coined the term 'sweetness and light' to describe the essence of culture, which he associated with the 'moral and social passion for doing good' (1869/1970: 205) and the 'endless growth in wisdom and beauty'. This was dependent on making 'the best that has been thought and known in the world current everywhere' (226) and included the idea of the disinterested pursuit of knowledge and the broadening of judgement through reading, observing and thinking (226). What makes this so important is linked to Arnold's belief that the pursuit of perfection was about the cultivation of the inner self, which involved the disavowal of 'external' forms of culture that satisfied base desires associated with material possessions, unhindered competition and the amassing of huge industrial fortunes.

However, while believing in the necessity of educating all members of society, if the ideals of his version of culture were to prevail it was necessary to rely on a few enlightened minds. The idea of culture being defined in this way has been of great interest to cultural critics because it restricts the notion to what is associated with 'high' or exclusive forms of culture chosen by a self-appointed social elite. But this model has attracted much criticism because of Arnold's conception, and the social basis, of 'anarchy'. This is because, while criticizing the shortcomings of all classes, Arnold was particularly hard on those he named the 'populace', complaining that by the 1860s the common people had lost their 'strong feudal habits of subordination and deference' and had come out of their poverty and squalor to assert themselves by demanding social and political rights, 'marching', 'meeting' and 'bawling' where they liked (231 and 254).

Thus, Arnold was against working-class demands for rights and equalities, which he saw as creating social unrest and thereby threatening anarchy. Consequently, Arnold embraced the power of the state that was to guarantee 'right reason' over personal liberty, and which would effectively smother popular political movements and disturbances through 'the principle of authority' (236). For this reason Arnold's notion of culture is not only linked to elitist attempts to confine it to the narrow tastes and interests of a self-elected minority but to reactionary anti-democratic thinking that actively resists political reforms.

The inheritance of Arnold's ideas about culture can be detected in the work of F. R. and Queenie Leavis who were instrumental in helping to establish the importance of English Studies at Cambridge University in the years following the First World War (see Inglis, 1993; Strinati, 1995; Storey, 2009a). Their emphasis on the cultural importance of establishing canons of great literature, the need for developing the critical tools necessary for an adequate analysis of it, and the belief in the positive transformative role of high literary culture place them firmly in the Arnoldian culture and civilization tradition. The affinity between their work and Arnold's is also brought out by F. R. Leavis and Denys Thompson's insistence on the importance of the minority to preserve 'the finest human experience of the past' in order to maintain the 'implicit standards that order the finer living of an age' (Leavis and Thompson, 1933/1977: 5). Again, this maintenance of cultural standards was something of a gladiatorial task carried out against what they saw as the debilitating effects of modernity.

For these writers part of the task of teaching English Literature involved the training of 'critical awareness' that would teach students to develop informed judgements and discriminate between great literary works (**minority culture**) and the trivial, debased and dehumanizing products of **mass culture**. The problem for the Leavises was that mass culture (or **popular culture** like popular fiction, music and films imported from North America) constantly appealed to the lowest common denominator and stunted the development and possibilities of consumers. Furthermore, the training of critical awareness was also necessary because the effects of popular forms of culture, including the popular press and advertising, were debasing not only the language but the emotions of those who consumed them (1933/1977: 5f.).

This explained and justified the importance of literary education, which was to train students to recognize these tendencies and consequences while broadening their minds and refine their sensibilities through the appreciation of great literary works. Again, cultural critics have questioned this reductive view of culture with its simplistic understanding of the habits of consumers while challenging the legitimacy of these self-elected arbiters of taste and morality, even if they have sometimes shared some of the Leavis circle's concerns about the effects of industrial capitalism (Mulhern, 1979).

However, while this narrow definition of culture can be challenged as reactionary and elitist (Turner, 2003: 35), the Leavisite approach also encouraged close (detailed) readings not only of literary texts but of advertisements and popular cultural forms. This adaptation was important for cultural analysis not only in terms of method but because it assumed that it was important to be able to read and understand the cultures of everyday life (even if it was only to assume their vast inferiority). The Leavises' role in establishing the journal *Scrutiny* (F. R. Leavis founded it in 1932) helped to create a forum for debate concerning not only literary-intellectual culture but what many felt were the evils of industrial capitalism and mass culture.

However biased this criticism may have been it has been seen as an important 'moment' (Inglis, 1993: 32) for literary-cultural analysis and this has led Terry Eagleton to assert (perhaps with some overstatement) that *Scrutiny* actually founded a certain kind of 'cultural studies' in England, 'as one of its most enduring achievements' (Eagleton, 1983: 34). But, as Eagleton has also asserted, the Leavisite project was absurd insofar as it seemed to be predicated on the idea that social decline could be averted by sensitive readings of *King Lear* (34). If Arnold could be seen as a reactionary elitist because of his resistance to any kind of working-class radicalism the Leavises can be seen as narrow-minded conformists insofar as they, according to Mulhern (1979: 331), systematically repressed politics from their particular bourgeois-inflected brand of literary-cum-cultural criticism. However, this criticism cannot be levelled at the next thinker I shall discuss: Theodor Adorno.

The Frankfurt School and the culture industry

Adorno was affiliated to the Institute for Social Research at the University of Frankfurt which, owing to the rise of Nazism in Germany (many of those affiliated were from the Jewish community), eventually relocated to Columbia University in New York (before moving back to Frankfurt in 1951). While many other important thinkers were affiliated to the Institute, I shall limit myself (mainly) to discussing Adorno's critique of mass culture (an idea he developed with Max Horkheimer) in relation to what he called the **culture industry**, because this has had a particularly important influence on how popular culture has been theorized and understood.

The Institute of Social Research is otherwise known as the **Frankfurt School of Critical Theory** because a number of the writers affiliated to it were influenced by Horkheimer's essay 'Traditional and Critical Theory' (1939/1982). What I want to argue here is that some of the general approaches of **critical theory** have filtered, directly or indirectly, into cultural studies. Horkheimer argued that the social sciences cannot be treated like the natural sciences because they cannot extrapolate general 'universal' laws from particular instances (as in the pure sciences). This was because knowledge produced in the social sciences is subject to the theories (or ideologies) that produce them; thus, it is necessary to be aware of the historical context in which research takes place. Also, critical theory should not be tied to fixed premises and, while being informed by Marxism, be open, flexible, self-critical and interdisciplinary.

The goal of critical theory (like much cultural studies) is akin to Horkheimer's Marxist-inflected idea that the aim of critical theory is 'the emancipation of human beings from the circumstances that enslave them' (1939/1982: 244). This is the ultimate end of Adorno's critique of the culture industry, which helped to establish the terms in which popular culture could be discussed and often condemned or dismissed by critics on the Left. Fundamental to Adorno's notion of the culture industry is that the rise of mass entertainment and mass communications within industrial capitalism led to the factory-like production of formulaic and predictable popular forms of culture motivated by profit and the dictates of consumer capitalism. What concerned Adorno were the effects of mass culture, which he argued functioned to pacify the exploited masses, accustoming them to the 'humiliating conditions' of their lives and perpetuating their economic inferiority, while impoverishing them materially, emotionally and intellectually. In short, it rendered consumers politically impotent (Adorno, 1991: 143f.).

A convenient way of illustrating Adorno's ideas is to refer to his early 1960s essay 'Perennial Fashion – Jazz' because it not only provides a concrete example of the culture industry but can help to elucidate Adorno's methodology. In this essay Adorno argued that in its initial stages jazz possessed some originality and merit. However, it was soon commercialized by the culture industry and was reduced to a set of standardized and predictable forms, which, while satisfying desire temporarily, ultimately frustrated it. At the same time its ephemeral worth was compounded by the constant pressure to appear new.

In terms of method, Adorno combined Marxist concepts with a number adapted from Freudian psychoanalysis (a common strategy in cultural studies). He argued that getting lost in jazz (or any kind of mass culture) was akin to ignoring the difficulties of the present by regressing back to a passive infantile stage. Adorno described this in terms of Freud's castration symbolism because all this disempowered the jazz aficionado (and musician). In this way jazz, in its hypnotic sameness, becomes like an addictive drug (Adorno, 1990: 126) where the jazz enthusiast, far from being a rebel, is a victim, a conformist compulsively consuming sameness camouflaged as variety (122).

Adorno's critique of mass culture was made possible by his notion of authentic art or culture where 'serious' forms of music offered genuine aesthetic and intellectual fulfilment (rather than offer the sensationalist and sentimental pleasures of mass culture), revealing an organic form where the detail expressed the complex whole. It provoked imaginative responses and challenged the audience or reader, instead of inciting escapism. It was also able to express utopian ideals for a better world rather than provoke the unreal dreams of wealth, power, ardent love and adventure of popular genres. Whereas Arnold feared that the 'populace' would bring about anarchy, Adorno saw the opposite: the consumers of mass culture are victims, and the passive resignation brought about by working under capitalism is intensified through the mindless entertainment provided by the culture industry (see Adorno and Horkheimer, 1947/1972: 142). The sinister image that Adorno conjured up of jazz lovers was one where their syncopated dance-steps actually resembled the goose steps of the Nazi shock troops – both were subject to dangerous manipulative techniques that moved and dominated the masses.

However, there are some resemblances between Adorno and the writers in the culture and civilization tradition. Adorno defended 'serious' (radical avant garde) culture against the threats of modern mass culture. For Adorno, Arnold and the Leavisite tradition authentic art possesses transformative power: it has the power to awaken critical awareness and offer genuine intellectual and aesthetic pleasures. What distinguishes Adorno's approach is his theoretical complexity and explicit Marxist convictions expressed in the idea that great art, through offering utopian alternatives for a better future, can serve to awaken the masses to rebel against servitude, exploitation and inequality.

Another difference is that Adorno, along with many Marxist colleagues, shared the concern that capitalism, through the culture industry, constantly threatened to drain authentic culture of its revolutionary, utopian potential by incorporating it into itself – this is one of the reasons he insisted on writing in a highly complex style, so it could not be appropriated by the capitalist system of domination (Adorno, 1966/1973). This anxiety about the way the capitalist system and its values and ways of thinking dominate society will be explored in many chapters in this book (particularly those on Barthes, Althusser and Jameson); however, here I shall stress the point that Adorno's conception of the masses as passive dupes and his denigration of popular styles of culture have received considerable criticism by specialists in popular culture. It is also possible to question the extent to which ordinary people are manipulated by popular forms produced within capitalism and, as Gendron (1986: 32f.) has observed, given the variety of the transformations within popular styles, arguments about standardization may not be very convincing. Also, the assertion that consumers are largely passive is simply assumed rather than demonstrated (Murdock and Golding, 1977: 18f.) and then there is the question of up to what point capitalism is able to neutralize all rebellion and resistance.

My overview by no means exhausts Adorno's theses and these criticisms are only a fraction of those that might be levelled at Adorno's theories; nevertheless, Adorno continues to be an important reference point for anyone analysing popular cultural forms and their relations to capitalism, consumerism and the creative industries. However, other writers affiliated to the Frankfurt School, like Walter Benjamin, offered a more positive image of mass-produced culture. In his 'The Work of Art in the Age of Mechanical Reproduction' (1936) he argued that in industrial capitalism the intensely individualistic contemplation of art objects (with their sacred 'aura') could be replaced by the possibility of collective appreciation of the new mass produced forms of film and photography in such a way that ordinary people were no longer excluded from the appreciation of the new forms (Benjamin, 1973: 237).

This democratizing possibility challenged the idea that mass-produced popular cultural forms and mass consumption were, in themselves, debased, inferior and dehumanizing. This is not to say that Benjamin was naively optimistic about all cultural production. When writing his 'Theses on the Philosophy of History' (1940) he was also capable of producing trenchant and suggestive phrases like: 'There is no cultural document that is not at the same time a record of barbarism' (Benjamin, 1973: 248). This challenges the culture as civilization thesis because here civilization is envisaged as the product of exploitation and suffering (we may see a pyramid or a cathedral as wonders or art but not think about the social, political and economic conditions in which they were produced). Other approaches that helped to challenge the idea that worthwhile culture was restricted to selective traditions of what were regarded as highly sophisticated works (and which included a less submissive and more positive role for working people) was provided by the writers I review in the next section. Each one helped to challenge the idea that being a member of the industrial classes was, per se, to be condemned to a trivial life of passivity and domination.

Culturalism(s)

The three writers I will discuss now (like those already mentioned) all began publishing before the institutionalization of a recognizable area of study known as cultural studies. However, they have all served as important precursors by helping to establish a sense of tradition and, especially in the case of Raymond Williams, serving to lay down some of the conceptual and methodological foundations of what is now cultural studies. It is customary to group these writers together under the label **culturalism** because they saw that ordinary people have been and can be active agents of change rather than passive dupes (the image that tends to be reinforced in the work of Arnold, the Leavises and Adorno). As Storey has emphasized, these writers were interested in the lived culture of ordinary people, which was assumed to be worth studying, while stressing 'human agency': that is ,'the active production of culture, rather than its passive consumption' (Storey, 2009a: 37f.).

Another reason why the 'culturalism' label is used is that it helps to distinguish these writers (who tended to put greater emphasis on history, individual experience and agency) from later cultural critics who embraced structuralism (see below), which tended to see people as shaped by cultural systems. However, while these writers *do* emphasize agency it is only a convenient label to describe work which, in many ways, has very different nuances, ends and themes. As Jenks (1993: 154) has stated, it is possible 'to overemphasize the communality of vision' between those defined as culturalists.

Richard Hoggart and *The Uses of Literacy*

The first of these 'culturalist' writers is Richard Hoggart, whose contribution to cultural studies is usually reduced to two principal events: the publication of his book *The Uses of Literacy* (1957) and his role as founding director of the Birmingham Centre for Contemporary Cultural Studies (1964): one of the institutions which most helped to establish a distinctive cultural studies identity in Britain (and which had a considerable influence on the direction that cultural studies would take in other parts of the world – see below). However, the publication of *The Uses of Literacy* helped to establish Hoggart as an important voice in discussions of the media, popular culture and the meaning and value of working-class life. One of the tasks he set himself was to study how the 'appeals of the mass publications connect with commonly accepted attitudes, how they are altering those attitudes, and how they are meeting resistance' (Hoggart, 1957/1958: 19). However, the book went beyond just the uses of literacy to consider what constituted being working class (in terms of education, work, clothes and accent, etc.) and many other aspects of working-class life and culture.

Hoggart's task was made easier because he was from a working-class family in Leeds and this enabled him to give an 'insider view' of working-class urban life, consciousness, culture and experience. In *The Uses of Literacy* he offered meticulous descriptions and considered the meanings of everyday events – this included everything from describing institutions like the working men's clubs to a day out at the seaside. For example, when portraying the seaside trip he showed detailed knowledge of the typical rituals that characterize the day out (147f.). As Graeme Turner has stated, Hoggart's drawing on personal experience tends to give an air of 'authenticity' to his depiction of working-class life in the pre-war period which is depicted as 'a complex whole, in which public values and private practices are tightly intertwined' (Turner, 2003: 39).

Significantly, the working-class rituals Hoggart described were not represented (as they might have been by the Leavises and some of the *Scrutiny* circle) as trivial and debased but as eloquent moments of 'a full rich life' made meaningful by a strong sense of community spirit. Far from passive, Hoggart saw the working classes of his youth as possessing 'a strong natural ability to survive change by adapting or assimilating what they want in the new and ignoring the rest' (32). In this Hoggart was helping to focus attention on cultures of everyday life that would become so important to what it meant to do cultural studies. However, if Hoggart went beyond the Leavises when describing the pre-1930s working-class culture, he still shared much in common with their views of mass urban culture when he gave his account of the mass entertainments of the decades following the 1930s.

When Hoggart was confronted by the influence of Hollywood films, rock 'n' roll music and popular forms of fiction (which, like the Leavises, he associated with Americanization) he feared that it was a corrupting influence on the more traditional values he associated with the working class of his youth. He was concerned, like so many of his contemporaries, about the creation of mass culture, which replaced older values with those of consumerism and mass consumption (24). Hence, when he described things like the popular romances, the milk bars and Teddy Boy culture of the 1950s he tended to give a less sympathetic, more distanced, one-sided and judgemental view (describing the Teddy Boys as 'shoulder waggling barbarians' or 'barbarians in wonderland' (1957/1958: 193). For some critics Hoggart's inability to apply his insights into the popular culture of the 1930s to the mass culture of the 1950s is the principal weakness of his book (Storey, 2009a: 40).

However, one of the main reasons why Hoggart was so concerned about these cultural changes is that he felt the older urban working class had developed a strong sense of resistance but, like the Leavises (and Adorno), thought of the average consumer of contemporary mass culture as 'hedonistic but passive' (250). This contrasted with his earlier belief that the traditional working classes took an active role in making, choosing and adapting culture to their own ends. Hoggart's anxieties came from his deep sympathies with the working class whose strength and independence were increasingly threatened by what he called 'competitive commerce'. He believed that this was a greater threat to the working classes because it was a form of subjection that promised to be more powerful than older forms of economic subservience 'because the chains of cultural subordination are both easier to wear and harder to strike away' (243–4).

Later cultural theorists, like John Fiske (following Odina Leal), would apply Hoggart's insights of 1930s working-class culture in a more consistent and general fashion, arguing that the social order 'constrains and oppresses the people, but at the same time offers them resources to fight against those constraints' (Fiske, 1992: 157). This view tends to reflect Hall and Whannel's understanding of youth culture (see below). However, if Hoggart assisted in helping cultural critics to reconsider the meaning and value of the working class then E. P. Thompson helped cultural historians to appreciate quite how the working class forged itself in the first place and to become more aware of radical working-class politics, struggles, movements and traditions.

E. P. Thompson and *The Making of the English Working Class*

Like Adorno, Thompson's work was informed by his Marxist background; however, while he showed a strong interest in theory (see Chapter 4 where I will review his criticism of and resistance to structuralism), he defined himself as a historian. His historical work that has had the most important impact on cultural studies is his *The Making of the English Working Class* (1963), which traced the formation of the working class between the years 1780 and 1832. These dates are important because they coincide with the rise of the Industrial Revolution and the moment in the nineteenth century when a working class could be said to be a historical force and a reality. It was between these dates that 'most English working people came to feel an identity of interests as between themselves, and as against their rulers and employers' (11).

The year 1832 is also of special significance because it was the date of the Reform Act that gave the vote to large parts of the middle classes but excluded the working classes. However, working-class consciousness had developed to such a point that some contemporaries (like Arnold, see above) feared the growing powers that the working classes were claiming for themselves. For Thompson, by 1832 the working class was 'the most significant factor in British political life' (11). One of the reasons why Thompson's study has become so important cultural studies is because he set out to explore the common interests, experiences, preoccupations and struggles of working people at a key moment in history. Although this was not the first book of its kind, it helped to refocus history in such a way that the working classes were central, rather than being considered passive observers drawn along by the external forces of historical change.

Thompson emphasized the idea of 'the making' of the working class because he saw his book as 'a study in an active process, which owes as much to agency as to conditioning'. Thus, the working class 'did not rise like the sun at an appointed time. It was present at its own making' (Thompson 1963/1968: 8). For this reason he is often referred to as a 'culturalist'. Thompson preferred to use the term 'working class' (instead of its plural) because it indicates the sense of solidarity and commonality of interests between different working groups, which were united by common experiences and struggles. Thus, the task Thompson set for himself was to rescue the working class (especially radicals) from 'the enormous condescension of history' (12), stressing the political radicalism and growing political consciousness necessary to the formation of a class. He did this by describing (among other things) the numbing work-discipline and rebarbative conditions that the workers suffered under industrial capitalism, relating how class consciousness grew out of demands for social and political rights, and narrating the heroic deeds, organization, popular revolts and other initiatives that would eventually lead to social and political change.

In this way Thompson was able to construct a theory of class. For him the working class is not a descriptive label invented by historians or sociologists but a 'historical phenomenon' that developed over time. Fundamentally, it is a relation dependent on difference and conflict. For Thompson, class 'happens' when people, as a consequence of common experiences, 'feel and articulate the identity of their interests as between themselves, and as against other men whose interests are different from (and usually opposed to) theirs' (8). From this point of view it does not make much sense to isolate one class without showing how its existence is dependent on, and in conflict with, other classes. In fact, Thompson argued that the ruling class was itself only properly consolidated as a response to 'an insurgent working class' (11), which was often violently punished for fighting for its rights and taking things into its own hands.

This way of thinking fits in with the Marxist idea of history as antagonistic; Thompson positing that class experience was 'largely determined by the productive relations into which men are born – or enter involuntarily'. For Thompson, class-consciousness was the way in which these experiences were filtered in cultural terms: 'embodied in traditions, value-systems, ideas, and institutional forms' (8). Whereas Adorno and Horkheimer (more often than not) wrote of the working classes in pessimistic terms, Thompson (albeit writing about the classes in earlier centuries) emphasized the heroism, bravery, resistance and capacity for struggle of women and men who put their lives at risk to promote the interests of working-class rights and equalities. In short, together with the work of Hoggart (and Williams), Thompson's account helped to emphasize the working classes as active agents of historical change.

Although (as stated above) Thompson thought of himself as a historian, his work comfortably fits into the cultural studies idiom because of the way it explores how alternative, popular radical cultures were produced through struggle, political agitation and resistance. This suggests at least three important components of cultural studies: its (almost) constant (but troubled) engagement with Marxist theory, its interdisciplinary predisposition, and its profound interest in forms of resistance and political struggle as legitimate objects of analysis and knowledge. All these themes would be considerably extended in the work of Raymond Williams.

Raymond Williams

Raymond Williams has had a major influence on the development of cultural studies, with John Storey (2009a: 44) describing the range of his work as 'formidable' and Terry Eagleton claiming that, given breadth of his work, conventional labels like political theorist, sociologist, social philosopher or cultural commentator are incapable of describing his work 'exhaustively or exactly' (Eagleton, 1984: 108). Furthermore, this body of work (produced over nearly 40 years of academic life) was constantly evolving. While always a committed and active member of the British Left his closer association with Marxist discourses towards the end of his life further complicate definitions of his work. Thus, I can only give a brief idea of some of the facets of Williams's work that have been of interest to cultural studies practitioners.

One aspect of Williams's work that has made a particularly strong impact has been his efforts to contextualize and offer adequate definitions of culture. In *Culture and Society* (1958) he explained that the organizing principle of his study was to be found in the insight that 'the idea of culture, and the word itself in its general modern uses, came into English thinking in the period which we commonly describe as that of the Industrial Revolution' (Williams 1958/1987: iii). Thus, he provided a historical basis for understanding culture by locating it in the social and political changes brought about under industrial capitalism. His basic approach was to give an account of a range of writers from the eighteenth to the twentieth century (from Edmund Burke and William Cobbett to D. H. Lawrence and George Orwell) who helped to provide a 'map' through which it was possible to perceive the 'wider changes in life and thought' that these writers echoed in their works (xiii). This enabled Williams to focus on the social-political, intellectual tradition that has helped to define modern, democratic, industrial society.

At a methodological level, a significant achievement of the book was Williams's demonstration of how a number of key words (like industry, democracy, art and culture) acquired new and important meanings in the last decades of the eighteenth and in the first half of the nineteenth century. In this way he was able to 'map' language historically in terms of important cultural transformations. He further elaborated this technique in his 1976 book *Keywords: A Vocabulary of Culture and Society* (revised edition, Williams, 1983a) – an important labour that has been continued with the publication of *New Keywords* (Bennett et al., 2005).

One important conclusion that tends to come out of this 'keywords' approach is that culture is not understood as a fixed category but a process; it is not a conclusion (Williams, 1958/1987: 295). As mentioned earlier, this indicates it is subject to historical forces and change. This idea was developed in Williams's later work *Culture* when he distinguished between dominant, residual and emergent cultures, where dominant forms and practices, at any given moment, co-exist with older forms and nascent possibilities which may be absorbed by, or challenge or supersede, prevailing trends (1981: 204–5). This way of thinking introduces the idea of culture where dominant forms are constantly in potential conflict with historical residues and emergent potentialities. Again, culture is seen as complex and dynamic, rather than as a series of objects with fixed and universal value.

The forces of historical change would also be a major theme developed in Williams's 1961 publication *The Long Revolution*. In this study Williams, while recognizing that the Industrial Revolution could be condemned for creating and perpetuating forms of exploitation, subordination, hardships and injustices, saw it as a vital force that would, through the great personal struggles of subordinated groups, bring about the reforms that would result in modern democracy. This is because Williams wrote of the Industrial Revolution as unifying three interrelated revolutionary processes: the democratic, industrial and cultural (1961/1992: x–xi). However, Williams, as the committed socialist that he was, argued that modern democracy (while it contained the voting rights, and improvement in working conditions, education and health reforms that had been fought and won) was in no way complete: it could only be a stage in a long revolutionary process, informed by socialism. The important thing here for the definition of culture is that these aspects were every bit as much a part of developing cultural life as contributions in the sphere of the arts. Looking at Hoggart, Thompson and Williams's contributions it is possible to get an idea of another key component of much work in cultural studies: the importance of politically engaged readings of culture which recognize the value and importance of everyday culture and of working-class life and activism.

Another important aspect of *The Long Revolution* was Williams's division of approaches to culture as the ideal ('a state or process of human perfection'), documentary ('the body of intellectual work' in which human thought and experience is recorded) and the social ('in which culture is a description of a particular way of life, which expresses certain meanings and values not only in art and learning but also in institutions and ordinary behaviour' (41f.)). This last approach extended the definition of culture in ways the previous approaches (which are closer to the Arnoldian–Leavisite tradition) would not have contemplated. From the social point of view an interest in culture would include not only the definitions included in the other approaches but everything from the structure of the family and the organization of production to 'the structure of institutions which express or govern social relationships' and the 'characteristic forms through which members of the society communicate' (42).

One important consequence of Williams's approach is that the understanding of modern culture could not be confined to the study of 'high' culture: popular mass culture was equally important. This meant that if modern conceptions of culture were to be linked to the social and political changes brought about by industrial capitalism (and the gradual struggle for reform) then cultural historians would have to attend to *all* the historical circumstances that produced the forms of art and life of industrial civilization. As Williams emphasized: 'a good living culture is various and changing, [and] the need for sport and entertainment is as real as the need for art' (337). Cultural studies practitioners have taken this very seriously: the study of popular culture and its audiences being one of the staples of analysis.

This was all part of Williams's classic definition of culture 'as a theory of relationships between elements in a **whole way of life**' (46). For Williams it was a 'fatally wrong approach' to assume 'that political institutions and conventions are of a different and separate order from artistic institutions and conventions'. For him, absolutes like politics, art, science, religion and family life 'belong in a whole world of active and interacting relationships, which is our common associative life' (39). This 'whole way of life' approach to culture was illustrated by Williams when he described the rise of the popular press in the 1840s. He showed how an adequate understanding of it would need to take account of all kinds of things like changes in infrastructure (the expansion of roads and railways, shops, etc.); the social character of the period (ideas, beliefs and values); the lowering of taxes on printed matter; the rise of literacy; and technical advances and industrial organization, etc. (54f.). Significantly, Williams did not dismiss the popular press as impoverished and impoverishing but saw it as part of an expanding, creative and vital culture.

Williams's work, then, has been fundamental in terms of a establishing a tradition of analysis that takes mass popular cultural forms seriously and which is not clouded by prejudice and simple value judgements. If Williams wrote important studies on the novel and drama, he also wrote (as indicated earlier), in a non-dismissive way, on advertising, the popular press, film, television and communications, exploring how these contributed to social, economic, political and cultural change. All this demonstrated his interdisciplinary and boundary-breaking approach to the analysis of culture (a legacy that cultural studies, in general, has continued to nurture).

If this were Williams's only contribution he would still be a major figure in cultural studies but his influence is even more profound. Williams's insistence that cultural analysis should take account of the processes of production and the social relations these imply helped to establish what has become known as 'cultural materialism' (Williams, 1980: 243). You will see that I insist on the importance of materialist approaches, especially in the final chapters of this book. Williams's relevance to cultural studies has also been maintained by his willingness to engage with the ideas of important Marxist theorists like Louis Althusser (see Chapter 4) and Antonio Gramsci (see below and Chapter 14). This was in the 1970s when cultural studies was in its infancy in Britain and

when important debates were raging about the importance and relevance of different Marxist approaches (see below).

There are many other aspects of Williams's work that could be emphasized but this should give an idea of the extent and importance of his books which, in the words of Stuart Hall, 'have no comparison among contemporary writing for range and stubbornness of critical intelligence' – in a body of work with 'an astonishing variety of modes of writing' (Hall, 1988: 20–21). These words are praise indeed coming, as they did, from a man who has been a key figure in terms of the way cultural studies has developed (especially in Britain).

The consolidation of cultural studies in Britain: Stuart Hall and the Birmingham Centre

In this section I shall discuss the importance of Stuart Hall's contribution to cultural studies within the context of the institutional consolidation of the area. Trying to do justice to Stuart Hall's impact and role is difficult: as Roger Bromley has argued, apart from Williams, Stuart Hall 'has been the most influential figure in British cultural studies' and, even outside Britain, his work 'has probably been more responsible than any other for the spread of the field' (Bromley in Munns and Rajan, 1995: 194). Thus, I shall limit myself to giving an idea of some of the ways Hall and the Centre for Contemporary Cultural Studies at Birmingham University have helped to shape some of the dominant questions and themes that have had a major influence on how the area has evolved.

Two reasons why Hall has been such a key figure is that, first, he was a prominent founding member of the New Left in Britain (a group of left-wing intellectuals influenced by Marxism but critical of Soviet Russia) and, second (in 1969), he became Director of the Centre for Contemporary Cultural Studies at Birmingham University. This was a position he held right through the 1970s. This was a crucial period for the rise of cultural studies and, as Turner (2003: 59) has observed, Hall 'oversaw a tremendous expansion of the theoretical base and intellectual influence' of the Birmingham Centre (inside and outside Britain). This expansion helped to bring about the multi-disciplinary character of much of cultural studies (Hall and his colleagues at Birmingham tended to maintain a respectful, if critical, dialogue with the social sciences). As Turner (2003: 62–66) has indicated, while the Birmingham Centre has been of particular importance (and can 'justifiably claim to be the key institution in the field') it was by no means the only hotbed of cultural analysis (important research was also being done elsewhere in Britain, in the US and other parts of the world). However, I shall use Hall's influence as a loose (if limited) indicator of wider changes and developments in what was gradually becoming a recognizable area of academic study.

Hall insists that the Birmingham Centre was a collaborative effort and a large number of his publications confirm this, many being co-authored. He also stresses that cultural studies has no clear origins, it being made up of 'multiple discourses', 'different histories', combining distinct methodologies and theoretical positions, 'all of them in contention'. The image Hall uses for cultural studies at the Birmingham Centre is 'theoretical noise': a cacophony of 'bad feeling, argument, unstable anxieties, and angry silences' (Hall, 1996a: 263). This helps to remind us that the Birmingham Centre (like any other) was a research forum and not a fully unified project. However, Hall, while insisting on this openness and plurality, stresses that cultural studies is not just anything: something is 'at stake' – it is related to pedagogies that try to make a difference in the world. It is linked to what Hall sees as the broad (and not too intensively policed) 'project' of cultural studies: 'intellectual practice as politics' (272) or, as Tony Bennett has emphasized, the area is committed to 'examining cultural practices from the point of view of their intrication with, and within, relations of power' (Bennett, 1992: 23) – something I will stress throughout this book and especially in the final chapters. The kind of cultural studies that Hall and his colleagues helped to engender is a set of practices which accept difference and conflict as a necessary part of what it means to practise cultural analysis. So, despite the 'noise', the Birmingham Centre provided an important institutional context in which scholars could be trained and in which something like a cultural studies group identity could develop. This is related to the production of 'organic intellectuals', which I shall comment on below.

Even before becoming director of the Birmingham Centre, Hall had already begun to help move the analysis of popular culture beyond the terms of the debate found in the work of the Leavises and Hoggart. In *The Popular Arts* (written with Paddy Whannel), rather than repeat the 'misleading generalizations' that reject mass culture per se, the authors argue that fine distinctions could be made *within* popular, mass culture (Hall and Whannel, 1964: 35f.). For Hall and Whannel it made no sense to compare pop music to Beethoven – different popular styles could be distinguished from each other. This could be done through informed choices to see if a popular cultural form was dependent on predictable, pre-digested formulas or was more innovative and able to challenge audiences and be emotionally rewarding.

Importantly, Hall and Whannel, when discussing popular styles of music, contextualized it in relation to things like the social, economic and political relations of those who listened to it (269). They also stressed the affective role that popular styles played in helping young people to channel their feelings and discussed how the music helped to distinguish **youth subcultures** from the adult world they were reacting against (through things like dance, fashion and slang) (214). In short, while recognizing that mass commercial culture was 'a lush grazing pasture for the commercial providers' it was within these commercially oriented cultures that they could express rebelliousness and non-conformity and establish a sense of identity. Mass culture could be seen as 'an expressive field' and a 'contradictory mixture of the authentic and manufactured' (276). They acknowledged that the rebellious teenager was a media construction but they also stressed that the pop phenomenon could not be reduced to its economic context.

In this way the authors were able to not only deal with questions of value and the commercial context but consider the social, emotional and psychological role of teenage culture. Despite their failure to oppose the mass culture critique by privileging and thus removing 'certain of the texts and practices of popular culture from the condemnation of the critics of mass culture' (Storey, 2009a: 54) their approach went considerably beyond those of the Leavises, Adorno and Hoggart. In this, along with Hall's collaboration with Tony Jefferson, *Resistance Through Rituals* (1976), and other publications that came out of the Birmingham Centre like Dick Hebdige's hugely influential *Subculture: The Meaning of Style* (1979), they helped to establish and consolidate the study of popular forms and youth subcultures (for the difficulties and deconstruction of the notion of popular culture see Chapter 6).

The work done under Hall at the Birmingham Centre also included studies on black Britain, politics, ideology, racism, the popular press, television broadcasting (including the news, current affairs, the power of the media), photography, deviancy, violence, crime, football hooliganism, poverty, law and order, class and education (for a fuller list see Hall, 1996a: 504f.). This does not exhaust all the themes and does not include the important theoretical legacies associated with the Birmingham Centre. As many of these will be the subject of subsequent chapters I shall limit myself here to listing some of the most important shifts and turns. These included a constant and uneasy engagement with Marxist concepts (see particularly Chapters 3, 4 and 13–15), the introduction of structuralist methods (see Chapters 2–4), which challenged the 'culturalist' model but, in turn, were challenged by deconstruction and poststructuralist theory (see Chapters 5–10). These approaches were often nuanced by the use of psychoanalytic theory (see Chapters 7, 8 and 10), and considerations of postmodernism (see Chapters 11–13). Within these broad theoretical approaches themes like cultural imperialism, post-colonialism (see Chapter 6) and questions of diaspora (which included questions of 'race' and ethnicity and identity) were developed. While this is only a rough approximation of the kind of work that was going on at the Birmingham Centre it should give an idea of the kinds of themes and theories that would help to consolidate the area and why they feature so prominently in this book.

Particularly important within debates about Marxism was the question of ideology and Antonio Gramsci's (related) notion of **hegemony**. Whereas more simplistic forms of classical Marxism tended to see the dominant capitalist class as exercising direct power over the proletariat (and related social classes), Gramsci's theory of hegemony (developed in the years leading up to and during the Second World War) contemplated the idea of power being exercised through negotiation and persuasion (Gramsci, 1971: 12). Part of the context for this was that a too rigid model of ideology was seen as incapable of explaining why members of the proletariat do not automatically side with social and political forces that seem to be more in tune with their economic and political needs and interests. Thus, in Gramsci's work, the winning of consent for a particular set of views took on particular importance. Gramsci maintained that politics in democratic societies could be seen in terms of groups or power blocs forging alliances to struggle over and win moral and intellectual leadership (57). The loosely aligned bourgeoisie did this by representing their ideas as 'common sense', and in the interests of all (and therefore tending to persuade ordinary people – and themselves – of their competence and right to govern (66)). This theory helped to challenge the idea that ideology functioned in some kind of overly coercive and deterministic way and explained how counter-hegemonic groups and forces could be assembled (an idea particularly attractive to Raymond Williams (1980: 34)).

This 'enormously productive metaphor' (Hall, 1996a: 267), then, questioned simplistic notions of class because beliefs, values and identifications could not necessarily be traced back to cultural-economic origins – although there would be dominant emphases. This idea of hegemony has been applied in many contexts, including the analysis of popular culture to describe how popular cultural forms are (de)valued, excluded from, and in tension with, the dominant (elite) culture (Hall, 1981: 448–9). It was in this context of discussions of ideology and hegemony that Stuart Hall understood one of the intentions of the Birmingham Centre as the production of what Gramsci designated **organic intellectuals** (see Chapter 15), who could theorize culture and transmit counter-hegemonic ideas both inside and outside the confines of academe (Hall, 1996a: 267–8). What has been called the 'turn to Gramsci' (Bennett, 1986: xif.) included this idea (mentioned at the beginning of this chapter) that those working in cultural studies could be theoretically informed but, at the same time, politically engaged, seeing 'intellectual practice as a politics' (Hall, 1996a: 272). This has become an important preoccupation in much of cultural studies and one I shall return to frequently, and especially when I discuss and use Gramsci's notion of hegemony in Chapters 14 and 15.

Feminism and race/ethnicity and beyond

One thought that may have occurred to some readers is that there are a number of glaring omissions in this thumbnail sketch to do with the role of women and questions of race/ethnicity. This is largely because it was not until the late 1970s that feminists and black scholars began to have any significant influence on the thematic directions cultural studies would take. It was not that they were silent; both broad groups had contributed to books like *Resistance Through Rituals*. The problem was one of emphasis. For example, feminist discontent with the male bias of cultural studies was manifested when the Women's Study Group at the Birmingham Centre published *Women Take Issue* (McRobbie, 1978). This book helped to redress this very important disparity and helped to put feminist research on a more even footing. In the book you are reading I have tried to keep a constant eye on themes of interest to feminist scholars, rather than dedicate just one chapter to the theme.

If *Women Take Issue* represented a concerted feminist intervention, *The Empire Strikes Back* (1982) helped to address what black scholars felt were serious omissions within cultural studies with reference to 'racist ideologies and racist conflicts' in Britain (Centre for Contemporary Cultural Studies, 1982: 7) – even if *Policing the Crisis* (Hall et al., 1979) and other publications had already touched on these themes. These are just some of the theoretical and thematic legacies that would be taken up and extended both in the Birmingham Centre, and beyond. Since the 1970s cultural studies has proliferated in many parts of the world and has opened itself to many other important questions concerning gender and its relations to sexuality (questions that will be discussed in greater detail in Chapters 7–10 of this book) and other themes like globalization, corporativism, the role of the 'new social movements' (see Chapters 13–15).

In fact, the sheer variety of topics and theories that are explored within the area can seem intimidating – as my references to Grossberg et al. (1992) tend to confirm. However, because my intention is to help you to grasp some of the most important theoretical currents in the field I cannot offer anything like a complete or convincing overview of the subject. For that it would be necessary to consult the impressive array of journals and books that have been and are being published in the area (for a selection of journals see the Further Reading section of this chapter). However, I hope the limited thumbnail sketch I have offered here will serve to show how the theories I shall discuss and demonstrate in the following chapters fit into the wider history (or 'founding mythology') of that loose miscellany of approaches known as cultural studies.

Summary of key points

This chapter has reflected on the notion of culture and emphasized the complex character of cultural studies by taking British cultural studies as a model for understanding how it has developed and been consolidated. Cultural studies has been seen to grow out of an antagonistic struggle against narrow ways of conceiving culture by looking at the culture and civilization tradition. This position has been contrasted with Adorno's and Horkeimer's conception of mass culture as dominated by the culture industry, Benjamin's idea that mass-produced images offered the possibility for new kinds of meaningful, collective aesthetic experience and the 'culturalist' approaches associated with Hoggart, Thompson and Williams. The consolidation of cultural studies in Britain has been illustrated through reference to the Birmingham Centre for Contemporary Cultural Studies under the tutelage of Stuart Hall. This has emphasized cultural studies' interdisciplinary character, its eclectic approach to theory and its conception of 'intellectual practice as politics'.

Further reading

Culture and cultural studies: Raymond Williams's *Culture and Society* (1958/1987), *The Long Revolution* (1961/1992) and *Keywords* (1983a) are a good starting point for definitions of culture within cultural studies. Graeme Turner's *British Cultural Studies* (2003) gives a detailed history of all the different twists and turns in the development of British cultural studies. To get a fuller idea of cultural studies it is worth consulting publications like Frow and Morris's *Australian Cultural Studies: A Reader* (1993) and Hartley and Pearson's *American Cultural Studies: A Reader* (2000). Of course, many nations have and are developing distinctive styles of cultural studies and to get some sense of comparison you might look at Mookerjea et al.'s *Canadian Cultural Studies* (2009) and Sarto et al.'s *The Latin American Cultural Studies Reader* (2004). In order to get an idea of where cultural studies is heading it is worth exploring titles like Graeme Turner's *What's Become of Cultural Studies?* (2011) and Lawrence Grossberg's *Cultural Studies in the Future Tense* (2011).

Adorno and the Frankfurt School: To get a more profound idea of Adorno's critiques of mass culture a good place to start is with his *The Culture Industry: Selected Essays on Mass Culture* (1991) and then explore his collaborative work with Horkheimer in *The Dialectic of Enlightenment* (1947/1972). Phil Slater's *Origin and Significance of the Frankfurt School: A Marxist Perspective* (1977) offers a critical overview of Adorno's approach to the culture industry and Gillian Rose's *The Melancholy Silence* (1978) can be used to get an idea of the history of the Frankfurt School and, in particular, Adorno's contribution. For a wider-ranging and detailed account of Adorno and other Frankfurt writers see Susan Buck-Morss's *The Origin of Negative Dialectics* (1977).

The culturalist tradition: Graeme Turner (1996), Dominic Strinati (1995) and John Storey (2009a) (all mentioned above) give useful overviews of Hoggart, Thompson and Williams and relate their work to the idea of culturalism. Two excellent introductions to Richard Hoggart's work are Sue Owen's number in the *International Journal of Cultural Studies* (2007) and her edited collection *Richard Hoggart and Cultural Studies* (2008). Harvey Kaye and Keith McClelland's *E. P. Thompson: Critical Perspectives* (1990) offers a series of essays which evaluate E. P. Thompson's contribution as both historian and activist. Raymond Williams's *Writing in Society* (1983b) gives an idea of the broad range of Williams's thought and erudition and the volume edited by Terry Eagleton, *Raymond Williams: Critical Perspectives* (1989), offers a series of chapters that help to explain Williams's projects and assess his relevance and importance.

The consolidation of cultural studies in Britain, Stuart Hall and the Birmingham Centre: Hall et al.'s *Culture, Media, Language* (1973/1980) is one of the best books available to get an idea of the scope of the work being done in Birmingham because it is a compilation of essays published by key scholars at the Centre. A book which combines key essays written by Hall himself and essays which assess his importance, influence and role at the Birmingham Centre is *Stuart Hall: Critical Dialogues in Cultural Studies* (Morley and Chen, 1996). This is particularly recommended because it also helps to get a sense of how cultural studies emerged in Britain and the kinds of themes, conflicts and directions which were taken at the Birmingham Centre. For the beginning of concerted feminist interventions see McRobbie's *Women Take Issue: Aspects of Women's Subordination* (1978, mentioned above) and for resolute challenges from black scholars see *The Empire Strikes Back: Race and Racism in 70s Britain* (1982, see above) and Paul Gilroy's *There Ain't No Black in the Union Jack* (1987).

Journals and websites dedicated to cultural studies: If you are new to cultural studies you might want to explore some of the major journals dedicated to the area. Most major journals offer the possibility of signing up for electronic tables of contents so you get notification when new issues appear. The choices are considerable, so I shall only list a few of the more general titles with a broad thematic base. To start you might choose one or more of the following:

Australian Journal of Cultural Studies
Continuum: Journal of Media and Cultural Studies
Cultural Studies
Cultural Studies: Critical Methodologies
European Journal of Cultural Studies
International Journal of Cultural Studies
Journal of Popular Culture
Journal of Cultural Research
Media, Culture and Society
Theory, Culture and Society

An alternative is to explore cultural studies websites that often have online publications and a host of resources and information. You might begin by the following, which are particularly well designed:

Cultural Studies-L Page: http://comm.umn.edu/~grodman/cultstud/
Cultural Studies Central: www.culturalstudies.net/
Voice of the Shuttle's Cultural Studies Page: http://vos.ucsb.edu/browse.
    asp?id=2709

2

Structuralism and the Linguistic Turn

Ferdinand de Saussure

Introduction

The next three sections are dedicated to some of the ways structuralism has been of interest to cultural studies. This chapter will introduce one of the founders of structuralism: Ferdinand de Saussure. It will start by contextualizing the publication of his key work and will discuss the way in which his theories have been mediated to the academic world. It will then introduce his revolutionary theory of the sign, describe his main concepts and demonstrate how they may be used in practice with relation to questions of gender and patriarchal forces.

Learning goals

- To appreciate how Ferdinand de Saussure's ideas have been communicated to the academic world.
- To understand Saussure's theory of the sign and how this relates to what he called semiology.
- To see how cultures can be seen to code reality through dominant binary oppositions and construct gender identities through them.
- To develop a firm conceptual basis in order to be able to see how structuralism can work in practice.

Concepts

The key concepts introduced in this chapter are: structuralism, theory of the sign, signifier, signified, semiology, the code, signification, syntagmatic and paradigmatic relations, langue, parole, binary oppositions and patriarchy.

Second-hand Saussure

Of all the theories that have influenced twentieth-century thought **structuralism** has been one of the most important and revolutionary. It is primarily associated with the Swiss linguist Ferdinand de Saussure (1857–1913), who is seen as the father of structuralist thought. Although structuralism was developed within linguistics, it has left its influence on many academic areas within the arts, not only on cultural studies but on other fields including Anthropology, Philosophy, Communications and Media Studies, Political Theory and Literary Studies (to mention only a few). I shall begin discussion of structuralism by outlining, very briefly, something of the publishing history of Saussure's key work: his *Course in General Linguistics* (1916/1959).

The first thing to emphasize is that Saussure's major work was not actually published by him in his lifetime (he died of cancer in 1913) but compiled from his lecture notes (given between 1907–11) by two of his ex-students (Charles Bally and Albert Sechehaye). At the end of their preface to the first edition they asked a very pertinent question: 'Will the critics be able to distinguish between the teacher and his interpreters?' (1916/1959). This, in turn, raises the question of the integrity of the ideas we attribute to Saussure. The importance of this is that Saussure's early reputation was based not on his own notes but these 'second-hand' ones. In fact, not only are there now two scholarly translations of his *Course in General Linguistics* (the second appeared in the 1980s (Saussure, 1916/1983)), there is also a volume (Saussure, 2006) that brings to light a Saussure manuscript that was thought to be lost but discovered in Geneva in 1996. These alternative editions, however, have not so much challenged the main lines of argument or the integrity of the principal concepts but raised questions about nuances of meaning and accuracy. However, although the discovery of Saussure's Geneva manuscript may be regarded as a more authoritative text, it was the first 1916 compilation of Saussure's lecture notes that helped to launch the structuralist revolution. Thus, it is to that earlier edition that I shall refer.

This contextualization helps to make us aware that referring to what might seem like a later more 'authentic' text actually ignores the particular historical transmission of 'Saussure's' ideas. From this point of view, discussions of 'Saussure's' *Course in General Linguistics* are not only complicated by the problem that the original text(s) were not written in English (which is the case of a substantial number of other theorists discussed in this book) but by the fact that the standard text that helped to establish Saussure's importance and reputation was itself assembled by Bally and Sechehaye. Given these factors (and critics' dependence on this earlier text) there is a special sense in which Saussure's *Course in General Linguistics* should be regarded as second- or even third-hand and very much the product of a complex chain of mediations.

Signs of Saussure: signifiers and signifieds

In terms of understanding what has become known as structuralism (a theory of language that emphasizes structure rather than reference – see below), perhaps the best place is to start is to review Saussure's theory of the **sign**, which has had so much influence on contemporary thought. Saussure's theory of the sign grew out of his reaction against what he felt was an over-emphasis in linguistics on describing language from a historical (or what he called a diachronic) point of view. The diachronic approach describes how meaning is made possible through etymologies, which describe the roots and development of words through time. However, what interested Saussure was how language functions at specific moments (what he called a synchronic approach), which actually helps to describe how meanings are possible at a more abstract level. For this he needed a workable theory of the sign. For Saussure the sign is made up of two parts: the **signifier** and the **signified**. The signifier is the *form* of the sign, made up by what he called 'sound-images' that can be spoken or written (Saussure, 1916/1959: 11), and the signified is the *concept* (or meaning) that is understood as resulting from the particular form. It is only the combination of the form and the concept that can be properly called the sign.

What was so revolutionary about all this was that Saussure was not only challenging the historical approach to language but the idea put forward by some linguists that language is a naming process – a 'list of words, each corresponding to the thing that it names' (65). What he argued, however, is that words (or linguistic signs) do not actually unite things and names, but sound-images and concepts (signifiers and signifieds). To clarify this point I will refer to the word 'pig' (Figure 2.1). What we see is that we have the word or sound pattern 'pig' (the signifier) linked to a concept evoked by the word (the signified).

THE SIGN	A. The **signifier** of language is a word or a sound-pattern	Pig
	B. The **signified** is the meaning, concept or idea	The concept of a mammal of pinkish hue, bristly hair, curly tail, that has short legs, cloven hooves and a cartilaginous snout used for sniffing and digging, etc.

Notice that the actual flesh and blood pig remains outside the theory of the sign

Figure 2.1   The sign according to Saussure

In order to clarify this model I shall explore the implications of Saussure's theory of the sign a little more. The same signifier can have more than one signified, and vice versa. What this means is that the signifier 'pig' can mean (signify) the animal, but it can also mean fat, greedy, smelly, dirty, rude, is a derogatory word for police officer, and it can refer to crude substances (like pig iron), or something that is difficult or unpleasant ('a pig of a job'), etc. As a verb it can mean to gulp food down, overeat, or gorge oneself (to pig out), to shape metal, to farrow – and this does not exhaust all the possibilities because there are other terms like 'pig headed', 'pig Latin', etc.

Alternatively, a signified can have more than one signifier. For example, the concept of a mammal of pinkish hue, bristly hair, curly tail etc. can take as a signifier the following word-images: boar, swine, hog, piggy, piglet, porker, shoat, grunter, etc. For Saussure the form may remain the same but the content may be different (or vice versa). Important to Saussure is that each signifier/signified combination, united in the sign, is indissolubly linked like the two sides of a coin or a piece of paper where 'thought is the front and the sound the back' (113).

However, Saussure was quick to point out that there is no objective relation between the two parts of the sign: the relations between signifiers and signifieds are purely arbitrary – there is no logical relation between ideas and the forms they take in a language – the sound-image 'pig' is the form the concept happens to take in English. These relations are conventional insofar that the sound-image of the word in English could just as well be represented by any other sequence of consonants and vowels (as it is in other languages: *cochon* in French, *cerdo* in Spanish, *Schwein* in German, etc.).

Of course, here I am discussing the sign in terms of words but signs that are made up of a signifier with a meaning attached to it may take other forms. At the simplest level (and according to a given culture), a raised middle finger may signify 'Up yours!', a bunch of roses, 'I love you', a wry face 'I'm suspicious of you or what you are saying'. Meaningful forms of communication can be created through a host of other signifying systems: the dots and dashes of Morse code, simple instructions through the use of different coloured lights (the traffic-light system), through the raised dots in Braille, the sign languages used in deaf communities, the positions of flags in semaphore, etc. – all can be reduced to systems which are made up of signifiers and signifieds.

Help File: sharpening your knives – searching for signifiers

Once you start to look for signifiers outside the obvious example of words you will find them everywhere. For example, in Spain in small towns you can still come across something which was once much more widespread. Knife sharpeners would announce their presence in a community by blowing a simple scale up and down on a flute-like whistle. This scale is a signifier which conveys a message akin to 'Bring out your blunt knives, the knife sharpener is in the vicinity'. There is no variation to indicate anything else like 'I'm leaving now'. This is a very limited signifying system based on either presence or absence (like the sound of an ice-cream van) and its difference from other sounds produced in the street.

Language as relational not referential

One important thing to notice in Figure 2.1 is that the actual flesh and bone animal remains outside the signifying system. For their meaning, signs *do not* depend on references to actual things but on their *relations* to other terms. That means that in the structuralist theory of the sign meaning is made possible because language is *relational*, not referential.

In this context Saussure emphasized something that would inspire many writers influenced by his work. Signifieds (concepts) are 'purely differential and defined not by their positive content but negatively by their relations with the other terms of the system. Their most precise characteristic is in being what the others are not' (117). Thus, a pig is understood because it is not a cow, a snorkel or a screwdriver, which means that in language 'there are only differences *without positive terms*' (120). According to structuralist thought, although we may not be conscious of it, every word in this book, or in any signifying system, functions according to these axioms. Every meaningful symbol is a signifier with its signified. Studying the relation between these two elements of the sign within a code is what Saussure designated '**semiology**' (although many critics use Charles Peirce's term 'semiotics' which is often used as a synonym for 'semiology' (Peirce, 1894/1988)).

Help File: semiology and the code

I wrote above that within structuralist thought every meaningful symbol is a signifier with its signified and that studying the relation between these two elements of the sign within a code is what Saussure designated 'semiology'. Saussure based the word 'semiology' on the Greek word for sign (*semefon*) and used the neologism to conceive of a 'science' that studied 'the life of signs within society' (hence its interest to areas like cultural studies). However, there is another important idea for structuralism expressed here which is the **code**. For Saussure this 'consists of a written set of strict rules of usage', otherwise known as orthography (Saussure, 1916/1959: 25). It is important to note that these codes govern *any* system that produces meaning, not just language.

One characteristic of structuralist thought, then, is the use of highly specialized terms like the signifier, the signified, semiology and the code. This is something that reflects that Saussure, and many later structuralists, tended to see themselves as scientists dreaming of being able to make objective statements about the nature of signs and the codes that govern them: the idea of semiology being to 'show what constitutes signs, [and] what laws govern them'. In fact, linguistics, for Saussure, would only form a part of the general science of semiology and the findings would later be extended to what Saussure called 'the mass of anthropological facts' (Saussure, 1916/1959: 16). This application of structuralist theory beyond its immediate use in linguistics is what has made it so relevant to the analysis of culture.

Of 'cartoon wars' signification and syntagmatic and paradigmatic relations

Having discussed the relations between the signifier and signified in more detail, I want to consider more fully what it means to say that in structuralist theory meaning is made possible because language is relational, not referential. On one level, what Saussure calls '**signification**' is a question of studying the *relations* between the two elements of the sign to show how they produce meaning with relation to codes (114). However, structuralism explains how language functions by showing how, at *every* level, it is the relations between elements which create the possibilities for meaning. As stated earlier, semiology actually shows that language functions *without* having to rely on language/real-world connections. What Saussure put forward is that signifiers and signifieds function within a closed sign system.

To explain Saussure's point that in signification 'everything is based on relations' (122) I will refer to what he regarded as two important forms of mental activity: '**syntagmatic**' and 'associative' (or what the linguist Roman Jakobson (1960/1981) called **paradigmatic**) relations. The first kind of mental activity is linear where signs are arranged in sequences. These units he called *syntagms* of which a minimum of two is necessary to create a syntagmatic chain. In language this works at every level from the phonetic to the syntactic structure. Phonetically, the English language has twenty-six letters which can be formed into combinations of consonants and vowels to form word-sounds. The same is true at the level of grammar. For example, the words 'is', 'hereditary' and 'death' can be organized into a meaningful chains to read 'Death is hereditary', 'Is death hereditary?', etc.

The other mental activity, the associative or paradigmatic relation, has to do with the total number of possibilities that can be used to substitute the terms organized on the syntagmatic chain. To explain this Saussure referred to what he called the 'inner storehouse that makes up the language of each speaker' (123). This where one element can be exchanged or substituted for another. To explain this let us take the alphabet. The alphabet is the storehouse from which letters can be chosen. For example, if the letters (or speech sounds) 'p', 'i' and 'g' are assembled in a row they create the word 'pig' – and if the vowels or consonants are exchanged for others it is still possible to get a meaningful syntagmatic chain in the form of other words like 'peg' or 'dig'. It is possible to see the same process at work when considering the storehouse of language (or vocabulary) we carry around with us – out of our repertoire of words, and in line with normative grammar (a code), we can make meaningful sentences.

I will take the sentence 'all generalizations are false, including this one' to demonstrate how this works (see Figure 2.2.). Appealing to our storehouse of language (the vocabulary at our disposal) this syntactic chain can be altered in all kinds of ways. Notice that any syntagmatic chain can be modified through the use of all the lexical choices at the speaker's disposal. In this diagram certain words can be exchanged for others and the sentence will still make sense. Thus, it is possible to see that meaning is made possible by the system (or code) that enables it. First, this is dependent on establishing a line of

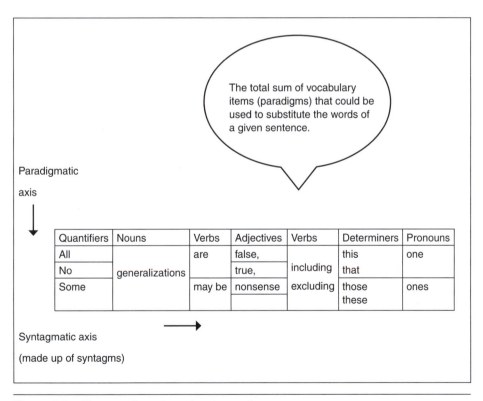

Figure 2.2 The paradigmatic and syntagmatic axes

syntagms on the syntagmatic axis that corresponds to a pre-existing word order (quantifier, noun, verb, adjective, verb, determiner, pronoun). Second, each item on the syntagmatic axis can be substituted for other terms that set up similar or new possibilities for meaning.

To illustrate these ideas in a different way (and show how they might work with relation to visual images), I shall refer to an episode from season ten of *South Park* entitled 'Cartoon Wars II'. It includes a scene which can be used to illustrate how systems based on the syntagmatic and paradigmatic axes produce meaningful structures with relation to another cartoon series, *Family Guy*. In this episode the writers of *Family Guy* are not depicted as humans but as manatees (aquatic animals with paddle-like flippers). These manatees are responsible for developing (the seemingly unconnected) plot lines of *Family Guy*. They do this through the manipulation of idea balls, which have a verb, a noun or a pop culture reference written on it, which are then dropped into a five part 'joke combine'.

So it is that a five-ball combination with the words 'laundry', 'date', 'winning', 'Mexico' and 'Gary Coleman' is turned into a typical *Family Guy* joke. Once these paradigms have been organized in a sytnagmatic line the conventions of a *Family Guy*-style joke are revealed. In this way Lois Griffin is seen saying to her husband, 'Peter, you didn't do the laundry today', and Peter Griffin answers, 'You think that's bad? You remember the time I won a date to go to Mexico with Gary Coleman?!' Here the viewer is presented with a flashback where a Mexican waiter speaks Spanish and Gary Coleman says, 'Watchoo talkin' 'bout, Willis' (his well-known catchphrase from the popular US TV sitcom *Diff'rent Strokes*). Thus, the episode of *South Park* shows how the random paradigms are organized into gags on a syntagmatic axis, and gives insights into how the surreal flashbacks that typify *Family Guy* are generated by a random code (which insists on combinations at any cost). Familiarity with the syntagmatic and paradigmatic axes enables them to be used to analyse any system of signification. Basically, as suggested above, the concepts drawn from the analysis of language can be applied to other domains. As an example I shall show how a semiological approach can be used to analyse the food habits of a particular culture.

Practice: food for thought – exploring semiology

While reading the following section you might experiment with the ideas of the syntagmatic and paradigmatic axes to help to analyse, interpret and explain the strange meal that is served and think about how different cultures organize the consumption of food.

Imagine you are somewhere in Britain and have decided to have lunch in what looks like a Chinese restaurant. A waiter approaches and asks you what you would like to eat. You tell him to surprise you. He agrees, and immediately charges you for the food you have not yet eaten (and reminds you that the tip is not included in the price). The next thing that happens is that you are brought a cup of coffee – confused, you look around at the other diners – no one finds this odd so you say nothing. Then you are given some bowls of fresh lychees with eggs and bacon. Then you are served plates of rice, a croissant, with marmalade and butter, chow mein, Chengdu chicken and shredded roast duck with jellyfish. Once you finish these dishes you are brought plates of Chinese salad, a glass of orange juice, muesli, milk, spring rolls and clam soup, followed by prawn crackers. Finally, you are asked if you want to eat in the restaurant or have a take-away.

Help File: more food for thought

If we start with the syntagmatic axis we can see that the order in which the food is served is wrong with relation to the dominant food habits found in Britain. It is important to realize that each culture will have its dominant practices that provide the norms against which oddities, challenges or mistakes or blunders can be measured. A waiter who charges customers *before* they eat a meal and then serves everything in reverse creates the kind of awkwardness of someone who reverses the syntax of a sentence. If someone said 'true be wouldn't it, fact a was it if even' instead of 'even if it was a fact, it wouldn't be true' (a phrase concocted by Theodor Adorno quoted in Jameson, 1991: 370), it would cause confusion or even be unintelligible. Other oddities appear when the order of breakfast, dinner and evening meal are confused or transgressed so that items from breakfast and are introduced at lunchtime.

Notice, also, that there are also inconsistencies at the level of the paradigmatic axis. Eating Chinese food in Britain (while not dominated by cast-iron laws) has its basic rules of choice and these are broken in a number of ways. Lychees are served with eggs and bacon, plates of rice and other typical main dishes are served with items associated with breakfast, like croissant, marmalade and butter. A structuralist analysis of these mistakes (or dissident acts) can help us to understand the cultural norms that are ingrained in the practices of everyday life. For example, the Mexican recipe for mole poblano, where chicken is served with a sauce made of (among other things) tomato, spices, nuts, herbs and chocolate, is not out of the ordinary. Yet for those not familiar with this combination of food-paradigms this

(Continued)

(Continued)

mixture of chicken and chocolate disturbs the conventionalized separation of meat and chocolate.

At the paradigmatic levels there are also significant variations which sometimes seem strange across different cultures. If the Spanish think it odd that some British and American tourists order coffee with their tapas (snacks), the British may baulk at a particular Spanish breakfast which consists of toasted bread, grated tomato – and fresh crushed garlic. These items are not necessarily contrary to British taste but are considered by those used to eating cornflakes, yogurt and muesli, and so on for breakfast as odd choices (paradigms). A consideration of paradigmatic relations can take you considerably further. For example, some British people will sometimes turn their noses up when they see certain items on the menus of some Chinese restaurants – things like deep-fried pigeon in spiced sauce, duck tongues served with tangerine peel, red-cooked duck's webs, cow's bronchial tubes served in a white wine sauce.

This negative reaction can be explained by saying that the paradigms have not been 'normalized' sufficiently among carnivores. The problem is not always concerned with whether or not a customer eats meat but *what* kind of animal is chosen to be consumed or what *part* of the animal is chosen as edible. In a country (and at a particular time and place) where rabbits are considered cuddly, furry pets the idea of killing and eating them may seem barbaric. There are local cuisines that serve rats, maggots, monkey brains, scorpions and all manner of other insects which may seem repulsive to those with other normalized food paradigms.

As a conclusion it is possible to say that having considered the syntagmatic and paradigmatic axes, we now have an elementary way of doing comparative cultural analysis which helps to explain and analyse how different cultures organize and normalize their eating habits.

Further practice

It is possible to invent other odd combinations and choices to explore how a particular culture organizes or normalizes the world. A simple way to start is to work out how traffic lights work by experimenting with the concepts of the signifier, the signified and the paradigmatic and syntagmatic axes (considering the colours as paradigms and the sequences as syntactical). These concepts can be used to think about clothes, and how social norms create common choices and how different combinations are related to factors like age, class, gender, region, sexuality and ethnicity to generate different effects and meanings. Then there are the rituals that govern courtship with their dominant conventions and gestures, etc. In the Further Reading section I have included some references on the semiology of fashion and the discourses of love.

By studying these multiple contexts it is possible to get an impression of our cultural identity or, to be more accurate, cultural *identities* because while there are dominant practices, values, beliefs, etc. these will, within the same geographical area, be in competition, or may co-exist, with many other forms of practices and beliefs that may be affected by things like age, class, gender, ethnicity, sexuality, region, religion and politics. Considering all these possibilities (and this by no means exhausts all the semiological possibilities that have been explored), it is not surprising that Stuart Hall claimed that the metaphor of rethinking social practices as if they were a language 'constitutes the theoretical revolution of our time' and has 'reorganized our theoretical universe' (Hall, 1986/1996: 145).

Coding reality, *langue* and *parole*

Given the above explanations, it should now begin to be clear why structuralists see the world in terms of complex sign systems – the anthropologist Clifford Geertz asserting that human beings live 'suspended in webs of meaning they themselves have spun' (1973: 5). As stated above, structuralist analysis does not need the referent or 'reality' to describe how sign systems work and, while it does not necessarily deny the referential world, it does pose important epistemological questions about how communities make sense of the world. That is, it helps to reflect on *how* we come to know what is regarded as reality. As John Fiske has said, the only way to make sense of 'reality' is through the codes of a particular culture:

> There may be an objective, empiricist reality out there, but there is no universal, objective way of perceiving and making sense of it. What passes for reality in any culture is the product of the culture's codes, so 'reality' is always already encoded, it is never 'raw'. (Fiske, 1987: 4–5)

Structuraltism, then, can help understand what passes for reality. Within the branch of studies known as Social Semiotics structuralist theory is often used to account for not so much what signs mean but *how* they mean. Of course, the *how* (discussing the laws and conventions that govern how meanings are made possible) often implies *what* things mean, or might mean – as should become clear as this chapter unfolds. Part of Saussure's great contribution to the analysis of culture is to be found in showing how a sign system governed by established codes (what he called *langue* or language) is able to produce meaningful words or utterances (*paroles* which, in spoken language, correspond to speech).

Once Saussure's ideas were in wider circulation it did not take long for scholars to use his insights and apply them to all manner of cultural manifestations to understand what are known as *signifying practices*. For example, the structural anthropologist Claude Lévi-Strauss showed that things like totemism, myths, kinship or cooking are systems that are structured like a language and can thereby be understood in Saussurean terms. That is to say, understanding is not so much about grasping the meaning of individual examples (of myth, etc.) but being aware of *how* meaning is made possible by the underlying cultural systems (rules, conventions, etc.) that *give rise* to these manifestations. I have already shown how it is possible to think about this with relation to eating habits but another relatively easy way of beginning to practice structuralism would be to experiment with Lévi-Strauss's idea that cultures make sense of the world through **binary oppositions**. These provide 'classificatory systems' upon which social realities are based.

Lévi-Strauss and the binary opposition

The question I want to address here is: what have binary oppositions got to do with classificatory systems? The answer is that cultures make sense of the world through distinguishing between opposites like life/death, good/evil, freedom/repression, natural/unnatural, love/hate, peace/war, etc. In *The Raw and the Cooked* Lévi-Strauss emphasized oppositions like nature/culture, raw/cooked, inedible/edible where one term is often taken to be positive and the other negative (Lévi-Struass, 1970). It is possible to adapt these ideas to see how a particular culture classifies and symbolizes the world. For example, certain foods may be considered only fit to eat if they are cooked (like meat, fish, potatoes, etc.), while others are regarded as edible without any special preparation (like fruit, some vegetables, etc.). In the case of fish, if it is commonly eaten cooked, it has to be subjected to various forms of manipulation to receive general social approval. A culture may have a negative view of fish if it is served in its raw state and consider the eating of it as inadvisable, dangerous or animalistic. Thus, the binary oppositions do not only classify but may have important cultural values attached to them.

It may be objected that some sushi dishes, where fish or meat is served raw, contradict Lévi-Strauss's idea of the binary codes. Yet it is important to recognize that binary codes are not necessarily valid across all cultures or in the same culture at different moments in its history. Also, not only do different cultures divide the world up in different ways but even in the 'same' culture there may be some variations in the way these simple oppositions work (although there are dominant trends). Many people in Britain demur at eating sushi but this kind of food has still made something of a cultural impact. In large geographical masses or, in the case of Britain where geographical size is less important but where multicultural values complicate monolithic definitions of culture, one would expect considerable variations in the way these binary oppositions function. Therefore, the universal for Lévi-Strauss is not to be found in the multiple examples (*paroles*) of normative conduct but in the habit of structuring the meaning of behaviour on the opposition itself (which is part of the way the *langue* functions). Another important point to consider is that binaries are not necessarily logical – they are culturally constructed and *perceived* as opposites.

To illustrate this I will take human beings as an example. There is a sense in which they can be seen as all belonging to the same species but they can be represented, understood or categorized in terms of opposites. Humans can represent themselves as being of different nations, classes, races, genders or sexualites, etc. (anything that can potentially create a sense of 'us' and 'them'). Classifications of these kinds can easily result in the perception of fundamental differences where a sense of right and wrong, good and bad, greater or lesser value can be attached to them. Once these have been established within a culture the simple binary can lead to complex sets of associations that become hardened into beliefs, which can be very hard to challenge or change. The social consequences of these binaries can be extremely divisive and damaging, ultimately leading to repression, exclusion, sexism, racism, homophobia and even genocide.

Here I shall elaborate a more detailed example that is highly relevant to cultural studies: how masculinity and femininity are culturally constructed through binary oppositions. Kaja Silverman makes the point that key oppositions and equations give rise to conceptual systems. These are the typical cultural codes where 'a term like "woman" is defined in opposition to a term like "man"'. These terms are aligned with an assortment of symbolic attributes (what Lévi-Strauss thought of as bundles of relations; Lévi-Strauss, 1963/1974) which spin off the original binary terms – men being given attributes like 'rational', 'firm' and 'strong', while women may be symbolized through terms like 'emotional', 'pliant' and 'weak' (Silverman, 1983: 36). For Lévi-Strauss this would be an example of an 'unconscious structure' (Lévi-Strauss, 1963/1974: 21) – a largely unrecognized socially constructed *langue* underlying these terms. Many feminists (Millett, 1970; French, 1985 – to name only two) refer to this particular structure as **patriarchy** and explore the way its representations magnify so-called differences in order to perpetuate the subordination of women.

Help File: patriarchy

Patriarchy is a contested term in feminism (and in gender studies in general) and not all feminist critics agree on how it functions or exactly how effective it is. However, Chris Weedon provides a very concise and useful definition:

> The term 'patriarchal' refers to power relations in which women's interests are subordinated to the interests of men. These power relations take on many forms,

(Continued)

(Continued)

from the sexual division of labour and the social organisation of procreation to the internalised norms of femininity by which we live. Patriarchal power rests on social meaning given to biological sexual difference. In patriarchal discourse, the nature and social role of women are defined in relation to a norm which is male. This finds its clearest expression in the generic use of the terms 'man' and 'he' to encompass all of humankind. (Weedon, 1997: 1–2)

Linguistic exchange and acts of power

The use of language, then, can be understood as being involved in struggles over meaning (what was called 'hegemony' in Chapter 1). Pierre Bourdieu's phrase 'every linguistic exchange contains the *potentiality* of an act of power' (Bourdieu and Wacquant 1992: 145) has often been quoted to emphasize how everyday language is involved in these struggles. Any seemingly innocent exchange of words can be seen as always already invoking the status quo and acting as a powerful hegemonic force over so-called free individuals. A witty play on this idea is expressed in John Agard's poem 'Listen Mr Oxford Don' where the poetical voice opens up the potentiality of an act of power:

> I ent have no gun
> I ent have no knife
> but mugging de Queen's English
> is the story of my life
> I dont need no axe
> to split / up yu syntax
> I dont need no hammer
> to mash / up yu grammar

(John Agard, 1985)

Conclusion: men and women are not natural facts

By way of conclusion it could be asserted, following Monique Wittig, that the terms 'men' and 'women' are not 'natural facts' but 'political categories' (Wittig, 1981: 17). Echoing Simone de Beauvoir, Wittig asserts that 'one is not born a woman' – one becomes one – one is culturally constructed as male or female. Wittig's point is that women and men are coerced to correspond, in mind and body, with 'the idea of nature that has been established for us' (17) and this involves not only questions of gender but also of sexuality – the heterosexual norm being the foundation that oppresses women in general but also the lesbian and the gay. Gender as 'nature' (and the binaries it implies) is not based on some neutral 'natural' ground but on the dominant (restraining heterosexual) discourses which construct it. It is normative heterosexual culture that creates the binary categories of man–woman, masculine–feminine.

In the following chapters I will come back to these important ideas but to conclude this chapter I want to stress that what we have here are cultural representations that are understood to be the products of an underlying system. It is common to assume that members of given cultures think in terms of their myths, whereas the structural anthropology coming out of Lévi-Strauss's writings tends to assume that it is not individuals who think in myths, but myths (cultural systems) that think individuals. If we extend this idea beyond a discussion of myth, this approach tends to challenge more traditional ways of thinking about culture (something I will discuss in much more detail in the following chapters). At this point it is convenient to return to Clifford Geertz's idea that human beings are suspended in webs of significance that they themselves have spun. From this point of view, Geertz understands culture to be those webs of meaning. By looking at the feminist ideas developed by de Beauvoir, Silverman and Wittig we can see how those webs of significance (culture) are often mistaken for nature (something else that will be highly relevant to the themes developed in later chapters).

Summary of key points

This chapter has introduced Saussure's concept of the sign as a combination of the signifier and the signified and shown how, in semiology, these concepts are linked to syntagmatic and paradigmatic axes and the notions of *langue* and *parole*. Structuralist linguistics has been described as the metaphor that informs a general science of semiology and the chapter has demonstrated how the key concepts can help to show how everyday culture can be analysed. By referring to Lévi-Struass's work, cultures have been seen to code the world through binary oppositions and this idea has been used to illustrate how feminist critics have shown how gender and sexuality do not originate in 'nature' but are products of (patriarchal) culture.

Further reading

Umberto Eco's *Theory of Semiotics* (1978) is for the more advanced reader because it is wide-ranging in its references and goes into considerable depth in terms of the idea of semiotics, critiquing it and bringing out all kinds of subtleties. Terrence Hawkes's *Structuralism and Semiotics* (1977) is one of the standard works in terms of introducing the main concepts. Charles Peirce's *The Essential Peirce: Selected Philosophical Writings* (1894/1988) (mentioned above) contains a number of concepts which can help to understand different signs (such as icons, indexes or symbols). Ferdinand de Saussure's *Course in General Linguistics* (whether it be one of the 1916 versions or the 2006 edition) is a must if you plan to carry out any detailed work based on semiology. *Social Semiotics* is one of the key journals that has kept structuralist approaches on the theoretical map dedicated as it is to publishing politically engaged papers that use methods inspired by (and related to) Saussure's ideas. See the Further Reading sections at the end of the following two chapters for more suggestions.

3

Semiotics

Umberto Eco, Roland Barthes and Stuart Hall

Learning goals

- To understand how a whole series of concepts can provide a model to understand popular cultural forms like novels, the press and advertisements.
- To appreciate how semiotics can help to understand ideology and how it functions.
- To be able to see how the key concepts work and develop the critical and interpretive skills to be able to put the ideas into practice.

Concepts

The key concepts introduced in this chapter are: denotation and connotation, coded and non-coded iconic messages, the message without a code, linguistic message, 'anchorage' and 'relay', ideology, the photographic message, 'photogenia', modern mythologies, semioclasm, first- and second-order semiological systems, motivation, encoding and decoding, preferred, negotiated and oppositional readings.

Introduction

Having introduced and illustrated some of the main concepts of structuralism in the previous chapter, this one demonstrates how structuralism has provided methods to interpret popular cultural forms and how it has been linked to the concept of ideology. Umberto Eco's analysis of Ian Fleming's James Bond novels is used to show how attempts have been made to boil popular forms down to their narrative structures. This chapter will also introduce some aspects of Roland Barthes' work, which provides a series of very useful concepts to show how structuralism can help to interpret images (from photographs to ads). This dovetails into Barthes' idea that contemporary ideology is a kind of 'mythology'. His classic reading of a photo of a black soldier is used to show how semiotic analysis has provided a method to consider what ideology is and how it functions. The final sections refer to Stuart Hall's theory of encoding and decoding in order to appreciate the complexities of semiotic readings.

Structuralism and 'bonding' with popular culture

As stated above, to begin I shall consider how structuralism has provided a method to interpret popular cultural forms. A good place to start is with the literary critic-cum-theorist and novelist, Umberto Eco, who attempted, in 'Narrative Structure in Fleming (1966), to account for the continued popularity of Ian Fleming's James Bond novels by trying to uncover the underlying narrative structures on which these popular fictions are based. This will give a taste of how structuralist ideas were applied to popular forms. In the essay under discussion Eco argues that Fleming's novels (what can be regarded as the *paroles*) are successful examples of a kind of '007' narrative systemization (at the level of the *langue*, or narrative codes).

If this looks like an effort to try to reduce narrative phenomena to a scientific system, it is. This is because a lot of early structuralists thought that they had discovered a reliable scientific method and Eco was revelling, to some extent, in this new-found approach (although in other works he challenged an oversimplistic application of structuralist ideas (Eco, 1962/1989, 1979/1981)). What he does in his 'Narrative Structure in Fleming', and which is typical of structuralist readings, is to establish a series of sequential oppositions on which he claims the novels are constructed. The common binary oppositions that Eco discerned in the Bond novels are:

- Anglo-Saxon moderation versus the excesses of Bond's enemies
- Bond's acceptance of discomfort and sacrifice versus 'the ostentatious luxury of his enemy'
- chance ('opportunistic genius') versus the less effective calculation of the enemy
- idealism and loyalty to his country versus greed. (Eco, 1966: 251)

Returning for a moment to the themes explored in the last chapter, Eco asserts that the narrative sequences in the Bond novels correspond to the syntagmatic axis, and that these are selected from a limited set of paradigms. Thus, in Eco's analysis paradigms are selected with relation to a dominant code which demands that Bond be sent on a mission to frustrate an elaborate plan by a fiendish villain of indeterminate nationality (certainly not English). Possible paradigms which will be hinged on this narrative code will include the following. Bond's principal antagonist will inevitably be involved in some dicey (but lucrative) business which promotes causes inimical to the interests of the West. 007 will strike up an erotic 'bond' (pun intended) with a beautiful woman who has to be emancipated from her past and who will fall into his arms – although he will leave her. Other predictable paradigmatic elements demand that Bond will be captured and tortured (not too much) and will eventually defeat his enemies; the main villain will, fittingly, suffer a gruesome death. The point is, all these elements (and quite a few more not mentioned) can be shuffled up to make a new novel out of what Eco calls 'imaginative laziness' (258).

For Eco, the secret of the novels' success is to be found in the variations played upon these predictable elements. Eco, reflecting the scientific confidence of the early structuralists, gave letters to each narrative segment – thus producing series like: A, B, D, B, B, E, C, B (where each letter stands for a discrete narrative sequence). In this Eco's analysis was influenced by the criticism of writers who are associated with what is known as 'Russian formalism' like Vladimir Propp (see below). These were critics who tried to establish scientific methods to account for the literariness of texts, rather than rely on the history of ideas, psychology or sociological explanations (see Steiner, 1984). Indeed, the Saussurean model (mixed with various other kinds of formalist criticism that attempt to isolate the unique structural features of texts) has been used and adapted by a number of critics to make sense of popular cultural forms. For example, Jim Kitses (1970) and Will Wright (1975) have both used structuralist approaches to explore the Hollywood Western genre. Just as Eco discerned patterns like Bond's acceptance of discomfort and sacrifice versus 'the ostentatious luxury of his enemy', etc., Kitses has shown (among many other things) how Westerns are also structured around simple binary oppositions like nature/culture, wilderness/civilization and the gun versus the rule of law. From the point of view of methodology this approach has proven to be a very useful interpretative tool. Before discussing how structuralism may be used to interpret text and image, I shall offer some advice on some possible forms of practice.

Notes on practice: propping up analysis

As a relatively easy practice exercise it is possible to take novels, short stories, a TV series, a comic, or a set of video games or popular film genres and see if they seem to be governed by the combination of more or less predictable narrative elements. This exercise will be easier if the analysis is limited to a single genre.

(Continued)

(Continued)

One possibility is to adapt the findings of the Russian formalist mentioned earlier, Vladimir Propp, to see how they may be adapted to a different genre. In his *Morphology of the Folk Tale* (1968) Propp reduced a large group of Russian folk tales to 31 basic narrative structures (character and action possibilities that he called 'narratemes'), thus establishing a typology that summed up all the narrative possibilities. These are all linked to a very limited repertoire of characters (related to spheres of action) that Propp reduced to seven. Rather than offer the 31 narratemes I will limit myself to the spheres of action. A couple of further points which may help analysis are: (a) a character may serve more than one purpose and (b) heroes in folk tales are usually men or boys (although the protagonist may be a girl if the tale deals with someone kidnapped or exiled). Thus, you may want (or need) to neutralize this gender bias in the following list. Here is a greatly simplified version of Propp's spheres of action:

1 There is some wicked or malevolent being (devil, dragon, bandit, stepmother, witch, etc.) who indulges in kidnapping people, stealing, declaring war, and wilfully causing damage and who will have to be overcome (or killed).
2 There is a donor – a fairy godmother figure (or an animal) who bestows on the hero a magical object to help him defeat evil and achieve his ends.
3 There is one or more (magical) helper (related to the donor in point 2) who befriends and aids the hero in his quest.
4 There is the object of the quest (the princess), and her father. These two figures serve to establish the basic outline of the narrative, providing the ends of the quest and the reward (the princess herself).
5 The dispatcher: the person who commands or requests the hero to go on a journey through threats and/or with the promise of a reward (riches, territory, the princess, etc.).
6 The hero who accepts the challenge, goes on the quest, overcomes all difficulties, fights and defeats the villain and gets the reward.
7 The false hero (who must be exposed or defeated) who tries to take credit for the hero's actions with an eye to the reward. (Adapted from Propp, 1968: 79–80)

Help File: propping up analysis and bonding with popular culture

It is interesting that Eco actually saw the narrative apparatus of the Bond novels as expressions of the 'most secure and universal principles' that put into play the kinds of 'archetypal elements' that have been successful in traditional tales. Thus,

Eco links the Bond novels to the fairy-tale elements highly reminiscent of Propp's categories. The character of 'M' in Fleming's novels is like the King of the fairy tale, Bond is like the hero sent on a mission, and the Villain would correspond to the Dragon. The Lady and the Villain are a version of Beauty and the Beast and it is Bond's role to rescue the Sleeping Beauty and, in doing so, 'restore her to fullness of spirit'. The opposition between the free world and the Soviet Union represents 'the primitive epic relationship between the Chosen Race and the Lower Race, between Black and White, Good and Bad' (Eco, 1966: 260). Eco usefully conceived the Bond plots as a series of predictable moves within a game (253), which helps to bring out the relations between the narrative code (*langue*) and the narrative moves (*paroles*).

If you choose to do some independent work you might see how far these can be extended to the material chosen and consider how you feel about using phrases like 'most secure and universal principles'. You might also think about what gets left out in this kind of analysis.

Structuralism and the rhetoric of the image: anchoring the image and making it speak

Up to now I have concentrated on how structuralism has been used with relation to popular narrative, but I shall now demonstrate how structuralism functions with relation to the analysis of images. To do this I will turn to one of the main names associated with the development of semiotic theory, Roland Barthes. Part of Barthes' contribution to semiotics is in how he analysed the nature of images and how they are deployed to create meanings. First, I shall refer to his seminal work 'Rhetoric of the Image' (Barthes 1964/1977) in order to develop a heuristic device that can be used to examine how static images (like photographs and ads) can be made to signify.

It might seem odd that Barthes applied the term 'rhetoric' to the image because the term is normally associated with oratory, that is, the art of using language to persuade, please or influence others. However, Barthes' use of the word is thoroughly appropriate because in this essay he analysed the persuasive power of images by exploring how they are constructed, how meaning is created around them, and how they function within culture.

To do this Barthes chose an image from a magazine advertisement (see Figure 3.1) where Panzani products (like pasta and tinned sauce) and tomatoes, peppers, onions and a mushroom are placed in or around a half-open string shopping bag. Barthes chose the ad because the image was deliberately chosen to provoke desire and sell a product. The background is red and this is played against greens and creams and whites which evoke the colours of the Italian flag.

Figure 3.1   Panzani advertisement

© Panzani Freres

The linguistic message: denotation and connotation

Barthes breaks down his analysis to explore what he calls **the linguistic message** and the coded and non-coded iconic messages. At the level of the linguistic message it is, of course, necessary to take account of any printed words that may appear in the ad (most ads have at least the brand name – even although a number of years ago some cigarette manufacturers experimented with leaving the brand name out). The linguistic message might be quite complex and include puns (which are an effective attention-getting device) like:

MUM'S TAKING US TO LEGOLAND®
SHE'S AN ABSOLUTE BRICK. (Quoted in Laviosa, 2005)

However, in the Panzani ad the only words are those printed on the packets and a number of the ingredients named as 'de luxe' and the brand name itself. At the most basic level it indicates the name of the manufacturer but Barthes notes that the brand name 'Panzani' also signifies 'Italianicity' – it conjures up a sense of being Italian through the very shape of the word. Of course, as Barthes emphasized, it is necessary to have the appropriate cultural knowledge to be able draw this conclusion.

At this point it is worth distinguishing between two concepts that Barthes uses. When a meaning is explicit, rather than produced through suggestion or association, he uses the term **denotation**. The literal naming of things is regarded as denotative and is associated with straightforward dictionary definitions. However, when meaning is produced through suggestion or association he uses the term **connotation**. Of course, the same word can have denotative and connotative aspects. For example, the word 'tribe' may be used denotatively to refer (literally) to the social division of people but it may, as Robert Moore has noted, assume a connotation of 'primitiveness' or 'backwardness', which is why many writers prefer to use words like 'nation' or 'people' when referring to Native American peoples (Moore in O'Brien and Kollock, 2005: 124). No phrase is intrinsically denotative or connotative because everything depends on interpretation. 'Water is square' may be read as utterly meaningless at the denotative level by a literal-minded person but highly suggestive by someone who treats the phrase as poetic.

Practice Exercise: Italianicity

It is possible to sift through ads to explore how connotations are produced and what meanings seem to be implied through references to different nations or groups of people. It is worth considering how these features help to construct or reinforce different national identities. The following Help File will offer some examples.

Help File: 'Frenchicity', 'Germanicity' – denotation, connotation and national identity

The use of connotation can be illustrated by the German car manufacturer Audi that has been using the phrase 'Vorsprung durch Technik' in their ads since the 1970s (roughly translated it means 'progress through technology'). In Britain, for example, the German language is not widely understood – so, why use a phrase like this?

(Continued)

(Continued)

For many people interested in cars, the look and sound of the words connote what can be called 'Germanicity': high-tech, high-quality engineering. Even in the company name 'Audi' both denotative and connotative meanings can be found – the denotative meaning being an explicit reference to the company itself. However, at the connotative level Audi can suggest things like 'cars of quality', 'cars built with safety in mind', 'cars for the rich', 'cars for people with taste', etc. Notice that even words or phrases that seem impenetrable can connote a sense of nation, quality, etc. (French perfume ads constantly play on the idea of French sophistication.) For Barthes, the image cannot be analysed without reference to the words around it – they will contextualize it and help to guide interpretation (something I will analyse in greater detail below).

The non-coded and coded iconic messages

In order to grasp the concept of iconic messages, it is necessary to understand that an icon is an image analogous to the thing it represents, like the statue or a photograph of a person. At the level of **the non-coded iconic message** we observe the simple objects that have been photographed or depicted (the bag, pasta, tomatoes, etc.). Barthes makes the point that objects have to recognized *before* secondary (connotative) meanings can be derived from them. In this context Barthes developed an idea that has been repeated many times: the non-coded iconic message is '*a message without a code*' (Barthes 1964/1977: 36). This might seem a contradiction but what Barthes emphasized here is that the simple, literal (iconic) recognition of objects is still a form of communication – it is still concerned with perception and knowledge. This point should become clearer when it is contrasted with what Barthes called **coded-iconic messages**.

Barthes argues that once the iconic message has been recognized (as a person, a packet of pasta, etc.) meanings (or signifieds) are made possible through the composition of the images. In the Panzani ad Barthes identifies the half-open string bag with its contents (the icons) as an image that connotes the return from the market (rather than the supermarket – the bag is not plastic). There is also the combination of colours, yellow, green and red, to intensify the sense of stereotypical 'Italianicity' and the suggestion that Panzani can provide all the ingredients for an Italian dish (and the possibility that the tinned sauce gains something from being combined with fresh vegetables). Thus, whereas the coded iconic message is subject to all kinds of deliberate patterning to create meaning, the non-coded iconic message signifies through simple recognition (it is chosen but not coded, only recognized for what it is).

Although Barthes distinguished between non-coded and coded iconic messages, he recognized that the two are experienced together, not separately; images are not recognized and *then* interpreted. What Barthes argues here is that the relation between them is like that of the signifier and signified. Thus, the value of separating them is only for the sake of analytical clarity, something that facilitates an understanding between the relations between the linguistic and iconic aspects of a message. (I shall have more to say about these relations when I introduce the idea of a second-order semiological system.)

The relation between linguistic and iconic levels: anchorage

Barthes' essay is made much more interesting by the fact that he considers the question of how the linguistic message functions with regard to what he calls 'the (twofold) iconic message' (38) To consider this he introduces two further concepts: **anchorage** and '**relay**'. To start with, anchorage is a very useful concept because it describes how the signifieds of the linguistic message steer the viewer towards the meanings desired by the advertisers by reinforcing or supporting the images through elucidation and selection. For Barthes images are '*polysemic*' (open to a variety of possible meanings). Anchorage attempts to restrict this openness by limiting interpretation: it is 'a kind of vice which holds the connoted meanings from proliferating' (39). This is typical (but not an invariable characteristic) of the use of images not only in ads but in newspapers, magazines, comic books and webpages (and even in moving images like film, etc.).

In this respect it is interesting to see how newspapers use carefully selected photographs of suspected criminals to give them a particularly sinister look. However, so that readers do not 'misread' the image (by thinking that the person depicted simply looks tired or unwell) and the newspaper can protect itself from libel the word 'assassin?' (with a question mark) may be appended to it. The careful choice of the image and the caption help to establish a meaning for the image and close it off to other interpretations. If the suspected criminal is then cleared of the crime the same photo can be used with a slogan like 'falsely accused' to re-anchor the image to suggest that the bags under the eyes and unshaven look are not now signs of guilt but of needless innocent suffering and exhaustion.

Practising anchorage: Triumph's 'wolf' and Magritte's 'pipe'

In 2006 the British motorcycle company Triumph advertised their Speed Triple using a photo of it and the caption: 'A wolf in wolf's clothing'. Here anchorage contradicted a literal understanding of the image and punned on a well-known saying (to remove any 'sheepish' references) to anchor the image in such a way that what might have

(Continued)

(Continued)

seemed an ordinary photo of a motorcycle connoted a wildly powerful machine. However, anchorage that contradicts the obvious can be taken in some interesting directions. René Magritte once produced a series of images of a pipe with the caption 'Ceci n'est pas une pipe' (This is not a pipe). This can be used to explore anchorage but also serve to make us more aware of its possible limitations or ambiguities.

Before reading on you might see if you can apply Barthes' notion of anchorage to this playful idea and consider how it might challenge it.

Help File: (anti-)anchorage and 'This is not a pipe'

The negation of what obviously looks like a pipe draws attention to the fact that it is a representation and not the thing itself. At first glance it seems absurd to claim that the image is not a pipe. Surely, the anchorage has got it wrong? The pipe as sign (the combination of signifier and signified) seems to speak for itself as an obvious icon, but the written phrase (the anchorage) can be seen to contradict the obvious commonsense interpretation. This opens up the possibility of something Barthes did not contemplate: the idea of 'anti-anchorage', where a linguistic strategy actually unhinges a predictable, seemingly self-evident reading by opening up other interpretative possibilities. Magritte's phrase renders anchorage ambiguous, even paradoxical – a closing down of the obvious interpretation of the iconic image in order to open up other possibilities. However, while anti-anchorage is possible, Barthes general point still holds: advertisers, newspaper editors, etc. commonly use anchoring tactics to try to restrict or even fix the meanings of images.

The relation between linguistic and iconic levels: relay

If anchorage functions as a restrictive or stabilizing force 'relay' relates to the way words can be appended to images to give a sense of progress through time. To improvise on Barthes' idea for a moment, in comic strips it is quite possible to convey a sense of movement through time without linguistic pointers (we see one action followed by another) but speech bubbles or captions can help to limit or define a sense of action in a more accurate way through phrases like 'see you tomorrow' followed by images of departure and then greeting, or captions like, 'later that day', 'two weeks later', 'ten years before', etc. Again, this device is not limited to static images: these linguistic pointers are also common in film. It is possible to understand 'relay' as a subset of 'anchorage' because it is still guiding interpretation. For practice this means that we must be aware of all the possible factors that may influence *how* the images are stage-managed by the use of words.

Barthes and 'The Photographic Message'

Barthes' essay **'The Photographic Message'** goes into some of the relations between the text and the image explored in 'Rhetoric of the Image', only it relates them to the way photographs are deployed in the press. Again, text, in the shape of headlines, captions and the press article itself, are seen as constantly influencing the way the image is understood (Barthes 1961/1977: 16). In this essay Barthes notes that press photographs look like pure denotation (a language without a code) because they appear to give a neutral and unmediated vision of reality as a kind of brute fact. However, Barthes argues they actually (like the images in advertising) carry (through connotation) a 'supplementary message' (17). The question I want to address here is, if the press photo is a language without a code, in what way can connotation be said to be constructed from or on it? What Barthes states is that apart from the depicted object (what he calls the first order of signification – see below) there are a series of techniques that can be used to influence how an image is interpreted. These are: (1) getting subjects to pose in specific ways; (2) the placement of objects in the frame; (3) the use of 'trick effects'; and (4) what Barthes calls **'photogenia'**.

The first three elements actually change the reality that is photographed, even though the photo may appear 'objective' or 'natural'. As is obvious to most people, the subjects of a photo can be asked to pose in various ways to influence interpretation. For example, a child who is asked to stare upwards with hands held together in prayer may signify innocence, saintliness, purity or spirituality, etc. Objects can be placed in the frame to connote certain things through association. For example, the child may be given a Bible or a candle to hold. All these cultural associations can be seen as part of a lexicon where the individual parts can be placed together to create syntactic patterns of conventionalized representations which influence interpretation. Trick effects, for example, are to do with the way photos can be manipulated but still appear true to life (something even easier to achieve today when a politician's head can easily be 'photoshopped' onto someone else's body for satirical effect). As hinted above, the reason it is easy to trick people with photos is that even when manipulated these 'tricks' are easily concealed owing to what Barthes calls the 'exceptional power' of denotation which confers upon photos a 'special credibility' (21–27).

Finally, the term 'photogenia' focuses on the role played by aesthetic factors. If posing, placement and trick-effects change the 'reality' of the image, photogenia describes how an image is 'embellished' through technical features like lighting, exposure and printing, etc. (23). For example, a photograph of an athlete can be blurred to convey the idea of extreme speed, lighting and exposure might be used to soften an image to lend a romantic tone, etc. In historical hindsight it might seem as if Barthes was stating the obvious in suggesting that it is naïve to see press photos as pure denotation, or as objective reflections of reality. However, it is worth recalling that Barthes was developing these ideas in the early 1960s when photography was still something of an arcane practice for most people. It was not so obvious for many of Barthes' contemporaries that these photographic strategies intervened between so-called objective reality and its photographic representation.

Practice: photographic messages

You might take a series of photos and consider the roles played by posing, placement and trick-effects that change the 'reality' of the image and photogenia (which describes how an image is 'embellished' through technical features like lighting, exposure and printing, etc.). You might start with photos where you would expect high levels of manipulation – like those used in advertisements or film posters. These ideas can then be experimented with to see how they may be useful when applied to moving images like films.

With relation to the tactics described above, Barthes also helped to highlight how the common stock of meanings was attached to certain images. If we return to the point about how the pose of a child praying can conjure up saintly innocence, it is possible to see that it draws on common images to convey a message beyond the simple denotation. Barthes' point was that photographs (and images in general) always have to draw on the knowledge of the viewer to connote something. If they do not, then the reading is either limited to the recognition of the object *as* object (pure denotation – which is rare) or completely arbitrary. This can be demonstrated with relation to an episode of *South Park*.

In episode eight (from season four) Chef wants the South Park flag changed because he thinks it is racist. He objects to the flag because it depicts a black figure being hung on the gallows by a group of white people who look like they are dancing round the hanged person (all the figures are represented in a minimalist way). Chef's mind is eventually changed when he comes up against the following situation. Stan, Kyle and their friends tell him they are against changing the flag and cannot see anything racist in it. Chef, scandalized by their failure to see the 'obvious', starts to rebuke them but suddenly realizes that for the kids it is not racist because they failed to see the stick figures as representing different racial groups – they just saw people. To use Barthes' terms we could say that the flag failed to connote the lynching of a black person to the kids because their common stock of cultural references did not make this reading available. The situation is resolved when the figures surrounding the (black) figure are replaced by people of different colours thus reflecting a multicultural community.

This scenario helps us to understand how important cultural background and knowledge are to how connotation is made possible. However, it also demonstrates that these connotations are not automatic and fixing meaning to images often needs the features Barthes discussed with relation to terms like 'anchorage' and trick effects, etc., if reading them is not to be an arbitrary process. It also tends to reinforce Barthes' point that pure denotation is practically non-existent (30f.), and that no image exists in an interpretive vacuum.

Semiology and ideology

To sum up a little: I have shown how it is possible to understand various aspects of culture by means of a whole series of concepts developed within structuralist thinking. While this might seem excessively formalistic, the points outlined at the end of the last chapter and Eco's analysis of the Bond novels suggest that semiotic analysis can go beyond formalistic explanations of how systems work and how meaning is made possible through them. It has done this by trying to uncover the ideological bases of these systems, and it is to this that I shall now turn.

Oversimplification Warning: ideology

We will see in this chapter (and subsequent chapters) that **ideology** is an exceptionally difficult term to define and for this reason I will not offer a simplistic general definition but gradually explore the notion as the chapters unfold.

We saw in the last chapter that humans can represent themselves as being of different classes, races, genders or sexualites, etc. and that these classifications can easily result in the perception of fundamental 'natural' differences where a sense of right and wrong, good and bad can be attached to them. We also saw that women are often defined in binary opposition to men. This illustrates how semiotic analysis can help to uncover the ideology of patriarchal structures that perpetuate the subordination of women. This ideology of patriarchy is also linked to Monique Wittig's claim that the terms 'men' and 'women' are not 'natural facts' but 'political categories'. As I shall demonstrate, this is very much in line with the way Barthes understood the workings of ideology – where 'culture' (or history) is constantly mistaken for 'nature'.

From this point of view, as Edward Sapir has observed, it is necessary to recognize that people do not live in an 'objective world' but 'are very much at the mercy of the particular language which has become the medium of expression for their society' (Sapir, 1929/1958: 69). This reflects Fiske's point that what passes for 'reality' is the product of the way cultures codify it. This raises the important question (as we will see when we come to discuss Althusser and Thompson in later chapters) of up to what extent people are at the mercy of the particular language, or the cultural systems, in which representations and meanings are produced. This, in turn, raises the question of the way ideology is produced within these structures.

So, one of the things that has made semiotic analysis of particular interest to cultural studies is its ability to explore how ideology is produced within signifying practices (if it only offered formalistic descriptions of the way meaning is made possible, it would only be of limited interest). One of the ways semiotics is able to shed light on ideology can be discerned with relation to Umberto Eco's observation that the Bond novels obey the traditional, archetypal, Manichean code of good versus evil where the world is understood in terms of simplistic opposites (Eco, 1966: 260). For Eco, the novels are ideological in the broadest sense of the term: their typical structures are little more than an apology for Western political ideals, which leave no room for a more complex understanding of West–East political relations. As Turner has stated in the context of the analysis of popular texts within cultural studies, the structuralist influence has come to mean that analysis is not so much confined to the structures of individual works but widened to focus attention on the 'wider structures that produced them' (2003: 17).

Eco, despite his formalism, can be seen to reflect this because, by considering the Bond novels as a whole, he shows that they are structured around ideology because they serve as a simplistic apology for Western political, economic and cultural values, beliefs and ways of life (they constantly privilege the British and their allies above ugly, if ingenious, communists, neo-Nazi criminals and other grotesque villains). So it is that Eco helps us to perceive 'wider structures' by showing how Fleming echoes the climate of the Cold War and reflects, through sometimes laughable caricatures, the dominant ideology of the West.

Semiology and ideology: the ideological contents of our age

In one of the essays reviewed above, 'The Photographic Message', Barthes finds ideological implications in the way images are subjected to technical and cultural manipulation. At the end of this essay Barthes, reflecting Marxist thought, sees ideology in terms of how cultural forms are indicative of the dominant beliefs and values of the ruling classes. Thus, he mentions the possibility of evaluating 'the ideological contents of our age' with relation to the 'code of connotation of a mode of communication' – in this case through the press photo. What this entails is an attempt to understand the forms that a society uses to 'ensure its peace of mind and to grasp thereby the magnitude, the detours and the underlying function of that activity' (Barthes 1961/1977: 31).

From this point of view, ideology can be unpacked, as it were, by looking at all those forms which reinforce the status quo and thereby perpetuate the ways of seeing and interests that are embodied within it. This is why he was always so suspicious of words like 'nature' because he suspected that something was always being hidden behind them (I shall come back to this in a moment). This leads us on to one of his most famous and accessible books, *Mythologies*, a collection of essays written in the mid-1950s for French literary magazines. It was revised in 1970 to include an academic essay called 'Myth Today' and has since become very important to the way cultural studies has theorized popular culture. It is a book which covers a great deal of ground analysing, as it does, things like sweating Romans in films, the face of Greta Garbo, the meaning of Einstein's brain, striptease, soap powders and detergents, margarine, toys, new cars, wine, milk, steak and chips, ornamental cookery and plastic (and this does not exhaust all its subjects).

(Bourgeois) Paris meets its match: Barthes and modern mythologies

Barthes' choice of title might seem odd; especially as myth is something that is habitually associated with dead religions. Yet, within structuralist thinking, Barthes used the idea to expose the class interests that are expressed in, and lay behind, the established order of things. In this way Barthes helped to revolutionize 'ideological critique' through an engagement with Saussurean concepts applied to the social world around him. By exposing what he called **modern mythologies** he helped to make semiotics a major form of ideological analysis. He did this by focusing on the products of mass culture and treating what he called 'collective representations' as sign systems. The end of which was to 'account in detail for the mystification which transforms petit-bourgeois culture into a universal nature' (Barthes, 1957/1972: 11). It is this that gives rise to the modern myth (Barthes' notion of petit-bourgeois culture should become clearer as the chapter progresses).

It may be objected that structuralism is not needed to demystify bourgeois culture. This is true but this brings me onto another important part of Barthes' approach. Barthes' idea was to combine denunciation with 'an appropriate method of detailed analysis', what he called '**semioclasm**' (8), a neat combination of semiotics and iconoclasm which was to provide a way of offering very close and methodical critiques of cultural phenomena. Structuralism helped to provide the concepts and the general method – linked of course to Barthes' own broad culture, intellectual subtlety and ingenuity. The exposé of modern 'myths' or bourgeois class interests (disguised in the culture of everyday life) involved being constantly aware of the obfuscation of nature and history. Discovering modern myths was made difficult because they resided in the 'falsely obvious', the taken for granted, or 'the-what-goes-without-saying' (10). Barthes, in a later essay, which summed up some of the propositions set out in *Mythologies*, explained that:

> myth consists in overturning culture into nature or, at least, the social, the cultural, the ideological, the historical into the 'natural'. What is nothing but a product of class division and its moral, cultural and aesthetic consequences is presented (stated) as being a 'matter of course'; under the effect of mythical inversion, the quite contingent foundations of the utterance become Common Sense, Right Reason, the Norm, General Opinion, in short the *doxa* [...]. (Barthes, 1971/1977: 165)

Barthes' basic method was to reverse this mythical inversion and expose these processes. In the essay he appended to *Mythologies* entitled 'Myth Today' he draws on Saussurean concepts to show how this is possible, defining myth as a kind of language but one which is a '*second-order semiological system*' (1957/1972: 113). In the last chapter I outlined Saussure's notion of the sign which is the combination of a signifier (a word or image) and a signified (a concept or idea which is evoked by the signifier). This is a **first-order** system. Barthes says that this first-order semiological system functions as the signifier of the second-order system.

To give an example of how these two orders relate to one another I will discuss the famous case that Barthes used to describe it (see Figure 3.2). Barthes is at the barber's and he is given a copy of the popular magazine *Paris Match*. On the cover there is a photo of a young black soldier in French uniform. His eyes are uplifted, and Barthes imagines that his gaze is probably fixed on the French flag. The simple recognition of the saluting soldier is the first-order semiological system but Barthes argues (drawing on his cultural knowledge) that this basic level is there to signify something else which reinforces the present socio-political arrangements in France:

> But, whether naively or not, I see very well what it signifies to me: that France is a great empire, that all her sons, without any colour discrimination, faithfully serve under her flag, and there is no better answer to the detractors of an alleged colonialism than the zeal shown by this Negro in serving his so-called oppressors. (1957/1972: 115)

To elaborate on this a little, the first semiological system refers to the signifier (the shapes of the photo on the page) and the signified (the recognition of a black soldier saluting French flag). The second-order system takes the signified of the first-order system (a black soldier saluting) and makes

Figure 3.2 Paris Match 326

© Lagardère

it into a signifier, which is given a culturally loaded meaning (the connotation, ideology or myth) and which is an apology for French colonialism. For Barthes, this is how modern myth functions: it restricts the signifying power of the signifier in the second-order semiological system by using it for a narrow (ideological) end. That is to say, the myth reduces the complexities of the existence of a black soldier in the French army by subordinating it to France's social, economic, political and imperial interests: he is reduced to a simple ideological (pro-imperialist) 'gesture' (121). It follows from this that the second-order semiological system is responsible for the myth.

The example of the black soldier typifies a semiotic reading of culture to expose the ruling ideologies that are constantly being circulated in the cultures of everyday life. Thus, an approach that looks like a mere formalism on the surface can help to generate engaged political criticism. For Barthes it is always important to recognize the interaction between the first and second orders of signification. The first order is like a car windscreen through which it is necessary to look to see a landscape but seems invisible or transparent if attention is only focused upon the landscape itself. It is impossible to see the second level (the landscape) without taking account of the first but it is always possible to choose to focus on the one or the other level for theoretical purposes (122). To be aware of this process is the job of semiotic reading because it is able to expose how modern myths are made possible. Given these fine distinctions Barthes, at this stage of his career, thought of semiotics as a science (109).

Myth, motivation and naturalization

For Barthes modern myths are 'motivated' (Barthes, 1957/1972: 117). **Motivation** can be explained with relation to a point made earlier about Saussure: that signifiers can have more than one signified and vice versa. The myth (or ideological message) is motivated because the concept (or signified) of the second-order system is drawn from the common stock of pre-existing meanings. What this means is that the ideological (imperialist) message behind the black soldier's salute could be expressed through a multitude of other signifiers. Barthes offers alternative possibilities like a French general pinning a medal to a one-armed Senegalese, or a French nun giving a cup of tea to a bed-ridden Arab (125–26). Each of these scenes is motivated by the same ideologically motivated message.

To explore this a little further, the 'falsely obvious', 'the-what-goes-without-saying' (10) within semiotics, is known as **naturalization**. As we know, women can be forced or coerced to take a secondary role in society, certain races or ethnicities can be forced into slavery or only given menial jobs, non-heterosexual relations can be seen as a perversion of what is normal etc.: this is something dependent on the way societies are shaped throughout history. This is often called 'contingent', meaning they could have developed in other ways. Thus, once colonial, patriarchal or class rule over other nations, genders or groups is an accepted everyday part of life (as a part of nature and the way things *should be*) it can be said that they have been 'naturalized'. For Barthes, people who do not see through this process of naturalization are 'myth-consumers' (128) and at the mercy of a 'certain regime of ownership' which is the bourgeois system (dominated by capitalist production, the exploitation of the proletariat and the values of consumerism) that sustains the various guises of the bourgeoisie (137–138).

If we are myth-consumers we are unwittingly hoodwinked by these myths which only help to reinforce images which support the status quo – society as it benefits the interests of those who dominate it. In this context Barthes sees bourgeois ideology as largely anonymous (it is not named as such except by intellectuals on the Left) and it is at work not only in the imperatives of consumer culture and the press but in justice, diplomacy, film, theatre, 'pulp literature', social ritual and conversation (like commenting on a 'touching wedding', talking about the weather, food, etc.). These are the norms by which myth consumers live where 'reality' seems to exist spontaneously, without a class origin, as if there is some kind of universal or 'Eternal Man, who is neither proletarian nor bourgeois' (139).

Coming back to the photo of the black soldier, ideology *does not* hide imperialism but states it. It does this in such a way that it makes it an innocent and largely unquestioned everyday fact of life – in this sense it serves to reassure the public and is able to depoliticize things (143). To put this another way, Barthes states that the bourgeoisie effectively 'hides the fact that it is the bourgeoisie' (never announces itself *as such*) and therefore produces myth. Open revolution announces itself 'and thereby abolishes myth' because it is not involved in the mystification of itself (147). It is possible to adapt an image from Slavoj Žižek to illustrate this. Žižek states that the right-wing intellectual is a conformist knave who 'refers to the mere existence of the given order as an argument for it, and mocks the Left on account of its 'utopian plans, which necessarily lead to catastrophe' (Žižek, 1997: 45). Following Barthes and Žižek, we could say that representing the status quo in this way is a perfect piece of modern capitalist mythology.

Barthes' reading of the society wedding helps to demonstrate how the values and practices of the dominant classes come to filter into everyday life (even if, for many, it may only function as a distant dream). Barthes argues that the 'big wedding' may seem a vital part of everyday life but actually has its origins in the bourgeois class ritual which unites marriage with the ostentatious parade and consumption of wealth (and which is disseminated through media like the press, film and popular literature). It is by 'spreading its representations over a whole catalogue of collective images for petit-bourgeois use' that the bourgeoisie is able to create the illusion of 'a lack of differentiation of the social classes'. For Barthes, at the moment a typist earning very little money '*recognizes herself* in the big wedding of the bourgeoisie' bourgeois ideology has effectively succeeded in extending itself (1957/1972: 140). Before I continue to discuss some of the complexities of encoding and decoding I will offer some advice on how some of these ideas might be put into practice.

Thus, from the point of view of Barthes' notion of ideology, subjects in society are coerced to see, think and behave in ways that reflect the dominant socio-political, economic system. This can be seen from the way baby clothes tend to stratify recent arrivals by colour coding them into 'feminine' pink and 'masculine' blue. A walk round most toy stores serves to demonstrate the ways in which children are exposed to the further stratification of the feminine and the masculine in terms of the way the shops are divided into separate territories of dolls and soldiers, etc., with the nebulous neutral area of pencils and plasticine in the middle.

Practice: working with modern mythology and orders of signification

As described above, Barthes called the signified of the first-order semiological system the signifier of the second-order semiological system and the signified of the second-order system is what Barthes referred to as signification – which is where modern mythologies are to be found. One simple practice exercise to explore modern mythologies would be to look for images that are clearly ideologically motivated (in the way the photo of the black solder is); another would be to invent some images for yourself. For example, images could be assembled that would seem to uphold the principles of capitalism. Here are some ideas: a business person handing out a cheque for charity; a boss and a union representative smiling and shaking hands; a technician representing a major oil company standing in front of solar panels; or a wind turbine against a blue sky and a green landscape.

Having done this you can offer a reading of your own images, describing the stages and explaining (using your cultural knowledge) how it is possible to arrive at a myth which can be said to support the status quo of capitalist society. Once the semiological systems are distinguished from one another it is possible to see the common myth behind the images I suggested above as something like: 'Some people might complain about consumer capitalism but, in practice, it's basically humane, responsible and it works!' Then you need to explain how this myth, this simple meaning, is always at the expense of a larger history which is repressed: that businesses may give money to charity but are not principally defined by altruism; that, although agreements are made by management and unions, their history is largely one of bitter conflict growing out of things like exploitation, poor work conditions, low wages and lay-offs; that while multinationals may invest some money in the environment they are the biggest abusers of it, etc.

Notes on further practice: operation margarine

For further practice you might try to test out some of the points that Barthes makes about the rhetorical forms that bourgeois myths take. They include things like inoculating the public against criticism by 'admitting the accidental evil of a class-bound institution the better to conceal its principal evil' (Barthes, 1957/1972: 151). This could be illustrated by my last point but Barthes exemplifies this through reference to an advertisement he saw for Astra margarine. It begins with an indignant cry: 'A mousse? Made with margarine? Unthinkable!' However, once the mind has been softened up through criticism it is then revealed as delicious, useful – and cheap. The moral is that your prejudice '[has] cost you dearly!' The margarine ad is like an allegory for how the same strategy relates to important institutions like the army and the church and how they are defended in films and novels. For example, Barthes notes that Graham Greene's play *The Living Room* begins with 'burning zeal' about the weaknesses, bigotry and 'self-righteousness and narrow-mindedness' of the church but ends by suggesting that, despite all its failings, the church 'is a way to salvation for its very victims' and so justifies itself through 'the saintliness of those whom it crushes' (39–41). It is possible, then, to look out for examples of 'operation margarine' in all areas of culture to see how far criticism is only put forward so it can be disarmed by a sense of greater good. For example, nuclear armaments (and nuclear power) are commonly justified by acknowledging some element of danger (especially post-Chernobyl and Fukushima), but this is often neutralized by the 'what is all this compared to its advantages?' strategy.

Practice and the privation of history

There is also what Barthes referred to as 'the privation of history' tactic that, as noted above with relation to the black soldier, empties signifiers of all history so signification can be limited. This can be explored with relation to war reports in the media where phrases like 'collateral damage' are commonly used. There is a very suggestive example of how war becomes naturalized and how myth works in Jean-Luc Godard's film *Pierrot le fou* (*Pierrot the Mad*, 1965). The two protagonists hear a report about how 115 men are killed in the Vietnam War. One of the characters, Marianne, says that she is saddened by the anonymity of the deaths, and about how the soldiers' lives evoke nothing more than a statistic. The signifiers are reduced to a simple calculation in such a way that it serves as an example of bourgeois myth at work. This manoeuvre is further compounded when her lover, Bernard (Pierrot), says 'C'est la vie!': it is the matter of fact response that normalizes the tragedy and transforms misfortune and complexity into 'that's life'.

Identification: transforming the Other into the self

Other tactics to be aware of are the processes of 'identification' which reflect the inability of the petit-bourgeois to imagine the Other: 'If he comes face to face with him, he blinds himself, ignores and denies him, or else transforms him into himself' (Barthes, 1957/1972: 152). From this point of view, 'delinquents', like the hooligan, the parricide and the homosexual (who seem to suggest difference to the bourgeois individual) are represented as 'going astray' from an essential (bourgeois) nature. Thus, it is possible to study how cultures are represented in films, books, news, etc. to see whether ways of life, customs, etc. are reduced to some essential nature that denies cultural difference. The obverse of this is *exoticism* where the Other becomes an oddity, a spectacle, 'relegated to the confines of humanity' and thereby no longer threatens the bourgeois view of the world (153). There is also the magic device of tautology which consists in mere repetition, like when someone answers the question, 'What is life?' with the answer 'life is life'. This strategy gestures at rationality but fails it, denies it, and imposes its irrational law through authority, not rational explanation. Just like war in Jean-Luc Godard's *Pierrot le fou*: that's the way the world is, things just *are*.

(Continued)

(Continued)

Allied to the last point is the strategy that assumes that things have an essential character but then denies that they can be reduced by language. Barthes offers the example of the theatre as a good example of this contradiction where, on the one hand, 'theatre is presented as an essence which cannot be reduced to any language and reveals itself only to the heart' yet, on the other, 'to describe the theatre intellectually is disparaged as 'scientism or pedantic' (154). Without referring to Barthes, Leslie Fiedler once showed how this functioned in the USA with relation to the denigration of comics. What he noticed was that the 'bourgeois hostility to popular culture' (Fiedler 1955/1972: 462) was dominated by middle-brow taste which looked down on comics but, at the same time, was equally ill-disposed towards intellectual culture that it did not understand: thus, the 'middlebrow reacts with equal fury to an art that baffles his understanding and to one which refuses to aspire to his level' (464).

Common sense alert!

The strategies outlined above are linked to what Barthes understood as the way myths reside in statements of 'fact' expressed as *common sense*. For Barthes, common sense is no more than a disguise for the interests that refuse any real explanation and that leave the established bourgeois social structures just where they are (Barthes, 1957/1972: 155). This is an important point because Barthes indicated in his preface to *Mythologies* that the starting point of his reflections 'was usually a feeling of impatience at the sight of the "naturalness" with which newspapers, art and common sense constantly dress up a reality which, even though it is the one we live in, is undoubtedly determined by history' (10).

Interpreting signs in the media: Hall's 'Encoding and Decoding in Television Discourse'

Some readers may be sceptical about some of Barthes' interpretations and, indeed, later chapters will show how poststructuralist thinkers (Barthes among them) have questioned structuralism as a reliable method. However, in defence of Barthes, he was aware that different readings are made possible according to the political beliefs of the perceiver. Yet he was confident he had unpacked the mythic content because he felt that he had the necessary cultural knowledge to see behind the use of language and images. Of course, he knew the image of the black soldier could be read in other ways – for example, while it may convey a mythic content it would be likely to provoke a more antagonistic response from the Left. But, as Barthes shows, that does not mean that a reader on the Left cannot see what the image is being used to signify – although this may be a complex affair.

This raises a very important question that is of great interest to areas like cultural studies: how is it possible to distinguish the between different potential meanings? Stuart Hall, in his essay 'Encoding and Decoding in Television Discourse' (in Hall et al., 1973/1980), can help to answer this question. Hall uses the language of structuralism to distinguish between '**encoding**' and '**decoding**' with relation to TV (although his ideas can be applied to all kinds of media). Hall challenges the simple encoding/decoding model which assumes that someone encodes a message in a particular medium and the receiver (in command of the necessary code) decodes it. By appreciating the complexity of the processes involved, including the idea of the audience (as something fragmented into distinct social groups rather than something homogeneous), Hall questioned the efficacy of the old encoding and decoding paradigm: in short, there could be no simple correlation between the emission and reception of signs.

Hall and preferred readings

The question to be answered here is how this relates to Barthes' method. Barthes was trying to isolate what Hall would call the '**preferred reading**' of a message (as a combination of image, voice and text). The question here is, is the audience positioned in such a way that certain meanings or experiences are made available (and others closed off)? Hall insists that visual media are encoded according to conventions but may not be decoded in the way that the makers of a TV programme (or any text) may have wished. However, this does not mean that just any meaning can be imposed: for example, it would be hard to justify an image of a dog licking a child's face (with no caption) as an injunction to commit murder. Barthes' ideas of myth insist on seeing images not only in relation to the way images are marshalled but also how they link to common meanings already circulating within society. Hall's ideas help us consider these things but also to speculate on the possibilities of alternative readings.

Alternative meanings and the 'Battle of Orgreave'

To give an example of what Hall is arguing I shall take an incident that Hall does not mention and then link it to his ideas. The incident is known as the 'Battle of Orgreave' which names a clash between coal miners and the police in South Yorkshire in June 1984 during the miners' strike of 1984–5. There was considerable controversy about the fights that broke out between police, who were required to protect a steel works from picketing miners, and the miners themselves who wanted to put the steel works out of action. Amid incidents of stone throwing, miners repeatedly tried to overcome the police cordon but they were repulsed.

What happened next is what caused the controversy. The miners' ranks were definitively broken and they were forced to retreat across a railway line. Much of the press emphasized the antagonistic role of the miners, although some claimed that the police brutally and deliberately attacked miners. In an emblematic photo taken by the photographer John Harris a woman named Lesley Boulton (a member of Women Against Pit Closures) is seen holding a camera and defending herself from a mounted policeman about to bring his raised truncheon down on her head. Boulton, and others, agreed that the miners at this point had no intention of attacking the police, yet the police chased and attacked the miners. That evening BBC1 put out a controversial report, complete with film of the incidents that showed miners attacking the police. Miners and some onlookers (including John Harris who took the photo (Harris, 2011)) claimed it was the police who actually attacked the miners – not the other way round. Harris, as a personal witness, confirms the exemplary behaviour of the miners and corroborates that Boulton was calling for an ambulance at the time of the attack, something that tends to support Seumus Milne's argument that the filmed events were reversed to buttress the claim put forward by the government of the then Prime Minister (Margaret Thatcher) that the militant miners represented 'the enemy within' that had to be rooted out (Milne, 2004).

The 'Battle of Orgreave' and preferred, negotiated and oppositional readings

The question I want to pose here is how Hall's ideas would help to theorize this. Hall distinguished between different possibilities for decoding visual texts: not only the 'preferred' but also the **negotiated** and **oppositional readings**. The preferred is what the producer (or programme makers) want(s) the audience to understand (the dominant-hegemonic position). The negotiated reading is what normally takes place – audiences are normally influenced by dominant codes and may accept much of the dominant, hegemonic interpretation of events but may also resist certain aspects of the preferred reading. A negotiated reading would also have to take account of the way personal experience and interests may influence interpretation. The oppositional (or counter-hegemonic) position is where the viewer understands the preferred reading being constructed but chooses a critical position (like Barthes did of the *Paris Match* cover). In the original BBC report the preferred reading is encoded with relation to the showing of the filmed events in the following order: (a) rioting miners; (b) police charging with batons; then (c) arrests. Added to this there is the verbal reporting (anchorage) which reinforces the above order of events.

From this it is possible to see that encoding the events in this way encourages the TV audience to decode the battle as being caused by the miners, and this fits in with the hegemonic reading (which Harris's photo challenges). If viewers decoded the message in these terms, then they would have been like Barthes' 'myth-consumers' who unquestioningly accept the dominant meanings of the events legitimated and conveyed by the producers of the codes. However, another possibility may be considered: if the BBC had reflected the order that miners (and other onlookers) insisted was the right one, an alternative encoded sequence would have been produced: (a) police charging with batons; (b) rioting miners; then (c) arrests, plus the verbal reporting. In this case the encoded message would have invited an alternative preferred reading which was critical of police behaviour. Nevertheless, Hall insists that a negotiated meaning is more likely: this is where there is no exact one-to-one relation between encoding and decoding because it is very difficult to guarantee that a vast TV audience will respond *exactly* as the programme planners would like – although with the correct sequencing, choice of photos, verbal reports they can go quite some way towards achieving this (Hall et al., 1973/1980: 135).

However, any deliberately oppositional reading would have to read against the grain of the preferred reading. In the above example on the miners' strike this would be someone who watches the original BBC news account but doubts the way the events are reported. We could imagine someone like Barthes who is sympathetic to the miners and who understands what it is the programme makers require the public to think but who, nevertheless, reads the message within some other critical frame of reference. Did the events *really* happen in this way? How much did media manipulation (of what seems like incontestable filmed reality) distort the events? Hall argues that the oppositional reading is typical of a person who 'listens to a debate on the need to limit wages but "reads" every mention of the "national interest" as "class interest"' (Hall et al., 1973/1980: 138). This takes us back to questions of ideology where a news service encodes events in such a way that they function to support the right-wing, anti-union government of Margaret Thatcher. The important thing about these reflections is that while there is always a certain autonomy in terms of how messages are decoded there are often coding practices which help to manoeuvre interpretation or restrict it in important ways.

Practising 'Encoding and Decoding in Television Discourse'

As a practice exercise you might record a series of news programmes to explore the different possibilities for decoding visual media and see if you can distinguish between what 'preferred', 'negotiated' and 'oppositional' reading might look like. The comments on the 'Battle of Orgreave' should help you to consider these possibilities. If you record different news reports of the same incidents (especially if the channels are not owned by the same media company) this may help to expose the different

(Continued)

(Continued)

rhetorics which help to create 'preferred' readings. You may explore reports across different media with distinct political affiliations (newspapers, magazines, TV news, blogs, etc.) to help you explore these themes. For example, John Harris has distinguished between five different responses to his photo of Lesley Boulton: (1) right-wing responses have suggested the photo was manipulated to make it look like a policeman attacked Boulton; (2) the policeman was just a 'rotten apple' in an otherwise good policing barrel; (3) that the police did a good job and that Boulton should not have been where she was; (4) interpretations more sympathetic to the miners saw the truncheon attack as a disturbing new trend in policing; (5) the attack on Boulton was typical of the policing of the mining communities (Harris, 2011).

Of course, not all critics have been convinced by Hall's theses, Shaun Moores questioning how we can ever really know when we have found the preferred reading (1993: 28), David Morley raising wider questions about how understanding influences interpretation (1992: 126f.) and Robert Stam insisting on a more complex notion of reading that accounts for more contradictory possibilities (2000: 233f.). However, while taking account of these problems, I would argue that Hall's concepts can help to explore *how* dominant readings are made possible (with relation to coding and decoding). You may want to rethink some of these issues after reading the chapters on poststructuralism.

This kind of reading can be seen within what Hall has termed 'the politics of signification' where the meaning of events has to be fought over because it is within signification that 'collective social understandings are created' and where these meanings can be contested (Hall, 1982: 70). From this point of view signification is a kind of hegemonic battlefield where meanings have real-world consequences. In the next chapter I shall continue to examine how structuralist thinking has helped to probe the institutional contexts and effects of ideology.

Summary of key points

In this chapter I have shown how structuralism has provided methods to interpret popular cultural forms, demonstrating how Eco analysed Fleming's Bond novels and reduced them to their narrative structures. Propp's concepts have been introduced to help with the task of practising this form of semiotic analysis. This chapter has also introduced the work of Roland Barthes to show how a series of very useful concepts can help us to interpret both texts and images and see how the public may be influenced to read them in dominant ways. Barthes' idea that contemporary ideology is a kind of 'mythology' has been discussed and his classic reading of a photo of a black soldier has been deployed to see how semiotic analysis works in practice. The chapter has also looked at the concepts that can help to consider what ideology is and how it functions. The final sections have considered Stuart Hall's theory of encoding and decoding and a reading of the 'Battle of Orgreave' has helped us to understand the complexity of the semiotic processes involved.

Further reading

Roland Barthes and semiotic readings of culture: Barthes' *A Lover's Discourse: Fragments* (1977/1979) can be seen as a kind of semiotic de-mythologizer, where love is broken down into what Barthes regarded as the image-repertoires that dominate the lover. Barthes' *Empire of Signs* (1970/1983) is ostensibly about Japan but is an object lesson in semiotic reading which treats Japan as a sign system, an 'empire' of (empty) signs. This is a good example of semiotics at its most playful and suggestive. Barthes' *The Fashion System* (1967/1985), like *Empire of Signs*, does not treat its subject as separate from semiotic systems – Barthes discussing garments and the photography of them as discourses. This book is worth exploring as a detailed and ingenious example of semiotic theory in practice which further develops the idea found in *Mythologies* that bourgeois values normalise and colonise culture. Barthes' *Camera Lucida* (1980/2000) moves well beyond Barthes' early semiotic explorations of images (in this case static and moving) but, in its more freewheeling meditative style, is still indebted to his structuralist roots and has a lot to say about how conventions attempt to fix the meaning of images and how they may be liberated. Tzvetan Todorov's chapter 'The Typology of Detective Fiction' (in his *The Poetics of Prose* (1977)) would help to isolate the main conventions of detective narratives from a structuralist point of view and would complement the references to Eco and Propp.

Stuart Hall's 'The Determination of News Photographs' (1981a) is inspired by Barthes' methods of reading and would complement my reading of 'The Battle of Orgreave'. Jack Lule's 'Enduring Image of War: Myth and Ideology in a *Newsweek* Cover' (1995) offers a practical reading of a *Newsweek* cover very much in the style of Barthes' reading of the cover of *Paris Match*. There are many books which use semiotic theory to discuss advertising. Beasley and Danesi's *Persuasive Signs: The Semiotics of Advertising* (2002) offers a thoroughgoing overview of the possibilities, looking at advertising as a signifying system within social discourse. Jean-Marie Floch's *Visual Identities* (2000) shows how ads can be analysed using semiotics as a method. He subjects ads by companies like IBM, Apple, Chanel and Waterman (pens) to close scrutiny. The strength of this book is in not only interpreting ads from a broadly semiotic point of view but that it is written with industrial advertisers in mind. Shaun Moores's *Interpreting Audiences: The Ethnography of Media Consumption* (1993) is recommended because, from an ethnographic point of view, it considers the power of media texts to determine meaning but also considers the importance of the multiple contexts (and the difficulties) of reception.

The representation of the miners in the media: James Curran and Jane Seaton (2009) *Power Without Responsibility: Press Broadcasting and New Media in Britain* is a useful source to consider the so-called free press in Britain, which includes detailed sections on the reporting of miners' strikes. Seumus Milne's *The Enemy Within: The Secret War Against the Miners* (2004) offers valuable insights into Margaret Thatcher's attack on the miners and the unions, bringing out the biased reporting, dirty tactics, slur campaigns and political chicaneries behind the scenes. See BBC South Yorkshire for the photo of Lesley Boulton and a brief account of the 'Battle of Orgreave'. It can be accessed at: www.bbc.co.uk/southyorkshire/content/articles/2009/03/02/lesley_boulton_orgreave_photo_feature.shtml

4

Ideology

Marxism and Louis Althusser

Learning goals

- To appreciate how Louis Althusser's thought is indebted to structuralist ways of thinking and how it differs from more 'culturalist' approaches.
- To understand the nuances of Atlhusser's conception of ideology and how it functions to create subjects in society.
- To become aware of the interconnections between the main concepts introduced.
- To see how the key concepts work and how they may be put into practice.

Concepts

The key concepts introduced in this chapter are: ideology, the ideological state apparatuses, the repressive state apparatuses, overdetermination, the material and imaginary aspects of ideology, interpellation, double reading, the problematic and symptomatic reading.

Introduction

This chapter introduces some of the ideas that cultural studies has found most useful in the work of the Marxist philosopher Louis Althusser, something which will involve detailed discussions of how Althusser's notion of ideology is indebted to structuralist ways of thinking. The chapter will be concluded by outlining the rift between the Althusserians and other Marxists, like E. P. Thompson, who were more committed to the idea of human agency.

Introduction: Althusserian structuralism

Louis Althusser was a French Marxist philosopher whose ideas have had a decisive influence on cultural studies. What is distinctive about his work is the way in which he combined Marx's writings with the structuralist ideas that were circulating at the time. Although his greatest influence was during the 1970s and 1980s he still remains an important source of concepts within cultural studies. This is particularly the case when questions of ideology are discussed. To begin my introduction to Louis Althusser's impact on cultural studies I will refer to Clifford Geertz's point that he did not think that culture was best seen in the more traditional terms of customs, traditions and ingrained habits, etc. but as 'a set of control mechanisms – plans, recipes, rules, instructions' that govern behaviour (1973: 44). If culture is seen as a 'control mechanism' this seems to suggest that it is deterministic (that is, that people are not free to choose but governed by social structures). However, the extent to which culture is a control mechanism depends on how much emphasis is put on the idea of the underlying rules of culture as a kind of *langue* in relation to particular cultural practices, which would be the *paroles*. This notion of culture is one reason why, when structuralist ideas first began to make an impact, not everyone was convinced by the new method, or the assumptions behind it (see the last section of this chapter).

Before I continue I want to stress that Althusser's re-readings of Marx are very sophisticated and my comments can do no more that scratch the surface. It is also worth noting that although Althusser's writings are often associated with structuralism, his relation to it is often very tangential and mediated not only through Marx's writings but though many other thinkers (primarily Engels, Freud and Jacques Lacan, but also others like Descartes, Spinoza, Leibniz, Hegel, Lenin and Mao). Furthermore, like most thinkers, Althusser's concepts evolved throughout his career (Montag, 2003: 77). Thus, my version of Althusser tends to reflect what cultural studies has tended to find of interest in his work. To begin a more detailed discussion of Althusser's definitions of ideology I will outline his distinction between repressive and ideological state apparatuses.

The ideological and repressive state apparatuses

Althusser, in 'Ideology and State Apparatuses' (from *Lenin and Philosophy and Other Essays* (1971)), begins by reiterating Marx's point that any given 'social formation' (like capitalism), in order to preserve itself from collapse, must develop effective mechanisms to perpetuate the social, economic and political structures upon which it is based. Thus, capitalism is not only characterized by the production of commodities and services but by the way it preserves and protects itself by ensuring fundamental rights to do with individual ownership and the right to employ people and amass huge private fortunes. At the same time entities like the education and legal institutions have to be managed carefully to ensure and maintain the privileges of those who have most to gain from the given arrangements. Thus, Althusser stresses that 'in order to exist, every social formation must reproduce the conditions of its production at the same time as it produces, and in order to be able to produce' (1971: 128). To explain this Althusser referred to the **ideological state apparatuses** and the **repressive state apparatuses**.

For Althusser, following the Marxist-Leninist tradition, the state is a 'machine' of repression, which permits the ruling classes to exercise power and secure their domination over the working classes, and thus subject the workers to capitalist exploitation and control (137). One of the questions that Althusser set himself to answer was how the capitalist machine functioned. To simplify, Althusser insisted that the state is an 'apparatus'. What this means is that it includes a series of instruments of social control like the legal system (allied to the police, the courts and the prisons); but it also includes the army, which functions as a 'supplementary repressive force' when the police services fail. Above all this 'ensemble' is the head of state, the government and the administration. All this, of course, functions 'in the interests of the ruling classes' (137). These are the repressive state apparatuses.

The ideological state apparatuses (or ISAs) are associated with religion, education, the family, law, politics, trade-unionism, communications (the press, radio and television, etc.) and culture (which includes literature, the arts, sports, etc.). These are linked to 'distinct and specialized institutions' which differ from the (repressive) state apparatus because they belong to the *private* domain. The state is conceived to be neither public nor private but above these distinctions; this is because 'it is the precondition for any distinction between public and private' (143–144). Althusser distinguishes between the two apparatuses because, as we shall see, the repressive state apparatus functions 'by violence' (not always but in the 'last instance'), whereas the ISAs function (not surprisingly) 'by ideology' (145).

Oversimplification Warning: state and ideological apparatuses

Althusser insisted that repressive and ideological aspects of the state apparatuses cannot be divided in any simplistic way. While the (repressive) state apparatus functions predominantly by repression, it still has a secondary ideological function because there is 'no such thing as a purely repressive apparatus'. At the same time, the army and the police also have an ideological dimension insofar as there are discourses which 'ensure their own cohesion and reproduction, and in the "values" they propound externally' (145).

(Continued)

(Continued)

On the other hand, the ideological State apparatuses also have a secondary repressive function, even if concealed or symbolic. Thus, 'there is no such thing as a purely ideological apparatus' (145). For example, schools, churches and other institutions have their modes of punishment (failure, expulsion, etc.) to discipline those who contravene the rules. This is also true of the family, or the cultural apparatuses like the press and cinema, etc., which all have their own internal and external controls and censorship, etc. Thus, it is possible to see why these, and other things like the legal system, can be seen as part of both the state and the ideological apparatuses.

Althusser develops his argument by stating that there is a principle that unites all the different ISAs: that is, the ideology of the ruling class. His reasoning is that given that the ruling class holds state power (normally 'by means of alliances between classes or class fractions') it follows that it also has at its disposal the ideological state apparatuses. In this Althusser's point reflects Antonio Gramsci's concept of hegemony (that I discussed in Chapter 1) with its insistence on alliances, persuasion and the winning of leadership. Althusser put it like this: 'no class can hold state power over a long period without at the same time exercising its hegemony over and in the State Ideological Apparatuses' (Althusser, 1971: 146). Thus, the ISAs, while separate, are intimately related to the repressive state apparatuses. If this were not the case the ruling classes would soon lose hegemonic control over the ideological life of the nation. For this reason the ISAs can be understood as the sites of (class) struggle because it is in them that ideological forces fight for control.

Practice: thinking through the apparatuses – school

The last few sections have outlined how Althusser conceives the structures in which ideologies have their existence. Through the repressive and ideological state apparatuses individuals are exposed to repressive and more persuasive mechanisms which are constantly functioning to regulate normative behaviour, attitudes and values. Within the 'concert' of ideological state apparatuses the school has a special position. This is because, in modern capitalist society, it takes children from all classes when they are infants and subjects them, when they are most vulnerable, to subjects that either prepare them or exclude them from the different employment hierarchies that help to perpetuate capitalism.

Althusser paints a scary, if realistic, picture of children inculcated with 'know-how' until, around the age of sixteen, a great mass of them are ousted into menial jobs. Little by little, the rest are primed to become technicians, white-collar workers, executives or intellectual workers, etc. Some become 'the agents of exploitation' (capitalists and managers), others the agents of repression (soldiers, police officers, politicians and administrators, etc.), and others professional ideologists (like priests 'of all sorts') (1971: 155–56).

This way of thinking helps to describe how all people are ideologically groomed to take up their role in class-based society. Thus, different groups are provided with the 'education' (or lack of it) needed to adopt different functions: of the exploited low-grade worker, the 'agent of exploitation' (entailing the ability to give workers orders and speak to them); of the agent of repression (with the aptitude to give orders and enforce obedience, or 'manipulate the demagogy of a political leader's rhetoric'), etc. All these roles have their appropriate 'virtues' attached like 'modesty, resignation, submissiveness on the one hand, cynicism, contempt, arrogance, confidence, self-importance, even smooth talk and cunning on the other'. Althusser also opined that these virtues are also taught in other institutions like the family, the church, the army, and in other purveyors of ideology like books, films, and even the football stadium. However, as Althusser contended, no other ideological state apparatus has, like the school, a captive audience of all classes of children for 'eight hours a day for five or six days out of seven' (156).

Althusser drew the conclusion that it is through this 'massive inculcation of the ideology of the ruling class that the *relations of production* in a capitalist social formation, i.e. the relations of exploited to exploiters and exploiters to exploited, are largely reproduced'. Yet, for Althusser, this ideological conditioning is largely invisible. The reason for this is that the ruling classes represent the school 'as a neutral environment purged of ideology' – an environment full of teachers who respect the 'conscience' and 'freedom' of the children who have been commended to them. Althusser saw ideology operating in the bourgeois image of the teacher who was represented as an exemplary figure, teaching through example, who set children on the enlightened path to 'freedom, morality and responsibility' through 'knowledge, literature and their "liberating" virtues' (156–57). In this way Althusser attemted to show *how* an ISA actually works on the lives and consciousness of different classes in society. To bring these ideas fully up to date, Althusser's idea of education as a neutral space has been further compromised in relation to the ways large businesses and the multinationals have increasingly privatized aspects of the public sphere (see Klein, 2000: 87f.; Monbiot, 2000: 281f.; Giroux, 2002; Lorenz, 2006) – a theme I shall address in the final chapters of this book.

The relative autonomy of the ideological state apparatuses

One of the most influential ideas that Althusser developed (and which, again, echoes Gramsci's model of hegemony) was that, whereas the repressive state apparatus centralizes all its parts 'beneath a commanding unity', the ideological state apparatuses 'are multiple, distinct' and 'relatively autonomous' in relation to the state apparatus. This is a very important point because it challenges the naive reading of Marx and Engels that assumes that the base (or economic infrastructure that establishes the exploitative relations between capitalists and workers) fully determines the superstructure (the realm of the ISAs). Althusser's model shows how the ideological and state apparatuses are interdependent. Thus, he gives a much more sophisticated idea of how the apparatuses function and this, in turn, helps to describe how conflict is possible at the ideological level. Again, echoing Gramsci, ideological conflicts are not only produced between the working classes and the ruling classes but may take place within the ruling classes themselves.

This idea is a more nuanced version of Marx and Engel's point that the class that rules at the social, economic, political level establishes its view of the world as the 'ruling *intellectual* force' (Marx and Engels 1846/1970: 64). This entails that the ruling ideas expressed by the ruling class are 'the ideal expression of the dominant material relationships' (64). A dominant class, then, not only subordinates non-ruling groups at social, political and economic levels but also in terms of how individuals perceive the world they live in.

Thus, Marx and Engels asserted that when the ruling class establishes itself it must, if it wishes to maintain its dominance, represent its own interests as if they were in the common interests of everyone. Moreover, these ideas have to be represented as if they are the 'only rational, universally valid ones' (66). This model of ideology supposes that the relations of subordination in the material base must be validated at the level of ideas and beliefs: that is, at the ideological level (of consciousness). If this were not the case, capitalist society would be in constant peril of extinction. Althusser agrees with this insisting that, 'in the final instance', the relations of production at the infrastructural level *are* decisive. However, what makes Althusser's account more nuanced is that he insists (like Gramsci) on the relative autonomy of ideology. That is to say, there is no simple causal or one-to-one relationship between the base and the ideological superstructure, or there would be no room for ideological struggle whatsoever and it would be very difficult to account for any kind of evolution or change in a given system.

Overdetermination and the imaginary and material aspects of ideology

This relative autonomy of the ideological state apparatuses leads onto another concept that has been very important to cultural studies: Althusser's use of the Freudian concept of **overdetermination**. Freud used the concept to explain that dreams or symptoms of neurosis could not be described by any simple theory of causation which assigned only one cause. That is to say, neuroses are not the products of *one* determining factor (Freud, 1955: 524, 508, 569).

Althusser reluctantly picked up this concept (1965/2005: 101) and developed it in various complex ways. I shall not go into all the ramifications here but sum up why this idea has been so useful within cultural studies.

Althusser's account of the intricate relations between base and superstructure is one of the reasons why critics like Raymond Williams found Althusser's work of particular interest. Williams insisted that determination should not be thought of as 'a single force, or a single abstraction of forces', but more as a process in which 'real determining factors' (like the distribution of power or of capital, inheritance, etc.) 'set limits and exert pressures' rather than function as simplistic mechanisms of control (Williams, 1974: 130). As Graeme Turner has said (2003: 54), Williams, in rejecting more mechanistic models of determination, preferred Althusser's idea of overdetermination because of the relative autonomy of the different cultural forces at play with relation to the repressive and ideological state apparatuses.

We are now ready to look at some of the implications of the relative autonomy of ideological forms. At the simplest level (as in the early Marx) ideology can be understood as 'the system of the ideas and representations' which dominate the minds of people or a social group (Althusser, 1971: 158). However, Althusser goes beyond this definition. This first thing to recognize is that ideology can be understood as a collection of *individual ideologies* like the ISAs (linked to class interests) or in terms of an abstraction that is 'eternal' and has no history. In order to understand this 'eternal' aspect it is necessary to recognize that Althusser was drawing, once again, on Freud because he links ideology to Freud's conception of the unconscious.

For Freud, the contents of the unconscious of each person may be different but all minds have an unconscious structure. So it is with ideology: ideology is a structure, its contents may vary but its form, like the unconscious, is always the same (161). It is like Saussure's theory of language: ideology is a structure or system which speaks us – we are subjects (like *paroles*) who are products of ideology (a kind of *langue*). However, Althusser emphasized that ideology creates the illusion that we are in control, that we have the freedom to choose but, to return to Geertz's phrase, we are really at its mercy, it is a 'control mechanism'. To move the discussion on a bit further I will now look at Althusser's argument that ideology has 'imaginary' and 'material' aspects.

Ideology as imaginary

One of Althusser's claims is that ideology has an imaginary dimension. While it is possible to conceive of ideology in terms of what is sometimes called 'false consciousness', where the population is duped into believing what is not true to serve the ends of priests, capitalist ideologist etc., Althusser proposed a more subtle model (1971: 162–4). Althusser's classic definition is that in ideology people do not express their 'real' relations to their conditions of existence, 'but *the way* they live the relation between them and their conditions of existence'. For Althusser this presupposes a real relation and what he calls an *imaginary* or *lived* relation. In short:

> Ideology, then, is the expression of the relation between men and their 'world', that is, the (overdetermined) unity of the real relation and the imaginary relation between them and their real conditions of existence. In ideology the real relation is inevitably invested in the imaginary relation, a relation that *expresses* a *will* (conservative, conformist, reformist or revolutionary), a hope or a nostalgia, rather than describing a reality. (Althusser, 1965/2005: 233–34)

Notice that Althusser distinguishes between a 'real relation' and an 'imaginary relation' (the 'imaginary relation' is indebted to Jacques Lacan's notion of the 'Symbolic' – see Chapters 7 and 8). The main idea is that it is the codes, conventions, rules, laws, etc. that enable individuals to have a 'relation' with the world they live in. Understanding, then, is not a question of having a one-to-one relation with an objective world but living a relation through a way of seeing it (this is ideology). Thus, the 'real conditions of existence' in a capitalist society, for example, may be described as an economic system based on things like the investment and exploitation of capital, resources and labour for the purposes of creating surplus profit which is unevenly distributed in social terms. This system is bolstered up by laws which protect the right to private ownership, etc.

Ideology (as the imaginary) is a question of *how* people relate to these basic conditions as conservative ('leave the system alone because it's the best there is'), reformist ('the system's right but it should be improved'), or revolutionist ('the system is exploitative, unjust and inhumane and should be replaced'). This helps to explain how members of the same class can relate to the 'same' world but in different ways. To simplify the issues, a left-wing worker sees the factory system and free-market economy in terms of capitalist exploitation and social injustice; the working-class Tory sees the same basic conditions but agrees with the capitalist employers that they are providing jobs and the best conditions for 'progress'. Graeme Turner offers a very concise view of Althusser's position:

> Althusser argues that ideology operates not explicitly but implicitly; it lives in those practices, those structures, those images we take for granted. We internalize ideology and thus are not easily made conscious of its presence of its effects; it is unconscious. And yet, the unconscious has, within many philosophical frameworks, been seen as the core of our individuality, a product of our nature. (Turner, 2003: 20)

As Turner suggests, if Althusser is to be believed, the unconscious is formed in ideology, 'from *outside* our "essential" selves'. This makes the notion of an essential self a 'fiction', an 'impossibility', and what we are left with is 'a socially produced sense of identity', a 'subjectivity' (20). It will be worth keeping this in mind when I discuss the work of Jacques Lacan.

The material existence of ideology

For Althusser, if ideology has an imaginary dimension, it can also be said to have material existence. To simplify Althusser somewhat, he argued that ideas are never 'spiritual', in the sense that they are cut off from (or above) the everyday material world. Thoughts, values and beliefs exist in relation to the apparatuses examined above. That is to say, they are linked to forms of action that are inserted into practices which, in turn, are governed by rituals. For example, the relations between religious belief and action can serve as a useful analogy for the way ideology functions in a more general sense. In the case of Christian religions, they have a set of beliefs linked to forms of action like getting baptised, confirmed, attending Mass, praying, doing penance, getting married, etc., all of which are highly ritualized. Thus, believers do not just believe *as such* but express this belief in various officially sanctioned practices. So it is that Althusser sums up his ideas by saying that actions 'are inserted into *practices*' and that these practices 'are governed by the *rituals* in which these practices are inscribed, within the *material existence of an ideological apparatus*' (1971: 167–68).

The same can be said for any set of beliefs. To believe in justice, it is necessary to 'submit unconditionally to the rules of the Law'. Without an apparatus or institutional base there is no practice and vice versa. Thus, everyday life is full of the material forms of ideological existence like a day at school or university, a political meeting, etc. The whole of life takes place inside ideological practices: there is no way out. While no one can escape it the only way to remain above it would be to practise the 'science' of Althusserian Marxism, which could distinguish between 'real' and 'imaginary' relations and science and ideology. This was something E. P. Thompson rejected (see below) and which Jacques Rancière (one of Althusser's early collaborators) criticized, believing that Althusser's distinction between ideology and 'science' was too rigid (Rancière, 1974).

Practice: ideology as material practice – who does the washing up?

With relation to the notion of ideology as a material practice, a relatively easy way to start practice is to explore the spaces around you like the domestic space (an ideological state apparatus). Questions like who cleans? who cooks? who gets up to clear the dishes? who throws out the rubbish? who cleans the car? etc. can be used to explore how common (material) practices imply larger ideological structures (see Walton, 2008: 213f.).

So, the materiality of ideology resides in the fact that belief systems, and the practices determined by those belief systems, are firmly rooted in the relations between the ideological and state apparatuses; ideology would have no materiality if no one actually acted according to those beliefs. This brings me to another important concept in Althusser's writings: that of **interpellation**. This will help to clarify Althusser's complex notion of ideology and how it functions.

Interpellation

Althusser's basic premise is that 'ideology interpellates individuals as subjects' (1971: 162). To see how this works it is necessary to take into account Althusser's contention that ideology functions in such a way that it 'recruits' subjects among individuals, or 'transforms' the individuals 'into subjects'. Althusser described interpellation as a kind of summons and his classic formula is to compare the way ideology works with the way the police hail suspects. Althusser's analogy assumes that the guilty individual, rather than someone else, will nearly always turn round when s/he hears the call: 'Hey, you there!' (174f.). It is at this moment that the individual becomes a subject. Although Althusser's dramatization only features one subject, his point is that *everyone* is interpellated in this way.

While Althusser's example has a sense of before and after, he stresses that ideology functions without this sense of succession: 'The existence of ideology and the hailing or interpellation of individuals as subjects are one and the same thing' (175). Attached to what we might call this allegory is that this hailing seems to occur outside ideology (it is in the street) but really it is inside it. This is because recognizing oneself is not normally thought of as being ideological – but to be a subject for Althusser is already to be in ideology. This leads Althusser to make the claim that 'those who are in ideology believe themselves by definition outside ideology'. This means, and this is crucial to Althusser's understanding of ideology, that one of its effects is to negate itself *as* ideology.

This brings me back to the idea that there is no before and after in ideology. Althusser's point is that:

> ideology has always-already interpellated individuals as subjects, which amounts to making it clear that individuals are always-already interpellated by ideology as subjects, which necessarily leads us to one last proposition: *individuals are always-already subjects*. (175–6)

While Althusser does not mention Saussure, this conundrum can be explained (as mentioned above) by referring to the ideas of *langue* and *parole* where ideology is the underlying structure and where *parole* describes the (individual) subjects who live the illusion that they are free. Unless you are a particular kind of (Althusserian) Marxist, you do not see the ideological underpinning that forges your consciousness and structures life at institutional levels. It is for this reason that Althusser claims that individuals are always-already subjects, even before they are born because they begin their lives within particular pre-established ideological configurations (176). Culture is already waiting for you at birth and, to use a metaphor from information technology, will not only boot you up but format you so you can function as a 'free' subject.

Thus, people may think they are free individuals but they are subjects, subject *to* the organization and material practices of ideology. Unless we are Althusserian Marxists, we are victims of 'misrecognition': we might think we pre-exist ideology and are above it but we are actually products of it. To be a subject is to be fully immersed in the rituals of everyday life (which are manifested in the smallest of ways from being recognized as unique individuals through the use of names, to recognizing one another by using handshakes, etc.). As *always-already* subjects, we 'constantly practice the rituals of ideological recognition, which guarantee for us that we are indeed concrete, individual, distinguishable and (naturally) irreplaceable subjects' (172–3). Ideology actually *is* this misrecognition of freedom, where we mistakenly think we are free. Getting at the (unconscious) structures behind these conscious rituals (and relating them to the class basis of society) is what Althusser regarded as part of Marxist science. Before going onto the next section, I shall offer some advice on how to explore some of these ideas in practice.

Practice: interpellation and ideology as material practice

One way to begin practice is to consider films like *The Truman Show* (1998) and *Toy Story* (1995) to explore how Althusser's concepts might be used. Below are a few pointers.

The situations of Truman Burbank and Buzz Lightyear help to emphasize a number of important ideas which arise from Althusser's notion of culture and the way subjects are interpellated. First, Truman and Lightyear illustrate Althusser's idea that subjects are always-already constructed in-so-far that they are born into particular cultural ideological situations which are the basis of their understanding, values and beliefs. Truman is brought up in a giant TV studio which he mistakes for reality just as Buzz Lightyear mistakes the blurb on his box for his particular reality as a space ranger (when he is only just another toy). Truman's life is dominated by everyday rituals (leaving for work, greeting the neighbours with trite phrases, buying his newspaper

(Continued)

(Continued)

or magazine, etc.) which constantly reinforce his sense of self (his ideological mis-recognition). Likewise, Buzz Lightyear's conversation is anchored by (but not limited to) certain clichéd phrases (like 'to infinity and beyond') which serve to strengthen his own identity. However, like Truman, his 'own' identity is an illusion. Both experience reality through the cultural narratives that give their lives meaning and they can be seen to be 'spoken' through their immersion in particular cultural/ideological systems that pre-exist them.

In the first part of *Toy Story* Lightyear insists on his version of reality, seeing the old head of the toys, Woody, as misguided. In this way the case of Lightyear exemplifies one of Althusser's contentions that within particular belief systems it is the beliefs of others that are often considered ideological, imaginary or illusory. Buzz's later consciousness of his condition (that he is a toy, not a real-life space ranger who can fly) – like Truman's (that he is living in a giant simulated reality) – can be seen as an allegory of the intellectual results of Althusserian 'science' where ideology can be penetrated by Marxist analysis. A film that unites the themes of *The Truman Show* and *Toy Story* is *Bolt* (2008) and this would be a good starting point to explore some of the themes explored in this chapter.

Barthes' interpretation of the grandiose wedding (that I discussed in the last chapter) can also be seen as another example of the rituals of material practice and interpellation. We saw that the big society wedding may seem a vital part of everyday life but, according to Barthes, it actually has its origins in the bourgeois class ritual which combines marriage with the ostentatious parade and consumption of wealth (and which is disseminated through media like the press, the romantic novel and film, etc.). At the moment a typist earning very little money '*recognizes herself* in the big wedding of the bourgeoisie' (Barthes, 1957/1972: 140) it can be said that she has been successfully interpellated. Of course, from Althusser's point of view this interpellation would have been complete long before this moment but this example can be seen as one of the ways interpellation constantly reinforces ideological existence.

The fact that these concepts can be so easily applied to film reflects, as I indicated at the beginning of this chapter, one of their principal uses in the 1970s and 1980s – their use within film and television criticism interested in the workings of ideology (see academic journals like *Screen*). However, you might use these basic interpretive strategies to explore other cultural forms like books, video games and adverts.

The Subject of the subject

In the context of interpellation, Althusser (again drawing on Lacan) brought out the ambiguities of the word '*subject*'. Althusser pointed out that the term is used to mean, in the first case, 'a free subjectivity, a centre of initiatives' where the subject is responsible for its actions and, in the second, 'a subjected being, who submits to a higher authority, and is therefore stripped of all freedom except that of freely accepting his submission' (Althusser, 1971: 182). To be a subject, then, is to have a sense of autonomy but also to be *subject to* the ideological and repressive state apparatuses. What we might call 'the system' is the *Subject* that 'subjectivizes' or makes possible the subject in the first place. To put this in seemingly paradoxical terms, the entry into a linguistic, cultural system (as a legal citizen) enables members of it to take up the position of a subject (like the subject of a sentence) and this gives the impression of freedom and power but this subjectivity is only made possible because the 'subject' is an object (in the system that gives it this perceived autonomy). The individual as subject is always subordinated to the ultimate Subject which appears as an object outside the self (this will be discussed at greater length in Chapters 7 and 8).

Thus, we have a paradox where individuals are interpellated as (free) subjects in order that they 'shall submit freely to the commandments of the Subject'. That is to say, subjects (under the illusion of being free) accept their subjection so that they can go about performing 'the gestures and actions' of their subjection, all by themselves (182). Thus, Althusser's model of ideology is one where subjects are actually self-regulating (something I will come back to in Chapter 9 on Foucault), and are all subjected to the Subject (181). It is this paradox which ensures the constant 'reproduction of the relations of production and of the relations deriving from them' which is ultimately warranted by the legal-political and ideological superstructure. Having dealt with the subject of the Subject, the next section will deal with three related concepts which have left considerable influence on cultural analysis: **double reading, the problematic** and **symptomatic reading**.

Reading culture with Althusser: double reading

In order to understand 'the problematic' and 'symptomatic reading' it is necessary to grasp what Althusser meant by 'double reading'. He explained this with relation to Marx's interpretation (in *Capital*, 1867) of the classical political economists (such as Adam Smith and David Ricardo). Althusser claimed that Marx performs a 'double reading' (Althusser and Balibar, 1968/2006: 18) where, in the first reading, Marx sees oversights, gaps and silences in the arguments of the classical economists. That is to say they fail to see things that Marx can.

The interesting point Althusser has to make is concerned with what he thought of as Marx's second reading. Here it is not a question of oversights and gaps but a problem of vision: 'what classical political economy does not see, is not what it does not see, it is *what it sees*; it is not what it lacks, on the contrary, it is *what it does not lack'* (21). Marx does not accuse Smith and Ricardo of getting things wrong – he claims they give *'the correct answer to a question that has just one failing: it was never posed'*. What Marx says is that *'it is the classical text itself that tells us that it is silent'* (22). An analysis of Marx's text should help to clarify this.

Marx described how classical political economists tried to verify the 'price of labour' and then asked the question, 'How is this price determined?' Marx explored how these economists understood the relations between labour costs and supply and demand, and analysed their conclusion that, if supply and demand are balanced, the price of labour would no longer depend on them, and thus could be determined as if they did not exist. Marx was interested in the way that these economists considered their own analysis as 'scientific', linked, as it was, to a strategy that considered averages based on data analysed over a number of years. In this way classical political economy assumed it had 'ascended from the accidental prices of labour to the real value of labour'. Out of this Marx developed the following point:

> It [classical political economy] then determined this value by the value of the subsistence goods necessary for the maintenance and reproduction of the labourer. *It thus unwittingly changed terrain* by substituting for the value of labour, up to this point, *the apparent subject of its investigations*, the value of labour power, a power which only exists in the personality of the labourer, and is as different from its function, labour, as a machine is from its performance. (Marx quoted in Althusser and Balibar, 1968/2006: 20)

The sentence picked out by Althusser for special comment is 'the value of labour is equal to the value of the subsistence goods necessary for the maintenance and reproduction of the labour' (22). Althusser shows that the problem for Marx is not that labour or labour relations are invisible but that the maintenance and reproduction of 'labour' does not seem to make proper sense. Althusser demonstrates how Marx's reading opens up these *'points of emptiness'* within what seems the fullness of the utterance. In answering a question never posed the phrase selected for special mention actually addresses a question about 'labour power' (to be found in the labourer) rather than simply focus on 'labour' in itself (23). This is why Marx wrote that this is like confusing the difference between a machine (akin to labour) and its performance (akin to labour power).

The (invisible) problematic

To develop these ideas a little further, Althusser demonstrated how Marx's double reading shows how a question that purports to be about labour inadvertently answers a question about labour power that is, in a playful paradox, 'present in an emptiness'. What is present in the emptiness of the abstraction is the *human* dimension of people grafting for a living; those whose lives depend on the capitalists and their exploitative system. So the classical political economists were, according to Althusser, 'blind' to what they 'saw' (23). The reason is because the classical economists were restricted by their old 'horizon' within which the new problem is not visible. This helps us to understand the idea of the 'problematic': the questions a text asks and attempts to answer *limit* its horizons but, at the same time, a text can border on issues which a sensitive (Marxist) reader can see but which the authors could not perceive themselves. This, in turn, opens up a new 'theoretical problematic' (24f.).

This introduces another key term: 'the problematic'. Reading with relation to the problematic entails reading texts with relation to their theoretical or ideological limits. This involves asking: What kinds of questions do they raise? How do they answer them? Do they speak of things their own horizons and limits prevent them from seeing? Althusser, however, goes even further, claiming that the objects which are stated but not visible are actually *forbidden* – they are 'repressed from the field of the visible' because the writers *do not wish* to see them (26). The intricacies of labour power were not something the economists wanted to consider as they were only interested in their own convenient (non-human) abstraction: 'labour'.

Symptomatic reading

This leads to the final concept I shall introduce in this chapter, what Althusser termed the 'symptomatic'. The symptomatic is a variation on Freud's idea that it is possible to interpret the manifestations of neurosis in such a way as to get back to the cause. Althusser's way of putting it is to say that Marx's second reading can be called symptomatic because it exposes 'the undivulged event in the text it reads, and in the same movement relates it to a *different text*, present as a necessary absence in the first' (28). So, in trying to offer a scientific analysis of 'labour', the classical political economists imply, through their texts, the existence of 'labour power' (a second repressed 'text' within the first). The presence of an answer to a question not formally posed is like a symptom just waiting to be diagnosed.

To sum up, Marxian 'double reading' looks for gaps and silences and the 'problematic' describes the theoretical or ideological limits of the text read. Then, there is the 'invisible problematic' which is a symptom manifested by (and repressed in) the original problematic which is revealed by 'symptomatic reading'. Thus, Marx measured the problematic visible in the writings of the political economists against the invisible problematic contained in them which reveals the symptom 'in the paradox of *an answer which does not correspond to any question posed*' (28).

Practising double reading: the problematic and the symptomatic

One way of exploring these concepts is to choose a film or an advertisement and try to decide where the ideological limits or horizons are to be found. To give an idea of how this might work here is a reading John Storey offers of Martin Scorsese's film *Taxi Driver* (1976). The film's plot, set in New York City, revolves around Travis Bickle, a late-night taxi driver who has returned from the Vietnam War (1955–1975). Seeing so much violent crime and prostitution he decides to take the law into his own hands, which results in him violently killing a number of people but also saving a young prostitute. Out of this plot Storey says a symptomatic reading of it would 'reveal a problematic in which answers are posed to questions it can hardly name'. The question here is, 'How does the veteran return home to America after the imperial horrors of Vietnam?' Storey's Althusserian interpretation reads this in the following way:

> At the heart of the film's problematic are questions relating to real historical problems, albeit deformed and transformed into a fantasy quest and a bloody resolution. A symptomatic reading of *Taxi Driver*, reading the 'symptoms' for evidence of an underlying *dis-ease*, would construct from the film's contradictions, its evasions, its silences, its inexplicable violence, its fairy-tale ending, the central and structuring absence – America's war in Vietnam. (Storey, 2009a: 73)

Storey's reading is justified because we never actually see scenes from the Vietnam War, only small details like a Viet Cong flag hanging up in Travis Bickle's apartment and occasional verbal references to it. This is a useful way of reading films and ads – seeing if small 'symptoms' point to larger themes which are not developed in any significant way. Storey outlines the case of car ads where cars are seen in 'nature', well away from congested streets and heavily polluted environments, because to confront these issues in any direct way would allow the criticisms 'to come between the car being advertised and any potential buyer'. In this way, possible criticism is answered 'without the questions themselves having been formally posed' within the text's problematic. Elsewhere (Walton, 2008: 213f.) I have shown how these ideas can be applied to old Marlboro cigarette ads which displace attention from a harmful contaminant onto iconic (and unpolluted) images of the American West (at the same time conveniently ignoring other questions concerning addictive additives, factory conditions, labour conditions and advertising specifically targeted at women and Third World nations).

These ideas can be extended to all kinds of ads where, for example, the product is placed in some kind of fantasy space. Even farm products advertised with relation to images taken from the countryside like cottages and farm animals, which we may assume to be products of a 'natural' environment, can be seen as posing an invisible problematic. This is because much commercial farming, with its genetically engineered products, intensive use of fertilizers, hormones and insect sprays, mechanized abattoirs, etc., offer innocent-looking bucolic images which can be read as symptoms of a highly industrialized, globalized and contaminating production base. These are the gaps and silences that can be explored behind the pastoral fables of the ads. Robert Kenner's film *Food Inc.* (2008) offers all kinds of insights into how advertisers habitually create images of the 'natural' world by cloaking genetic engineering, intensive use of fertilizers, hormones, insect sprays, etc. Many of these ads could be prime targets for symptomatic readings.

E. P. Thompson verus the Althusserians and the triumph of structuralist approaches

Althusser's structuralist-inflected brand of Marxism created a set of controversies because writers like the historian E. P. Thompson put great emphasis on the power of individuals and groups to actively change the world they lived in. As described in Chapter 1, this latter approach is commonly termed 'culturalism' and it stressed the importance of human agency, human values and human experience (Storey, 2009a: 37). Thompson's view, as expressed in his *The Poverty of Theory* (1978/1995), is that structuralism (especially as practised by those influenced by Althusser) is 'wholly self-confirming', a pseudo-science circling around its 'own self-perpetuating and self-elaborating procedures'. In short, it is 'a sealed system in which concepts endlessly circulate, recognise and interrogate each other' (17).

Another of Thompson's objections was related to a basic assumption in structuralism that things can be explained through understanding the structural rules that lay behind them. This took the emphasis off the individual acts and struggles of actual people in history and put it on the processes that organize cultures. Thompson, as a Marxist historian, was scandalized by the idea that another Marxist thinker could believe that people were '*structured* by social relations, *spoken* by pre-given linguistic structures, *thought* by ideologies' or '*gendered* by patriarchal sexual norms', etc. (206).

Historically, structuralist thinking coincided with the rise of what is known as the New Left in Britain and the expansion of the Birmingham Centre for Contemporary Cultural Studies under the tutelage of Stuart Hall (see Chapter 1) which helped to incorporate Althusser's ideas into British cultural studies (as did the widespread use of his ideas in the film journal *Screen* – see above). What preoccupied Thompson in this paradigm shift was that history seemed to have got lost. He felt that, in the work of the structuralist Althusserians, theoretical practice had become an obsessive and tail-biting end in itself. So, while Thompson and the Althusserians were both writing in the Marxist tradition they had very different ways of practising Marxist criticism.

Structuralism, Althusser and Marxism as science

For Thompson, theory should always be provisional, exploratory, never complete, always subject to the world outside. He claimed that Marxism, in its theoreticist Althusserian guise, had nothing to say about the actual lived world, and (locked in its theoretical obsessions) could not offer any (empirical) way of finding out about it (226). In Althusser's work (and that of his followers) Thompson only saw a highly questionable and one-sided mechanistic approach and attacked what he felt was the spurious, overblown and misleading assertion (or pretension) that some kind of 'Science' was being practised (227). In stating this he was reflecting the view of many Marxists (and non-Marxists) who refused to see Marxism (as politics or a form of intellectual analysis) as scientific. As stated above, critics like Jacques Rancière were not persuaded by Althusser's distinction between ideology and Marxist science (Rancière, 1974)

Thompson also objected to what he called the enormous emphasis the Althusserians placed on ideological modes of domination (described above). For Thompson, Althusser put so much emphasis on ideological domination that he felt it destroyed 'every space for the initiative or creativity of the mass of the people', resulting in an elitist approach where only an 'enlightened minority of intellectuals' could struggle free from domination (250). Nevertheless, it would be the structuralist Marxists who would win the day during the 1970s and much of the 1980s. However, the questioning of the scientific basis of structuralism and attempts to push thinking beyond its paradigms would pose serious challenges to structuralist-based approaches by those commonly known as poststructuralists (who, despite these critiques, had little in common with Thompson's brand of Marxism). It is to those thinkers that I shall be turning in the following chapters.

Summary of key points

This chapter has shown how Althusser's ideas are indebted to structuralist ways of thinking and how they were in conflict with 'culturalist' approaches that emphasized human agency. Althusser's definitions of ideology have been reviewed with relation to his distinction between ideological and state apparatuses and these have been linked to his notions of the material and imaginary aspects of ideology. Other key ideas like overdetermination, interpellation, the problematic and symptomatic reading have been outlined and illustrated.

Further reading

In-depth critiques of Althusser's ideas and influence: Ted Benton's *The Rise and Fall of Structural Marxism: Althusser and His Influence* (1984) is a respectful and detailed critique of Althusser's ideas and legacy, which defends Althusserian ideas from what Benton feels were appropriations which distorted them. Warren Montag's *Loius Althusser* (2003), while tending to emphasize Althusser's interest to literary studies, reflects his wider interest to cultural analysis.

Works which are indebted to Althusser's theories: As mentioned above the academic journal of film and television studies *Screen* featured many articles inspired by Althusser's work in the late 1970s and early 1980s. If your library has copies you might explore some back numbers, perhaps beginning with Mulvey's essay (see below). Pierre Macherey's *A Theory of Literary Production* (1978) is a systematic application of Althusserian theory to literary forms. A good starting point would be to read how Macherey (in Chapter 3) adapted Althusser's ideas to argue that the 'unconscious' of Jules Verne's science-fiction fantasies can be read to reveal the contradictions of French colonialism. Laura Mulvey's 'Visual Pleasure and Narrative Cinema' (published in *Screen* in 1973) is a classic essay that combines feminism, Althusser, semiotic theory and psychoanalysis to study the way women have been represented in classic Hollywood films, which are seen to function to satisfy the erotic needs of the male gaze. Mulvey reprinted the ground-breaking essay (revised her arguments and responded to critics) in 'Afterthoughts on 'Visual Pleasure and Narrative Cinema' in *Visual and Other Pleasures* (1989). Judith Williamson's *Decoding Advertisements: Ideology and Meaning in Advertising* (1978) shows how concepts taken from Althusser's work can be usefully applied to the world of advertising.

5

Poststructuralism

Roland Barthes and Jacques Derrida

Learning goals

- To understand poststructuralism (and deconstruction in particular) not as a complete departure from structuralism, but as an extension and critique of Saussure's theory of the sign.
- To see how facets of Roland Barthes' writings can prepare the way to understanding key ideas in deconstruction.
- To grasp a number of key (anti-)concepts in Jacques Derrida's work.
- To become aware of the basic steps of Derrida's deconstruction of the privileging of speech over writing to appreciate how it works in practice.

Concepts

The key concepts introduced in this chapter are: poststructuralism, the death of the author, intertextuality, deconstruction, 'différance', difference and deferral, trace, structure, the transcendental signified, the metaphysics of presence, logocentrism and phonocentrism.

Introduction

The following two chapters build on the chapters on structuralism but also challenge some of their basic assumptions to show how poststructuralist reading techniques have radically questioned fixed meanings and essences. This chapter introduces poststructuralism by showing how a number of themes developed in Barthes' writings can be associated with deconstructive strategies. The chapter then goes on to illustrate Derridean deconstruction with relation to a number of its key (anti-)concepts. This serves as preparation for the following chapter, which will show how deconstruction has been adapted to practice with relation to questions commonly considered within cultural studies like class, race/ethnicity, gender, sexuality and the post-colonial.

Poststructuralism and deconstruction: a few preliminary remarks

As John Storey has noted, **poststructuralism** 'is virtually synonymous with the work of Jacques Derrida' (Storey, 2009a: 126) and the name Derrida gave to his general philosophical strategy: '**deconstruction**'. Before I go on to discuss Derrida's work I shall make a few comments about the historical situation in which the ideas were developed. The rise of deconstructive criticism grew out of the discipline of philosophy in the wake of the revolutionary incidents in France in May 1968. Since then deconstructive strategies have been gradually taken up in many branches of the humanities in other parts of the world. Since the 1970s deconstruction has gradually become part of the common currency of cultural studies, and for that reason alone it is necessary to be familiar with it. Without knowledge of deconstructive thinking it would be very difficult to understand the contemporary intellectual climate. Notwithstanding, Derrida has proven to be a controversial figure and his writings have provoked both great enthusiasm and condemnation: he has been hailed one of the greatest thinkers of the twentieth century and been accused of being absurd, nihilist, ahistorical, insubstantial, muddle-headed and politically quietist (among other things) by some of his harshest critics (Donoghue, 1976; Searle, 1977; Krieger, 1979; Graff, 1980; Habermas, 1987; Wolin, 1991).

Those coming to Derrida's work for the first time might find it quite a challenge. This is partly a question of style (he could be very playful linguistically and formally) and partly a question of his very nuanced and lengthy finely-spun arguments thoroughly grounded in Western traditions of thinking. Ideally, you should be familiar with Saussure (as you now are) and other linguists, ancient Greek philosophy and the Germanic tradition ranging across Kant, Hegel, Nietzsche, Husserl and Heidegger, as well as having a passing knowledge of other thinkers like Freud, Rousseau, Edmond Jabès, Emmanuel Levinas, Michel Foucault, Jacques Lacan, Philippe Sollers, John Austin and John Searle.

However, my aim here is not to draw out all the philosophical implications of Derrida's work because this is not an introduction to deconstruction for philosophy graduates. Thus, I will limit myself to an outline of a number of what have become key concepts within cultural studies. However, even a modest aim of this kind is hazardous, given the complexity of Derrida's thought. What I aim to show in the next two chapters is that within cultural studies certain useful concepts have been *adapted* from Derrida's work, often in non-specialist ways (this will be evident when I review Stuart Hall's use of deconstruction in the following chapter). A careful reading of Chapters 2 to 4 of this book should make an introduction to deconstruction easier because these have already introduced some key ideas necessary to understanding how Derrida's ideas relate to structuralism (I shall indicate these connections as I go along). Before continuing, however, I will clarify what the 'post' of post-structuralism means by referring back to Barthes' notion of modern mytholo-gies and hint at deconstructive themes by introducing Barthes' notion of **the death of the author**.

The 'post' of poststructuralism, Barthes, and the mythology of the de-mythologist

In the most general terms, poststructuralism refers to the work of writers who continue to use concepts taken from Saussurean linguistics, but who subject them to radical questioning. However, at times, thinkers who hardly use structuralist terminology are associated with poststructuralism. On the surface this may not seem to make sense. However, because some thinkers, like Michel Foucault, share certain thematic interests with those described as poststructuralist, their work is often classified under the same label. For example, Chris Weedon (1997) regards Foucault's work as poststructuralist for thematic reasons, even though she recognizes that the term 'does not have one fixed meaning but is generally applied to a range of theoretical positions' (19).

In this chapter, and the following one, I shall concentrate on writers who self-consciously use structuralist notions to question structuralism and take it elsewhere. That means I will leave writers like Foucault for later chapters which will indicate some of the thematic connections between Foucault and poststructuralist approaches. On the other hand, the critic Jean Baudrillard, who self-consciously used structuralist theory, will be discussed under another convenient label – that of postmodernism – because he is commonly discussed and thematized within the sets of discourses known as the postmodern. There is a lesson to be learnt here: the labels we create, although they may often make sense, are, in the final analysis, a categorical convenience.

The question I want to address here is: what are some of the common ways that writers commonly considered poststructuralist question structuralism? To help answer this question I shall refer back to Roland Barthes, a writer who, as will be seen, is very difficult to label. As described in Chapter 3, in *Mythologies* Barthes set himself the task of unmasking and defining bourgeois myths in 'methodical fashion' (1957/1972: 10). This approach linked him to the scientific claims that characterized much structuralist thinking. For many practitioners, it seemed as if there were, at last, a series of concepts and a method that could guarantee a certain level of reliability. The unpredictable slipperiness of subjective interpretation could be replaced by a more organized rational objectification of language and other cultural phenomena. If you go back to Chapter 2 you will see that Saussure conceived of a 'science' that studied 'the life of signs within society' and that he, and later structuralists, dreamt of being able to make objective statements about the nature of signs: the idea of semiology was to show 'what constitutes signs' and 'what laws govern them' (Saussure, 1916/1959: 16).

As we saw with relation to the conflict between E. P. Thompson and Althusser, by the 1970s structuralist approaches were revolutionizing critical practice and displacing what were considered outmoded approaches concerned with human agency. So, why is Barthes so hard to label? Barthes, like many thinkers, did not develop a set of ideas and then stop thinking – his later thought develops in ways that challenge his earlier more obviously structuralist work. In his autobiography *Roland Barthes by Roland Barthes* he describes how he needed to move beyond the scientific assumptions in structuralism in order not to become theoretically fossilized (Barthes, 1975/1977: 70f.). Yet even in an early work like *Mythologies* it is possible to detect a certain uneasiness concerning scientific objectivity. In his preface of 1957, before the structuralist revolution really hit Europe and North America, he stated that there may be 'a mythology of the mythologist' (1957/1972: 11).

While Barthes did not go into much detail he seemed to be aware that demythologizing bourgeois myths may itself be a kind of fiction insofar that, while he was confident that he was exposing multiple forms of bourgeois ideology, these readings are, in the final instance, *his* readings. This belief in producing objective scientific statements through structuralist method might be thought of as the 'mythology of a de-mythologist'. This is because Barthes was aware that those who seek to de-mythologize may actually re-mythologize by putting exaggerated confidence in their ability to create objective facts beyond personal interests, passions and obsessions. The questioning of this disinterested view promised by so-called objective science has become very important to what have become poststructuralist approaches. In fact, Barthes stated that he did not agree with the belief that there is the objectivity of the scientist, on the one hand, and the limited subjectivity of the writer, on the other. He lived the contradiction of the two (11), able, in the same book, to write in terms of 'objective analysis' *and* admit that 'form is always there to *outdistance* the meaning' (122). This introduces an element of, to use something of a clichéd term, 'slippage' into what may have seemed an effort to fix meaning through semiological analysis. It is this consciousness of having to live with theoretical contradictions that could be said to characterize the deconstructive thinking of Jacques Derrida and poststructuralist thinking in general.

Readers as writers, the death of the author and 'authoricide'

Barthes' essay entitled 'The Death of the Author' is also very useful in terms of introducing themes which echo motifs found in deconstructive thinking. This is because of what the essay has to tell us about the relations between authors, interpretation and the (de)stabilization of meanings. In this essay Barthes makes the point that the figure of the author is a modern phenomenon arising from around the time of the Middle Ages, insofar as in pre-modern societies (what he calls 'ethnographic societies') stories were recounted by mediators. Barthes stresses that in the Middle Ages emphasis was placed more on the skill of the narrator rather than on the 'author' as 'genius'. With the rise of capitalism and its emphasis on things like individualism, the image of literature to be found in ordinary culture is 'tyrannically centred on' the life, tastes and passions of the author (Barthes, 1968/1975: 143).

Barthes' basic point is that while it was (and still is) common to refer to the author in order to try to establish the meaning of a work, the moment something is written down 'the author enters into his own death' (143). Once we accept that the 'Author-God' is not 'in' the text but absent, then authors cannot be referred to in order to fix meaning. That is, to assign a text an 'Author' is 'to impose a limit on the text' to impose on it a 'final signified' (147). Although Barthes does not mention Nietzsche in this essay, it is like Nietzsche's proclamation, 'God is Dead!' If God exists and created the world with a meaning then it is always possible to refer back to its maker but if God does not exist then the world has no intrinsic meaning outside the meanings we create with relation to our common ways of engaging with it.

Here, Barthes cleverly inverts the way authors are usually understood – that is, they are normally thought to come *before* the work. However, Barthes says our notion of the author grows *out of* the text(s) we read – thus 'the modern scriptor is born simultaneously with the text' (145) and is thereby a textual *effect*, not a cause. Once the figure of the author is considered dead (conceived of as an effect) it can no longer act to ground a text's meaning and, thus, interpretation becomes an 'anti-theological activity that is truly revolutionary' (147). That is to say, meaning is liberated and can no longer be anchored to a writer's intentions.

In this way the reader is properly born, and reading is not the uncovering of fixed signifieds but a form of writing. As in secular thought, God (the author, meaning as authorial intention) is created by humans (readers), rather than the other way around. Barthes concludes his short essay with these words: 'we know that to give writing its future, it is necessary to overthrow the myth: the birth of the reader must be at the cost of the death of the author' (148). Through what might be called 'authoricide' it is possible to focus on other things which are relevant to the production of texts, like a consideration of the way writers relate to genre and all the other forms, idioms, conventions and styles which inform a text. This would also include acknowledging all the social and cultural forces that influence the writing of a text, which may or may not be part of an author's knowledge (something Barthes would explore in his book *S/Z* (Barthes, 1970/1975)). The consequences of what I have called 'authoricide' is another facet which is often linked to poststructuralist approaches.

Of intertextuality, authoricide and suicide

Before going on to discuss Derrida, I want to bring out a couple of other ideas in Barthes' essay 'The Death of the Author' because they can further help to prepare for deconstructive styles of thinking. Another of Barthes' claims, which is related to the ideas expressed above, is that a text 'is not a line of words releasing a single "theological" meaning' but 'a multidimensional space in which a variety of writings, none of them original, blend and clash'. The text, he asserts, is a 'tissue of quotations drawn from the innumerable centres of culture' and these multiple writings enter into 'mutual relations' and are focused on the reader (Barthes, 1968/1975: 146). The reader here is visualized as 'the space on which all the quotations that make up a writing are inscribed' and a text's unity is not to be found in its 'origin but in its destination' (148).

What Barthes was expressing here is related to what in another essay ('From Work to Text') he referred to as 'the intertextual' (Barthes, 1971/1975: 160), commonly known as **intertextuality**. At the basic level this is how one text can incorporate others into itself, where one book quotes another or, to draw on cinema, where a film incorporates into itself another film (at the extreme level this where films like *Scary Movie* are almost entirely made up of references to other films). These are often considered classic forms of intertextuality but Barthes' point is more profound. What he was saying with phrases like a text is a 'tissue of quotations drawn from innumerable centres of culture' is that *language itself* is radically intertextual.

To enlarge a little on what Barthes says it could be stated that all writers (and speakers) have to draw on words, phrases, tags, sayings, proverbs, names, people, movements, literary, historical, philosophical texts, films, TV, ads (cultural references of all kinds), etc. These serve as a kind of dictionary that a writer uses to create a text (this latter term understood in the widest possible sense). All these elements (which can be usefully associated with Saussure's paradigmatic axis) coalesce and interact together as a 'tissue of quotations' that have to be made sense of in the reader's or viewer's mind.

In this way it is possible to see that texts are all part of a vast and complex textual universe in which writers have to immerse themselves in order to produce a work. You might always have thought of texts and films, etc. as unique, undivided, integrated wholes which are products of author-director-geniuses.

However, Barthes' emphasis on intertextuality questions the integrity of the text *as text* – that is, even before possible sources, influences or citations are considered (which in themselves may challenge the idea of a text hermetically sealed off from other texts and sources). From Barthes' point of view the author is now less a romantic genius producing a uniquely original text than the means by which these intertexts are forged into the multiplicity that is the 'work'. In 'From Work to Text' Barthes said that it is wrong to associate the intertextual with so-called origins like sources and influences because 'citations' are part of the unavoidable fabric of the language we use. In this way they are 'anonymous, untraceable, and yet *already read*: they are quotations without inverted commas' (Barthes, 1971/1975: 160).

To sum up for a moment, in Barthes' notion of intertextuality authors no longer ground the meaning of a text, they write a work but the impression we have of them is always a *product* of acts of reading. The text is no longer unique or undivided but a tissue of citations: intertexts in the widest possible sense that have their realization in the minds of readers. This means that there is no longer *a* meaning to be found like a gem hidden away in the text – texts are open to the meanings generated by readers and other external factors – another idea which is very important to poststructuralist ways of understanding textuality and identity.

However, before I go on to discuss deconstruction (I hope you notice how I am constantly deferring deconstruction's arrival – an irony you should understand by the end of this chapter), I will introduce one more relevant idea found in Barthes' 'The Death of the Author'. When we think of the role of a 'scriptor' (rather than an 'Author' with real feelings, passions and impressions, etc.) who cannot be referred to in order to ground a text's meaning, then we are faced with 'the book itself' which is 'only a tissue of signs, an imitation that is lost, infinitely deferred' (Barthes, 1968/1975: 147). That last phrase 'infinitely deferred' introduces the important idea of **deferral** – *this* is the language of deconstruction (very much influenced by Derrida) where definitive meanings are constantly delayed. But before I move on I will just postpone deconstruction a little longer to consider a few possible exercises for practice.

Practice: of intertextuality, authoricide and suicide

You might think about the death of the author and its implications not only for reading literary texts but all cultural forms including reading Barthes (and even this book).

One way of exploring the death of the author is to focus down on your own habits of writing and reading. When you next write a letter, an e-mail, an SMS, an essay, short story or contribute to a blog, etc. think about Barthes' notion of intertextuality.

First, write in your normal way without being too self-conscious. Afterwards, try to become aware of each word you used, your phraseology, images, cultural references in terms of being part of a 'tissue of signs'. Try to recall where certain phrases or uses may have originated – and attempt to become aware of the radical intertextuality beyond just quoting or referring (directly or indirectly) to other forms of writing. Then try to imagine what image of you (as author) another reader might construct from what you have written (or give it to a friend to read). You might rewrite your text to try to produce different possible implied personalities of your authorial voice and think about how you achieved this. Again, you might test these out on other readers to see how well you succeeded and explore why you may or may not have produced the required effects – asking your readers to describe what effects your language had on them. Remember, language, while dominated by rules, is public and, as the American New Critics insisted, a text cannot be reduced to the intentions of the author because they are never *in* the text (Wimsatt and Beardsley, 1946). The next step is to practise 'authoricide' and reread what you have written with relation to the idea of the death of the author (or the author as 'scriptor'). How does it change your assumptions about the text?

Following this you might try reading something completely new (or watch a TV series or listen to a song) and visualize yourself as 'the space' on which all the elements that make up the piece of writing, the series or the song 'are inscribed'. What are your reactions? What associations are there? In what ways do you think you may have read the text five or ten years ago? What kinds of assumptions do you bring to your understanding? For example, if you go to a coffee shop with some friends and you say, 'I'm dying for a cup of coffee', what do you think they would understand? Why? Now, imagine you write a book of poetry and you are at the book launch. You are asked to recite one of your poems and, after a suitable pause, you declaim a one-line poem: 'I am dying … for a cup of coffee.' Then you stop and wait for applause. What would you think of someone who rushed to a local café to get you a cup of coffee? What might these things suggest for the identity of the text with relation to the act of reading? Think about the importance of the context, conventions and the idea that a text's unity is not to be found in its origin but in its destination. In what ways does this change your conception of it?

In what ways do these ideas affect your idea of the author of the book you have in front of you? Can you speculate on why my first name might be written as Davoid (I will play on this idea again later in the book)?

Jacques Derrida: '*différance*', deferral and trace

What I plan to show in the following sections is that the themes developed in Barthes' work will help to understand some key ideas within deconstruction.

Before I continue, however, here are a few words of caution. Jacques Derrida's term 'deconstruction' is not something that can be easily defined – it is a convenient, all-inclusive label. As I hope to show, any attempt to stabilize a text or, in this case, a whole body of writing, militates against the very idea of deconstruction and defies its main premises. Furthermore, Derrida's published work spanned more than forty years and, although there are common traits running through it, as Gayatri Spivak has noted, he often developed and revised his work (1999: 423f.). To call Derrida a 'poststructuralist' is also another convenient label because he never acknowledged belonging to any such group. However, as I will show, he worked with, and critiqued, some of the basic concepts developed by Saussure and in at least this sense it is justified to talk about his work in this way.

To introduce deconstruction I want to start with one of Derrida's best-known concepts: **différance**. Once I have introduced and explained it I shall discuss deconstruction as a possible method. Those familiar with the French language will recognise that Derrida has changed a letter in the French word *différence* (the 'e' has become an 'a' – I will explain why later) and will know that, depending on the context, the word can mean 'to differ' or 'to defer'. What I have called a concept is, for Derrida, actually an 'anti-concept' which is 'neither a word nor a concept' (Derrida, 1972/1982: 3). The reason (to ignore all the subtle, playful and painstaking elaborations and qualifications he develops before getting to this point) is that it conjures up 'to defer' and 'to differ' *at the same time*. The anti-concept teaches us something about all signs – they are all subject to **difference** and constant **deferral** (we saw that Barthes used this latter term).

These are two key ideas in deconstructive thinking and for this reason I will go into considerable detail about them. We know from the chapter on Saussure that the word 'pig' only means what it does because it differs from other words and that for it to make sense as a sign this signifier needs a signified (or set of signifieds). We also saw that meaning is always dependent on difference: signifieds (concepts) are 'purely differential and defined not by their positive content but negatively by their relations with the other terms of the system'. Their chief characteristic was 'in being what the others are not' (Saussure, 1916/1959: 117). Thus, a pig is understood because it is not an aardvark or a tea bag, which means that in language 'there are only differences *without positive terms*' (120).

However, Derrida, while drawing on Saussure's concept of the sign (with the emphasis on the idea that 'there are only differences *without positive terms*') complicates it. The sign is now no longer a signifier and a signified like the two sides of a piece of paper (like Saussure thought of it) – but is radically split. *Différance* seems to embody both possible meanings of the term and neither. One way to understand this deconstructive conundrum is to say that if Derrida's term really does mean 'to defer' and/or 'to differ' then its meaning *is not* deferred and it *does not* depend on difference (it has a fixed identity). Yet if it is subject to difference and deferral, it cannot have a fixed meaning. This point can be generalized to apply to any word – not just Derrida's neologism. For example, if a child asks me to define the word 'liberty' and I define it as 'a state of being free' and the child replies, 'Yeah, but what does a state of being free mean?' I would have to turn this signified into more signifiers which would require further signifieds.

I could go on like this ad infinitum (or just go round in circles) because there would never be a point at which I could stop this endless process where signifiers demanded more signifieds. According to this way of thinking, meaning is indefinitely postponed (deferred). Thus, it is possible to talk about meaning effects. Signs seem to mean something but they are always caught up in *différance* so that no one ever arrives at a final term outside the linguistic system that could stabilize this infinite regress. There is always what Derrida termed a 'supplement', a surplus an 'exterior addition' that threatens the integrity of a discourse and can never be fully tamed (1967/1997: 144f). John Storey has put the case very well when he says that if you look up a word in a dictionary you are referred to other words which then need to be looked up – a process creating 'a relentless deferment of meaning'. It is only when words are used in specific discourses and read in particular contexts that this endless signification may come to a temporary halt but, in the final analysis, even a well-defined context cannot halt the potentially endless play of signifiers (2009a: 127).

In this way it is possible to see that Saussure's neat concept of the sign is destabilized through this play on the two senses of the French word. This kind of thinking can be seen as poststructuralist because it is clearly indebted to Saussure's concepts but goes beyond them to challenge the idea that language can be stabilized through the neat unification of signifier and signified. I might emphasize again at this point that I have enormously simplified Derrida's arguments in a very un-Derridan way. I have (ironically) imposed a set of signifieds on an ambiguous term which is supposed to function to undermine this very project – and reduced a whole essay to a few paragraphs.

It seems, then, that meaning is both present and absent. If Derrida alerts us to the slippery nature of the sign he knows, at the same time, that the only way of getting these ideas across is to play the meaning game he challenges. He has to be a member of the devil's party, as it were, to articulate his anti-concepts. This is why he sometimes put 'words under erasure' (an idea he got from Heidegger) – that is, he wrote them but crossed them out.

This is linked to his concept of the **trace** where signs (of all kinds) are a 'mark of the absence of a presence, an always already absent present', and where they serve as 'the lack at the origin that is the condition of thought and experience' (Spivak in Derrida, 1967/1997: xvii). What this means is that signs always assume the absence of the thing being named. That is the point of language and thought: its starting point is that it has to work independently of any grounding presence. So it is that Spivak claims of Derrida that he teaches us that 'we must learn to use and erase our language at the same time' (xviii), an idea I will expand on in the following sections.

Structure, the transcendental signified, the metaphysics of presence and logocentrism

To delve a little deeper into Derrida's ideas, I will look at the essay that helped to put his deconstructive thinking on the map: 'Structure, Sign and Play in the Discourse of the Human Sciences'. In this essay Derrida pointed out the importance of the idea of **structure** within Western thinking, stating that it functions by way of providing a centre, a 'point of presence' or 'a fixed origin'. In this way it not only orients, balances and organizes a discourse but permits and limits its play (its ability to signify indefinitely) (Derrida, 1967/1978: 278). If we come back to the idea that in language 'there are only differences *without positive terms*' we know that the concept (or meaning) of each signifier is postponed indefinitely within the structure of a discourse. In this respect, one of the things that Derrida puts forward in 'Structure, Sign and Play' is that to stop this infinite regress it would be necessary for there to be what he referred to as a **'transcendental signified'** – something outside the system that could somehow suspend this play (280).

A 'transcendental signified' is anything that could limit the endless deferral of meaning. Without one the play of meaning is (potentially) extended indefinitely. One way would be to refuse Barthes' death of the author and dream of a situation where authors, as origin, could finally fix the meaning of an utterance or piece of writing. Derrida calls this dream **the metaphysics of presence** (281) which, he argues, has a long history in Western thinking. Derrida develops this idea in many different aspects of his work but one way of understanding it is to refer to another of Derrida's essays, 'The End of the Book and the Beginning of Writing', which is the first chapter of his groundbreaking work entitled *Of Grammatology*.

Outlining the idea of the 'metaphysics of presence' will show how deconstruction works in practice. My aim here is to focus not only on the ideas Derrida puts forward but on what Derrida *does*, because this will help to show how deconstruction *works*. What he does in the essay just mentioned is to perform a deconstruction of something that he sees fundamental to how Western thinking tends to conceive of truth. Derrida points out, by referring to thinkers like Plato, Aristotle, Rousseau and Hegel, that Western philosophy gives greater importance to speech rather than to writing.

Derrida points out that in Aristotle's work spoken words are seen as symbols of mental experience and written words are 'the symbols of spoken words'. This is because the voice, 'the producer of *the first symbols*, has a relationship of essential and immediate proximity with the mind' (Derrida, 1967/1997: 11). Derrida's point is that in the Western philosophical tradition speech is privileged over writing because it is understood to be at one with the mental processes (thoughts, pure being) that generate it – that is, *before* writing, reading and interpretation. Writing is downgraded in Aristotle (and the Western tradition in general) because it is distanced from the origin which is the mind (the *logos* as thought or reason). This is what Derrida terms **logocentrism**, a defining characteristic of Western thinking where meaning is grounded in the metaphysics of presence, and where presence (and speech) are privileged over absence (and writing).

This privileging of presence over absence was something already found in Plato's *Phaedrus* where Plato argued that writing suffers from a similar disadvantage to painting. Representations in painting may resemble beings but if they are asked a question 'they maintain a solemn silence' (Plato, c. 370 BC/1973: 97). For Plato, the same can be said with relation to writing. Furthermore, according to Plato, writing is no guarantee of wisdom because it does not prove that writers really know their subject; it is a poor substitute for speech. Only in the spoken word can individuals prove that they possess understanding, wisdom and truth (and speakers can clarify and answer you back). Again, we see an insistence on the importance of the *logos*, of being self-present which is opposed to the inferior condition of absence or non-presence.

Thought as structured through polarities of this kind and the privileging of one term over another is something that Derrida sees everywhere in Western forms of thinking (philosophical or otherwise) with common dichotomies being based around things like: man versus woman, mind versus matter, soul versus body, presence versus absence, truth versus error, being verses nothingness and identity versus difference, and so on. As Barbara Johnson has written of Derrida, within Western thinking these dichotomies are not treated equally: 'the second term in each pair is considered the negative, corrupt, undesirable version of the first'. Thus, 'absence is the lack of presence, evil is the fall from good', etc. so that the two terms are not simply opposed but 'are arranged in a hierarchical order' which gives the first term *priority* over the second. What these hierarchies do is to 'privilege unity, identity, immediacy, and temporal and spatial *presentness* over distance, difference, dissimulation and deferment' (Johnson in Derrida, 1972/1981: viii). One way of understanding deconstructive thinking is to see how Derrida collapses (without necessarily inverting) these hierarchies.

Logocentrism and the metaphysics of presence: further connections

However, before discussing further (anti-)concepts I want to consider some further implications of the word 'logocentric'. We have seen that to say that Western thinking is 'logocentric' is to stress that meaning is commonly thought to emanate from the *source* of language (that is, the mind of the speaker or writer, the *logos*) rather than admit, like Saussure, that meaning does not have its source outside language but is made possible by the rules that govern it and that are shared by those who use it. The 'metaphysics of presence' describes this tendency to assume that meaning is present to itself at the moment of enunciation and is dependent on something extra-linguistic – namely, the *presence* of the speaker at the time of the utterance. Thus, meaning in language is promised by something which is not strictly part of the 'materiality' of language itself (it is 'meta' – above or beyond language itself).

For Derrida meaning is an *effect* of language and can never be said to be *in* it or somehow prior to it (in the intention of the speaker). As stated, presence is metaphysical in the sense of being outside or above the materiality of the sign – for Derrida it cannot be the origin and ground of meaning. This tendency of assuming meaning is independent of, or beyond, the language we use can be typified when someone says, 'I know what I mean, but I can't put it in words' as if the meaning of a phrase is present to the speaker but is incommunicable. However, for Derrida (following Saussure) meaning is dependent on the linguistic conventions and codes that govern the production and reception of language, not on the intention of the speaker or on feelings of self-present meaning *prior* to articulation.

From these reflections Derrida offers a meticulous analysis of Heidegger's notion of being where he shows that being, rather than 'being' prior to language is, again, an effect of it. That is, being can only be posited *within* a system of signs. This assumption is one of the characteristics that unites much structuralist and poststructuralist thought and is reminiscent of the conflict I reviewed in the previous chapter between Thompson and Althusser. There we saw that Thompson was scandalized by the idea that people could be thought to be '*structured* by social relations, *spoken* by pre-given linguistic structures, *thought* by ideologies', etc. (Thompson, 1978/1995: 206). Having reviewed terms like 'logocentrism and 'the metaphysics of presence' I shall now explore related deconstructive concepts. For Derrida, if Western thinking is dependent on 'logocentrism' and 'the metaphysics of presence', it is also 'phonocentric'.

Phonocentrism

Phonocentrism comes from the Greek word *phōnē* (referring to speech or sound) and Derrida uses it to indicate (as we saw above) that in Western thinking there is the tendency to privilege speech (as closer to the origin of production, the being of the speaker) over writing (understood as being secondary and thereby cut off from the origin that gives an utterance its meaning). Thus, speech is given priority over the written word because it is seen as more authentic. In this context we have another of Derrida's deconstructive manoeuvres. What Derrida does is to collapse the distinction between speech and writing. Derrida writes: 'The exteriority of the signifier is the exteriority of writing in general' the point being that 'there is no linguistic sign before writing' (14).

Derrida's argument is that because the spoken word is seen as arising from the self-present core of the self (being) writing is understood as something outside of being (it is non-self present), and complicated by the secondary processes of production and interpretation. In the Western tradition of thought 'to be' is to be self-evidently present to the self (this is logocentrism) and this is associated with the speaking voice (this is phonocentrism). However, for Derrida *all* uses of signs are dependent on the same linguistic rules that govern and structure language. Thus, as hinted above, you are no closer to the meaning of a phrase in speech than in writing because this meaning does not *precede* the act of speech, it is a consequence of using language. In 'Structure, Sign and Play' Derrida states that presence is actually lost in the sign, whether written or spoken (Derrida, 1967/1978: 281).

This is very close to Barthes' idea of the death of the author – you may speak or write something but the moment the words are free of your mouth or pen you are erased in them (and, as stated earlier, interpretation becomes an 'anti-theological activity that is truly revolutionary'). For Derrida this is all implied in what has been translated as 'trace' (mentioned earlier). The sign itself (whether written or spoken) indicates an absence. If words are thought of as footprints they are signs or traces to be interpreted: they do not carry within them an essential meaning but merely open up a space for interpretation. The trace, then, is 'the simulacrum of a presence that dislocates, displaces, and refers beyond itself' (Derrida: 1967/1973: 401).

This seems to imply that signs signal a kind of authorial absenteeism and this brings me back to Barthes' notion of the intertext. At the beginning of the chapter we saw that Barthes defined the text as a 'tissue of quotations drawn from innumerable centres of culture' arguing that *language itself* is radically intertextual. This means that all writers (and speakers) have to draw on words, phrases, tags, sayings, proverbs, names (cultural references of all kinds), etc. which serve as a kind of dictionary of resources that writers use to create a text and that readers use to engage with it. These are the networks of 'quotations' that confront the reader as a 'text'. Derrida's notion of the text echoes this when he writes of Plato's writings: 'In a word, we do not believe that there exists, in all rigour, a Platonic text, closed upon itself, complete with its inside and its outside' (Derrida, 1972/1981: 130).

As in Barthes, this compromises the identity of the text as a stable, unproblematic and unique entity. The title of the book from which this quotation has been taken is *Dissemination*, which reflects another important theme that reinforces the idea that texts, and language itself, are part of radical processes of interaction which complicate the notion of the unique, integral (self-enclosed) text. The complex, sedimented histories of words, phrases, tags, etc. disseminate meanings in terms of both the production and reception of 'the text'. If the text is stabilized it is because all these possibilities are repressed or relegated to the margins (another theme in the Derridean tradition that I shall discuss in more detail in the following chapter).

~~Conclusion~~: returning to *différance*

Finally, I want to come back to Derrida's anti-concept of *différance*. I made the point earlier in the chapter that if you are familiar with the French language you will notice that Derrida replaced the letter 'e' with an 'a' in the French word *différence*. Understanding the significance of this change in spelling is one of the keys to understanding deconstruction. The word, as it is pronounced in French, cannot be distinguished from the unchanged word '*différence*' which shows that writing can actually exploit linguistic resources that cannot be detected in speech without further elaboration. To get the point over while speaking you would have to say something like: when I say the word *différance* I mean you to understand it as if it had an 'a' interposed between the 'r' and the 'n' of the third syllable instead of the expected 'e'. This is at least one example of where writing cannot be reduced to speech, as its inferior copy. However, this should not lead us to conclude that Derrida is arguing that the act of writing actually precedes speech. That might seem an obvious conclusion but Derrida resists it.

While deconstruction does overturn the privileged term (speech) it does not seek to put the other (minor or secondary) term in its place. If you go back to the section in Chapter 2 where we looked at Lévi-Strauss's idea that cultures make sense of the world through 'binary oppositions' (nature/culture, raw/cooked, etc.), you will see that these provided 'classificatory systems' upon which social realities are based. Derrida attacks the basis of these binaries by finding, through very close reading, what he calls '*aporias*': loose ends, or logical inconsistencies in any system of thought. Once you recognize that speech is dependent on the same underlying structures as writing (the particular grammatological rules that Derrida calls '*archi-écriture*' or 'proto-writing' (Derrida, 1967/1997: 291)) you have found a way of undermining the simple binary which contains a privileged term. The point is, however, not to fall into the trap of privileging writing over speech. If you do, it can only be for the strategic ends of emphasizing a point (Derrida, 1967/1997: 99f.).

To conclude, these basic manoeuvres have influenced many areas in the humanities (not just philosophy) and particularly cultural studies and literary criticism. The theory that comes out of this is that reading 'must always aim at a certain relationship, unperceived by the writer, between what he commands and what he does not command of the patterns of the language that he uses' (Derrida, 1967/1978: 158). This means that deconstruction looks for inconsistencies (*aporias*) and paradoxes through exploiting a text's own blindnesses and contradictions – a technique that resembles, to some extent, Althusser's notion of the 'problematic'. This technique of reading is similar to what in philosophy is called 'immanent critique'. This requires a full immersion into the logic, assumptions and rhetorical procedures of a given piece of writing which is then undermined according to its own internal contradictions (or, in Derrida's terms, *aporias*), rather than be subjected to a set of critical premises which are understood to be imposed from the outside (see Harvey, 1990: 5f.).

Reading the above sections you may get the impression that I have revealed the method of deconstruction. While it can be, and has been, reduced to a method, Derrida was at pains to insist that deconstruction is more like a local intervention that cannot be reduced to a simple set of moves. Having said that, it is possible to break down some common strategies as a means of trying out some of the concepts for yourself. And it is in this spirit that you should read the first part of the following chapter, which includes a heuristic (a tool for thinking with) to help you. A final point: you should now realize why I stated earlier that any introduction to Derrida's work contradicts the premises of deconstruction. This is because any attempt at stabilizing the term denies the difference and deferral that militate against its stabilization in the first place. But this is one of the contradictions that deconstructive thinking forces us to live with.

Practice

The next section will show how deconstruction has been useful to various approaches associated with cultural studies but, as a preliminary exercise, you might analyse why I have written and erased the word 'conclusion'. This should help you to focus on some of the key ideas outlined in this section.

Summary of key points

This chapter began by considering the idea of poststructuralism and showing how a number of themes developed in Barthes' writings (like the de-mythologist, the death of the author and the notion of intertextuality) can be associated with deconstructive strategies. The relationship between structuralism and poststructuralism has been described as one not based on complete rupture but of continuity and critique. The chapter has also demonstrated how deconstruction works with relation to (anti-) concepts like 'différance', 'logocentrism', 'phonocentrism' and 'the metaphysics of presence'. A concentration on the basic steps of Derrida's deconstruction of the privileging of speech over writing has helped to show how deconstruction may work in practice.

Further reading

Barthes: Graham Allen's *Roland Barthes* (2003) provides a very accessible overview of the entire Barthes oeuvre and Allen goes into fine detail concerning Barthes' concepts and how he developed them. If you found the practice section 'Of intertextuality, authoricide and suicide' and the complexities of the interpretive issues particularly interesting you might explore Andrew Bennett's reader *Readers and Reading* (1995). The notion of intertextuality was coined by Julia Kristeva; her *Desire in Language: A Semiotic Approach to Literature and Art* (1980) should help to give an idea of its scope and implications.

Derrida: James Smith's *Jacques Derrida: Live Theory* (2005) is an accessible introduction to Derrida's work which also includes some discussion of the ethics of deconstruction. Feder, Rawlinson and Zakin in their *Derrida and Feminism* (1996) have compiled a collection of essays which discuss Derrida's work with relation to feminist debates. The last chapter of Derrida's *Limited Inc.* (1988) includes an interview (which was really a written exchange) with Derrida where he clarifies his deconstructive philosophy in highly readable terms. If you find Derrida's work daunting, a good place to start is with his *Positions* (1972/1987), which is collection of three interviews with Derrida where he outlines his thinking in a language which avoids the rigorous, playful, challenging and difficult style he adopts in most of his essays and books.

6

Doing Deconstruction

Techniques for Practice

Learning goals

- To be able to see how a rudimentary form of deconstruction may be practised.
- To understand how deconstructive techniques can be applied in various ways according to themes like contesting patriarchal power, challenging the idea of the 'popular', questioning subaltern consciousness and undermining simplistic narrative accounts of the (imperialist) nation.
- To appreciate how cultural studies has used deconstructive techniques and consider its possible 'dangers' and limits.

Concepts

The key concepts introduced in this chapter are: heuristic, popular culture, high culture, historiography, post-colonialism, 'dissemiNation', two interpretations of interpretation and 'arbitrary closure'.

Introduction

This chapter breaks down the steps of the deconstructive technique described in the last chapter and offers a heuristic device to aid thinking about how deconstruction might be practised in an engaged, self-consciously political way. This is done by applying it to the way in which masculinity and femininity have been constructed and this leads on to a consideration of the possible strengths and weaknesses of deconstruction as an approach. This is followed by three sections which show how deconstruction can be, or has been, adapted to cultural studies. The first section reviews Stuart Hall's 'Notes on Deconstructing "The Popular"' (1981b). The second illustration shows how Gayatri Chakravorty Spìvak deconstructs subaltern consciousness, and the third how Homi Bhabha applies deconstructive techniques to the notion of the (imperialist) nation. Thus, the two latter sections also introduce important aspects of post-colonial criticism. Further notes on practice discuss how to apply deconstructive thinking to earlier parts of the book, particularly Barthes' reading of the black soldier on the cover of *Paris Match* and his arguments in *Mythologies*. This section also reflects on the scope and implications of using deconstructive thinking. The chapter is concluded by a discussion of Stuart Hall's idea of 'arbitrary closure' and its significance for the practice of cultural studies.

Practising deconstruction: a heuristic

I said at the end of the last chapter that, even though deconstruction can be (and has been) reduced to a method, Derrida was at pains to insist that it is more like a local intervention that cannot be reduced to a simple set of moves. Having said this, I will break down some of Derrida's common strategies into a **heuristic** (a tool for thinking with) which will help to sum up some of the key ideas outlined in the last chapter while offering a scheme that can be used to think with deconstruction (see table 6.1). Before I continue, however, a caveat that reflects a point I made in the previous chapter: the following section should be read with a sense of irony because it reduces and stabilizes deconstruction in a way that Derrida would probably have seen as counter to the general principles of his thinking.

Deconstructing patriarchal power

From the point of view of practising cultural studies this heuristic, this simplified version of deconstructive technique, can be used to address all kinds of cultural privilege based on questionable binary structures. In this section I shall show how this might work with relation to an important theme already developed in this book: patriarchal power. In Chapters 2 and 3 we saw how Kaja Silverman argued that key oppositions give rise to conceptual systems based on typical cultural codes where women are defined in opposition to men. It is this binary structure that feminism challenges. This privileging of one term over another which reflects conventional, established relations of power, is, as Derrida explained in *Positions*, always based on a 'violent hierarchy' where 'one of the two terms controls the other'. To deconstruct the opposition is, in the first

Table 6.1 Practising Derrida's deconstruction: a heuristic

Here is a breakdown (in four stages) of what Derrida does in 'The End of the Book and the Beginning of Writing' (1967/1997).

1 First of all we need to isolate the problem that Derrida addresses. Very simply it is possible to say that it is that Western thinking tends to be *logocentric* (grounded on the 'metaphysics of presence') and *phonocentric* (speech is given priority over the written word).

2 It is necessary to isolate the binary oppositions to be dismantled. We can split these up into oppositions according to the privileged and the non-privileged (or secondary) terms:

Privileged binary terms:	Non-privileged (secondary) terms:
Presence (linked to being)	Non-presence
Speech	Written word
Language fully present to the self	Language not fully present to the self

3 We can then analyse the binary oppositions showing how a deconstructive technique collapses these binaries by finding *aporias*, loose ends and/or logical inconsistencies in the system of thought. We can then divide our comments into two columns: a critique of the privileged terms and comments on how to deconstruct the binary oppositions.

Derrida's critique of the privileged terms

A Being is seen as preceding, or beyond, language, because it provides the locus and foundation for truth and understanding (*logocentrism*). It functions as a kind of 'transcendental signified' – an anchor external to language which holds all meaning together. The traditional figure of the author (and her or his intentions) can serve this purpose.

B This *logocentrism* is dependent on *phonocentrism*: speech is always privileged over writing because the spoken word is considered closest to being because it issues from this being/centre (self). The idea is that at the instant of speaking the meaning of the utterance is immediately and fully present to the speaker's consciousness. Again, the self-present self functions as a 'transcendental signified' – an absolute foundation, outside language, which gives a stable centre to make truth possible.

Derrida's deconstruction

A Being, or the self, as something present to itself cannot function outside language. To say the 'self' or talk about 'being' as beyond signification makes it 'metaphysical' (this is the metaphysics of presence). This is absurd because although 'being' cannot be reduced to a word or concept it is tied to language insofar that it cannot be articulated outside it.

B According to structuralism, what creates meaning is not the presence or consciousness of the speaker (or immediate access to intention) but the underlying conventions of language. This '*archi-écriture*' is necessary for both the spoken and the written word; therefore, at the instant of speaking the meaning can be no more immediately present or reliable than written language. There cannot be a 'transcendental signified' (a self/being) an absolute foundation outside. So, spoken or written, language has no stable centre of being on which to rely. Being is articulated through signification, not something prior to it.

4 *Conclusion*: despite a bias in Western thinking, speech cannot be privileged over writing but nor should writing be privileged over speech because, in order to function, they are both dependent on the underlying conventions of language.

place, 'to overthrow the hierarchy' but, as seen in the previous chapter, without allowing the subordinated term to predominate (Derrida, 1972/1987: 4f.).

Once the binary structures and the hierarchies of power have been isolated it is necessary to think about how they can be dismantled. That is to say, there is the need to be aware of the privileged and non-privileged (secondary) binary terms (see point two above). For example, women, as Silverman emphasized, have traditionally been *defined against* the 'rational', 'firm' and 'strong' characteristics given to the privileged male. For this reason women are symbolized by terms like 'emotional', 'pliant' and 'weak' (Silverman, 1983: 36) and, in De Beauvoir's terms, seen as the 'second sex' and gendered 'Other' (Beauvoir, 1949/1984).

Derrida would want to insist that the binaries are mutually dependent, reflecting the Saussurean idea that concepts are purely differential and defined negatively with relation to other terms: their main characteristic being 'what the others are not'. However, whereas structuralism provided the means to recognize the way cultural systems function to produce meaning, deconstruction goes a stage further because it *undermines* the systems themselves and (this is where a more politicized deconstructive reading comes in) makes us aware of the way a system functions to privilege certain individuals, races, classes, sexualities, etc. over others. In this way Monique Wittig's assertion that 'men' and 'women' are not 'natural facts' but 'political categories' (Wittig, 1981: 17) can be applied to other terms like 'heterosexual', 'white', 'upper class', on the one hand, and 'gay/lesbian', 'black' and 'working class', on the other – in fact, any opposition that perpetuates subordination. At this point a deconstructive way of thinking would collapse the primary binary oppositions by finding *aporias* – the loose ends and/or logical inconsistencies in the system of thought. To illustrate this I shall use an essay by the feminist historian Sherry B. Ortner ('Is Female to Male as Nature is to Culture?' 1972/1995) to show how *aporias* might be tracked down and deconstructed (where necessary, adding to her arguments).

While Ortner does not claim to deconstruct the binaries upon which women and men are commonly represented across cultures, her essay can help to show how they may be challenged. In an attempt 'to explain the universal secondary status of women' Ortner argues that women are devalued in diverse cultures because they are represented as being closer to 'nature' while men represent themselves as being closer to 'culture' (Ortner, 1972: 504). As a first deconstructive move it might be observed that in these arguments the culture–nature binary has already been compromised insofar that if men are, in some way, closer to culture then this seems to evoke being cultured as more 'natural' to masculinity. In this way 'nature' has already slipped across the continuum into its binary opposite.

The reason that Ortner repeatedly finds to support the claim that women are closer to nature is that their physiology is seen as more directly involved with 'the crucial function of transforming animal-like infants into cultured beings' (505). Thus, women are generally associated with mothering functions (to ignore the multiple roles that women are actually expected to perform) and confined to the 'domestic unit' which is 'one of culture's crucial agencies for the conversion of nature into culture, especially with reference to the socialization of children' (505). Here we see another *aporia* within the patriarchal socio-political model because Ortner argues that women, as educators, are actually crucial to the way culture perpetuates itself through the gender most associated not with culture but with nature.

Ortner concludes that, of course, women are no closer to nature (or culture) than men but their lives are repeatedly restricted through the way they are represented and that these representations have important ideological and political consequences. Of course, this kind of identity politics is not enough and it can only be a starting point. For change to be brought about institutional and symbolic changes must be initiated: laws and social institutions have to be transformed, as well as cultural symbols and assumptions. It might be argued that deconstruction, as a tool that can be used to challenge cultural symbols and assumptions, can play a part in bringing those changes about. I have emphasized how deconstruction can work as an effective tool to challenge sexist assumptions; however, in this context Chris Weedon has helped to bring out the strengths and weaknesses of deconstructive readings. She argues that while deconstruction theorizes 'the discursive context as the relationship of difference between written texts' and insists that 'non-discursive forces are important' it does not 'spell out the social power relations within which texts are located'.

Weedon shows how deconstruction can make us aware that the signifier 'woman' can signify anything from angel, career woman and romantic heroine, to victim, successful wife and mother and irresistible sexual object. This helps us to appreciate that the term is always open to 'constant rereading and reinterpretation'. However, feminist poststructuralism 'must pay full attention to the social and institutional context of textuality in order to address the power relations of everyday life' (Weedon, 1997: 25). I would argue that Ortner's style of feminist anthropology (while too reductive in its attempts to look for universal causes) goes some way towards addressing the social and institutional contexts of these power relations. Further potential weaknesses of deconstruction for feminism are also brought out when Weedon writes:

> While its stress on the plurality and non-fixity of meaning is a helpful move beyond criticism which attempts to identify one true meaning, the implicit assumption that there is a free play of meaning not already located in a hierarchical network of discursive relations denies social power by rendering it invisible and in so doing reaffirms the status quo. Deconstructionist approaches to textual analysis which share a disregard for the wider historically specific discursive context of reading and writing and the power relations which structure the literary field itself do not meet feminist needs. The interests which inform deconstructionist criticism as a purely textual criticism are generally the unacknowledged interests of individual readers, most often those supporting white middle-class patriarchy. (160)

Weedon, then, sees deconstruction as going beyond criticism which tries to fix meaning in a simplistic way but she is sceptical about interpretive play for its own sake. She wants to relate interpretation to the social forces that influence the way literary texts are read. As a feminist she is aware that the way texts are made to mean is very much dependent on a series of male-dominated institutions that establish the basic limits of interpretation. While readers are reading texts as 'free play' they are not encouraged to consider the politics of reading.

If the implications of these possible weaknesses are applied to other areas of interest concerned with class, sexuality, race/ethnicity, the post-colonial, and age, etc. it is important to stress that deconstruction needs to be handled with care in case it becomes an intellectual tool which may end up reaffirming the world as it is. In the following sections I shall introduce deconstructive approaches that illustrate ways of using it that *do* tend to focus on the 'wider historically specific discursive context of reading and writing' as a means of challenging the status quo.

As a concluding point, one effective way of understanding the potential power of deconstruction is to refer to Gayatri Spivak's view that deconstruction (in the context of post-colonial oriented studies) 'cannot found a political program of any kind. Yet in its suggestion that masterwords like "the worker" or "the woman" have no literal referents, deconstruction is a political safeguard' (Spivak, 1990: 104). I shall return to Spivak and how deconstruction might aid 'post-colonial' debates a little later but before I do I shall refer to a useful and influential essay by Stuart Hall which shows how deconstructive thinking can be used to consider the politics of 'the popular'.

Help File: post-colonialism

This is a complex and contested term (Williams and Chrisman, 1993: 1f.) which tends to focus on the historical, economic, political and other cultural legacies of imperialist expansion.

Further adapting deconstruction to cultural studies: Stuart Hall's 'Notes on Deconstructing "The Popular"'

For an area like cultural studies, while the reading of complex philosophical texts is common, the ideas are often not developed for *directly* philosophical ends but adapted to particular ends. A very effective example of this kind of adaptation is Stuart Hall's essay 'Notes on Deconstructing "The Popular"' (1981b). The first thing to notice is that Hall, apart from using the word 'deconstruction', avoids (for the most part) the complex anti-concepts associated with Derrida's style of argumentation. In this sense, he takes advantage of a deconstructive way of thinking, but I would not call it an example of full-blown deconstruction. That would require all kinds of plays on words, formal experimentation and the stylistic nuances associated with Derrida – and recognition of how the discourse in which Hall writes is ultimately undermined by its own rhetorical procedures.

What I want to emphasize here is that it is possible to see that Hall performs, as his title indicates, a deconstructive manoeuvre. To demonstrate this I shall impose on his essay the deconstructive steps I set out in the heuristic above. Hall's first step is to outline the problem. He does this by considering the term '**popular culture**' and concluding that 'there is no whole, authentic, autonomous "popular culture" that lies outside the field of force of the relations of cultural power and domination' (Hall, 1981b: 512). To maintain the high versus popular culture distinction is to assume that they are fixed binary domains whereas they are culturally constructed and fought over. This means that culture is not free of politics and power. A sense of the high and low is a question of hegemonic struggle (Gramsci's term for the way cultural forms are fought over – see Chapter 1 and below). That is to say, there is no intrinsic high or low culture before institutionally grounded value judgements get to work on cultural forms.

Hall's next step is to set up what we can understand as the main terms of a deconstructive manoeuvre. Hall maintains that in order for proponents of **high culture** to maintain the binary distinction they have to assume the existence of something outside the realm of the most valued cultural forms. This outside is what is excluded from the centre. While Hall's direct source is Antonio Gramsci, this is a very Derridean way of thinking. One of Derrida's book titles is *Margins of Philosophy* (1967/1984) and it reflects Derrida's constant awareness of what is excluded from the middle – that which has to be denied in order for the structure to remain in place. In the case of structuralism it is the play of *différance* that has to be pushed to the margin and (for Hall) in the case of high culture, it is all the cultural products or practices that need to be proscribed.

Hall's (deconstructive) point is that the maintenance of high culture is actually dependent on the very thing it excludes. The choices are really about a struggle for cultural hegemony and the so-called high and low forms are not dependent on absolute difference but chosen from the available forms. The low cultural forms are constantly threatening the integrity of high culture from the margins (an artist like Andy Warhol with his Campbell's soup cans and Brillo Pad boxes can be considered trash or an integral part of the artistic tradition). We see here how the simple binary collapses. High and low forms are relational and interdependent and can change historically. Hall refers to the history of the swastika to show how it changed from being a religious symbol (associated with the official culture of various ecclesiastical classes) to becoming a key Nazi symbol, later becoming a symbol within neo-Nazi groups (with ambiguous class relations). Subsequently, it became a rather more ambiguous symbol within the punk movement, and a symbol of counter-hegemonic culture. Mediating his deconstruction through Gramsci, Hall insists that there is no absolute link between class and so-called popular culture – the relations are negotiable and the term 'popular culture' is unstable.

To go a little beyond the terms of Hall's arguments, certain hybrid forms of culture further blur distinctions between official and unofficial, popular and high culture. For example, Monserrat Caballé, a prestigious Spanish opera singer, managed to get a hit single with 'Barcelona' by collaborating with Queen's Freddie Mercury. This can be seen as an indeterminate cultural form which lies somewhere between the common distinction made between high and low culture. John Storey (2009a: 6–7) discusses how Luciano Pavarotti's recording of Puccini's 'Nessun Dorma' (None shall sleep) and his two albums of arias got to the top of the British album charts – something else that posed a challenge to the high (elite) and low (mass) cultural distinctions.

Then there are popular TV series like *Twin Peaks* created by 'quality' film-makers like David Lynch that, again, challenge the simple binary oppositions. From this point of view it is possible to see how Pop 'art', like Andy Warhol's use of everyday objects (see above) and Roy Lichtenstein's blowing up of comic-book images, compromises the notion of 'high culture' through what is its excluded other. As we have seen, deconstruction typically looks for these ambiguities or *aporias* to show how forms can be undermined through their own inconsistencies. There will be more discussion of these phenomena and how they collapse the high/low distinction in later chapters on postmodern culture.

To conclude this section, Stuart Hall's use of the term 'deconstruction' helps to show that it is a useful conceptual tool. While deconstruction has not always enjoyed a very comfortable place within cultural studies (some critics like Weedon (above) feeling it may end up reaffirming the status quo and others accusing it of being too theoreticist) it is possible to see, as Gary Hall has argued, that it has an important place in cultural studies insofar as it can help to think through 'some of the problems and paradoxes in its complicated relationship to politics and the political' (Hall and Birchall, 2006: 32). In this section I have shown how deconstruction can help to illuminate patriarchal forms of power and how high culture is a cultural construction with a political dimension. In the next two sections I will illustrate how deconstruction has served as a useful tool with relation to debates centred on **historiography**, **post-colonialism** and nation and narration.

Gayatri Chakravorty Spivak and deconstructing historiography

Gayatri Chakravorty Spivak (an important translator of Derrida's works) wrote an essay entitled 'Subaltern Studies: Deconstructing Historiography' where she deconstructs what she calls (playing on Derrida's 'metaphysics of presence') the 'metaphysics of consciousness' (1985/1996: 212). Spivak's deconstruction is an appreciative but critical intervention into the work of the Subaltern Studies collective that began writing in the 1980s. This was a group of historians, inspired by the work of Ranajit Guha, interested in re-reading Indian colonial history. Like Hall's reading above, Spivak's intervention can help to show how deconstruction may work with relation to possible *aporias* (in this case within historical writing). One of the problems that Spivak addresses with relation to the Subaltern Studies group is its attempt to give expression to the consciousness of insurgent groups. It is worth noticing here that Spivak is sympathetic to the project she is analysing but a deconstructive approach helps her to spot very special kinds of weaknesses in it.

Help File: historiography

While the standard definition of this word relates it to the study or writing of history it is often used to describe the writing of more traditional historians who assume that historical narratives can more or less reflect the past in objective ways with relation to periods and movements (for challenges to this, apart from this chapter, see the chapter on Foucault and those dealing with postmodernism).

The emphasis of the group on subaltern consciousness grew out of dissatisfaction with historical narratives that recounted the history of India that put the emphasis on the political consciousness of elite groups, who were understood to have led resistance against British colonial rule. Just as E. P. Thompson attempted to reconstruct British history by showing how the working classes, through developing consciousness of themselves and their predicament, were active agents of change (1963/1968), so the Subaltern Studies group attempted to recoup the lost consciousness of non-elite groups during the uprisings in India under British imperial rule. Broadly speaking, this interest required the Subaltern Studies scholars to explore not only the uprisings, rebellions and subversive behaviour against colonial rule but also the discourses produced in and around these political occurrences. This emphasis on exploring the margins rather than the centre to subvert more traditional notions of history is very much in keeping with poststructuralist tendencies. However, within this general strategy Spivak perceives structural weaknesses which she felt needed to be addressed.

The 'problem' of subaltern consciousness for Spivak is that the discovery and investigation of a subaltern or peasant consciousness is really a question of deducing it from uprisings and acts of rebellion. There is no actual evidence of consciousness *itself*. This is linked to what seems to be a 'positivistic project' (one based on empirical observation) that would lead 'to some *thing* that can be disclosed'. For example, rebellious peasant action is read as reflecting a 'single underlying consciousness'. However, for Spivak this is not subaltern consciousness itself but consciousness extrapolated from counter-hegemonic action (1985/1996: 211). For her, subaltern consciousness is a 'methodological presupposition' (212) rather than something actually found in the materials studied.

To explain this further, Spivak points out that the collective, while seeking subaltern consciousness, admitted that it is 'never fully recoverable', that it is 'effaced even as it is disclosed'. This is because it is 'irreducibly discursive' (212). (Even if there were abundant textual evidence this would probably be a problem for Spivak because it would still be discourse and not conscious-ness *as such*.) The collective's strategy not only fails because there is no 'empirical' basis for a single underlying consciousness but is destabilized by Derrida's point about 'trace': the sign (whether written or spoken) indicates a profound absence. What this deconstruction reveals is that historians of subaltern 'consciousness' (or of anything else) must be aware of the 'historio-graphical' aspect of their work: the principles and methods that enable them to construct a sense of history. Failure to do this opens them up to a decon-structive reading that undermines the project through close attention to the rhetorical inconsistencies (*aporias*) that are built into the project at its outset. It might be stated that historiographical consciousness of a different kind is necessary to become aware that consciousness of subaltern consciousness is not possible.

One might object here that Spivak's deconstruction seems at odds with the kind of politicized readings that the Subaltern Studies collective were attempting. Surely, constructing a sense of subaltern consciousness would help to challenge narrow, official, hegemonic views? This might be answered by stating that, in the final analysis, no argument really helps a cause if it has serious intellectual flaws. Furthermore, it is better to recognize these pos-sible weaknesses for oneself rather than have them pointed out by those whose histories are considered questionable. Also, Spivak's arguments tend to pose the general question about whether anyone can, or should, speak on behalf of the subordinated. By constructing a sense of subaltern conscious-ness one is attempting to speak for a community which has (and had) no real voice.

Homi Bhabha and 'DissemiNation'

I shall now introduce an essay by the post-colonial theorist Homi Bhabha entitled 'DissemiNation: Time, Narrative and the Margins of the Modern Nation'. The main concept that governs this essay, '**dissemiNation**', while not relying so much on deconstructing binaries through *aporias*, is, as Bhabha acknowledges, very indebted to Derridean deconstruction (and wit). It also draws on Bhabha's personal experience of migration. In this essay Bhabha attempts to formulate 'the complex strategies of cultural identification' and forms of 'discursive address' that, in the name of the 'people' or the 'nation', function to make them the subjects or objects of a series 'of social and literary narratives' (Bhabha, 1990: 292). (This might remind you of Althusser's notion of 'interpellation' discussed in Chapter 4.) Bhabha explains that narrative strategies create the discourses that effectively unite populations under the idea of the nation through terms like common culture and community which make 'a one out of the many' (294). Within this project Bhabha effectively deconstructs the discourse of the nation by insisting on the 'temporal dimension' of national identity within the geographies of the ex-colonial powers. In the following section I will trace the steps of this deconstruction to show how it functions.

In his deconstruction of the imperialist nation, Bhabha plays on the Derridean idea of 'dissemination' (Derrida, 1972/1981), where, as seen in the previous chapter, meaning is never fixed but dispersed or scattered. Bhabha plays on this to create the witty term 'dissemiNation'. This term sets up the possibilities for seeing how the official idea of the nation is disseminated in various ways. For Bhabha the 'nation', although represented as a totality (as it is constructed in official discourses), is 'a space that is *internally* marked by cultural difference and the heterogeneous histories of contending people, antagonistic authorities, and tense cultural locations' (Bhabha, 1990: 299).

The nation which is narrated as 'a one out of the many' is a kind of 'double-writing', a 'dissemi-*nation*' because within the narrative fiction of the unified nation-state (what Benedict Anderson has called the 'imagined community' (Anderson, 2006)) are all the cultural differences and fragmented histories and conflicts that are disguised by the unified image (Bhabha, 1990: 299–300). The nation, like the poststructuralist sign, is radically split. To explain this Bhabha quotes Salman Rushdie's phrase from *Satanic Verses*: 'The trouble with the English is that their history happened overseas, so they don't know what it means' (317). Thus, we see how the imperial margin (the exploitation that happens or happened 'overseas') is actually fundamental to the identity of the metropolitan centre. This is linked to Bhabha's use of Mikhail Bakhtin's idea of the 'chronotope' – the time-place – which requires us to be aware of the spatial and temporal dimensions of narrative (Bakhtin, 1986). In terms of time, Bhabha points out that national(ist) discourses use the idea of the origin, the national past, within the present as a way of creating a sense of identity through continuity. A particular view of the past is installed into present time to maintain and perpetuate a sense of national identity.

In terms of space, the nation is usually conceived of as a very particular geographical area – Britain, for example, has geographical limits. However, Britain's imperial past, as we see in the Rushdie quotation, annexed 'other' geographical spaces to itself, generating complex political, economic, cultural relations with 'other' 'nations'. The implications of this generate important questions. Where is the identity of the 'nation' in all this? Britain, as a 'nation', is disseminated – what might seem to be its core is dispersed. And what can be said of the 'nations' annexed to its imperial 'centre'? Where does their national identity begin and end (in the past, the present and the future)? Hardly surprising, then, that Bhabha coins the neologism 'dissemi-Nation'. To conclude this section I would like to add a few comments on the general use of deconstruction in cultural studies, before coming back to Derrida and offering some advice on practice.

It would be easy to score points off Hall, Spivak and Bhabha by pushing deconstructive theory to the limit by deconstructing their interventions by exposing how their discourses could be destabilized by the radical play of *différance*. But this would defeat the point of a cultural studies-inflected critique. This is what distinguishes much cultural studies from professional philosophy: it tends to err on the side of radical political critique. The value of deconstruction is that it forces us to become intensely aware of how discourses function but it can also throw all thought into disarray, into endless speculation and doubt, or into constant impasse. That is its strength from a broadly poststructuralist point of view but (as Weedon stressed) it is also its weakness from the more pragmatic political point of view. In this chapter I have shown how three writers use it but harness its more radical and internecine potential. So it is that some of the basic assumptions of deconstruction have seeped into the general practices of cultural studies but cultural studies uses these assumptions in such a way that it does not necessarily undermine itself at the same time. Hall, Spivak and Bhabha use deconstructive techniques but do not allow them to question the status of their own discourses.

This acceptance of the radical possibilities of deconstruction, but disciplined by strategic restraint, was echoed by Stuart Hall (in another context) when he insisted that 'politics is impossible' without what he called '**arbitrary closure**' (Hall, 1996a: 137). This insists on using theory, even 'wrestling' with it, but not becoming a slave to it (280). This, I would argue, has been the way in which cultural studies practitioners have generally incorporated deconstructive techniques into their work. The alternative is to flirt with the danger of deconstructing yourself and depoliticizing your critique by emptying it out of all content (something even Derrida resisted).

The danger of deconstruction

I shall conclude this chapter on deconstruction by summing up the 'dangers' of the approach, reviewing Derrida's 'interpretation of interpretation', and offer some further advice on practice. First, I want to emphasize, as should be obvious by now, that any text is apt to be flawed by its own inconsistencies and *aproias*, etc. If, as was suggested earlier, Derrida's deconstruction can be seen as a form of immanent critique it is one which should (ideally) come with a warning on the box:

DECONSTRUCT AT YOUR PERIL BECAUSE YOU MAY END UP FALLING INTO THE VERY ASSUMPTIONS THAT YOU ARE AT PAINS TO DECONSTRUCT!

This danger was emblematically illustrated when Derrida deconstructed an essay by Jacques Lacan on Edgar Allan Poe's 'The Purloined Letter'. Following this the literary critic Barbara Johnson deconstructed Derrida's deconstruction of Lacan (Derrida, 1975/1987, Johnson, 1977). The next obvious step would be to deconstruct Barbara Johnson's deconstruction of Derrida's deconstruction of Lacan, doing everything in your power (through self-reflexivity and plays on words, concepts and form, etc.) to constantly alert the reader to the play of *différance* in your own writing (for examples see Derrida, 1972/1981: xvi–xvii). A question this raises is whether there would be any value in repeating this manoeuvre ad infinitum. As mentioned above, cultural studies tends to resist this infinite regress. This goes some way to explain why deconstruction has had a somewhat uneven recognition within cultural studies – some readers in the area include short texts by Derrida but many leave them out. Yet it is interesting that, while Derrida is not always required reading, writers who are quite clearly in the deconstructive tradition (like Spivak and Bhabha) are included in readers, and Derrida is often discussed in introductions. In cultural studies Derrida seems both there ... and not there.

This ambiguity is theoretically appropriate and revealing. This suggests that students of cultural studies need to be aware of deconstruction if they are to be prepared to engage with contemporary thought. Yet deconstruction is still, to some extent, seen as marginal, or even new. This is highlighted by the inclusion of a chapter by Gary Hall on cultural studies and deconstruction in a recent book entitled *New Cultural Studies: Adventures in Theory* (Hall and Birchall: 2006). Deconstruction is (still) 'new'! It seems almost to have slipped in by the back door. The explanation for this goes back to the way Hall used a deconstructive technique to reflect upon the politics of the popular. Readings inspired by Derridean strategies seem more relevant to the projects of cultural studies than direct deconstructive philosophical speculations *as such*. Cultural studies generally sidesteps the stylistic particularities and full consequences of deconstruction's radical programme.

However, having said this, deconstructive reading includes within itself a kind of safety valve for those who want to resist its more radical effects in the shape of what Derrida called 'double reading'. As noted earlier, at one level it challenges *logocentrism* and *phonocentrism*, insists on *différance* and indeterminacy, and pulls apart discourses according to inconsistencies, contradictions and paradoxes. However, at another level, Derrida admits that there is no way to transcend these problems – the effects of meaning are dependent on the assumption of a centre, a self (however illusory it is), that provide anchor points from which to start. There is a sense in which even if you do not believe in the cake, there is no other option, you have to eat it – that is, if you want to communicate anything. This brings me to Derrida's notion of **two interpretations of interpretation**.

'The End of the Book and the Beginning of Writing': two interpretations of interpretation

Derrida, in his essay 'Structure, Sign and Play in the Discourse of the Human Sciences', insists that there are 'two interpretations of interpretation' (1967/1978: 278f.). The first 'dreams of deciphering a truth or an origin which escapes play and the order of the sign'; the other one 'affirms play' and tries to go beyond 'man' – man 'being the name of that being who, [...] has dreamed of full presence, the reassuring foundation, the origin and the end of play'. (292) So what deconstruction announces is the end of this dream of stability, closure, absolute truth and the beginning of the free-play of signs; in short, of writing over the (fossilized) book. This was something echoed in a section of *Of Grammatology* entitled 'The Beginning of the Book and the End of Writing' (1967/1997) and, although he does not state it, Derrida was actually playing on the title of one of Heidegger's essays called 'The End of Philosophy and the Task of Thinking' (1964/1978). What the two essays share in common is an attempt to go beyond what counted as philosophy at the time and take it somewhere else through new forms of thought.

Of course, it is possible to interpret this emphasis on 'play' in terms of assuming that by using deconstruction a text can be interpreted in any way the reader wants. However, Derrida was more cautious – while deconstructive thinking tends to push beyond attempts to limit the signifier it also acknowledges that without limiting factors (the 'double reading' mentioned above) there would be no means of communicating any kind of message (Derrida, 1988: 144f.). Derrida realized that there would be no point putting forward a theory which would be so 'permissive' that the theory 'itself' would get lost in a free-for-all, 'absolutely anything goes' attitude to the text. Just because final closure is always suspended does not presuppose that any meaning can be imposed on a text – there is still the necessity of finely arguing a case that attends to particularities and conventions. To say that Martin Luther King's famous 'I have a dream' speech is an incitement to do more gardening would be laughably arbitrary (unless you had very sophisticated and convincing arguments to support the claim).

To bring these sections to a close, I shall come full circle and return to the idea expressed in Barthes' 'The Death of the Author': that is, that once the text is finally freed from the tyranny of the intentions of the flesh and blood author we are faced with 'the book itself' which is 'only a tissue of signs, an imitation that is lost, infinitely deferred'. I think we are in a better position to understand this now.

Practice: deconstructing *Mythologies*

As a practice exercise I shall refer you back to the sections in the last chapter that dealt with Barthes' reading of the black soldier on the cover of *Paris Match*. Here is the passage in full:

> I am at the barber's, and a copy of *Paris-Match* is offered to me. On the cover, a young Negro in a French uniform is saluting, with his eyes uplifted, probably fixed on a fold of the tricolour. All this is the *meaning* of the picture. But, whether naively or not, I see very well what it signifies to me: that France is a great Empire, that all her sons, without any colour discrimination, faithfully serve under her flag, and that there is no better answer to the detractors of an alleged colonialism than the zeal shown by this Negro in serving his so-called oppressors. I am therefore again faced with a greater semiological system: there is a signifier, itself already formed with a previous system (*a black soldier is giving the French salute*); there is a signified (it is here a purposeful mixture of Frenchness and militariness); finally, there is a presence of the signified through the signifier. (Barthes, 1957/1972: 115)

Armed with some of the concepts you have picked up in these last two chapters, you might see if you can deconstruct Barthes' argument. If you do this, try to think how you can apply concepts like *différance* (as difference and deferral), the idea of a transcendental signified and look for possible *aporias*. An important point to consider is that the flag that Barthes' mentioned is assumed from the context; it is not actually shown in the photo. Also, you might think about how Barthes' 'The Death of the Author' and his later intertextual approach might undermine his reading of the photo. Finally, you might evaluate the different approaches and explain your feelings about deconstructing Barthes' ideological reading. The following Help File will offer some ideas.

Help File: how to deconstruct Barthes' reading of *Paris Match* (and yourself in the process)

In the first place, while Barthes' argument depends on two levels of signification it ultimately deciphers the truth of the image which, to use Derrida's words, 'escapes play and the order of the sign'. Notice the word 'probably' when Barthes writes that on the cover 'a young Negro in a French uniform is saluting, with his eyes uplifted, probably fixed on a fold of the tricolour'. Barthes has to assume the existence of a symbol of the ideological apparatus (he could have imagined the soldier staring up at a general or colonel on a raised platform, etc.) in order for his reading to function. Notice that

(Continued)

(Continued)

he uses a concept that was reviewed in the last chapter: 'anchorage'. He anchors the image by conjuring up what he assumes to be the key to 'semioclasm' – the demythologizing of the image. Barthes could be said to be blind to this *aporia* at this point in his essay, even though, as stated above, he does say in his preface that there may be 'a mythology of the mythologist'.

Barthes interpretation of the black soldier saluting the flag can be said to rely on a kind of paradoxical 'metaphysics of absence' insofar as Barthes' argument relies on something which is not inside the frame of the photo': the flag itself. The flag can be seen as the 'absent-presence' – it is assumed in order that the main coordinates of the interpretation can function. Just as myth has to narrow down possible meanings, so does Barthes. The point here is not to empty out Barthes' insights into contemporary culture but to show how his argument depends on the very thing that Derrida's 'Structure, Sign and Play' (and Barthes' own 'The Death of the Author') challenges: there is the tendency to decipher a truth or an origin 'which escapes play and the order of the sign'. Barthes, for the sake of a politicized reading, does not start out with this premise for if he did the 'undecidability' of the photo' would scupper his project before it began. However, while it is possible to insist that the ultimate meaning is always subject to the infinite play of difference and deferral, many cultural practitioners would probably want to insist on the value of Hall's 'arbitrary closure' (and Derrida may well have appreciated Barthes' attention to convention and detail).

If we take up Roland Barthes' idea of intertextuality we expect language to be a 'tissue of quotations drawn from innumerable centres of culture' that have to be made sense of in the viewer's or reader's mind. On the one hand, this might help to reinforce Barthes' reading of the photo, but it would depend on how far *his* reading could be generalized. On the other hand, it could seriously question the integrity of a single reading which seeks a single truth or meaning.

As far as your evaluation of the different approaches is concerned, some readers may not feel comfortable about deconstructing Barthes' argument. However, Derrida's admission that deconstruction cannot be treated as a free-for-all opens up a space for accepting a reading like Barthes' interpretation of the black soldier – but with reservations. This opens up the question of the ethics of reading, a subject of great interest to Derrida (for example, Derrida, 2002, 2005, 2006). Yet deconstruction would be very self-conscious and wary about accepting a single reading as if it were a final truth (however attractive it may seem).

To conclude, while this is by no means a complete introduction to Derrida's work it should give an idea of how it might be used within cultural studies. Furthermore, this chapter should also aid the understanding other approaches associated with poststructuralism (and postmodernism) like the following two chapters which look at the work of the (post)structuralist psychoanalyst, Jacques Lacan.

Summary of key points

This chapter has introduced a heuristic device to demonstrate how a simplified form of deconstruction can work in practice, and Stuart Hall's 'Notes on Deconstructing "The Popular"' has been used to show how a deconstructive technique has been adapted to cultural studies. Likewise, in the context of post-colonial criticism, essays by Spivak and Bhabha have also shown how concepts drawn from deconstruction have helped to analyse the problem of subaltern consciousness and the complex identity of the (imperialist) nation. This chapter has been concluded by looking at the scope and implications of using deconstructive thinking within cultural studies (by reviewing Hall's notion of 'arbitrary closure') and Derrida's contribution has been summed up by referring to his two interpretations of interpretation and the interpretive implications of adopting deconstructive techniques.

Further reading

Derrida's (1994) *Aporias (Meridian: Crossing Aesthetics)* is an extended meditation on death but also explores the limits and contradictions of philosophical texts. This is not recommended as a book directly of interest to those practising cultural studies but as a means of understanding the idea of *aporia* which has only been touched upon in the most general way in this chapter. *Deconstruction in a Nutshell* (1996), like *Positions* (Derrida, 1972/1987), is a book which features Derrida discussing his own ideas. In this case it is the record of a round-table discussion that took place at Villanova University in 1994. Derrida and Bernard Stiegler in *Echographies of Television* (2002) reflect on 'teletechnologies' (from the TV to the internet) and their impact on philosophy and politics – subjects very close to cultural studies' interests. Simon Critchley's *The Ethics of Deconstruction: Derrida and Levinas* (1992) offers an extended analysis of ethics and deconstruction defending Derrida as an ethical philosopher. A book which uses a very playful version of deconstruction to critique the Disney empire and focus on the themes of race, gender and sexuality (in the broader context of the global ambitions of the USA) is Eleanor Byrne and Martin McQuillan's *Deconstructing Disney* (1999).

7

Psychoanalysis

Jacques Lacan

Learning goals

- To appreciate how Jacques Lacan's writing fits into poststructuralist ways of thinking.
- To understand something of the complexity of Lacan's thought.
- To be able to begin to start thinking with a number of key concepts and see how they can be used in practice.

Concepts

The key concepts introduced in this chapter are the subject, subjectivity, desire, the mirror stage, the Imaginary, the Symbolic, the big Other, *objets petit a*, need, the Real, the Name-of-the-Father.

Introduction

The following two chapters will be concerned with the French psychoanalytic critic Jacques Lacan and will show how a number of concepts associated with his work have been adapted to cultural analysis. The first two sections of the present chapter describe Lacan's ambiguous relation (and increasing importance) to cultural studies, while referring to a number of Derrida's concepts to prepare the ground for Lacanian analyses. The following sections introduce Lacan's notion of the subject, the importance of what he calls the 'mirror phase' and a series of other key concepts that have proved useful to cultural critics.

Preliminaries

Jacques Lacan's writing, like Derrida's, has an ambiguous relation to cultural studies – while some critics embrace the Freudian tradition and the implications of Lacan's work, others reject it or maintain a relation of uneasy acceptance. The relation between cultural studies and Lacanian psychoanalysis is complicated, to some extent, by what counts as cultural studies, or what is considered central to it in terms of canonical authors. A quick survey of introductory texts reveals that Lacanian-inflected analysis (like deconstruction) is definitely on the menu, but not always a main dish – as can be deduced from important introductions like Strinati (1995), Barker (2000) and Turner (2003) – works which mention Lacan but dedicate relatively little space to his ideas. On the other hand, John Storey's influential *Cultural Theory and Popular Culture: An Introduction* (2009a) relates Lacanian concepts to readings of popular culture and sees Lacanian thought as having had 'an enormous influence on cultural studies, especially the study of film' (79). This interest is reflected in the accompanying reader (2006b), which includes one of Lacan's key essays on 'the mirror stage' (see below). As Yannis Stavrakakis has said, 'over the last ten to fifteen years, psychoanalysis, and especially Lacanian theory, has emerged as one of the most important resources in the ongoing re-orientation of contemporary political theory and critical analysis' (2007: 1). It is interesting to note in this context that while the scientific basis of psychoanalytic theory has often been questioned (Webster (1986) seeing it as a pseudoscience and Popper (1963) as 'unfalsifiable') it continues to be used in arts subjects because it is often considered to have considerable explanatory power (regardless of its scientific validity).

Lacan's ideas, then, (while not always seen as fundamental) are becoming common currency in cultural criticism and for this reason (as in the case of deconstruction) it is necessary to be familiar with them. Given what has been called the 'preposterous difficulty of Lacan's style' (Mitchell, in Lacan, 1985: 4), evolution and extent of his work, my discussion of his ideas will be streamlined to demonstrate how they fit into poststructuralist ways of understanding identity and show how they have been adapted to analyse diverse aspects of culture.

Lacan, lack and identity: Lac(k)an

As an entry point into Lacan's work, I will start this section by summarizing how a deconstructive approach would consider identity. If Derrida's deconstructive ideas were applied to notions of gender, race, sexual or national identity, or even to an understanding of the self, each of these identities would be decentred through deferral and difference (*différance*) and the idea of 'trace', where identity is dependent on what is excluded. As already suggested (post)structuralist notions of identity take into account Saussure's idea that signifieds (concepts) are 'purely differential and defined not by their posi- tive content but negatively by their relations with the other terms of the sys- tem', and that their chief characteristic was 'in being what the others are not' (Saussure, 1916/1959: 117).

The implications of this are very important in terms of understanding iden- tity (especially from the Lacanian point of view): identity is seen negatively in the sense of it being defined in terms of what it is not. This implies that there is no essential identity and that at the core (if this word makes any sense) there is nothing – a lack. As will be shown below, this is one of the reasons why Lacan's work is considered poststructuralist. From this point of view my name might be (or even should be) written as Davoid Walton because it would indicate a void or empty space where the unified self might be consid- ered to be. It is a signifier requiring a signified which turns into a signifier and so on ad infinitum (it might be said that signifiers are 'signie defiers' – they resist final closure). Just as I have changed my name to Davoid, Lacan's name might be changed to Jacques La(k)can because this places 'lack' at the centre of Lacan (which poses questions not only about the identity of the man but his writing).

Oversimplification Warning

Lacan's work is notoriously demanding, complex, often stylistically ambiguous and conceptually enigmatic (something not helped by Lacan's tendency to give his con- cepts subtlely different meanings according to shifting contexts and his occasional reduction of key concepts to a series of algorithms). For these reasons it would be unfair to suggest that in a short chapter I can reflect much of the sophistication of Lacanian theory. One other factor that should be kept in mind is that Lacan's thought was based on his combinations of Freudian psychoanalysis and various strands of structuralism (see below) and was not designed primarily as cultural theory, but as a therapy to cure neurosis. Given the curative role of psychoanalysis we cannot expect to find a neatly packaged theory conveniently awaiting the cultural critic – for this reason Lacanian ideas have to be adapted to particular theoretical circumstances. A further factor to consider is that Lacanian concepts, unsurprisingly, have been defined and understood by different critics in very different ways.

The 'subject' of Lacan and the grammatical origins of subjectivity

One of the reasons why Lacan is considered poststructuralist is because (while he draws on Saussure's ideas) he tends to challenge the structuralist model of language; another is that he revises how the self is understood. This latter point is reflected in his use of the term **'subject'** instead of 'self'. The reason for this is that, like Freud, he resisted the idea that individuals are in some way 'given': that is, that the self is some sort of coherent, stable, unified whole governed by reason. The psychoanalytic approach tends to challenge the dominant idea of the self as promulgated though the dominant Christian traditions of understanding which see the self (as soul) as the unique indissoluble centre of being. In psychoanalysis the self is divided by conscious and unconscious forces where reason is constantly undermined by **desire** (see below). Coming back to Lacan's use of the word 'subject', it is a reminder of the importance of language in the construction of the self.

One of Lacan's theories is that the 'subject' (self) is an effect of language. For Lacan it is only with the entry into what he called **the Symbolic** (language, culture, any system through which meanings can be produced – see below) that **the subject** or self can be said to come into being. What this means in structuralist terms is that we find a subject position within a closed relational system. So, we might be the subject or object of a sentence as I/he/she versus me/him/her, etc., something which helps to explain Lacan's way of understanding **subjectivity** (what it means to be a subject or self).

For his notion of subjectivity Lacan drew not just on the Freudian (and Saussurean) tradition but on the work of linguists like Roman Jakobson. Lacan was influenced by Jakobson's discussion of 'shifters' (pronouns like 'I' and 'you'). Lacan repeats Jakobson's idea that the first-person personal pronoun ('I') 'designates the subject of the enunciation, but it does not signify it' (Lacan, 1966/1977: 298). This means that the first-person pronoun only indicates the grammatical subject but does not refer to an actual flesh and blood person; it is effectively an empty signifier – a 'shifter' (Jakobson, 1957/1971). Lacan put it like this:

> The articulation of language calls into question, first of all, the issue of the subject of the enunciation. The subject of the enunciation is definitely not to be confused with the one who takes the opportunity to say of himself *I*, as subject of the utterance. When he has to talk about himself, he calls himself *I*. It simply means *I who am speaking*. The *I*, as it appears in any utterance, is nothing more than what we call a *shifter*. (Lacan, 2008: 85)

These ideas can be clarified further with relation to Émile Benveniste who (like Jakobson) argues that the first person pronoun 'I' is an empty signifier insofar as it has no signified until a person uses it and this only indicates that someone is enunciating something: 'Each I has its own reference and corresponds to a unique being who is set up as such' (Benveniste, 1971: 218). Users occupy the subject position of a statement which is a grammatical position which does not, in itself, convey positive content. Benveniste also asserted that it is in and through language that humans are constituted as subjects, 'because language alone establishes the concept of "ego"'. In this way, 'subjectivity' is the capacity of speakers to posit themselves 'as a subject' and is thereby a property of language (1971: 224).

If the idea of being the subject of a sentence gives a sense of control, the relegation to that of the object may give a sense of subservience or powerlessness. If we can be subjects with the feeling that we control our world (like the grammatical subject can be said to govern a verb) then we can also be 'subjects', as in members of a state: that is, subject *to* society's customs or laws; subject to forms of domination, rule or authority (as shown in Chapter 4 on Althusser). Here we can see that a subject may feel empowered. on the one hand, or, on the other, 'de-centred' (an important term in poststructuralist criticism, as we saw from the last chapter) – that is, ousted from a privileged place at the centre and consigned to the margins or to a place of insignificance or relative weakness. I will now explore how this works with relation to other important ideas in Lacanian theory.

'The Mirror Stage'

I want to return to the idea that the self is an effect of language. This might seem as if Lacan converts everything into mere words – that there is nothing beyond signs. However, Lacan did not go that far – from his point of view it is not that there are only words or signs, but that the self has no meaning without relation to the symbolic network of language and representation in which a self can be conceived. Lacan's classic essay 'The Mirror Stage as Formative of the Function of the I' (Lacan, 1966/1977: 1f.) can help to understand how this works. Very simply put the mirror stage is to do with how a child undergoes identification with 'itself'. For example, before a child learns to use language it is in the pre-linguistic stage (a world of image rather than thoughts or concepts, called '**the Imaginary**' – see below). Before its gradual entry into language (the Symbolic) the child begins a process of self-identification, and this is where the mirror comes in.

Lacan compared the difference between the way a monkey and a child (of around six to eighteen months) respond to their images in a mirror. When a monkey sees its reflection, at first it is fascinated by the moving object, but once it realizes that the image is 'empty' it soon bores of the game. However, in the case of the child the fascination continues which helps it establish an 'imaginary' relation between itself and the world around it. Lacan wrote of this reflection as the *I* (of the self) in a 'primordial form' (2), before the acquisition of language. This sounds as if Lacan is saying that the child's relation with its own image is in some way an illusion. To some extent this is true but it is important to see that the term 'imaginary' is used in more than one way. First, the child is immersed in a world of *images*, before language can situate it properly as a subject. But, at the same time, the image is imaginary in the sense of being 'discordant' with its 'own reality' (2) – a distorted image of the self which is a fantasy.

Lacan explained this by referring to a baby of around six months. In the first place it is entirely helpless: it is unable to stand up or walk and has few motor skills. But on seeing its image in a mirror, it will lean forward as best it can to stare at itself. The image that it sees of itself in the mirror is a unified totality (which may be called a *Gestalt*) which looks fully synthe-sized and coherent, something which tends to disguise that it is, in reality, uncoordinated, defenceless and lost in what Lacan calls 'nursling depend-ence'. For Lacan, the child identifies with its image and invests it with nar-cissistic desire (fascinated self-love) but it is a purely imaginary (fantasy) relation between bodily self and spectral image – it is an unrealistic 'ideal-I' or 'ideal-ego' (2). The image of the self (as a totality), far from reflecting the child's awkward, helpless state, actually suggests the opposite and leads to illusion because the child *identifies* with its misleading coherent image. This narcissistic fantasy of the unified self will become a permanent part of the psyche in what Lacan calls, in another context, 'the Imaginary' (35). The Imaginary not only describes how subjects identify with their self-image (the self as an object of the gaze) but also how people identify with others: in short, the images (fantasies) we entertain about ourselves and others. From the very beginning, then, there is a mismatch between what we are and what we see, and this 'what we see' leads to a form of delusion because we are, in a sense, structuring the self on a misnomer. What I see as me, is fundamental to the way I conceive the self – but this 'me' is not me, just an image, an icon, a *Gestalt*.

The big Other

We have seen that the self begins to know 'itself' through an idealized identification with an external specular image (in what in Lacanian terms is **the big Other** (Lacan, 1973/1979: 129)). Ironically this identification, while symbolizing 'the mental permanence of the *I*', is a form of alienation from the self and an identification with something which is not the self but only *stands* for the self. The image of the unified self, then, is a fantasy that develops into 'the armour of an alienating identity, which will mark with its rigid struc-ture the subject's entire mental development', meaning, as suggested earlier, that these imaginary projections of the unified self are a permanent part of psychic life (Lacan, 1966/1977: 2). In terms of 'the armour of an alienating identity', for Lacan the very fact that subjectivity is produced in language means that the subject is permanently split off from the materiality of its being. That is why Lacan habitually represented the subject as an 'S' with a bar through it: $ (Lacan, 1966/1977: 269–70) – signifying the split subject.

Help File: the big Other

Slavoj Žižek describes the big Other as the place of the symbolic order. A useful way of thinking about it is to see it in these terms:

> First of all, the 'big Other' appears as a hidden agency 'pulling the strings', running the show behind the scenes: divine Providence in Christian ideology, the Hegelian 'cunning of Reason' (or, rather, the popular version of it) [...], the 'objective logic of History' in Marxism-Leninism, the 'Jewish conspiracy' in Nazism, etc. [...] This reference to the big Other is of course in itself radically ambivalent. It can function as a quieting and strengthening reassurance (religious confidence in God's will; the Stalinist's conviction that he is an instrument of historical necessity) or as a terrifying paranoiac agency (as in the case of the Nazi ideology recognizing behind economic crisis, national humiliation, moral degeneration, etc., the same hidden hand of the Jew). (Žižek, 1992: 39)

In short, all those symbolic structures that make organization and meaning in human life possible (including language) are located in the big Other.

Lacan asserts that at the point when the mirror stage comes to an end (at around eighteen months) the 'specular *I*' becomes a 'social *I*' – although it is a mistake to think that the specular (imaginary) dimension is finished: the only change is that the child is now at a new stage in its development. However, (to go beyond Lacan's essay on the mirror stage) the pre-symbolic imaginary stage will from now on operate as a kind of ideal state of one-ness before the subject became divided from itself (like Freud's oral stage where the child is comfortably cocooned at the breast-feeding stage). This transition will create a desire to return to this state of plenitude, which can never be fulfilled. This results in frustration and a gnawing sense of lack. As Lacan stated, 'I is an other' (Lacan, 1966/1977: 23), and it is possible to use this phrase to emphasize that the self, while seeming to account for something interior, cannot but posit itself through something exterior (systems of representation that pre-exist it). The 'social *I*' is our introduction into these cultural systems which give meaning and which we use to make meaning. So, in a neat paradox, the inside is really the outside (part of the big Other).

Outside inside: Lacan and *objets petit a*

To sum up, the 'social *I*' is connected to the acquisition of language but before the child enters the symbolic system of language it has no way of distinguishing itself from the world around it. Take, for instance, the things most important to the well-being of a baby. Lacan assumes that its first years are associated with a close attachment to the mother (of course, it could be otherwise). Here the child is dependent on those things which it needs to survive; for example, if it is breast fed it will depend on the breast for nourishment. Apart from its fundamental needs it may be dependent for its comfort on other things like its mother's voice, her gaze, etc. This is one thing many critics and theoreticians have found useful in Lacan's writings – the importance of things that are experienced as parts of, or complements to, the self and not understood or experienced as separate from it.

These things are called ***objets petit a***, which, once distinguished from the self, are experienced as missing complements to the self. The general point is that (during the pre-linguistic stage) because the baby cannot conceptualize, it cannot distinguish the breast, voice, gaze (or bodily excretions) from itself. In Freudian terms the baby is in a 'pure' state of undivided being or plenitude.

Help File and ideas for practice: *objet petit a*

The term *objet petit a* is short for *objet petit autre* (literally 'the little object of the other') which can be understood as anything which is outside the self (voice, gaze, etc.) but not perceived as such. According to Alan Sheridan (who has translated a number of Lacan's works into English), Lacan refused to define the term, leaving readers to make up their own minds (Lacan, 1973/1979: 282). The way I have defined it here does not exhaust its usages and my understanding has been influenced by Kaja Silverman's way of seeing it (1983: 156f.). Silverman offers a reading of Orson Welles's film *Citizen Kane* that can help to show how the concept might be used. She argues that Welles organizes the whole film round an *objet petit a*:

> That object is of course the sled named 'Rosebud' with which the young Charles Kane is seen playing early in the film, as his mother watches him from the window of their house. At this point in the story Charles obviously identifies strongly both with the sled and his mother, whose gaze he seems to solicit as he plays. The events which follow rupture his relationship with both, and constitute Rosebud, at least at the manifest level, as 'the most profound lost object.' Throughout the rest of the film he is shown obsessively collecting objects in a vain attempt to compensate for its loss, a loss which he experiences as an amputation. (Silverman, 1983: 157)

This way of reading can be adapted to the analysis of very different forms of culture or cultural processes. For example, it is possible to consider how Lacanian concepts

(Continued)

(Continued)

might help to interpret regionalism, nationalism and the resistance to them. Why would a region want to break away from the whole? From the point of view of the *objet petit a* the nationalist groups can be seen to be seeking for oneness or plenitude. That is, rather than be a minor part of a much bigger whole, the breakaway nation-state signifies completeness in itself and thereby obtains a sense of full identity. The nationalist dream is often based on a sense of lost identity insofar as it is usually based on the idea (fictional or real) that it was once integral and free. On the other hand, why resist a region's desire to become an independent whole? It can be understood as the fear of losing an integral part of the symbolic whole, which reduces the sense of power and oneness that comes with the feeling of greater totality. It can be suffered rather like the trauma of losing a limb. Of course, an analysis of this kind would have to be linked to the importance of political, economic and military factors because it reduces everything to psychological motives. However, as a starting point for analysis, these ideas can be applied to any circumstance where individuals or groups are involved in situations of loss and yearning.

Subjectivity and gender

We have seen that prior to the mirror phase the baby is in a 'pure' state of being with no boundaries between itself and the Other (understood here as what is 'outside' but is not yet conceived as such). However, once the child begins to distinguish itself from others or the world outside it can be said to have made its first steps into the Symbolic. Once the child begins to acquire language it can be properly said to be a 'subject' – but this becoming a subject will come at a price and lead to frustration. This is not only because (at the mirror stage) the baby becomes alienated from itself (through identifying itself with its image), but because at this moment *all things* will become alienated from it through its immersion into the Symbolic.

To explain this I shall refer to what Lacan called **the Real** (the child's own being and the world prior to its symbolization – see below). Lacan's basic point is that with the entry into the symbolic system of signs the Real is forever blocked off. The immersion in the Symbolic means that everything is now filtered through signifiers – once we become immersed in language there is no way back to an unmediated 'organic', undifferentiated 'self'. The materiality of the Real is elusive because it always has to be symbolized and is thus always something other than its symbolic representation. As Lacan explained: 'the being of language is the non-being of objects' (Lacan, 1966/1977: 263). This involves the 'lack' I mentioned at the beginning of the chapter: all signs presuppose the absence of the objects they are supposed to symbolize. As indicated above, even the sign for the self, the personal pronoun 'I', is empty:

it functions in language, not because I am somehow 'in' it, but because it gives me a subject *position* within language.

One consequence of this is that the subject, or individual, is doomed to a state of lack, because the full presence of undifferentiated being at the pre-linguistic stage can never be recovered (unless someone by accident or illness collapsed into a vegetative state). The introduction into the Symbolic also stratifies individuals in terms of gender (in terms of the linguistic pronouns 'he' and 'she') and these gender distinctions will also lead to a sense of lack and further frustration because these limit the free expression of instincts. In part this is linked to Freud's idea that all civilized societies impose laws against incest, which means that Oedipal desires have to be carefully policed. Added to this is the fact that societies also have normative sexual codes or laws which pigeonhole individuals and, as indicated in earlier chapters of this book, the very fact of being regarded as 'male' or 'female' will mean that there are also normative (restrictive) forms of behaviour developed around these simple binaries.

In this context, Lacan's pun on the word *l'hommelette* can help to clarify this. This term can mean 'little man (or person)' and also refer to an omelette where a broken egg moves in all directions. The broken egg is like the state before the entry into the Symbolic – at this stage sexuality is not culturally divided, it is in an unstable directionless state. However, with the entry into the Symbolic the 'little person' is consolidated and becomes a gendered being, and thus a sense of undivided oneness (with its indefinite 'pure libido' or 'life instinct') is 'lost in sexuality' (Lacan, 1973/1979: 197–8). At this point cultures impose norms on these gendered subjects where they are subjected to expectations in terms of general behaviour and may be coerced in terms of sexual orientation. In this Lacan agreed with Freud that sexuality (in the early stages of life) is 'polymorphously perverse' (undefined, heterogeneous) and went on to add that it is expressed in the 'networks of the signifier' (177). From this it is possible to see how the Symbolic, as the repository of cultural codes, is what accounts for gender, rather than the reference to biological attributes. This is enormously important for critics interested in questions of gender and sexuality (see below and Chapter 10 on Judith Butler).

To explore the notion of gender a little further I want to come back to the complex Lacanian notion of the sign and consider a phrase Elizabeth Wright has used in the context of describing Lacan's work: 'words are not the property of those who use them' (Wright in Jefferson and Robey, 1982: 129). This idea is linked to the way Lacan both used and challenged Saussure's conception of the sign (thus aligning him with other poststructuralists). Lacan, like Derrida, challenged Saussure's assertion that words and concepts form a one-to-one relation like the two sides of a coin. Signifiers are, in effect, constantly converted into signifieds which, in turn, are converted into signifiers. This, as we know from deconstruction, is a never-ending process that makes signification a very slippery phenomenon indeed.

To illustrate how this poststructuralist notion of language impacts on the understanding of gender I will refer to one of Lacan's anecdotes. Lacan describes how a train arrives at a station. In the train are a brother and sister who sit face to face next to the window. 'Look,' cries the little boy, 'we're at "Ladies!"'. 'Idiot!' replies the little girl, 'Can't you see we're at "Gentlemen"' (Lacan, 1966/1977: 152). This little story, with its double misunderstanding, demonstrates that because of the arbitrary relation between signifier and signified we can never be certain that the words we use will be understood or used as we intend them to be. Language, in the Lacanian view, is always open to the constructions that others put on it. Yet Lacan makes another interesting point in this context when he writes:

> Ladies and Gentlemen will be henceforth two countries towards which each of their souls will strive on divergent wings, and between which a truce will be the more impossible since they are actually the same country and neither can compromise on its own superiority without detracting from the glory of the other. (152)

Notice here that Lacan realizes that gender is something already culturally marked out in advance and will separate the two individuals into opposing gender camps (detaching them in an artificial way from their ambiguous polymorphous beginnings). He also claims, rather enigmatically, that they are really travelling towards the same country (one which will arbitrarily 'gender' them). He also sees that once individuals are trapped in gender distinctions there can be no cessation of hostilities. This can be read to mean that it is the entry into the cultural systems of the symbolic that causes the divisions on the grounds of gender. This opens up the possibility that gender is not fixed and that things could be otherwise, something I will explore with relation to Judith Butler's work (in Chapter 10). To continue this discussion of subjectivity and the construction of the self in language I will consider the following question: am 'I', according to the ideas outlined above, the same self as that of which I speak or think?

In order to answer this question Lacan radically rewrote René Descartes' postulation, 'I think, therefore I am'. For Descartes, this was an absolute starting-point, a kind of point-zero from which to start his philosophical programme by affirming his own being. However, Lacan rewrote this as 'I think where I am not, therefore I am where I do not think' (Lacan, 1966/1977: 166). This can be read in different ways. For example, as shown earlier, when someone uses a 'shifter' the word does not designate an actual person – the word 'I' only produces the effect of a speaking subject. Thus, wherever I am, it is not in language, and wherever language is, I am not. According to this way of thinking, although language situates us, gives us a subject position, and while subjects may live the illusion of possessing a coherent self, it is endlessly deferred through the defiles of the signifier (a point that will be elaborated on further in the next chapter).

Oedipus, the unconscious as a linguistic phenomenon, and the Name-of-the-Father

Above we saw that Lacan agreed with Saussure that language has meaning, not because it refers us to a referential world of things but because it is *relational*. Meaning is possible only because of difference ('pig' means porcine animal because it is not an aardvark, etc.). However, it would be more appropriate here to choose words like 'mother', 'father', 'brother' and 'sister' because the Oedipus conflict has an important role to play. Not only does the subject come into being with the entry into the symbolic order of things, but so does the unconscious. This leads to a very important idea in Lacanian thinking: that the unconscious 'is structured in the most radical way like a language' (Lacan, 1966/1977: 234). In order to understand the connections between language, the unconscious and the Oedipus complex it is necessary to reflect a little more on Lacan's notion of the subject. What is fundamental to being a 'subject' is not only the entry into the Symbolic but that which brings about the possibility of differentiating the self from others: what Lacan called '**the Name-of-the-Father**' (related to the 'Law of the Father', Lacan, 1966/1977: 67, 165–66).

This concept is not related to the actual father but the law the father symbolizes. An easy, if simplified, way of looking at this is to imagine what happens to the infant boy in classical Freudian terms (I will ignore the more complex scenarios of orphans, etc.). The boy's first object of desire will be the mother, and what comes between this desire and its realization, in the Oedipal scenario, is the prohibition of intimate relations with the mother. The term 'the Name-of-the-Father' designates the cultural taboo which imposes the law against incest: the child finds itself positioned within a rule-bound symbolic system as 'son' – a familial relation which carries with it certain sexual prohibitions. Vital to differentiation are the simple binary oppositions of male versus female and the categories of son versus mother, daughter versus father etc. As emphasized above, the entry into language implies not only familial ties and regulations, but also gender distinctions and the regulation of desire.

Help File: the Name-of-the-Father

If the Name-of-the-Father is not the actual flesh and blood father nor is it the particular image of the father that individuals may have of him: it is purely symbolic of the law (Lacan, 1966/1977: 199). As Green and LeBihan point out, the Name-of-the-Father in French is the *nom du père* and thus there is 'a pun in French on the sound of the word *nom* which is indistinguishable from the word *non* when spoken. The *name* of the father is also the *no* of the father' (1996: 164), and thus introduces authority through prohibition. This authority, although repressive is, from the Lacanian point of

(Continued)

(Continued)

view, necessary to provide the indispensable stability (through order) so important to psychic health.

The reason for this is that the laws (like a grammatical system) create the necessary structures which enable the organization of psychic and social existence. The renunciation of the mother and the acceptance of the 'no' or Name-of-the-Father enables entry into the Symbolic. This, while creating the circumstances for the Oedipus complex, is also the great enabler because, as Lacan states, it is the entry into the symbolic structures of language (represented by the Name-of-the-Father beyond the intimate one-to-one relation with the mother) which links 'subjects together in one action', human society being made possible by 'the existence of the world of the symbol [...] on laws and contracts' (Lacan, 1975/1988: 230). This represents the 'superimposition of the kingdom of culture' on unruly nature (Lacan, 1968: 40). Were it not for the authority and stability symbolized by the Name-of-the-Father psychosis would be the result.

I will come back to the Name-of the-Father and the stability of the psyche in the next chapter when I consider what Lacan referred to as 'master signifiers', which function to provide the basic coordinates of identity (I will also refer back to it when I discuss postmodernism and Fredric Jameson).

Taking the above points into account it is possible to see how the Oedipus complex and the unconscious fit in to the symbolic relations that the Name-of-the-Father sets up. Following Lacan (and using an Oedipal pun), language and the Oedipus complex can be seen as intimately related. The reason for this is that without the linguistic/symbolic/cultural system with its categories of 'mother', 'father', 'son' and 'daughter', etc. an incest taboo would make no sense (Lacan, 1966/1977: 65).

To see where the unconscious fits in to this model it is necessary to return to the idea that the unconscious is structured like a language. What this means is that the unconscious is not a pre-existing thing but the product of relationships arising from the Oedipal dynamic – following Freud, it is understood as coming into being because it is necessary. Once taboo relationships are produced through the symbolic order of things Oedipal desires are one consequence and, for the psychic health of the individual, must be repressed. The unconscious, then, would be unnecessary were it not for the subject positions and repressive taboos of the symbolic order – and the assumption that (to remain healthy) individuals need to be protected from the repressed desires. However, while (in healthy people) the mechanisms of repression protect the conscious mind (the ego) from forbidden desires, it does not mean that the work of repression goes on silently in the background (see below).

The unconscious is like Saussure's *langue*: it does not exist in some mysterious way prior to being immersed in culture but it is a product of culture. It is an underlying structure that is the product of adapting to (in this case) repressive cultural forces. Just as the absorption of grammatical rules of language create the possibilities for expression so the adaptation to societal rules structures the unconscious, which then acts as a productive mechanism. Lacan put it like this: the signifier is 'a new dimension of the human condition in that it is not only man who speaks, but that in man and through man *it* speaks (*ça parle*)' (1966/1977: 284). Here it is possible to see how Lacan influenced Althusser's way of understanding ideology where subjects in society are conditioned to see and think in ways that reflect the dominant socio-political, economic system. We saw that it was this way of thinking that provoked E. P. Thompson's outrage at the idea that another Marxist thinker could believe that people were '*structured* by social relations, *spoken* by pre-given linguistic structures, *thought* by ideologies' or '*gendered* by patriarchal sexual norms', etc. (Thompson, 1978/1995: 206). In this Thompson was reacting against Althusser's adaptation of Lacan's adaptation of Saussure to create his particular theory of ideology.

Coming back to the Lacanian unconscious, it is an underlying structure that is the product of adapting to repressive cultural norms and laws and functions as a dynamic and creative force. For example, repressed desires will manifest themselves in symptoms produced by the unconscious in phenomena like dreams, jokes, slips of the tongue, mispronunciation or, where neurosis is present, in things like tics, compulsive behaviour and irrational fears. This way of thinking helps to explain the origins of Oedipal desire and how desire (in general) can be understood as an inter-subjective phenomenon.

Desire as an inter-subjective phenomenon

We have seen that the production of subjects is a result of the entry into the Symbolic, and it is at this moment that desire also comes into existence, including (and especially) the Oedipal. The symbolic order creates the circumstances for the Oedipal crisis because its laws are repressive and, as explained above, what is repressed manifests itself in symptoms. Yet, as Lacan was at pains to emphasize, the unconscious is not to be confused with an actual part of the brain; it is 'neither being, nor non-being, but the unrealized' – representing, then, those desires which are blocked off from the conscious mind (Lacan, 1973/1979: 30). What is unrealized is not located *in* the brain, as such, it is a product of inter-subjective relations.

Lacan once wrote that 'man's desire is the desire of the Other' (Lacan, 1973/1979: 235f.), which has many implications in his work. However, at a basic level desire is not to be understood as a 'natural', spontaneous force but something that is generated with relation to others in society. One common example is the child (or adult) who wants something because other people want it. In terms of Oedipal relations, Lacan theorizes that children desire to be that which they perceive the mother or father to desire. For example (to reduce the possibilities to one example), the young Oedipal boy not only desires the mother but desires to be desired by her and tries to become the object of her desire (which he comes to understand is the father). Thus, Lacan writes of the awakening of 'desire for the object of the other's desire' (1966/1977: 19).

Therefore, desire does not pre-exist the entry into the Symbolic; however, this assertion is more nuanced than may seem on the surface. What Lacan was *not* saying is that at the pre-linguistic stage there are no organic needs; what he underlined was that after entry into language (the Symbolic) organic **need** is mediated through the signifier (which is not the need but its representation). Lacan expressed it like this: 'need has to pass through the defiles of the signifier' (264). This channelling of need through the symbolic order of language results in desire. Desire is our way of articulating these primary needs in symbolic form, but as I said above, this also has a cost. The cost is a further sense of lack (hence my spelling of Lacan's name as 'Lac(k)an').

This is because once need is articulated through the symbolic register any attempt at satisfying it is doomed to failure. It is the gap between the need and its articulation that brings about desire. This can be summed up in Lacan's phrase 'the moment in which desire becomes human is also that in which the child is born into language' (103). Chris Weedon puts it nicely when she writes, 'desire is subject to the constant deferral of satisfaction equivalent to the constant deferral of meaning in language' (Weedon, 1997: 50), a phrase which shows the connections between Lacan's conception of desire and post-structuralist (and more specifically, deconstructive) thinking. The origin of organic needs are to be found in 'the Real' (described above) but the symbolic expression of need as desire is what leads to constant deferral, frustration and lack. To conclude this chapter I shall make a few more observations about the Real as a final piece of preparation for the material in the following one.

The Real

Earlier we saw that the Real is not 'reality' (which is a representation of the Real) but the material thing upon which language (or any representational system) is working and which always lies outside it – what can be described as that which lacks the lack: 'The lack of the lack makes the real' (Lacan, 1973/1979: ix).

Practice: interpreting the Real

Elizabeth Wright has suggested a useful way in which the concept of 'the Real' may be used to interpret things like film. The following interpretation is typical of the way literary, cultural and film critics have used Lacan's theories outside their direct clinical contexts:

> The Real turns up in man's relation to desired objects. It makes its appearance because the signifying system is revealed as inadequate: the desired object is never what one thinks one desires. What one imagines, according to psychoanalysis, is always the primordial lost object, the union with the mother.

> To take an example, in Luis Buñuel's film, *That Obscure Object of Desire*, the desired love-object was represented by two actresses playing the one role. They had the same name, Conchita, but one could see that they were really different; what the women actually were – the Real – did not correspond to the imaginary picture the lover had of them. This is an analogy of what actually happens: the Real never fits comfortably into any conceptualization. Hence Lacan's point that the Real is impossible to grasp; it must be different from what words say it is. (Wright in Jefferson and Robey, 1982: 121)
>
> Thus, if we come back to the Imaginary, we can see that there is never a one-to-one relation between our identifications with self and others and the Real. As Fredric Jameson has observed, Althusser incorporated this idea into his way of thinking by stating that the Real is an 'absent cause' (Jameson, 1981: 35) – a materiality which is out there, and that upon which ideology is working, but never present.

Summing up the Symbolic, the Imaginary and the Real: returning to Althusser

In order to conclude, I shall consolidate the distinction between the concepts of the Symbolic, the Imaginary and the Real by referring back again to Althusser's use of Lacan. As we have seen, in the pre-symbolic, pre-Oedipal state, individuals have their being in the undivided materiality of the Real. This is lost in 'the mirror phase' when young children begin to identify themselves with an image that is (mis)taken for the self. This is the Imaginary: the identifications and images that we use to orient ourselves in the world. The complex symbolic structures that enable this organization are all parts of the Symbolic. One way of understanding the Lacanian Imaginary, Symbolic and Real is to review Althusser's model of ideology as 'the imaginary relationship of individuals to the real conditions in which they live' (Althusser, 1965/2005: 233–34).

We saw that Althusser distinguished between a 'real relation' and an imaginary (lived) relation. Althusser's 'imaginary relation' (which coincides with ideology) involves both the Imaginary and the Symbolic – this is because it involves identifications, on the one hand, which are made possible by the codes, conventions, rules and laws, etc., on the other. These two axes enable individuals to have a 'relation' with the world they live in. Understanding, then, is not a question of having a one-to-one relation with an objective world as such but living a relation through ways of seeing it (ideology). Thus, the 'real conditions of existence' in a capitalist society are described as an economic system based on things like the investment of capital bolstered up by the right to private ownership, etc. Ideology (as imaginary relations constructed in the Symbolic) is a question of *how* different groups or individuals relate to these basic conditions – as conservative, reformist or revolutionist, etc. This helps to explain how members of the same class can relate to the 'same' world but in different ways.

For Althusser there were 'real relations' that can stand as a measure to gauge different ideological positions (this is the role of Marxist science); however, in terms of Lacan's insistence on the failures of symbolizing the Real, it might be said that Althusser's sense of the real is less ambiguous in this respect. However, when it comes to theorizing the self their theories are more aligned. As Graeme Turner has argued, Althusser's model of ideology operates 'not explicitly but implicitly': living in those practices and structures we take for granted. Thus, ideology is internalized and unconscious. And yet, as Turner says, 'the unconscious has, within many philosophical frameworks, been seen as the core of our individuality, a product of our nature' (Turner, 2003: 20). The connections between Lacan's and Althusser's positions are brought out very well when Turner writes:

> If Althusser is right, then, our unconscious, too, is formed in ideology, from *outside* our 'essential' selves. For Althusser, the notion of an essential self disappears as a fiction, an impossibility, and in its place is the social being who possesses a socially produced sense of identity – a 'subjectivity'. This subjectivity is not like the old unified individual self; it can be contradictory, and it can change within different situations and in response to different kinds of address. We rely, in fact, on language and ideology to instruct us in how we are to conceive our social identities, in how to be a 'subject'. (20)

Thus, what we may think of as the coherent self – what we experience as the intimate and unique core of our individuality – is a fiction because the ultimate reality of the self is constructed outside in the big Other.

Practice: thinking with 'Lacanthusserianism'

Adapted versions of Lacan's Imaginary, Symbolic and Real can be used to interpret all kinds of cultural forms and situations which do not necessarily reduce all interpretation to the Oedipal drama. For example, at the beginning of Roberto Rossellini's film dealing with the consequences of the Second World War, *Germany, Year Zero* (1948), he has the camera depict actual images of the terrible destruction of war – in this case, Berlin. From the Althusserian point of view the emphasis would be on how the images are read by different groups structured within specific ideological contexts. For the sake of argument, the conditions of war (like the conditions of capitalism) can be taken as the Real (the absent cause upon which the Symbolic works). However, when the camera captures devastating images of bombsites and develops a filmic narrative around them this is not the Real but the way the absent cause is structured in the Symbolic. For the Allies these images (this is Rossellini's position) are seen as symbols of the dreadful injustice and brutality that are a direct consequence of fascism (even though the Allies themselves inflicted the damage on that particular city). Yet for the Nazis similar scenes of their own bombing raids were typically read as symbols of the triumphant might and justice of the Nazi war machine. Although we may prefer Rossellini's version, both these readings can be seen as 'the imaginary relationship of individuals to the real conditions in which they live'.

To try to get a more nuanced idea of the way these concepts may work, it is worth comparing these images of Berlin with others from the Second World War. Whatever terrors and suffering were unleashed in the Real (by things like the Nazi Holocaust, what has been seen as the Allies' indiscriminate bombing of cities like Dresden, and the atomic bombs dropped on Hiroshima and Nagasaki) the 'realities', defences and condemnations are constructed in the Symbolic. The Real as 'absent cause' permits multiple interpretations precisely because it can never be adequately or fully present in the Symbolic. This does not mean that cultural critics and historians do not have argumentative protocols at their disposal to evaluate different claims. For example, it is possible to counter neo-Nazi revisionist arguments that attempt to minimize Nazi atrocities; however, the gaps between what Raymond Williams called 'lived culture' (1961/1992: 49) (which would be how individuals engage with the Real) and its symbolization create the possibilities for difference, ambiguity and disagreement.

Of course, dominant representations will enter into the Imaginary so that, while Winston Churchill can be seen by some historians as ultimately responsible for the indiscriminate and inhumane bombing of Dresden, he can still be constructed as a (flawed) saviour and national war hero in the popular Imaginary. This is an image, which, while public, helps consolidate a positive notion of the private self because the self-image is partially constructed with relation to the image of the great nation led by illustrious heads of state. In this way it is possible to see how powerful identifications can be created in the Imaginary that cross over the public–private, interpersonal divide. Much more could be done with these ideas (and I shall explore them further in the next chapter) but this should give an idea of some of the ways Lacanian notions can be adapted outside their immediate psychoanalytic context. The notion of history outlined here will be relevant to postmodern theory discussed in Chapters 11 to 13.

In conclusion, Lacan's constant problematizations of identity and insistence on the role of the Symbolic in dividing the subject from the Real, have led to his being considered as one of *the* canonical poststructuralist thinkers. In this chapter we have seen how some of Lacan's concepts can be applied to the interpretation of films like *That Obscure Object of Desire, Citizen Kane* and *Germany, Year Zero* but in the following chapter I will show, after considering some related concepts, how Lacanian ideas may be used to elucidate (more fully) the concept of gender and be further applied outside the immediate confines of psychoanalysis.

Summary of key points

This chapter has introduced a series of key ideas associated with Jacques Lacan and has illustrated how they might be adapted to cultural analysis. Different sections have outlined and illustrated the grammatical origins of subjectivity, the importance of what Lacan called the 'mirror phase' and concepts like the Imaginary, the Symbolic, the Real, the big Other and the *objets petit a*. The chapter has also considered the role of the Name-of-the Father in establishing the symbolic matrices that make the subject possible and produce the Oedipal taboos and the effects of gender distinctions. Later sections have considered other key notions such as need and desire, and examples have been given of how some of the concepts might be used in practice.

Further reading

Lacan's *Écrits: A Selection* (1966/1977) is the usual starting point for getting a broader idea of Lacan's work. This is a collection of Lacan's seminars and, while some are difficult to read for the non-specialist, many of Lacan's key ideas are introduced and developed. Kaja Silverman's *The Subject of Semiotics* (1983) includes a very useful account of Lacanian theory. Juliette Mitchell and Jacqueline Rose's introductions (they write one each) to Lacan's *Feminine Sexuality: Jacques Lacan and the École Freudienne* (1985) provide in-depth and historically aware discussions of how Freud and Lacan's ideas relate to contemporary debates concerned with sexual identities. The texts that follow these introductions are essential reading for anyone interested in sexuality from a Lacanian perspective. Ann Kaplan's *Women and Film: Both Sides of the Camera* (1983) shows how some aspects of Lacan's work has been useful to film theory in the way it combines Freudian psychoanalysis with semiology; however, Kaplan redresses what she sees as the male bias in the Freudian tradition.

Slavoj Žižek, in works like *Looking Awry: An Introduction to Jacques Lacan Through Popular Culture* (1991) and *Enjoy Your Symptom: Jacques Lacan in Hollywood and Out* (1992), has done as much as anyone to show how Lacanian thinking can be applied outside the immediate context of clinical psychoanalysis. Žižek offers series of readings of films and other popular cultural forms. However, Žižek's approach is not only focused on the seeming object of analysis (like film or novel) because the object of his interpretation is not only popular culture but Lacanian psychoanalysis itself: just as Lacanian concepts illuminate popular culture so popular culture helps to illuminate Lacanian concepts. The following chapter will introduce a number of studies which are worthy of further study.

8

Applying Lacan

Techniques for Feminist and other Forms of Cultural Analysis

Learning goals

- To understand a number of key Lacanian concepts already introduced in greater depth.
- To be able begin to synthesize the ideas of different writers like Saussure, Althusser, Derrida and Lacan and see how their ideas are related through common ways of thinking (without losing sight of differences).
- To see how a series of Lacanian concepts can be used in practice with a view to developing critical independence.

Concepts

The key concepts introduced in this chapter are master signifiers, the Phallus, penis envy and the subject supposed to know.

Introduction

This chapter consolidates the concepts introduced in the last chapter and further demonstrates how they can be used in practice. It starts by going into more detail about how Lacanian concepts relate to seeing gender as being culturally inscribed. It also looks at how Lacan's concept of the Name-of-the-Father can be used in practice with relation to what Lacan calls the 'master signifiers'. Practice is illustrated through references to a number of (in)famous psychological experiments carried out at Yale University and the antics of two anti-corporate activist-pranksters known as 'The Yes Men'. Further practice is illustrated by showing how feminists have engaged with Lacanian concepts like the Phallus. The final sections consider Kobena Mercer's point that certain kinds of psychoanalysis have become a Eurocentric master discourse and the chapter is concluded by considering a number of points of connection between poststructuralist writers like Derrida and Lacan. In a final irony the notion of poststructuralism itself is questioned by the very theories that are put forward in its name. The chapter will not have formal practice sections because the whole chapter deals with the question of how to produce readings with relation to key ideas.

Anchoring the self: the master signifiers

In the last chapter I discussed how Lacan radically rewrote René Descartes' 'I think, therefore I am' as 'I think where I am not, therefore I am where I do not think' (Lacan, 1966/1977: 166). We saw that Lacan's reformulation of the cogito argument undermined the Cartesian foundation of the self. This led to the conclusion that, although language situates the subject within the Symbolic, and even though subjects may live the illusion of the coherent self, the self is endlessly deferred through the defiles of the signifier. All this is connected to what in Lacanian terms is called the 'castrating' effect of language. Rather than conferring power on the user, the entry into the Symbolic leads to the prohibitions mentioned in the last chapter while at the same time bringing about lack, the loss of a sense of undivided being and the alienation of subjects from 'themselves'.

However, just as Lacan believed that the stabilizing structures associated with the Name-of-the-Father were essential to psychic health (see the last chapter) he also held that human beings needed what he called **master signifiers**, which function to provide the basic coordinates of identity (Lacan, 1991/2007: 92f.). For example, most people define themselves with relation to their gender, nationality, religious or non-religious belief, class, profession, political affiliations, sexual preferences and so on. Around these master signifiers (what might be called, adapting Laclau and Mouffe (1985: 112), 'nodal points') are clusters of secondary signifiers of defining characteristics (people may think of themselves as decent, sincere, independent, honest, etc.). For Lacan both the master and secondary signifiers provide necessary coordinates for the self but he emphasized, in line with his use of structuralism, that these signifiers only give the illusion of meaning because none of them have positive content and no ultimate signified – they are all dispersed through other signifiers.

While all this seems to endlessly repeat the themes of lack and the decentring of the self it is important to recognize that all these master signifiers and their satellites *do* have a positive role to play. If a person does not inter-nalize the basic rules laid down in the symbolic order (the laws symbolized by the Name-of-the-Father) the result would be psychosis. This would be like learning a whole lot of words but having no grammar to organize them – the effect would be disastrous and reality (like the sentence without grammar) would be a discontinuous chaos of isolated units or experiences. The subject would have no coordinates in order to function and the unconscious would be 'present but not functioning' (Lacan, 1981/1993: 208). These themes of castration, stability, loss and control have often been theorized through the Lacanian concept of the **Phallus**, which has generated much discussion, espe-cially in feminist circles and it is to this that I shall now turn.

Lacan, feminism and the privileged signifier: the Phallus

The first question I want to address is, why talk about the Phallus (with a capital letter) and not call it the penis? This is to distinguish the concept from the actual genital organ. From the Lacanian point of view the Phallus, like the Name-of-the-Father, is symbolic (although there are obvious connections to be made between the concept and the male appendage insofar as it relates to traditional patriarchal societies). The first thing to understand about this complex idea is that nobody possesses the Phallus as such – not even men. Yet, although women lack male genitalia, both sexes can aspire to what the Phallus represents and without regard to 'the anatomical difference of the sexes' (Lacan, 1966/1977: 282).

However, like any signifier, the Phallus cannot be reduced to any simple meaning. At the simplest level it symbolizes things like power, authority, secu-rity and authenticity of meaning, or undivided wholeness of being (prior to representation) which people desire, but ultimately lack. The Phallus can be equated with the Name-of-the-Father because, by being associated with the exercise of authority, it has a stabilizing function. In short, the Phallus func-tions in the same way for both sexes – no one possesses the Phallus but seeks what is typically represented *by* it in patriarchal cultures.

Furthermore, Lacan, in a seeming contradiction, posited the possible 'castration' of men – and women. That is to say, if anyone one can take up the *position* of power or authority, they can also lose it – hence be castrated. Thus, Lacan could, without any contradiction, write of a 'phallic mother' or of a girl or woman taking up (or being deprived of) the Phallus (282). These are some of the reasons why the concept has been of interest to those interested in gender and sexuality (see below and the following chapters). Yet the very image of male genitalia as a symbol of this kind within Freudian thinking has sparked much controversy within feminist debates about the construction of gender.

As Danielle Ramsey has stated, one of the reasons why many feminists feel (and have felt) hostile to Freud's work is that, like Simone de Beauvoir, they see his ideas as a product and perpetuator of the patriarchal society into which he was born. While Freud has been seen as shattering taboos and sexual repressions, feminist critics have challenged 'his contentious view of female identity as marked by passivity and in particular penis envy, a life-long feeling of psychic inferiority and physical lack' (Ramsey, 1999: 133).

Help File: penis envy

Within his general theory of psychosexual development, Freud posited that when children reach the genital phase (at around three years old, having passed through the oral and anal phases) their principal focus is on their genitalia. This is the phallic stage because the penis becomes of prime interest to *both* sexes. Boys, desiring the mother (emotionally and sexually) but recognizing that they are in direct competition with the father for possession of her (and having discovered the pleasures of the penis), will now suffer castration anxiety. That is to say, if they are aware that they possess the penis they also realize it can be removed – by the figure who is the chief rival for the mother's affections. For girls, psychosexual development is more complex because at this stage, to develop in the normative heterosexual way, the girl will have to redirect her libidinal instincts from the mother and onto a figure of the opposite sex. The first object of her libidinal desire will be the father. It is at this stage that the girl comes to see that she lacks the penis and she will, in all likelihood, desire the penis and all that it represents. This is the phase Freud denominated 'penis envy', believing that 'envy and jealousy play an even greater part in the mental life of women than of men' (Freud, 1933/1964: 125.). The lack and the envy will lead girls to turn away from the mother and despise her (and herself and other women) for being deficient in this respect (Freud, 1923–1925/1961a: 144); the male reaction to the recognition of the lack of the penis may vacillate between 'horror of the mutilated creature or triumphant contempt for her' (Freud, 1923–1925/1961b: 252).

While Freud was aware that associating women with weakness and passivity and men with strength and activity was 'obviously an inadequate empirical and conventional equation' (Freud, 1949/1989: 70) it is hard to defend him from the reductionist view that women envy the penis. Freud's near contemporary, Karen Horney, while not rejecting the notion outright, pointed out the gender bias of the notion and the cultural factors that were sufficient for the explanation for envy, without the need to have recourse to insisting on the lack of the Phallus (Horney, 1967). Furthermore, as Kate Millett has observed (echoing Horney's view), 'surely the first thing all children notice is that the mother has breasts, while the father has none' (Ramsey, 1999: 137).

This rejection, however, has not stopped feminists from exploring and using Freud's ideas, and radical feminists like Juliet Mitchell have argued that far from claiming that women were inferior to men Freud offered the means to understand 'why women were constructed as such in a patriarchal society' (137). If classical Freudian psychoanalysis has received a mixed reception in feminist circles then a similar fate has befallen Lacan's work, which has been seen as able to provide 'insight into the psychic routes of patriarchy' by some feminists but, for others, is considered 'deeply misogynistic' (133). Even though the concept of the Phallus is not specific to men (although drawing its symbolic power from patriarchal social organization) feminists like Chris Weedon have argued that:

> Lacanian theory employs an anatomically grounded elision between the phallus and the penis which implies the necessary patriarchal organization of desire and sexuality [...] Men, by virtue of their penis, can aspire to a position of power and control within the symbolic order. Women, on the other hand, have no position in the symbolic order, except in relation to men, as mothers, and even the process of mothering is given patriarchal meanings, reduced, in Freud, to penis envy. (Weedon, 1997: 53)

These are some of the reasons why feminist thinkers like Nancy Chodorow, Hélène Cixous and Luce Irigaray have gone beyond Freud and Lacan and, in the case of Irigaray, developed 'a radical theory of the feminine libido, based on female sexuality and auto-eroticism, which celebrates the female body in separation from men' (54). Thus, it is possible to see that the psychoanalytic legacy in cultural criticism, whether its emphasis is on the penis or the Phallus, is a contested site of struggle. Feminists may usefully be seen as involved in a hegemonic struggle (see Chapter 1) over the representation of the psyche and the body and what this means in terms of women's subordination in patriarchy.

However, other critics, like the feminist philosopher Judith Butler, while critical of some of Lacan's ideas, have played on the penis/Phallus distinction in order to analyse heterosexual inter-personal relations, which do not necessarily imply that women are always subordinated to men. Butler makes the point that 'being' and 'having' the Phallus denote 'divergent sexual positions', or even impossible positions within language. What she means is that to 'be' the Phallus is to function as the signifier of the desire of the Other, that is, the heterosexual object of masculine desire. Women who are objects of masculine desire 'supply the site to which it penetrates' – they signify the Phallus through being its absence and thereby confirm it. This sets up a paradox whereby 'the one who lacks the Phallus is the one who *is* the Phallus' because power is wielded by the one who does not possess it. The masculine subject 'has it' as such but needs the feminine Other to confirm it in her own being (Butler, 1999: 56). This presents a seeming paradox: if you desire to be desired (a classic Lacanian formulation) then you want *to be* the Phallus as the object of the other's desire. In heterosexual relations, as a man you have and you want to be the Phallus, while as a woman you have not got the Phallus but you are the Phallus, etc.

It is hardly surprising, then, that the Phallus is seen as the privileged signifier in the Lacanian system. This is not only because it can give the *effect* of stabilizing meaning and afford the symbolic position of power but because it represents the law symbolized by the Name-of-the-Father. As discussed in the previous chapter, were it not for the authority and stability symbolized by the Name-of-the-Father, psychosis would be the result. It is hardly surprising, then, that authority figures and authority itself are powerful forces in human relations.

The master signifier and the Name-of-the-Father in practice: from electrocuting thy neighbour to The Yes Men

In the following sections I shall show how Yannis Stavrakakis has offered an interpretation that can help to show how some the Lacanian concepts introduced might help to explain the relations between blind obedience and forms of social control. I will begin with a simple observation by Wilhelm Reich developed in the context of trying to explain the mass psychology of fascism where large numbers of people are prepared (or are even willing) to give up personal responsibility and be subordinated by others:

> What has to be explained is not the fact that the man who is hungry steals or the fact that the man who is exploited strikes, but why the majority of those who are hungry *don't* steal and why the majority of those who are exploited *don't* strike. (Reich, *Mass Psychology of Fascism*, in Stavrakakis, 2007: 169)

This raises general questions about orthodoxy, conformity, surrender and obedience and why people may even submit themselves to (or become active agents in) authoritarian regimes. Many answers have been offered both inside and outside psychoanalysis (including the Frankfurt School – see Chapter 1) but I shall limit myself to some of the examples discussed by Stavrakakis. The first example involves 'the two anti-corporate activist-pranksters' known as 'The Yes Men' who have set up (among many other things) a bogus World Trade Organization (WTO) website in order to dupe representatives of the corporations and expose what they believe to be their questionable business ethics and basic lack of humanity. The website created by The Yes Men (Jacques Servin and Igor Vamos, otherwise known as Andy Bichlbaum and Mike Bonanno) was so realistic that it was mistaken for the official WTO site. So it was that they received invitations to speak as representatives of the actual WTO and began attending business meetings and conferences all over the world. As Bichlbaum and Bonanno observe, they intended to shock and ridicule through presenting official economic theory and policies (based around things like free trade and globalization) 'but presented with far more candour than usual, making them look like the absurdities that they actually are'. At other times they simply 'ranted nonsensically' expecting to kicked out, silenced or jailed. 'But no one batted an eye. In fact, they applauded' (The Yes Men, 2004: 8, and quoted in Stavrakakis, 2007: 170).

While it is not true that 'no one batted an eye' – when The Yes Men posed as Exxon Mobil and National Petroleum Council representatives in Canada they were (eventually) removed after describing and recommending a new technology to turn human flesh into a new Exxon oil product called 'Vivoleum' (see *Scoop*, 2007) – many of their absurd pranks were accepted, it seems, on the grounds that they represented the appropriate authorities. It seems obvious that The Yes Men would get caught out but the surprising thing is that on similar occasions they could not get the so-called experts to *dis*believe them (The Yes Men, 2004: 8). According to Stavrakakis, one way (excluding things like direct coercion) to explain these situations is to is refer to the idea of the Name-of-the-Father:

> Obviously, the Oedipal structure implicit in the social ordering of our societies, the role of what Lacan calls 'the Name-of-the-Father' in structuring reality through the (castrating) imposition of the Law, predisposes social subjects to accept and obey what seems to be emanating from the big Other, from socially sedimented points of reference invested with the gloss of authority and presented as embodying and sustaining the symbolic order, organising reality itself. (Stavrakakis, 2007: 169–70)

Another example which suggests a similar dynamic is associated with the (in)famous psychological experiments carried out by Stanley Milgram at Yale University in the early 1960s, where hundreds of volunteers were asked to punish other people by subjecting them to (what the volunteers thought were) powerful electric shocks. What surprised Milgram was the number of people prepared to continue to administer high levels of fake shock treatment, even though the actor-victims displayed great discomfort or even begged them to stop. Milgram's explanation for this obedience was that 'it is not the substance of the command but the source in authority that is of decisive importance' (Milgram in Stavrakakis, 2007: 173).

The Lacanian explanation: the Name-of-the-Father

Stavrakakis sees Milgram's explanation for the experiments he carried out as being akin to Lacan's position. This is because even before the experiments started those who were required to apply the electrical current gave themselves up to a scientific authority figure. For Stavrakakis this set of relations helps to explain this blind obedience in the examples discussed and 'lends support to the Lacanian understanding of the Name-of-the-Father, the signifier representing authority and order, as instituting the reality of the subject' (Stavrakakis, 2007: 173–174).

It is possible to link this back to the mirror phase and the entry into the Symbolic because this 'founding moment of subjectivity' is associated with symbolic castration (with its prohibition of incest) that 'disrupts the imaginary relation between mother and child and permits our functional insertion into the social world of language'. That is to say, 'the command embodied in the Name-of-the-Father offers the prototype of symbolic power that structures our social reality in patriarchal societies' (174). Recent events have shown how these relations still exercise power in shocking ways. For example, the torture of Iraqi prisoners in Abu Ghraib, by democratic nations, helps to underline that the displacement of personal responsibility onto symbolic authority figures is still very relevant to the contemporary world (Stavrakakis 2007:172; see also Bruner 2005: xi–xiii).

The Lacanian explanation: the subject supposed to know

All this links in with another useful concept in Lacan's thinking which is **the subject supposed to know**. We saw in the previous chapter that Lacan rewrote Descartes' 'cogito ergo sum' argument but he also pointed out that Descartes, in order to develop his argument, fell back on the notion of God (what ultimately promises the truth of the self is the existence of God). For Lacan this was odd considering that Descartes was trying to whittle knowledge down to one undeniable statement based on the self: if I can affirm the self at least I know I exist. However, Lacan points out that the argument relies on a 'sleight of hand' where 'what Descartes means, and says, is that if two and two make four it is, quite simply, because God wishes it so. It is his business' (Lacan, 1973/1977: 225). What Descartes effectively does is to displace the locus of knowledge away from himself (the *cogito*) onto the deity who functions as 'the subject supposed to know' (225).

This notion can be seen to function in all kinds of situations. For example, Slavoj Žižek talks about how it is common for people to believe in something because others are assumed to do so. One of the ways Žižek demonstrates this is to refer to an anthropological anecdote where so-called 'primitives', on being questioned about certain superstitious beliefs they were reported to hold, replied that 'some people believe', thus 'immediately displacing their belief, transferring it onto another'. For Žižek, 'in order for the belief to function, there has to be some ultimate guarantor of it, yet this guarantor is always deferred, displaced, never present in persona' (complemented by 'a subject who is supposed to believe'). Thus, we only need to presume the existence of 'the subject supposed to know' in the shape of others who just happen to believe or 'in the guise of the mythological founding figure who is not part of our experiential reality' (Žižek, 1998). Žižek exemplifies this in a humorous anecdote about the physicist Niels Bohr who replied to a visitor who expressed surprise that he had a lucky horseshoe on his door by saying that, of course, he was not superstitious, but that he had heard it still worked even if you did not believe it (Žižek, 1997/2005).

Thus, people might 'believe' in something (or anything) because, despite their own doubts, they assume someone (or an absent group or some symbolic figure) actually believes it to be true (this is what is behind phrases like 'they say', 'some people believe', 'I've heard', etc.). This can be explored with relation to the figure of the psychoanalyst in psychoanalysis, the teacher or professor in education, the doctor or specialist in medicine, the guru in mystical belief, and the scientist in the laboratory (see below). 'The subject supposed to know' is linked to the Name-of-the-Father because s/he functions as a symbol of the law, which has a phallic function in stabilizing discourse.

Returning to Stavrakakis and the Harvard experiments on the 1960s, the scientist who is able to get people to apply electric shocks can be seen as 'a subject supposed to know' who commands obedience through authority. However, as Žižek notes, this person does not even need to exist. However, there is also another dimension that Stavrakakis brings out from psychoanalytic thinking which is the 'emotional tie' that the volunteers felt toward the man they believed was the scientist responsible for the experiments. Milgram noted certain feelings of compassion towards the experimenter but little sympathy towards those they believed to be the guinea pigs receiving the electric shocks. Milgram interpreted this reluctance on the part of his volunteers to hurt the experimenter's feelings as part of the 'binding forces inhibiting disobedience' (Milgram, in Stavrakakis, 2007: 176). Stavrakakis concludes that there are two major points that Milgram can contribute to this inquiry:

> First, obedience to authority has a lot to do with the symbolic source of the command and very little with its concrete (rational or irrational, factual or fictional) content. Second, our attachment to this symbolic source is, to a large extent, extimate [both inside and outside] to the symbolic itself. Beyond the formal force of the symbolic command, Milgram reveals a lot about the more positive aspects of attachment and obedience to power structures.

Hence Stavrakakis emphasizes the importance of how affective ties (the will not to offend the one who is supposed to know) may override more rational considerations to the point of permitting extreme cruelty. At a general level, what Stavrakakis and Žižek demonstrate is that Lacan's theories can be applied to all kinds of social situations in order to fashion readings which are deeply indebted to, but not necessarily restricted to, their clinical psycho-analytic contexts. However, not all of Milgram's volunteers subjected themselves to the authority figure (just as not all The Yes Men's listeners allowed themselves to be taken in by their pranks). This suggests that while these theories can help to explain psycho-social phenomena they are by no means completely reliable or able to be universalized. Thus, before going on to conclude this chapter, I want to evaluate psychoanalytic approaches in the light of a point Kobena Mercer makes.

Oedipus (culture) bound

Within the context of reading racial fetishism (where the white gaze represents the naked black body), Mercer questions what he sees as the Eurocentricism of Freudian and post-Freudian theory. For Mercer, the increasing use of psychoanalytic concepts and their extension into other cultural contexts outside their European origins is something that critics should be very wary about. While Mercer admits that 'feminist appropriations' of psychoanalysis have been 'profoundly enabling', what concerns him is when these concepts and their assumptions are applied to questions of 'race'.

In this case 'universalist pretensions can be disenabling' because 'they preempt the development of pluralist perspectives on the intersections of multiple differences in popular culture' (Mercer, in Evans and Hall, 2001: 446). What concerns Mercer is the manner in which 'a certain kind of psychoanalysis' has become a 'master discourse' but one in which the 'ethnocentrism of classical Freudian theory remains unquestioned'. Here he sees a similarity between European colonialism and the dominant discourse of psychoanalysis:

> While the concept of fetishism is suggestive precisely because it connects the economic and sexual contraflow of ideological investments, it is also problematic, for its roots in European thought lie in the colonizing discourses of missionaries and anthropologists on 'primitive religions'. [...] The Greek tragedy of Oedipus, as the grand narrative upon which desire-as-lack or 'castration' is based, is culture-bound despite the universalistic claims staked out for it. Other cultures may be patriarchal, but does that mean they produce an Oedipal sexuality? (446)

The theories I have been exploring and illustrating up to now (and any theory) may seem to offer insights into *all* cultures (and certainly have some explanatory power) but Mercer helps us to become more aware that we may end up fetishizing the theory itself so that it becomes an overarching colonial enterprise which imposes very particular forms of Western thinking on the whole world (simplifying both itself and the other).

Points of connection: poststructuralism, Derrida and Lacan

By way of summary I want to refer back to deconstruction to help understand some of Lacan's ideas and consolidate some key ideas in poststructuralist approaches. Just as there was no one-to-one-relation between signifier and signified for Derrida so it is for Lacan. Both writers show how signifieds are constantly collapsing back into signifiers but, at the same time, there is no way of thinking beyond language to something which would somehow escape the slipperiness of signification. We saw in the chapter on deconstruction that, according to Derrida, we are no closer to the 'originary' meaning of a phrase in speech than in writing because meaning does not *precede* the act of speech, it is a product of it – again, the same can be said of Lacan's approach which never loses sight of 'the defiles of the signifier'. In Derrida's 'Structure, Sign and Play' we saw that that presence is actually lost in the sign (Derrida, 1967/1978: 281) and this very much echoes Lacan's view. We saw that this was very close to what Barthes' expressed in 'The Death of the Author': someone may write a text or speak but the moment the words are free of the speaker's mouth or pen the author is erased in them. Meaning, then, is not governed by intention or self-presence but according to how words are interpreted in the Other (the repository of all symbolic possibilities and interpretive codes and resourses).

Yet there is another point of connection that is very important which has to do with what Derrida called 'double reading'. We saw that while deconstruction challenges *logocentrism* and *phonocentrism*, insists on *différance* and indeterminacy and finding all kinds of inconsistency, contradictions and paradoxes (*aporias*), we also saw that there was no way to transcend them. The effects of meaning are dependent on the assumption of a centre (however illusory it might be) that provides a kind of anchor point from which to start. As stated in Chapter 6, there is a sense in which even if you do not believe in the cake, there is no other option but to eat it. This reflects something very similar in Lacan. It is easy to overemphasize lack and misrecognition, but it is also necessary to recognize the importance of the Symbolic and its laws as establishing the parameters for subjectivity and the system of communication that makes it possible in the first place. For Lacan, the Imaginary does not only describe the self-images we rely upon (originating in the mirror phase) but also includes the idea of us establishing the basic coordinates of the self that actually *enable* our functioning in the world (including the master signifiers). If this did not happen, as we saw above, the result would be psychosis.

Thus, in both writers, the idea of grammar as a set of enabling structural coordinates is also fundamental. We saw that Derrida's deconstruction of the speech/writing binary was dependent on the idea that they are both dependent on the same underlying structures: a grammatological set of rules that Derrida called '*archi-écriture*' or 'proto-writing' (Derrida, 1967/1997: 291).

This idea can give us an insight into Lacan's notion of the Symbolic because the unconscious is structured like a language in sofarthat it behaves according to the laws of desire (for the lost mother-object) that govern it (which have their origins in the big societal Other). Returning to Saussure for a moment, it is possible to say that there is a kind of *langue* (the symbolic fully internalized) that is responsible for the *paroles* that are produced (mental characteristics, especially neurotic symptoms for the psychoanalyst).

In the last chapter I described what would happen if Derrida's deconstructive ideas were applied to national identity or notions of the self. I said that the self would be decentred, subject to the play of deferral and difference and founded on 'trace', where identity is dependent on what is excluded. To put a Lacanian twist on this, the chief characteristic of the self would be in emptiness, where I think where I am not, and I am not where I think.

These characteristics are those which are often emphasized when the word poststructuralism is used. However, it is possible to consider Derrida's and Lacan's challenges to identity with relation to the notion of poststructuralism itself. If this is done according to these theories of signification, it would be undermined and deconstructed. For example, the writer I shall be discussing in the following chapter, Michel Foucault, is one that may problematize the idea of poststructuralism because, as already stated in earlier chapters, his work does not grow directly out of the paradigms associated with Saussurean linguistics yet he is commonly grouped with thinkers like Derrida and Lacan. This brings me back to a point made in an earlier chapter: poststructuralism as a label is an academic convenience – however, it is an important one which describes some of the most significant contemporary approaches to cultural analysis.

Summary of key points

This chapter has consolidated a number of key Lacanian concepts and has demonstrated how they can be used in practice. It began by considering how gender is culturally inscribed and looked at how Lacan's concept of the Name-of-the-Father can be used in practice with relation to 'master signifiers'. Practice has been illustrated with reference to the way feminists have engaged with Lacanian concepts like the Phallus, and the idea of 'the subject supposed to know' has been applied to the (in)famous psychological experiments carried out at Yale University and the mischievous interventions of 'The Yes Men'. The final sections have considered Kobena Mercer's contention that psychoanalysis has become a Eurocentric master discourse and the chapter has been concluded by considering points of connection between poststructuralist writers like Derrida and Lacan. To conclude it has been suggested that the notion of poststructuralism itself may be undermined by the very theories that have been put forward in its name.

Further reading

Relevant to the further reading for this chapter are Silverman (1983), Mitchell and Rose (in Lacan, 1985) and Žižek (1991, 1992) (all mentioned in the further reading for the last chapter). Jane Gallop's *The Daughter's Seduction: Feminism and Psychoanalysis* (1982) engages with Freud's and Lacan's legacies for feminism and challenges Juliet Mitchell's defence of Freud. For a series of meditations on Freud and penis envy see Luce Irigaray's *Speculum of the Other Woman* (1985). For The Yes Men see their two films *The Yes Men* (2003) and *The Yes Men Fix the World* (2008) which complement Andy Bichlbaum and Mike Bonanno's *The True Story of the End of the World Trade Organization* (The Yes Men, 2004) which outlines their infiltrations and subversions of several global free trade forums. These can be seen as forms of 'culture jamming' which I discuss in Chapter 15.

As indicated in the Further Reading section of the last chapter, one of the critics who has most helped to stimulate interest in how Lacan's ideas may be used beyond their immediate psychoanalytic contexts is Slavoj Žižek, who often combines Lacanian ideas with those of other thinkers like Kant, Hegel and Marx to offer trenchant (if often controversial) critiques of not only popular cultural forms but the contemporary world. Four titles (out of many) which demonstrate how a broadly Marxist-Lacanian approach can help to meditate on the problems of contemporary capitalist ideology, the crisis of democracy, the environment, violence and terrorism post-9/11, the current financial crises (backed up by arguments spun around references to everything from Gonzo porn to *Avatar*, *Kung-Fu Panda* and *Big Brother*) are *Welcome to the Desert of the Real* (2002), *First and Tragedy, Then as Farce* (2009b), *Violence: Six Sideways Reflections* (2009a) and *Living in the End Times* (2010). A book which considers Žižek's work and includes an interview with Žižek is Rex Butler's *Slavoj Žižek: Live Theory* (2005). *Contingency, Hegemony, Universality: Contemporary Dialogues on the Left* (Butler et al., 2000) brings together three thinkers who debate contemporary politics (and answer one another) using a wide range of poststructuralist theory (Žižek's interventions are very indebted to Lacan).

9

Discourse and Power

Michel Foucault

Learning goals

- To see why Michel Foucault's work has been associated with poststructuralist approaches.
- To understand the importance of discourses to Foucault's ways of thinking culture and to appreciate how they systematically form the objects of which they speak.
- To grasp how reason, truth, knowledge and power interrelate in Foucault's writings.
- To see how the discursive approach helps to illuminate Foucault's ideas about history and gives insights into how he approached surveillance and modern constructions of sexuality.

Concepts

The key concepts introduced in this chapter are: the critique of reason, knowledge, truth, power, discourse, anti-essentialism, self-regulation, surveillance, the Panopticon, genealogy and the history of sexuality.

Introduction

This chapter will begin by discussing the status of Foucault's contribution to cultural studies and go on to introduce Foucault's 'discursive' approach to cultural analysis and his critique of reason. This will be followed by a discussion of how Foucault theorized the relationships between knowledge, truth and power and this will be illustrated with reference to his ideas on self-regulation, surveillance and control. The chapter will then return to the discursive side of Foucault's work by exploring the idea of 'man' as a construction within the discourses of the sciences. This will serve as an introduction to Foucault's theory of history, which will be developed through dominant themes which he elaborated in his history of sexuality. The general approach is to connect Foucault to writers already introduced and prepare the way for an understanding of how Judith Butler united Foucauldian approaches with those of other poststructuralist thinkers.

Situating Foucault and his contribution to cultural studies

Different introductions to cultural studies will nearly always feature references to the work of Michel Foucault, especially those focused on the relations between discourse, knowledge and power, constructions of gender and sexuality, and the evolution of punishment, discipline and surveillance. I say Foucault will 'nearly always' be mentioned because this is not always the case; however, his influence has become so pervasive that anyone working within cultural studies is obliged to have at least some awareness of his work.

One of the reasons that Foucault is difficult to place is that his work crossed over many different subject areas. He wrote on subjects as varied as the connections between madness and civilization (1961/1967), the rise, and consequences, of the human sciences (1966/1974), the history of discipline and punishment and the birth of the prison (1975/1977) and the history of sexuality (1976/1990, 1984/1990, 1984/1986). Each one of these studies (and this only scratches the surface of his work) shows how the rise of the modern state is linked to the ways in which various aspects of life have been rationalized and controlled through discourses.

What has made the task of situating Foucault especially difficult is that his work has been associated with diverse intellectual movements. The fact that Foucault was a French intellectual making a name for himself from around the mid-1960s has led critics to associate his work with structuralist critics like Lévi-Strauss and Barthes (even though Foucault defined himself as an 'anti-structuralist' (Foucault, 1980: 114)). The difficulty of situating Foucault is summed up by Strinati who, like Chris Weedon (see Chapter 5), groups Foucault with the poststructuralists, arguing that his ideas are 'central to the critique of structuralism and Marxism', but also sees him as a sociologist and historian of knowledge (1995: 249). Foucault has even been defined as a deconstructionist (Dosse, 1997: 234f.) and a postmodern thinker (Sarup, 1993: 58f.; Cahoon, 1996: 360f.). Yet Foucault rejected all these labels and offered alternative, albeit related, ways of thinking about culture. I will now begin to look at how this may make sense.

Foucault: the critique of reason and the irrationality of rationality

The following sections introduce Foucault's discursive approach to knowledge and regimes of truth and show how they are always implicated in circuits of power. This is done by focusing on a number of key works which explore the rise of the clinic, discipline, punishment and the social, psychiatric regulation of madness. In doing this I hope to show that his ideas challenge identity in similar ways to what we have seen in the work of Althusser, Derrida and Lacan, while reflecting themes that are commonly associated with postmodernism (which will be the subject of later chapters). The first thing I want to emphasize about Foucault is his **critique of reason**. He can be said to mount not only a massive attack on all the rationalizing processes of modernity (the rise of the modern state) but also on the uses of argumentative reason without, however, rejecting reason *per se*. While realizing that the abandonment of reasoned argument would only result in the risk of 'lapsing into irrationality', Foucault proposed to ask a series of questions he regarded as central to critical thought:

> *What* is this Reason that we use? What are its historical effects? What are its limits, and what are its dangers? How can we exist as rational beings, fortunately committed to practising a rationality that is unfortunately crisscrossed by intrinsic dangers? (Foucault, 1984: 248–249)

The intrinsic dangers of which Foucault writes bring us to what can be considered the 'irrationality' of reason. Foucault cited the case of social Darwinism, where Darwin's theories were used for racist ends to privilege certain European nations over those considered inferior and therefore ripe for 'civilization'. For Foucault, this kind of thinking became one of 'the most enduring and powerful ingredients of Nazism'. The paradox is that social Darwinism was a kind of irrationality, but an irrationality that was at the same time 'a form of rationality' (249). What social Darwinists do is to take the idea of evolution, as the survival of the fittest, and then reapply it to the social, political world in which they live. The following is a simplified version of the kind of arguments they put forward: only the strongest are capable of adapting and surviving. We are the survivors. We rule through our superior strength and intelligence. Therefore, we rightly rule over the rest: other classes, women, other nations, etc.

The social Darwinists, then, use forms of 'reason' (they use arguments based on a 'scientific' source) but this 'reason' (arbitrarily and unjustifiably transferred from one context to another) is in the service of racism, sexism and all kinds of domination: it is 'reason' that serves the narrow interests of a dominant group. From this point of view reason is not above politics or power; it is an argumentative tool which can be put to all kinds of uses from arguing for libertarian politics to justifying slavery, torture and concentration camps. Reason, then, is not as innocent as it might seem – and nor is **truth**.

Truth as a thing of this world: knowledge, discourse, truth and power

For Foucault the uses of reason are bound up with the notion of truth. Truth is sometimes thought of as something other-worldly, the product of disinterested intellectual effort. But one of the reasons why Foucault is often grouped with structuralist (and postmodern) thinkers is he was deeply sceptical about the notion of truth. For Foucault truth was a meaningless concept unless it is tied to the systems which produce it. In his essay entitled 'Truth and Power' Foucault argued that truth is never outside **power** and so challenged the idea that it was 'the reward of free spirits' who had 'succeeded in liberating themselves'. He saw it as a thing very much of this world. Truth is not discovered, it is 'produced' through 'multiple forms of constraint' and it 'induces regular effects of power'. All this sums up Foucault's notion of **discourse** – which has had such an enormous influence on cultural analysis:

> Each society has its regime of truth, its 'general politics' of truth: that is, the types of discourse which it accepts and makes function as true; the mechanisms and instances which enable one to distinguish true and false statements, the means by which each is sanctioned; the techniques and procedures accorded value in the acquisition of truth: of those who are charged with saying what counts as true. (Foucault, 1980: 131)

This makes it sound as if truth (like reason), far from being innocent and good, is in some way manufactured, oppressive and even sinister. The general point that Foucault makes is that power cannot exercise itself without reference to domains of **knowledge**, or regimes of truth (which constitute discourses). For example, the production of knowledge in universities might seem innocuous but the state continuously uses knowledge (some of it produced in academic environments) in order to exercise power over its subjects. Of course, 'knowledge' itself does not exist in a vacuum, it has to be generated – it being tightly controlled by the institutions that produce it (see below).

If we take a subject that was very important to Foucault, criminality, it is not possible to lock someone up for being a criminal without several domains of 'knowledge' that can be used within institutional contexts which can define, isolate and give legitimacy to forms of social control. In this way it is possible to see how discourses of knowledge are involved with **power**. Let us take the case of someone who kills a number of people because he or she believes the deaths are sanctioned by a voice in their head. This person may be considered a murderer killing in cold blood, or criminally insane and therefore not responsible for their actions.

Here we might consider how many different kinds of people with specialized forms of knowledge, moving in distinct institutions, would be necessary for someone to be considered a cold-blooded murderer or criminally insane. The list might include, apart from the police and detectives, doctors, psychiatrists, social workers, members of the legal profession, the penal system and criminologists. All the professionals generate forms of knowledge which are linked to the exercise of power over individuals (what Foucault called 'a bio-politics' (1976/1990)). So it is that Foucault described truth in contemporary Western societies as being the product of discourses (systems which produce forms of knowledge like medicine, biology, psychiatry, the political sciences, economics, etc.) which are institutional and produced in officially recognized research centres.

Each discipline/area has its way of ordering the world (which may overlap with other areas) and establishing under what conditions something can be considered true or false. Thus, Foucault emphasized the processes of normalization, regulation and surveillance (see below) with relation to the institutions which control discursive practices or regimes of truth. What this means is that 'truth' is not just there in some mystical way: it has to be produced in discourse and that discourse has to be regulated and monitored, that is, subject to normative controls (which establishes what counts as knowledge, who can produce it, how is it produced and what is its scope and limits, etc.). A hint of the power of discourses can be seen in the way John Storey describes language as discourse: it *enables* us to speak, *constrains* what we can say, *constitutes* us as speaking subjects 'it situates and produces my subjectivity: I know myself in language. I think in language; I talk to myself in language' (Storey, 2009a: 128).

As Storey goes on to say, different discourses can be applied to the same subject, like film, but each one would open up certain questions and close off others (like Althusser's 'problematic'). Thus, film can be constituted in different ways according to distinct discourses being seen as a commodity (within Economics), have relations to literary sources (in Literary Criticism), as a historical document (within History), etc. It might be said that every discipline *disciplines* its object. As stated above, Foucault dedicated a whole series of books to how regimes of truth are established (through discourses) and how they function, often to the detriment of individuals in society (Foucault, 1961/1967, 1966/1974, 1975/1977, 1976/1990, 1984/1986, 1984/1990). In Foucault's work, then, the emphasis is not so much on how meaning is produced within discourses (as in linguistic approaches like structuralism) but on their 'exterior dimensions': something which concentrates on 'the fact and the conditions of their manifest appearance', the 'transformations which they have effectuated' and the terrain where they 'coexist, remain and disappear' (1978: 15).

To sum up these points, Foucault analysed how different discourses work to isolate human subjects, divide them, classify them and label them. These processes are those that unite knowledge and power in the sense that they facilitate forms of social control where bodies can remain free or be imprisoned or isolated in psychiatric wards, etc. For Foucault 'power and knowledge directly imply one another': 'there is no power relation without the correlative constitution of a field of knowledge, nor any knowledge that does not presuppose and constitute at the same time power relations' (Foucault, 1975/1978: 27). Yet it is worth remembering that he did not conceive of power as a necessarily (or wholly) top-down phenomenon where a monarch, a group or a class dominate others (Foucault, 1980: 98). While often emphasizing how power is exercised over individuals, Foucault saw power as exercised *through* people. Power is something that moves and is produced at every level: for Foucault 'power is everywhere' (Foucault, 1976/1990: 93). This means that for Foucault it is necessary to 'try to discover how it is that subjects are gradually, progressively, really and materially constituted through a multiplicity of organisms, forces, energies, materials, desires, thoughts etc.' (Foucault, 1980: 97). In this way it is possible to study how power is exercised (not just by the powerful) and the way it moves in complex ways with relation to multiple contexts.

Foucault's nuanced understanding of power goes beyond this because he also emphasized the way subjects are coerced in subtle ways where the modern state is seen to produce subjects who actually regulate themselves, rather than be intimidated into conformity by direct violence and torture. Foucault associates the rise of the modern state with an increasing reliance on the internalization of values and **self-regulation**. This provides a thematic link with Althusser's idea (see Chapter 4) that subjects of ideology (under the illusion of being free) accept their subjection so that they can go about performing 'the gestures and actions' of their subjection, all by themselves (Althusser, 1971: 182).

Foucault, like Derrida, analysed the uses of forms of reason: while it is valuable and necessary to intellectual effort, it cannot realize the dreams of universal truth or certainty. Foucault makes us aware of reason, truth, power and knowledge not only as productive forces but emphasizes their negative effects on human subjects. For these reasons Foucault's ideas have been of enormous interest to critics interested in all kinds of emancipation (whether on the grounds of class, gender, sexuality, the post-colonial, etc.).

Self-regulation, surveillance and control: Foucault and Bentham's Panopticon

To explain how the modern state is seen to produce subjects who actually regulate themselves through the internalization of values and self-regulation I shall refer to Foucault's reading of Jeremy Bentham's design for a prison which the latter named 'the Panopticon'. Foucault, in *Discipline and Punish*, uses the British utilitarian philosopher's 1787 design as an example of how, from around the eighteenth century in Europe, social mechanisms of control shifted from the body to what Foucault called the 'soul' (Foucault, 1975/1978: 16). The soul is not a metaphysical concept but refers to how forms of discipline were gradually transferred from the public spectacle of torture and private incarceration in the dungeon (in the feudal age of monarchs) to forms of punishment and control which worked on behaviour through the more subtle means of mainly non-corporeal mechanisms directed at the mind of the prisoner: on 'the thoughts, the will, [and] the inclinations' (16).

Bentham's plan built all the (non-communicating) prison cells around a central tower in such a way that the prisoners were always visible to the guards but the guards were not visible to the prisoners. The reason for this was that it did not matter if the guards were there or not – the important thing was that the prisoners *thought* the guards were there (or may be there). In this way, rather than exercise control through physical violence or coercion the prisoners regulated *themselves*. They become, to a great extent, their *own* guards – in this way the mechanism of control can be said to shift from the body to the 'soul'. So it is that the Panopticon is seen by Foucault to produce subjects who actually regulate themselves, rather than be intimidated into conformity by physical maltreatment and torture. This is the model for the modern state which is seen to rely on an internalization of values and self-regulation.

There is an important lesson here in terms of the way power functions in the modern state. The 'major effect' of the Panopticon is 'to induce in the inmate a state of consciousness and permanent visibility that assures the automatic functioning of power. There are wider implications to this model because, as Foucault indicates, Bentham envisaged the same system being adapted to other spaces to ensure regulation and control:

> If the inmates are convicts, there is no danger of a plot, an attempt at collective escape, the planning of new crimes for the future, bad reciprocal influences; if they are patients, there is no danger of contagion; if they are madmen there is no risk of their committing violence upon one another; if they are schoolchildren, there is no copying, no noise, no chatter, no waste of time; if they are workers, there are no disorders, no theft, no coalitions, none of those distractions that slow down the rate of work, make it less perfect or cause accidents. (Foucault, 1975/1978: 200–1)

From these trends in the seventeenth and eighteenth centuries Foucault saw what he called 'the disciplinary society' (209). Foucault's observations on the differences between more violent discipline and punishment and mechanisms of power which encourage self-regulation open up questions about the extent to which **surveillance** techniques have become part of everyday life. At this point we could come back to Wilhelm Reich's point (mentioned in the last chapter) that what needs to be explained is not the fact that people who are hungry steal or that those who are exploited strike, but 'why the majority of those who are hungry *don't* steal and why the majority of those who are exploited *don't* strike' (Reich, in Stavrakakis, 2007: 169). Foucault's use of Bentham's 'Panopticon' might go some way to explain this. The question is: up to what point is this the case in contemporary societies?

Practice: Panopticon and surveillance society

As a short practice exercise you might try to imagine in what ways Foucault's idea that 'invisibility is a guarantee of order' (200) may help to regulate the society in which you live. In the Help File below I shall offer some suggestions and a critique of this idea.

Help File: Panopticon, surveillance, resistance and de Certeau

Some of the most obvious ways in which populations are encouraged to be self-regulating are related to the uses of CCTV, where the ever-growing presence of cameras in places like shopping malls, stations and banks may work as a deterrent for criminal activity. Open-plan interiors in schools, offices and other work areas may also lead to certain self-regulatory practices and the widespread use of radars on the roads (whether they are switched on or not) have generally slowed down traffic, something which suggests that the presence of technology in itself has an effect on behaviour. Since the events of 9/11 the use of surveillance has been intensified by many governments in the West who are investing increasingly larger amounts of money in information gathering technologies to regulate and control citizens.

However, self-regulation, owing to the perceived presence of an authority, may not be so revolutionary in the Christian world as it might seem. The idea of an omniscient God, who is aware of all human action, motive and thought, already functioned through the institution of the church, long before the rise of the modern state. Bentham's Panopticon could be said to intensify the same principle through exploiting architectural form.

Something else that may be considered is the possibility that the mechanisms of the Panopticon and surveillance systems might actually be appropriated by the very people they are designed to control. To illustrate this idea I shall look at a Spanish film directed by Daniel Monzón called *Celda 211* (2009). As the title indicates, the film is a drama that deals with a rebellion that takes place in a prison. From the perspective of the Panopticon, what is striking is that the prisoners appropriate the surveillance system for themselves. That is to say, they are constantly aware of the CCTV system which acts as the eyes through which the authorities (and the audience) see what the prisoners are doing. They know where the cameras are and use them for their own benefit to communicate with the prison authorities (and manipulate them by 'performing' in front of, or covering, the lenses). They could be said to act in front of them because they know that extreme acts of violence will have the maximum effect if they are seen by the authorities.

(Continued)

(Continued)

This opens up a different set of possibilities for interpretation based on the work of Michel de Certeau. In his book, *The Practice of Everyday Life* (1988), de Certeau explored the way ordinary people resist or subvert mechanisms of control. For Certeau (and other writers like Merquior, 1985) Foucault's surveillance model is too reductive. De Certeau criticized Foucault saying that his method was one of 'first, *cut out*, then *turn over*' (62). What he meant by this was that Foucault cut out a particular practice associated with the Panopticon principle and over-generalized it in such a way that it explains everything. In this way he converts society into a wholly oppressive place of vigilance where no one seems to be able to escape the discipline society. The irony is that Foucault's own discourse becomes 'theoretically Panoptical, *seeing everything*' (63). However, to argue in Foucault's favour, he did maintain that where there is power there is also resistance (Foucault, 1976/1996: 95); nevertheless, his use of Bentham's Panopticon tends to emphasize the supremacy of surveillance and control.

This opens up an interesting debate concerning the extent to which individuals live in asphyxiating conditions of surveillance and to what extent people are able, as in *Celda 211*, to subvert societal disciplines and controls.

I shall now take this idea of discourse a little further and in another direction. One of Foucault's claims was that: you cannot remove power from knowledge and reason, you can only become more conscious of the way power and reason function together in producing knowledge and social control. In considering Foucault's claim that 'man is a recent invention' I want to start showing why Foucault's work is sometimes associated with what is called postmodernism.

Man as a recent invention! 'Man' in the discourses of the sciences

One idea that Foucault develops which seems particularly postmodern (although Foucault did not describe it as such and rejected the label) is that 'man' is a comparatively recent invention. Foucault made this provocative, even outrageous, claim in *The Order of Things* asserting that, within the context of European culture since the sixteenth century, 'man is an invention of recent date' and one, perhaps, 'nearing its end'. What Foucault points out is that if, in some kind of catastrophe, the scientific discourses in which human beings have been described were to disappear 'then one can certainly wager that man would be erased, like a face drawn in sand at the edge of the sea' (Foucault, 1966/1974: 386).

What this suggests is that there is no human 'essence' but that what a given society understands human beings to be at any given point is a product of the kinds of discourses that it produces about itself (this is associated with what is regarded as **anti-essentialism**). Foucault went on to claim that discourses are 'practices that systematically form the object of which they speak' (Foucault, 1969/2002: 54). This idea has been enormously suggestive, and links Foucault's work thematically with traits that many critics associate with both poststructuralism and postmodernism (Sarup, 1993), and can be applied to any domain of knowledge. To give a more detailed idea of how this anti-essentialist claim might work in practice, I will discuss Foucault's Nietzschean notion of history.

Goodbye to identity! The dissolution of 'history' and the genealogical approach

Another area of Foucault's thought which has been drawn into postmodern discussions is his Nietzschean view of history. Foucault takes a series of Nietzsche's writings and extrapolates from them a theory of history which he names '**genealogy**'. Very simply put, genealogical analysis resists more traditional accounts of history that assume it is a coherent narrative; the genealogical approach prefers to see history as a complex human construction. Once again, we see how practices 'systematically form the object of which they speak'. To illustrate this I shall start with the following quotation where Foucault outlines some of the key ideas of genealogy as he sees it:

> In short, genealogy demands relentless erudition. Genealogy does not oppose itself to history as the lofty and profound gaze of the philosopher might compare to the molelike perspective of the scholar; on the contrary, it rejects the metahistorical deployment of ideal significations and indefinite teleologies. It opposes itself to the search for 'origins'. (Foucault, 1984: 77)

There are three basic points which Foucault, with the help of Nietzsche, develops here. First, the historian of a genealogical approach does not adopt the more traditional role of the all-seeing 'objective' writer mediating events beyond personal interests and obsessions. Second, history cannot be understood as teleological, that is, it is not ineluctably moving toward some fixed end (Christian apocalypse, Hegelian totality or Marxist revolution). Third, history cannot be reduced to finding 'origins': they are understood as multiple, fragmented or lost – history does not precede historical discourse, it is a product of it. Historians might search for the origins of the Second World War but these always imply earlier origins and so on ad infinitum.

Another factor that tends to align Foucault's work with the many thinkers who are considered as postmodern (and/or poststructuralist) is his notion of identity. If history cannot be traced to clearly recognizable origins or seen as working towards fixed ends, this has profound consequences in terms of establishing any kind of identity, whether it be personal or historical. As Foucault explains, those who try to fix identity through descent are seeking for unification or a coherent identity but the genealogist aims to study 'numberless beginnings' in such a way that it 'permits the dissociation of the self, its recognition and displacement as an empty synthesis, in liberating a profusion of lost events' (81).

In seeing identity as fragmented and dispersed, no longer reducible to the old notions of stability, it is possible to see how Foucault's ideas have been linked to those of the later Barthes, Derrida and Lacan. What all share in common is a deep suspicion of foundational truths (based on some kind of unproblematic origin) and essentialist views of identity which assume it exists as a collection of essential features which can be uncovered through analysis (this is why I used the term 'anti-essentialist' above). In the context of trying to fix history through lineages, Foucault argues that the genealogical approach 'fragments what was thought unified: it shows the heterogeneity of what was imagined consistent with itself' (82).

What this means is that all the old ideas of intelligible historical movements, and immutable historical laws must be abandoned for the genealogical approach, which is constantly questioning the so-called truths of history and searching for what has been left out of the historical tales that historians tell. This involves putting historians back into history so that they no longer claim to be offering a disinterested view and recognize that they always write from a particular place and in a particular moment. They cannot pretend to objectivity or neutrality as if the past were a series of 'facts'.

The genealogist, then, is not in the business of constructing coherent narratives of history legitimated by claims of truth and objectivity, but working in the opposite direction: s/he is something of an iconoclast challenging the idea that historical discourse can mediate the past. As we saw earlier, Foucault insists that truth is the product of discourses, not something that precedes them. The genealogist challenges the idea of continuity and universal laws, preferring to expose the discontinuities and lack of historical forces by focusing very carefully on incidents. Coherent identity is another myth to be consigned to the past, as is the idea of discovering absolute truths – all is conditioned by personal interests and the kinds of questions asked.

Practising genealogical history: everything you wanted to ask about Foucault but were afraid to ask (Eric Cartman)

In Trey Parker and Matt Stone's *South Park* there is an episode (season one, episode 13) where Eric Cartman seeks his missing father. The episode can be seen as an allegory of Foucault's attitude to truth, identity, reason and the genealogical approach to history. Cartman's mother explains how she met his father at a drunken barn dance. The first man she kissed was a Native American, Chief Running Water. On hearing this, Cartman dresses up as a Native American and looks for his father. Chief Running Water explains that Eric's mother was with him but that he is not his father because she went off with the black American Chef. In the next scene we see Eric complete with an Afro hair-do and speaking in the argot of the black American rapper. Yet a quick visit to Chef reveals that Carman's mother left him to kiss other characters like his teacher, Mr Garrison, and even the entire American football team of the Denver Broncos (in fact nearly everyone has had some romantic or sexual encounter with Cartman's mother).

It is possible to see this as allegorical because we see that Cartman's identity changes according to what he *thinks* explains him as an origin. Reason searches for truth in fixities but gets lost in a multitude of possibilities and false starts. His present and future are dependent on this attempt to stabilize his identity through a search for some kind of foundation. However, his identity, centred on a series of lost origins, dissolves. The truth of the self is dependent on this effort to find a narrative that can explain him. The moment he thinks he is Native American or black American, his cultural references and allegiances change (once he transforms himself into a rapper he despises the Native Americans). Cartman's struggle to define the self through historical origins and shifting symbolic allegiances ironically results in the dissolution of the unity of the subject.

Cartman can be said to be trying to construct a discourse of the self founded on notions of origin, clarity and continuity, but all his efforts fail and he merely looks ridiculous (this very much reflects the Nietzschean ironizing that influenced Foucault). Cartman, like Foucault's traditional historian, is not searching for knowledge in a disinterested way: he is obsessed by origin as truth (although he does not mistake truth for a teleological goal); his identity is like 'man as a recent invention' – it is the product of explanatory discourses. His search for the self seems to confirm Foucault's attack on essentialism: Cartman has no essential identity, it is dependent on who he thinks his father is – this is the foundation that ultimately fails. At the end he is still at the beginning: his exploration of identity, truth and origin has resulted in a series of temporary constructions, all of which have proven to be defective.

Finally, this little allegory can be used to reflect on concepts like poststructuralism and postmodernism and how erroneous it would be (ironically from a 'poststructuralist' or 'postmodernist' perspective) to suggest that these concepts (or anything else) has an essential identity. From this point of view, the postmodern, etc. is not something essential, with a fixed unproblematic identity, but something which has to be constructed, like Eric Cartman's father, in discourse.

Genealogy: a further note on practice

As far as practising the writing of history is concerned you may find some of these ideas troubling. For example, when reading about the Holocaust or other brutal assaults on

(Continued)

(Continued)

human dignity, you may be more inclined to accept the kinds of conventions that Foucault is at pains to challenge. You may want to acknowledge that there are 'truths' about the barbaric treatment of peoples and that there is some coherence or a set of objective facts to back up the condemnation of the perpetrators of repression and torture. Yet the genealogical approach would not attempt to establish truths, origins or objective facts. Rather, it would tend to intervene to challenge accounts which attempt to construct a sense of an objective, seamless history with clearly defined origins all leading towards an inevitable conclusion. Like practising deconstruction, it is worth considering that the approach has far-reaching implications which may challenge the very bases of our thinking in ways that we might find uncomfortable. This abandoning of historical certainties is very much in keeping with postmodern views of history (see Further Reading); however, this style of reading has not entirely undermined the possibilities of understanding the past, it just problematizes the writing of it.

Foucault and the history of sexuality

To conclude this chapter I want to return to Foucault's notion of discourse and continue the debate on history with relation to the idea that 'practices systematically form the object of which they speak'. For this I will discuss Foucault's important contribution to our understanding of the **history of sexuality** where, in his first volume on the subject, he shows how, in the nineteenth century, sexuality was gradually made into a 'science' and thereby became subject to legal, medical, political and educational controls. Foucault's history of sexuality is a discursive approach which resembles that of *Discipline and Punish* because, like the case of criminality, sex is seen to be constructed within discourses which produce the official 'scientific' knowledge and truths which enable the social control of the sexualized body (the 'bio-politics' mentioned above). Again, Foucault emphasizes the relationships between the production of knowledge (about sex) and power – and the way discourses function to regulate, objectify and normalize sexual behaviour (1976/1990: 6f.). Foucault actually proposes that the history of sexuality 'must be written from the viewpoint of a history of discourses' (69).

However, Foucault's arguments about the policing of sexuality sometimes take unexpected turns. He argues that if there have been repressive functions there was also what he calls 'a discursive explosion' (17) which challenges the 'repressive hypothesis' which holds that Western societies since the eighteenth century have been characterized by repressing certain kinds of sexuality and silencing discussion of it. Foucault articulated this in a paradoxical way by saying that it was his aim to examine a society which had castigated itself for more than a century for its hypocrisy and which spoke 'verbosely of its own silence' and took 'great pains to relate in detail the things it does not say' (8). This means that if everyday social relations (like those between parents and children, teachers and pupils, etc.) were characterized by tact and discretion (18) this was not the case in terms of official analytical discourses or specialized forms of knowledge which effectively managed or policed sex (24) within a wider matrix of bureaucratic and institutional controls.

There are two further aspects I want to emphasize in Foucault's first volume of *The History of Sexuality*. The first is that it is possible to see the proliferating discourses as an attempt to circumscribe sexual activity within a 'strict economy of reproduction' and 'reproduce labour capacity' and 'perpetuate the form of social relations' so that sexuality would be 'sexually useful and politically conservative'. The second is that 'our epoch has initiated sexual heterogeneities' (36–7). What this entails is that, after the eighteenth century, discourses on the normative sexuality practised by married couples faded into the background to be replaced by the 'peripheral sexualities' of children (for example, masturbation) and the 'unnatural' or 'perverted' practices of 'those who did not like the opposite sex', and the ill, the mad and the criminal classes (38–9). The initiation of 'sexual heterogeneities' implies that society, while producing discourses on these 'peripheral sexualities' that created powers over them (through surveillance and separation, etc.), did *not* seek to eradicate them as such.

Once again, 'power' is the key word here. This can be illustrated with relation to Foucault's reading of the discourses produced about masturbation. Foucault argued that while enormous effort seemed to go into the elimination of the 'vice' of masturbation, it was a task that was 'bound to fail'. This led Foucault to speculate that masturbation 'was not so much an enemy as a support' whose continued existence aided the technologies of social control. The discourses that condemned and sought to root out a child's inevitable and burgeoning sex drive had the effect of increasing power over the mind and body (42f.).

Oversimplification Warning

Much of Foucault's history of sexuality is speculative and he constantly tries out ideas by asking multiple questions. Thus, Foucault's history of sexuality, in line with his genealogical thinking, is not a stable set of 'facts' but a tentative probing.

The homosexual as a recent invention

Returning to Foucault's argument that man is a recent invention, it is also possible to state that the homosexual and lesbian are recent inventions. Foucault explained that the sodomite existed prior to the homosexual as an aberration condemned by the Christian church but homosexuality (and all other sexual practices considered 'perversions') was the product of nineteenth-century discourses on sexuality:

> We must not forget that the psychological, psychiatric, medical category of homosexuality was constituted from the moment it was characterized – Westphal's famous article of 1870 on 'contrary sexual sensations' can stand as its date of birth – less by a type of sexual relations than by a certain quality of sexual sensibility, a certain way of inverting the masculine and the feminine in oneself. [...] The sodomite had been a temporary aberration; the homosexual was now a species. (43)

All this is a part of the medicalization of sex which links into another Foucauldian claim: that this medicalization was not so much about repression (although it would include prohibition) but *production* (105). Scientific discourses actually produce new 'subjectivities' creating new subjective spaces for different sexual orientations. In this way it is possible to see that if, on the one hand, sex had been made into a science, the body, as mentioned above, could then be subjected to legal, medical, political and educational control. Thus, once a new 'condition' or 'disease' is produced ideological forms of control can categorize, marginalize, judge, condemn and/or 'treat' the affected individuals. On the other hand, this all helped to initiate the subject positions of 'sexual heterogeneities' (43).

So, a man once condemned as a sinning sodomite would become a diseased and perverted homosexual and same-sex relations (given names like auto-monosexualist or homosexual) would be classified along with zoophiles, mixoscopophiles, gynecomasts and dyspareunists (to name only a fraction of the different sexual conditions that were subject to analysis and treatment) (43). However, at the same time there was 'a visible explosion of unorthodox sexualtities' which, even though dependent 'on procedures of prohibition', actually ensured 'the proliferation of specific pleasures and the multiplication of disparate sexualities' (49) and the 'solidification and implantation of an entire sexual mosaic' (53).

And yet, in a further twist, Foucault claimed that all these medical discourses were part of a 'science of evasion' because they refused to speak of 'sex itself' by concerning themselves with 'aberrations, perversions, exceptional oddities, pathological abatements, and morbid aggravations'. Thus, the medical discourses were subordinated to 'the imperatives of a morality' which disguised itself under a 'medical norm'. Here again, it is possible to see the relations between the use of 'reason' and the production of knowledge, truth and power. This is because the 'pornography of the morbid' set itself up as 'the supreme authority in matters of hygienic necessity' promising public health by cleansing society of venereal disease, 'defective individuals, [and] degenerate and bastardized populations' (53–54). If the biology of reproduction seemed to conform to pre-established scientific norms, the 'medicine of sex', which sought to create knowledge out of sexual aberration, was a 'stubborn will to unknowledge' which evaded the 'truth', the obvious evidence of sexuality that it studied. That is to say, it isolated all kinds of sexual practices but discounted them as perversions of a singular normative sexual 'truth' rooted in monogamous, marital, heterosexual relations.

Taking into account the wider implications of Foucault's history of sexuality it is possible to see that sexual practices have not always been understood, judged or controlled in the same way. For example, in ancient Greece and Rome all kinds of sexual possibilities between men were known and practised but were not subject to official condemnation or control – nor were they considered psychological complexes, nervous disorders or physical illnesses. Foucault made the point that in various parts of the world (like China, Japan, India, Rome or in Arabo-Moslem cultures) sex is, or has been, associated with the art of pleasure, not as something to be subjected to medical controls and regulation (see the *Kama Sutra*) (57), although he did not argue that the *ars erotica* (the erotic arts) completely disappeared from Western discourses on sexuality.

Following Foucault, these observations have led cultural critics to talk of sexual identities as culturally or 'historically constructed' (105) and consider questions of the social production of subjectivity. Foucault went further than this by suggesting that in just a few centuries 'a certain inclination' has led Western societies to direct the question of what it is to be human to sex: that is, 'sex as history, as signification and discourse' (78). To sum up, the exploration of the regulatory production of sexuality in Foucault's work (and the culturally productive possibilities of prohibition) has extended themes already introduced in the chapters on Lacan and will prepare you for the next chapter which will continue discussion of Foucault with relation to Judith Butler's ideas on 'gender trouble'.

Summary of key points

In this chapter we have seen that, like Derrida, Foucault has helped to develop ideas that help to question the foundations of the self, knowledge, truth and reason, and this has provided arguments to challenge all forms of essentialism. Thus, Foucault, like Barthes, Lacan, Althusser and Derrida, rejects essentialist versions of reality, preferring to concentrate on cultural, historical, philosophical constructions of it. Reality is not so much denied as seen as the product of the way discourses interconnect with power. It is this which aligns his work with both poststructuralism and postmodernism. These themes and others like self-regulation, surveillance and control have been explored with relation to Foucault's use of Bentham's 'Panopticon' and these have been complemented by Foucault's theory of history as genealogy and his history of sexuality.

Further reading

Foucault (general): A good place to get a broad idea of Foucault's scope is to explore Paul Rabinow's *The Foucault Reader: An Introduction to Foucault's Thought* (Foucault, 1984). This contains key essays and a number of useful interviews. To get a more profound idea of Foucault's notion of the way knowledge intersects with truth and power see his *Michel Foucault: Power/ Knowledge. Selected Interviews and Other Writings* (1980). This is a collection of interviews with Foucault where he set out his ideas in a highly accessible form. Michael Kelly's *Critique and Power: Recasting the Foucault/Habermas Debate* (1994) is a very useful collection of essays including a number by Foucault which pits his theories concerning power against those of Jürgen Habermas (who will be discussed in Chapter 11). This book illustrates how Foucault's ideas continue to be relevant to contemporary political debates but also indicates where critics see weaknesses in his approaches.

Foucault and history: As indicated in this chapter, Foucault has been seen as a key influence over poststructuralist and postmodern approaches to history. Attridge et al.'s *Post-Structuralism and the Question of History* (1987) is a reader that pulls together a host of controversial (postmodern) approaches to history (and challenges to the postmodern view). Hayden White's *Metahistory: The Historical Imagination in Nineteenth-Century Europe* (1973) and *Tropics of Discourse* (1978) are classic works in this genre as is his *Figural Realism* (1999) – they all draw attention to the problems of writing history and complicate the distinctions made between literary and historical writing. Keith Jenkins has been a tireless advocate of postmodern approaches – see his *Re-thinking History* (1991), *The Postmodern History Reader* (1997) and *Refiguring History* (2003).

Foucault gender and sexuality: Foucault's writings have been of enormous importance to many studies concerned with how men and women are represented within heterosexually biased cultures and those that deal with questions of homophobia. A related area is one focused on sexual identities and the HIV/Aids epidemic, which often analyses homophobic attitudes. Susan Hekman's *Feminist Interpretations of Michel Foucault* (1996) is a collection of essays on Foucault which gives an idea of his importance to feminist thinking and discussions concerning gender and sexuality. Hekman's introduction offers a very cogent overview of Foucault's importance. Jeffrey Weeks's *Sex, Politics and Society: The Regulation of Sexuality since 1800* (1989) is a very detailed Foucauldian approach to the subject stated in the title. The book was first published in 1981 but I recommend the second edition because it includes an extra chapter on discourses constructed around AIDS. Kenneth MacKinnon's edited collection *The Politics of Popular Representation* (1992) is just one of many books which reflect the enormous influence Foucault has had on research into gender, sexuality and AIDS.

10

Gender and Sexuality

Judith Butler

Learning goals

- To appreciate how Judith Butler's work on gender and sexuality dovetails into Foucault's discursive approach.
- To see how Butler's ideas link to other poststructuralist writers (like Lacan and Derrida) in terms of the way she theorizes identity, particularly with relation to gender and sexuality.
- To see how some of the key ideas might be put into practice.
- To begin to get an idea of how poststructuralist approaches can be thought of as postmodern.

Concepts

The key concepts introduced in this chapter are: sex, gender, sexuality, gender sub-version, gender as performative and postmodern feminism.

Introduction

As this is the last section on poststructuralist theory Butler's theorization of gender is used as a way of summing up a number of dominant themes that have been introduced in the earlier chapters. The chapter begins by describing the importance of Butler's project and pointing out how her work can be seen as growing out of Foucault's. Later sections are dedicated to explaining how

Butler adopts a radical discursive approach to gender and how she challenges normative heterosexual notions of gender and, through an engagement with other feminists like Esther Newton, Monique Wittig and Gayle Rubin, effectively deconstructs gender as a binary structure. The final sections consider her idea that gender is 'performative' and that it is dependent on repetition and historical 'sedimentation', as well as outline the possibilities for gender subversion and feminist politics. Possible critiques are also considered with relation to the way the ideas might work in practice.

Judith Butler and the weave of theory

The North American feminist philosopher Judith Butler is well known for her poststructuralist interventions into questions of gender, political and queer theory, ethics, hate speech and censorship (among others). However, this chapter will be limited to a discussion of her influential study *Gender Trouble* (1999), which has had an influence on many areas of the humanities. Butler's meditations on gender reflect Foucault's hypothesis that 'the project of a science of the subject has gravitated, in ever narrowing circles, around the question of sex' (1976/1990: 70). We will see that Butler is also interested in what Foucault expressed as 'the truth of the subject in the other who knows' and the knowledge that subjects are supposed to possess but are not aware of. For Butler, like Foucault, there is no 'natural property inherent in **sex** itself' but truths are made possible 'by virtue of the tactics of power' (70). You may notice that Foucault's formulation echoes a theme discussed in the chapters on Lacan: the truth emerges with relation to the other who is supposed to know – another feature which links Foucault's work to what has become associated with poststructuralist ways of thinking. Butler, then, takes up important themes developed by Foucault in his 'science of the flesh' (70) and thus situates herself theoretically with those thinkers commonly thought of as poststructuralist.

Troubling gender through poststructuralist theory: the project

One of the reasons why Butler wrote her ground-breaking book *Gender Trouble* (1999, first published in 1990) was to criticize 'a pervasive heterosexual assumption' in the feminist theory of the time. What she noticed was that it tended to restrict the meaning of **gender** 'to received notions of masculinity and femininity' and set up 'exclusionary gender norms' which where often homophobic. Her perception of her writing as opposing 'regimes of truth' (including a strategy that resists setting up a new normative 'gendered way of life' as a model), linked to an effort to open up new possibilities for gender (1999: vii–viii), is something else which puts her firmly in the Foucauldian tradition.

If Butler's approach is aligned to Foucault's it also engages with what she calls 'French poststructuralism' because she critiques a number of important French poststructuralist feminists (like Julia Kristeva and Monique Wittig) who had considerable influence over the direction feminism was taking in the 1980s. She is also aware that the term poststructuralism lumps together disparate writers who may or may not share things in common. Butler emphasizes that her approach to the various strands of poststructuralism is not to apply them in a formalistic way, where they are cut off from social contexts and political aims, but to 'subject these theories to a specifically feminist reformulation' centred on gender (ix). Some of the basic questions Butler addresses are about how non-normative sexual practices call into question the stability of gender linked to questions like, what is a woman, or a man? That is to say, if gender is not understood as 'consolidated through normative **sexuality**' (xi), then is it 'troubled' or destabilized through queer sexual practices?

For Butler, the problem for those who practise non-normative sex is that they tend to fall outside orthodox gender distinctions. For example, it has been suggested that a transsexual cannot really be described as a 'woman' or a 'man' but must be defined in terms of transformation or 'in-betweenness'. Then there is the case of lesbians who claim that 'butches' have nothing to do with being a man and others who claim that their 'butchness' is or was 'only a route to a desired status as a man' (xi–xii). These examples suggest that the normative categories of sexuality and gender simply fail to capture all these positions in their descriptive net and that words like 'butchness' do not indicate an unproblematic relation between the choice of sexual partner and perceived gender identity.

Oversimplification Warning: sex, gender and sexuality

In Butler's work it is important to distinguish between sex, gender and sexuality. Sex is a question of distinguishing between male and female (which usually relies on the establishment of biological differences, the isolation of particular chromosomes, hormonal characteristics, internal and external reproductive/sex organs, presence or not of hair, the structure of the body, etc.). Gender describes the characteristics that a given culture understands as masculine or feminine, dependent on social interactions and the assimilation of social norms, while sexuality concerns how individuals are classified with relation to sexual attitudes, orientation, choices and behaviour, which are often used to define what is intrinsically or properly male of female. Gender can be thought of as 'the cultural meanings that the sexed body assumes' (10) yet this sexed body is not something that exists prior to culture. As we will see below, the simple binaries of man and woman, male and female do not describe objective features; they are themselves cultural constructs.

In Foucauldian fashion, Butler subjects gender to a set of probing questions in order to show how the concept is often treated as if it were an 'interior essence'. The problem with this is that it creates 'an expectation that ends up producing the very phenomenon that it anticipates' (xiv). Thus, there is no essence of gender waiting to be discovered (through sexual practice or anything else): as in Foucault, gender is produced in regulatory discourses. Butler challenges the idea that two sexes translate into two genders: gender itself becomes a free-floating artifice, with the consequence that man and masculine might just as easily signify a female body as a male one and vice versa (10). This means that Butler, like Freud, emphasized that pure masculinity and femininity are 'theoretical constructions of uncertain content' (Freud, 1923–1925/1961c: 258) and 'not to be found either in a psychological or biological sense' (Freud, 1905/1953: 220).

Gender, then, cannot be stabilized with relation to normative, heterosexual relations, or any other relation whether it be lesbian, gay or bi, but neither do queer sexual practices or the transformative gender-bending categories of drag, transgender or transsexuality necessarily destabilize the notion. The reason is that these sexualities and practices can be understood within the dominant discourses to be aberrations, which only serve to reinforce the heterosexual norm. Thus, fundamental to the way 'men' and 'women' have been defined, is the assignation of fixed sexual roles.

Butler, Freud and Foucault: gender troubled

One of the aspects of *Gender Trouble* that has been of most interest to cultural studies is Butler's claim that gender is performative. In order to explain this I shall begin by outlining how Butler challenges an important assumption in Freudian psychoanalysis. As already mentioned in previous chapters, Freudian psychoanalysis considers that the incest taboo operates as a founding moment of civilization because it introduces the primary laws upon which social, sexual organization is based. We saw in Lacan's work that the incest taboo is seen to provide the foundations for the gendered subject. However, if we look at the structure of the heterosexual norm from Butler's point of view she detects something *prior* to this taboo.

Butler argues that there is a homosexual taboo that *precedes* the Oedipal taboo and that it reverses the Freudian 'causal narrative'. The point Butler makes is that the primary dispositions of masculinity and femininity are actually *effects* of a law regulating sexuality. Gender 'dispositions' are actually 'traces of a history of enforced sexual prohibitions' (1999: 82–3) which are hidden (and repressed). What this means is that there are no essential sexual 'dispositions' prior to the laws which regulate them – in a Foucauldian manoeuvre we can see that law/discourse mistakes its categorizations for something essential that precedes it. Thus, gender categories involve the mistaking of the effect for the cause. Here it is useful to return to the Barthesian notion that culture is constantly mistaken for 'nature'.

This observation has wide-ranging consequences for an understanding of gender and sexuality because the dominant presumption that the gender categories of 'man' and 'woman' are ineluctably linked to 'masculine' and 'feminine' heterosexual practices, behaviours and dispositions is radically undermined. In Derrida's terms (and Derrida is an important theoretical source in Butler's work), all these categories would have to be written 'under erasure'. This argument is reminiscent of a number of ideas I introduced in Chapter 2. There I described Monique Wittig's notion that the terms 'man' and 'woman' are not 'natural facts' but 'political categories' (Wittig, 1981: 17) and that 'one is not born a woman' – one becomes one – one is culturally constructed as man or woman. I also discussed Wittig's point that women and men are coerced to correspond, in mind and body, with 'the idea of nature' that has been established for them (17). From this Butler argues that the heterosexual norm is the foundation that oppresses women in general but also the lesbian and gay communities (and this could be extended to bisexuality). Gender as 'nature' (and the binaries it implies) is not based on some neutral 'natural' ground but on the dominant (restraining heterosexual) discourses which construct it. In this context Butler borrows from the work of Gayle Rubin (1975) to make the point that the incest taboo is not only a prohibition of sexual relations with intimate family members but serves also as a sanction, a coercive measure, that controls the free play of sexual desire and consolidates heterosexual desire as a sexual norm.

The reason for this is to do with the way cultures reproduce themselves. In Western cultures, the institution of exogamy (marrying outside the immediate family circle) functions to preserve 'the particular social identity of the kinship group' (Butler, 1999: 93). Thus, it is possible to see, as in Foucault, how the control of sexuality is fused with the movement of wider political power. Butler goes on to apply a Foucauldian idea to Rubin's claim that before the incest taboo, and the transformational processes that render biological males and females into gendered men or women, children contain 'all the sexual possibilities available to human expression' (Rubin in Butler, 94). Foucault's idea is that there is no sexuality *before* taboos or the law because the law produces *both* heterosexual and homosexual positions (although there may be a certain ambiguity in his later work (123)).

All this is linked to Foucault's claim that the regulation of sexuality through heterosexual discourses actually produces the thing it claims to be discovering – homosexual desire is not, in itself, repressed, something that needs to be uncovered as an object of medical or clinical analysis. It is conceived as aberrant, non-normative, 'a complex', etc. and *produced* in normative discourses in such a way that 'repressed desire' is circulated in the discursive spaces that are opened up for it. Following Foucault, Butler recognizes the productive possibilities of the 'prohibitive law' (92) and sees gender categories linked to sexuality as de-essentialized. Thus, Butler agrees with Foucault that the body is not 'sexed' in any 'significant sense' before 'its determination within a discourse through which it becomes invested with an "idea" of natural or essential sex' (117).

In this way it is possible to see how Foucault's and Butler's positions entail a radical discursive approach to explain sex, gender and sexuality.

(Again, Foucault's ideas are drawn into a debate which is self-consciously poststructuralist.) This has connections with Lacan's claims that gender is something constructed culturally and that it is the entry into the Symbolic that causes divisions on the grounds of gender. This opens up the possibility that gender is not fixed and that things could be otherwise, an important idea in Judith Butler's work. All this has implications for subversive, non-normative sexuality because if this is possible it will only be realizable from within the laws expressed within given cultural matrices. That is, only when the law 'turns against itself and spawns unexpected permutations of itself' will the 'culturally constructed body' be liberated – not to some kind of 'natural' past but to 'an open future of cultural possibilities' (119).

A lesbian is not a woman

In this context Butler develops a series of important ideas (that will help to throw light on the idea of **gender as performative**) through an engagement with Monique Wittig's writing on gender. For example, Wittig makes the provocative statement that 'a lesbian is not a woman'. This entails that the word 'woman' exists only as 'a term that stabilizes and consolidates a binary oppositonal relation to a man' – that relation being heterosexuality (143). Witttig's claim is that non-reproductive lesbian relations transcend the binary opposition between woman and man and that, therefore, lesbians have no sex (144). These assertions are dependent on recognizing that Wittig understands sex distinctions as categorical fictions serving the purposes of reproductive sexuality. Get rid of procreative sex and 'man' and 'woman' no longer have their descriptive power, for there would be no point in naming them as such (Wittig, 1981). Following Wittig (and de Beauvoir), Butler uses this to argue that 'one is not born female, one *becomes* female' (just as one is not born male) and that to be lesbian creates a third gender category, which 'radically problematizes both sex and gender as stable political categories of description' (Butler, 1999: 144).

However, if lesbianism offers certain radical possibilities Butler is careful not to oversimplify 'heterosexuality', as she feels Wittig does, by seeming to believe that only non-heterosexual identities can bring about the end of the 'heterosexual regime'. What Butler argues is that it is extremely problematic to assume the 'systemic integrity of heterosexuality' and conceive of other sexualities as 'outside' the 'heterosexual matrix'. This is partly because lesbian and gay culture can be understood as 'embedded in the larger structures of heterosexuality', even if they are understood as having subversive or 'resignificatory' relationships to it (154). Also, heterosexuality is not necessarily as simplistic as it may seem because there are 'structures of psychic homosexuality within heterosexual relations' and vice versa (155). For example, cross-gender fantasies may be played out within 'normative' heterosexual relationships (and vice versa).

Butler also challenges Wittig's idea that to be lesbian or gay is 'no longer to know one's sex' because these practices render sex 'an impossible category of identity'. Yet, as Butler illustrates, in practice these positions do not necessarily abandon traditional gender categories. She cites the case of a femme lesbian who explained that 'she likes her boys to be girls' meaning that the category of 'being a girl' serves as the context which resignifies 'masculinity' within a 'butch' identity. Thus, a sense of 'masculinity' is thrown into relief against a culturally recognizable 'female body' (156) – even if the terms masculine and feminine are destabilized 'as they come into erotic interplay' (157).

Of course the same can be adapted to gay, bi or heterosexual relations so that there are multiple ways in which the categories can be adapted to sexual desire and gratification. We see here that *a sense of* sexual identity is relevant, but it is unstable and in constant play. These identities only seem to mean something as *relations* to one another, and this brings us back to the contexts of (post)structuralism. The integrity of gender identities (like any identity) is dependent on a series of relations, exclusions or absences (163f.), which create the fragile and fictitious sense of self, but which is potentially threatened by that which is excluded or left in the margin. These ideas not only help us understand how Butler's approach is related to deconstruction and Lacanian psychoanalysis but, as mentioned above, also serve to prepare us to appreciate her claims about gender being performative.

Gender and performativity

In order to explain gender as 'performative' Butler uses Foucault's idea (Foucault, 1975/1977: 28f.) that in the modern prison the basic strategy is not to repress desire but to oblige the bodies of prisoners to 'signify the prohibitive law as their very essence, style, and necessity' (Butler, 1999: 171). Prisoners, then, have their criminality inscribed on them in such a way that it becomes the very essence of their being. Criminality, which is embodied in law, is projected onto the body and becomes its meaning. What Butler does is to use this idea of inscribed meaning and adapt it to explain how gender functions.

Butler's basic argument is that gestures, acts and desire generate 'the effect of an internal core or substance,' but this is produced *on the surface* of the body, through 'the play of signifying absences that suggest, but never reveal, the organizing principle of identity as a cause'. These acts and gestures, etc. are 'performative' because the essence or identity that they seem to express are 'fabrications' created and upheld through 'corporeal signs and other discursive means' (173). Here I shall consider some of the main implications of Butler's line of reasoning.

First, as mentioned above, the body has no gender essence which precedes its introduction into the discourses which describe it, inscribe it and regulate it (something that fits in with poststructuralist thinking). To put this simply, carefully selected features associated with femininity or masculinity within normative social discourses (like heterosexual desire, breasts, vaginas, penises, testes, manifestations of aggressive behaviour, passivity, etc.) are used to signify some interior essence. But, as described above, this inner essence, which seems to be described by the discourses, is actually a product of them. In some ways this is reminiscent of Lacan's idea that the introduction into the Symbolic stratifies us in terms of gender because are we distinguished from one another by the pronouns 'he' and 'she', and these cultural distinctions limit the free expression of instincts. What seems the inside (the gender core) is actually a product of the outside because social discourses project regulatory normative features onto the body in such a way that they seem to be discovering an essence. This creates the curious situation where the law which determines gender is effectively hidden from view. This brings us back to gender politics because the gestures, acts and desires selected by the discourses to form the illusory gender core are 'maintained for the purposes of the regulation of sexuality within the obligatory frame of reproductive heterosexuality' (173).

To improvise around this idea for a moment: whenever a woman is called 'butch' or a man 'effeminate' or when people who practise same-sex relations are thought of as perverse, unnatural, sinning against a church, or suffering from complexes, this reflects the normative heterosexual matrix that polices gender and sexuality. These are not innocent or neutral 'scientific' descriptions but culture mistaken for 'nature' which serve as oppressive value judgements. It would be equally possible to say something like: 'People behave in many different ways, have distinct and variable sexual orientations and desires (or no sexual desire at all) – full stop. In this way there is only behaviour and desire, etc.' From this point of view, terms like butch, effeminate, homosexual, etc. would not really make sense. In this way we are better able to see that they are cultural constructions which depend on some prior normative, regulatory definition of gender.

Drag, not such a drag: deconstructing gender

Butler's use of Esther Newton's anthropological studies takes us closer to the idea of gender as performative. What Butler found interesting in Newton's work (Newton, 1972) was the idea that the structure of impersonation uncovers one of the main mechanisms through which gender is constructed and maintained. This brings us back to the play between the inner and the outer because Newton maintains that drag is a 'double inversion' that indicates that appearance is illusory. Drag (male cross-dressing) suggests the outside is feminine but the inner essence is masculine yet, at the same time, it suggests the opposite: that the outside (the body as gender) is masculine and the inner essence is feminine.

From this Butler suggests that drag subverts the differentiation between inner and the outer psychic space and the idea of some 'true gender identity' based on behaviour. The value of drag, cross-dressing, sexual stylizations of butch/femme identities is that they often parody the idea of a primary gender identity (Butler, 1999: 174). This can help us to understand what Butler has in mind by calling gender performative. This is because the performance of cross-dressing complicates the distinction between 'the anatomy of the performer' (conditioned by male or female genitalia) and 'the gender that is being performed' (which is the opposite of the anatomy of the performer) (175).

Thus, drag sets in motion and plays on three dimensions of gender identification: the sexual anatomy of the performer, gender identity and the performance of gender. While some feminists may baulk at the idea of drag creating a culturally loaded and simplistic image of women it has the value of revealing the significant aspects of gendered experience which are 'falsely naturalized as a unity through the regulatory fiction of heterosexual coherence'. In this way drag exposes 'the imitative structure of gender itself – as well as its contingency' (175); the latter meaning that there is no necessary relation between sex, gender and behaviour. Important to this way of thinking is that there is no authentic original woman (or man) that is being copied: gender is a fantasy, a collection of culturally loaded attributes. What gender parody reveals, then, is that it is 'an imitation without an origin' (175), something which echoes a common poststructuralist assumption and looks forward to the kind of postmodern thinking that I will explore with relation to writers like Jean Baudrillard. These ideas are, to some extent, reflected in something Andy Warhol (1975/2007: 41) once wrote:

B: Is that a female impersonator?
A: Of what?

Oversimplification Warning: gender as performance

A common mistake when thinking about gender as performance is to think that whatever you perform is gender, as if it is malleable. In terms of gender, you cannot, Madonna-style, reinvent yourself at will. As Angela McRobbie has warned, *Gender Trouble* has often given rise to 'simplistic and celebratory readings' which reduce it to the banal (2005: 85). Butler's point is that while gender is a fiction or construction it is subject, as in Foucault's writing, to policing strategies. Gender may be performed according to personal desire, but its normative aspect will be a product of how it is produced within the discourses and institutions that have the power to establish its characteristics and limits (what Althusser would call the ideological apparatuses). Of course, individual behaviour will help to negotiate these characteristics and limits at any particular historical moment.

The implication of all this is that gender is now conceived of as the repeated performance of certain chosen traits which stand for being woman or man.

Traits, then, are made to *perform* gender. This could be said to introduce a certain theatricality into gender: you are not in essence a man or a woman but become one, are coerced into being one, through a kind of normative cultural script. This model undermines heterosexual coherency which is constructed within cultures and which is mistaken for an inner essence or truth. Drag, while it reflects 'hegemonic, misogynist culture', serves to denaturalize and recontextualize gender meanings while imitating 'the myth of originality itself' (1999: 176) because both drag and 'original' genders are fundamentally imitative. Here it is possible to see how deconstructive and Lacanian thinking is echoed in Butler's work. Gender, as some kind of original essence, is caught up within a signifying chain which endlessly displaces identity from one trait/trace to the next. Gender is to be found in this ritual of repetition; without it there is no gender. This is why Butler (echoing Freud and Lacan) thinks of gender as a failure: it is an ideal that no one can live up to and can never be fully internalized (176–79).

Practice: gender, performativity and contingency

It is possible to improvise around these ideas by commenting on what Butler regards as the contingency of gender. Given this model of performative gender, it is possible to imagine a society where *other* traits could be chosen as the principal features of 'normal' sexual relations. There might be endless ways that gender could be culturally constructed (if it were not abandoned altogether) yet each one of these constructions would be doomed to fail because they would all, in some way, force human beings into a categorical grid which is a simplification of multiple differences while being normative and (possibly) punitive.

If gender is performative then we have to consider up to what point it is the product of imitation and what is operating on imitation to create the prescriptive rules of behaviour. If girls and boys (taking these categories as cultural constructions and not pre-discursive essences) see others behaving in certain ways, up to what point is the copied behaviour nothing more than that? If feminine and the masculine are really more to do with emulation than essence, how do the normative gestures, behaviour and traits become consolidated in the first place? Why can a woman swing her hips or a man roll his shoulders and be thought of as 'natural' or authentically female or male? Why might the opposite signify non-woman, non-man? At what point do these become significant signs of gender? This chapter should help you to begin to pose these kinds questions (even if it cannot offer convenient answers).

You might also consider whether you think any society could be constructed on a gender-free basis and, if it so, what kind of system it would imply. Could it be that gender needs to be challenged but is, at the same time, a necessary fiction? You might remember Derrida undermining logocentrism and phonocentrism but arguing that it can never really be fully overridden. Or, as in Lacan's writings, is the (heterosexual) law necessary to sustain a symbolic system upon which some kind of identity is made possible in the first place? Asking these questions will not only help you consider Butler's ideas but engage with poststructuralist strategies in a wider sense.

Something else you might consider are the implications of Anne Fausto-Sterling's claim that, from the biological point of view, there is reason to believe that there are not just two sexes, or three (if we include male, female and hermaphrodite), but five (Fausto-Sterling, 2000). This is based on the idea that there are various intermediary states where 'women' have ovaries but with vestiges of male genitalia and vice versa. However, while this claim challenges gender as a simple binary (biological) opposition it does not provide an answer to all the arguments put forward by writers like Foucault and Butler. This is because they would probably want to insist that the five genders are still conceived within the general limits of the old fixed gender binary. Also, Fausto-Sterling's biological observations still leave the question open for those who are not biologically defined as 'intersexual'.

Genealogy and gender: gender as historical sedimentation of corporeal styles

Reviewing these basic arguments it is possible to see how Butler uses (as she openly acknowledges) a Foucauldian genealogical technique. This is because she sees gender traits of the 'real woman' or 'natural sex' as the products of historical sedimentation (which involves a genealogical approach to the subject). This means that a set of selected and ideologically loaded 'corporeal styles' are gradually mistaken for the truth of gender, which involves a 'natural configuration of bodies into sexes existing in a binary relation to one another' (1999: 178).

From this point of view gender can be seen in the repetition of bodily gestures, movements and styles which are built up in society over time. Gender performance is a *public* act that constantly reinforces a sense of gender identity for both performers and audience. For Butler, the distinction between expression and the performative is crucial. If gender attributes are not expressive of some inner essence but performative this means that there is no pre-existing identity 'by which any acts or attribute might be measured' (180). This bears a resemblance to the idea of identity found in Lacan's work when he says 'I'm like he whom I recognize to be a man, and so recognize myself as being such' (Lacan (1966/1977: 23). A 'man' does not seem to pre-exist in any fundamental way, Lacan is 'like' someone who recognizes himself as a man in terms of the culturally constructed *image* of a man.

Practice: gender and corporeal style. 'Boys' don't cry

Films like *Boys Don't Cry* (1999) can help to explore the performative aspect of gender and its value as a concept. The film is loosely based on the life of the transsexual Teena Brandon who, anatomically a woman, identified herself as a man (and has been referred to in the press since her death as Brandon Teena). Her transformation into a male was so successful that she passed as male and had several relationships with women, including Lana Tisdel, who (until Brandon was exposed as being biologically female) did not suspect Brandon was also a woman. Unfortunately for Brandon, s/he had befriended a couple of violent ex-convicts. When they discovered she was biologically a woman she was violently raped and killed by one or both of them (at the time of writing the case is still unresolved).

The fact that Brandon was convincing enough to be accepted as a man raises important questions about gender as an inner essence. If s/he could pass as a man between men and women, this would suggest that her gender performance as a male was the key to her being accepted as a man. When I say 'gender performance' I do not mean that she was necessarily 'acting' but referring to behaviour that would be regarded as normatively male. Following Butler, this suggests that a set of selected and ideologically loaded 'corporeal styles' were mistaken for the truth of gender. This, in turn, may lead us to consider how important 'corporeal styles' are to the way gender functions *as* identity. The fact that Brandon was eventually suspected of not being a man by her murderer(s) suggests that the performative dimension was not as convincing as it might have been. However, it is significant that the two men who raped her ultimately sought the truth of her gender identity by stripping her, which suggests that, in the last instance, the biological configuration of the body is commonly seen as the ultimate sign of gender. One might speculate on what these men might have done or thought if they had discovered a hermaphrodite body. In what ways might this reinforce or question gender as performative?

Another factor worth thinking about is that when Brandon was discovered as anatomically female, this provoked such a violent reaction that s/he was murdered (like other transgender victims like Matthew Shephard, Gwen Araujo and Chrissy Lee Polis). It is worth speculating on why Brandon's behaviour provoked this violence. Are performative gender norms so ingrained in some men that their disturbance threatens the integrity of the male psyche? Another interesting detail of the Brandon case is the controversy surrounding a number of comments made by Hilary Swank, who played Brandon in the film based on Brandon's later life. Swank referred to Brandon as 'he' when she received an Oscar for the role she played. This provoked criticism from Brandon's mother, who insisted that Brandon was a woman pretending to be a man to protect herself from the abuse she had suffered as a child (*Guardian*, 29 March 2000). In turn, this provoked some transgender activists to claim that Swank's use of the masculine pronoun was correct.

It can be argued that this tends to reinforce Butler's point that gender may not be seriously destabilized by queer sexual practices. In the aftermath of Brandon's tragic murder, we end up with a situation where gender distinctions are fought over and thereby reinforced by heterosexual norms, rather than radically questioned or undermined. Transgender still seems to function within the media and in everyday language as an aberration or a deviation from the heterosexual norm. Yet the film itself can be seen as part of the hegemonic struggle to challenge prejudice and promote the acceptance of non-normative sexual practices and diversity. This is the task of activist groups who have campaigned for tolerance on the grounds of sexuality (including those like avaaz.com that have initiated campaigns to counter the 'corrective rape' perpetrated as a 'cure' for lesbianism).

Gender subversions

This brings me to Butler's arguments about how the gender binary might be subverted. The theoretical manoeuvre that Butler performs here is reminiscent of Foucault's when he claimed that discourse not only restricts but, at the same time, produces new 'subjectivities', creating new subjective spaces for different sexual orientations (Foucault, 1976/1990: 105). Butler posits the possibility of subversive gender identities in the following way. She argues, like Foucault, that the rules governing signification not only restrict but 'enable the assertion of alternative domains of cultural intelligibility'. This means that if new possibilities for gender subversion are possible it can only be *within* the practices of repetitive signification (185), something that Butler has been at pains to emphasize (1993: 95f.).

So, what would subversive repetitions look like? It is here that we come back to parodic practices like drag where bodies can 'become the site of dissonant and denaturalized' performances that serve to unmask that the 'natural' is itself performative (Butler, 1999: 186). It is in 'hyperbolic exhibitions' that the emptiness of gender categories can be revealed for what they are. Before I conclude with some comments on the implications of Butler's ideas for feminist criticism and postmodernism I shall explore how some these ideas might be put into practice.

Practice: drag, hyperbolic exhibitions and subversive repetitions

The idea of hyperbolic exhibitions and the possibilities of subversive repetitions can be explored with relation to the outrageous 'I'm a lady' sketches in the British television series *Little Britain*. The actor David Walliams plays Emily Howard, a very

(Continued)

(Continued)

unconvincing transvestite, who seems an obvious man who outrageously insists that he is a lady. Here is a man with typical male attributes like bodily hair and stereotypical 'male' interests like playing football, pretending to be a particular kind of woman. In this case a refined, upper-class lady who looks like she has walked out of the nineteenth century with flouncy frocks and an obvious wig – a representation that falls well within the traditional limits of what generally counts as a woman. The repetitive joke is that Emily (really Eddie) is forced to acknowledge that he is a man.

From Esther Newton's point of view this cross-dressing would suggest that the outside is feminine but the inner essence is masculine while suggesting the opposite: that the outside (the body as gender) is masculine and the inner essence is feminine. Butler would add that this drag performance questions that there is a 'true gender identity' based on behaviour. As far as Butler's parodic performance of gender is concerned this kind of humour, while in some ways only reinforcing gender distinctions because the male and female are clearly demarcated, underscores that all gender *is* a performance. The humorous failure of the transvestite can be read as the fate of *all* gender: it is bound to fail. The twist is that the failed transvestite is not necessarily the failure of homoerotic desire, which seems to survive intact (while played by a heterosexual actor). This (and all drag performance) initiates and plays on the three dimensions of gender identification: the sexual anatomy of the performer, gender identity and the performance of gender.

In some ways another *Little Britain* character is even more interesting (and plays on the three dimensions just mentioned). This is Bubbles DeVere (played by Matt Lucas). My reading is based on the recognition that Lucas makes no secret of being gay. The character of Bubbles is represented by Lucas as a posh, grossly overweight, sexually voracious older woman who seems to live permanently in a spa (a site where the perfect body aesthetic is sought after). Yet DeVere's (latex) body, which we usually see fully naked, breaks all the canons of contemporary feminine body aesthetics. It is possible to see this as symbol of how bodies are inscribed with meaning.

What we have here is a gay man playing a woman chasing various men (usually for financial gain or some other advantage). Thus, this is not just cross-dressing but a kind of body swapping where gender is parodied not just by the heterosexual male (as in the case of David Walliams) but by an actor whose sexual orientation poses a challenge to heterosexual norms. Thus, a whole set of multiple signs are assembled which confound the reinforcement of gender distinctions that we saw in the above example concerning Emily Howard. Here we have an actor (male), who clads himself in a female body who pursues other men. There is a double gender performance here. At the level of the actor's gender and sexuality the audience is presented with a homoerotic performance of one male pursuing same-sex relations. However, at the fictive level there is a normative MANifestation of heterosexual desire, with DeVere pursuing male partners.

However, the humour seems to also depend on the overweight body as a normative sign of unprepossessing female ugliness. This can be read as a highly ambiguous set of relations where gender subversion has been made possible *within* the standard practices of repetitive signification but also sets up structures of failure. The double performance of this kind of parody can be said to throw gender categories into disarray. This is because DeVere is ambiguously both male and female (which complicates gender as 'in-betweenness'), homosexual and heterosexual, both non-normative and, at the same time, a failed symbol of orthodoxy. This double performance of cross-body dressing further complicates the distinction between 'the anatomy of the performer' (conditioned by male or female genitalia) and the double gender that is performed. Again, added to this we have the possibility of drawing the conclusion that there is no essence or final truth of gender but that gender *is* a performance, but one which ultimately fails.

I have offered these interpretations as a way of illustrating possible practice and to aid in the understanding of some of the implications of Butler's notion of gender as performance. However, while these exercises are useful, there would be no point in endlessly illustrating the theory in this way. Of more interest would be to explore the limits or possible problems with the idea of the concept itself. For example, you might consider how ideological change or weakening opens up expressive spaces, but also keeps gender distinctions/binaries firmly in place. If you focus on the way alternative sexualities have impacted on culture since the 1990s, you can see that gay and lesbian styles have gradually taken on a certain cutting-edge chic, yet the standard gender binary is still very much in place.

We may, following Susan Bordo, ask exactly how subversive gender games are. If Butler doubts the power of queer practices and transgender to destabilize normative gender, Bordo doubts the power of parody to undermine the binary frame of gender (292f.), feeling that drag performance and cross-dressing, etc. seem 'far less destabilizing of the "binary frame" of gender' than those which do not attempt parody in the first place. The idea is that if a transgender person seems convincingly male or female and then turns out not to be what s/he seems, this may more undermining of gender than more obvious efforts to subvert the category.

Gender performativity tends to emphasize the discursive regimes that regularize gender and sexuality but has less to say about how the discourses get loosened up through lesbian and gay movements, the way clothes manufacturers latch onto alternative images, how music, TV and film help to challenge and 'renormalize' sexual identities, etc. Like much (post)structuralism the theories do not really focus very well on how change is possible through time. Rather, they tend to concentrate on how things are at a particular moment, with relation to historical sedimentation. This reflects Saussure's preference for synchronic, rather than diachronic, analysis (see Chapter 2). However, as we have seen above, Butler's ideas can be said to provide the means to better understand how subversions are possible. Like Bordo, however, you may be concerned that poststructuralist approaches, while very capable of theorizing the relations between representation, politics and power, are not very effective at actually changing the institutions themselves which govern the social world in which we live (277f.). This takes us onto Butler and gender politics.

Gender trouble and feminist politics

As mentioned above, one problem for Butler is that feminist discourses often oversimplify questions of sex and gender in such a way that the sex categories 'woman' and 'man' function to ground feminist discourses in an uncritical way. This is unfortunate because these foundational identity categories 'simultaneously work to limit and constrain in advance the very cultural possibilities that feminism is supposed to open up'. For Butler there has to be a recognition that identity is an *effect*, that it is *produced*. This assertion could lead to misunderstanding insofar as it may lead to the conclusion that Butler is claiming that identity is 'fatally determined' or 'fully artificial and arbitrary', but she does not draw this conclusion (187). Because discourses shape identity does not mean that they are completely determined or that the traits that are highlighted are totally artificial.

Butler does not go into detail on this point and it would be of interest to explore how far it is possible to understand the limits between the cultural forces working on gender distinctions and what is left when the cultural factors are removed (or if they can be). However, Butler's insistence on discourse has led some critics to criticize her work for being too dependent on discourses and reducing gender to them in such a way that the body seems to get entirely lost in the process (Bordo 1993: 38). Another possible criticism is that Butler's deconstruction of identity is also a deconstruction of politics, but she resists this conclusion. Butler insists that 'it establishes as political the very terms through which identity is articulated' by questioning 'the foundationist frame in which feminism as an identity politics has been articulated' (Butler, 1999: 189). Yet Butler's notion of gender as performance has led critics to link her notion of gender to what is known as the postmodern subject and the postmodern body – what Susan Bordo regards as **postmodern feminism** (Bordo, 1993: 215f.). To end this chapter I shall, very briefly, consider these notions as a transition to the next.

Postmodern bodies, postmodern identities, postmodern feminism

For Bordo, when gender is thoroughly fragmented by class, race, 'historical particularity' and 'individual difference'; when its meaning is 'constantly deferred' and 'endlessly multiple'; when it is rendered 'useless as an analytical category' (215), then we are in the presence of postmodern feminism. This has opened up some fierce debates within feminism concerning the (in)efficacy of the kinds of approaches I have been outlining in this and previous chapters (see Nicholson, 1990; Bordo, 1993).

In previous chapters I have discussed many of the thinkers broadly defined as poststructuralist (including Foucault) who share a very similar attitude towards identity as fundamentally fragmentary, endlessly multiple and constantly deferred. However, here these features are described as postmodern. This brings me back to a point I made when discussing Foucault: writers can be thought of as key postmodern thinkers and/or poststructuralist philosophers (even if, in the case of Foucault, they hardly use structuralist concepts). If Foucault can be claimed as poststructuralist or postmodernist and Butler can be described as poststructuralist and postmodernist, this suggests that the terms are not mutually exclusive.

This reinforces the idea that these terms are academic conveniences and do not necessarily describe clearly defined and easily distinguished theories. Thus, in the chapters to come (which look at a number of key thinkers associated with postmodernism), you will see that poststructuralist approaches, with their sceptical (discursive) notions of reason, history and identity – and manifest deep suspicion of foundational truths and essences – are often understood as major features of postmodernism. What is understood as postmodernism is itself made up of a complex series of discourses which defy easy definition but, despite categorical ambiguities, the term can help us to understand a lot about twentieth- and twenty-first-century cultures.

Summary of key points

This chapter has shown how Butler's project is linked to Foucault's and how it relates to poststructuralist approaches. Butler's deconstruction of gender has been emphasized through her radical discursive approach which challenges normative heterosexual notions. The chapter has also emphasized Butler's belief that there is no essential masculinity or femininity prior to the laws which regulate them – and that discourse mistakes its categorizations for something essential that precedes it. Her idea that gender is performative has been outlined and critiqued and we have seen how the some of the main concepts might work in practice while exploring the possibilities for gender subversion and the relations between gender 'trouble' and feminist politics and postmodernism.

Further reading

In this chapter I have focused on some of the key ideas in Butler's *Gender Trouble* but her books *Bodies that Matter* (1993) and *Undoing Gender* (2004) extend, consolidate and reconsider her earlier book. *Bodies that Matter* considers the materiality of the body and how it is caught up in discourses of sexuality and gender and illustrates her ideas with reference to films and short stories and extends her arguments to include the category of race. The essays *Undoing Gender* are part of a project to relate the problems of gender and sexuality to persistence and survival, which engage with 'New Gender Politics' (a combination of movements concerned with transgender, transsexuality and intersex that are articulated within feminist and queer theory). It also considers the question of violence with relation to things like transgender. Butler's *Giving an Account of Oneself* (2005), while not principally concerned with gender, is a profound meditation on ethics which includes valuable discussion on how subjects are constituted socially and the limits of responsibility. Angela McRobbie's *The Uses of Cultural Studies* (2005) contains a short but wide-ranging chapter on Butler's engagement with feminism and psychoanalysis. For detailed discussions of postmodern feminism see Linda Nicholson's *Feminism/Postmodernism* (1990). Stryker and Whittle's *The Transgender Studies Reader* (2006) and Hines and Sanger's *Transgender Identities* (2010) both contain collections of essays which extend many of the themes discussed in this chapter. The journal *Sexualities* provides a rich source of essays on feminist and queer theory, gender, sexuality and new gender politics as do *Body and Society* and *Studies in Gender and Sexuality* (to name only three of a considerable range). Beatriz Preciado's *Manifiesto Contra-Sexual: Prácticas Subversivas de Identidad Sexual* (*Contra-Sexual Manifesto: Subversive Practices of Sexual Identity*) (2002) is one of the most provocative analyses of gender and sexuality to appear in the last decade (reviews of the book in English can be found online and the English translation should be available soon). Another provocative book that should be available soon is Preciado's *Testo Yonqui* (2008) (which roughly translates to 'testo(osterone) junkie'). It also deals with questions of gender but also analyses the role of the pharmaceutical companies and pornography within capitalism. *Manifiesto Contra-Sexual* can be read in French because it was originally published in that language.

11

The Postmodern Condition

Daniel Bell, Jean-François Lyotard and Jürgen Habermas

Learning goals

- To appreciate how Daniel Bell's and Jean-François Lyotard's notion of contemporary society is rooted in important changes in the mode of production concentrated on information technology and the commodification of data and knowledge.
- To understand how Lyotard's conception of the postmodern condition is dependent on incredulity towards metanarratives and how this produces a crisis in how knowledge is legitimated and valued.
- To appreciate the political implications of Lyotard's insistence on language games and little narratives as an alternative to overarching grand narratives.
- To understand how Lyotard distinguishes between modernism and postmodernism in the arts and what implications this has for writing and understanding.
- To be aware of the rift between Lyotard and Jürgen Habermas in terms of their varying political and intellectual stances and the way they relate to the project of modernity.

Concepts

The key concepts introduced in this chapter are: the post-industrial society, the postmodern condition, the crisis of (or incredulity towards) metanarratives, legitimation, the grand narrative, performativity, little narratives, delegitimation and communicative rationality

Introduction

This chapter begins with some reflections on the difficult concept of post-modernism and then, as a way of contextualizing Jean-François Lyotard's general approach to the postmodern condition, reviews Daniel Bell's definition of contemporary society as the post-industrial. The chapter then looks at Lyotard's idea that the postmodern condition is a question of the crisis of metanarratives and analyses a series of other key ideas while exploring the political implications of Lyotard's work. As stated above, Lyotard's distinctions between modernist and postmodern approaches to art are explained and this is explored through an alternative introduction. The chapter is concluded by examining and comparing Lyotard's position with that of the Marxist critic Jürgen Habermas.

Postmodernism(s): an exasperating but necessary term

Of all the concepts introduced so far 'postmodernism' is probably the one that has been most widely used in so many different contexts. It is one of those words that is often employed with no contextualizing frame to make sense of the way it is being used, Hans Bertens writing of it (and other derivatives like postmodernist and postmodernity) as 'an exasperating term' (1995: 3). Terry Eagleton has made the point that the word 'postmodernism' typically refers to some form of contemporary culture, whereas the term 'postmodernity' is often used to refer to a specific historical period (Eagleton, 1996, vii) – but there is by no means wide agreement on this (for this reason Eagleton ignored the distinction).

The reason why the word has not been abandoned in academic debates is because it has become crucial to the cultural, historical, intellectual and aesthetic description of the second half of the twentieth century. For example, Fredric Jameson, while seeing the concept as 'internally conflicted and contradictory', insists that, 'for good or ill, we cannot *not* use it' (Jameson, 1991: xxii). One way out of this impasse is to adopt Brian McHale's strategy of considering that 'there "is" no such "thing" as postmodernism', if this is understood as being 'some kind of identifiable object' in the world, 'possessing attributes about which we can all agree' (McHale, 1992: 1).

This might be taken to imply that questions about postmodernism are a waste of time but McHale goes on to say that the same can be said about all kinds of terms but this does not stop us from taking them seriously. One way of thinking about postmodernism (and all its derivatives) is to adopt a 'constructivist' approach which assumes that 'data do not exist independently of a theory that constitutes them *as* data' (2). This means that critics should not assume the unproblematic existence of a period but negotiate a set of features that are to be considered pertinent to it. In this way 'postmodernism' can be used to make sense of various facets of the world and organize it according to a number of key concepts. This will be my approach. In this context Jameson observed that because postmodernism is so complex it is not something to be defined at the beginning of a study but at the end. Following this, I shall not attempt any facile overarching definition at the outset but try to give a sense of what it can mean, or has been made to mean, as the following three chapters unfold.

However, if we accept, following Raymond Williams, that it is possible to study *how* a society at a given moment in history constructs or canonizes itself by searching for meaningful patterns within a particular culture it is also important to recognize that the chosen features are always part of 'the selective tradition'. And this selective tradition is always a limited *version* of a particular culture (Williams, 1961/1992: 49–50). Thus, with this in mind, in the following chapters I shall limit my discussion of postmodernism (and its derivatives) to a number of dominant ways it has been employed to under-stand various kinds of culture and intellectual currents in (mainly) Western societies since the late 1950s and early 1960s – but without forgetting that this is a selective tradition and by no means describes everything about the so-called period.

Before I go on to discuss the post-industrial society, I want to return to what Susan Bordo defined as postmodern feminism. We saw that feminism can be defined as postmodern when it is thoroughly fragmented by class, race, 'historical particularity' and 'individual difference'; or when its meaning is 'constantly deferred' and 'endlessly multiple', or even rendered 'useless as an analytical category' (Bordo, 1993: 215). When identities of all kinds are theorized in this way they are commonly thought of as reflecting postmodern ways of thinking, and we will come back to this way of thinking in later sections. However, poststructuralist theory is not the only way of defining the postmodern. One important way of doing so is to refer to significant changes in the economic infrastructure linked to new technologies and ways of think-ing and organizing society. This is what the French philosopher Jean-François Lyotard referred to as 'the postmodern condition' (see below), and it is to this way of thinking that I shall now turn by discussing Daniel Bell's concept of the **post-industrial society**.

For whom the Bell tolls: the coming of the post-industrial society

The 'post-industrial' is a term popularized by the sociologist Daniel Bell in his influential and speculative study *The Coming of Post-Industrial Society* (1973). For Bell the post-industrial society is distinguished from the pre-industrial (an 'extractive' economy based on agriculture, mining, fishing, timber and other resources such as natural gas or oil) and the industrial (based on forms of fabrication based on energy and machine technology). A post-industrial society is founded on computers and telecommunications where knowledge replaces material goods as the most important commodity for production and exchange. If industrial society was based on machine technology, capital and labour, post-industrial society is underpinned by intellectual technology, information, knowledge and services (Bell, 1973: xc). Much of what Bell speculated upon is now a social, economic reality. In advanced capitalist societies there are now more people who know how to send an e-mail than farm a field.

Bell emphasized that in the computer age knowledge and data are made into commodities and stressed that whereas in industrial societies commodities are produced, exchanged, sold and consumed this is not the case with information and knowledge; they can be constantly circulated. It is important, however, to remember that just as industry has not done away with agriculture the post-industrial society does not replace industrial society, it is defined as the major productive force of the economic and social world. Bell did not use the word 'postmodern' but the post-industrial as the computer age has become one key way in which postmodernism has been theorized and understood.

There are many more implications to Bell's post-industrial society but, as a means of linking his ideas to the next section, I want to emphasize one more aspect of his theory: that is, his prediction of a change in attitudes towards science. Bell argued that science would be increasingly subordinated to 'state-directed goals' and would be valued for its utility. This means that knowledge would be functional rather than be valued for its own sake (xcv). This is something that became an important part of Jean-François Lyotard's conception of what he called, in an eponymous title, *The Postmodern Condition* (1984, first published in 1979), which diagnoses what he accepted as the post-industrial society (37).

Lyotard, the postmodern condition and the crisis of metanarratives

Lyotard's classic formulation of the postmodern condition grew out of a report on the influence of technology on knowledge he was commissioned to write for the Quebec government (Lyotard, 1984: xxv). The book's subtitle is 'A report on knowledge' because Lyotard reflects upon the changing conditions of knowledge taking place towards the end of the 1970s. Much of this 'report' deals with the history of science from a philosophical perspective but most critics in cultural studies have focused on a number of key ideas to do with 'legitimation', 'metanarratives', 'grand narratives' and 'performativity'. My introduction will ignore some of the more technical aspects of philosophy to reflect these themes.

Lyotard began his book by defining postmodernism. This is the state of culture seen with relation to 'the transformations which, since the end of the nineteenth century, have altered the game rules for science, literature and the arts' within the 'most highly developed societies'. Lyotard's basic strategy was to position these transformations in the context of what he calls 'the crisis of metanarratives' (xxiii). Before I discuss the crisis I will explore what he meant by **metanarratives**. Lyotard made the point that in modern societies science is not just a case of seeking for the truth of things, 'stating useful regularities', etc., it is also under an obligation to legitimate 'the rules of its own game'. These justifications of itself as knowledge are what Lyotard thinks of as discourses of **legitimation**. Thus, they carry within themselves the discourse of 'philosophy' which he refers to as a 'metadiscourse' or metanarrative.

Legitimation and the grand narrative

When a science legitimates itself with relation to a metanarrative or metadiscourse (a justificatory discourse outside itself) Lyotard understood it as making an appeal to a **grand narrative**. What he meant by this was that knowledge does not exist in a vacuum; it can be justified by appealing to some larger narrative which assumes that the production of knowledge is in the best interests of 'the people', or humanity as a whole (30f.). To simplify Lyotard's arguments, these narratives of legitimation are of two kinds: political and philosophical.

The political forms of legitimation hark back to the Enlightenment and justify scientific knowledge in terms of the way it contributes to helping humanity emancipate itself from the tyranny of monarchs and the superstitions of the church. The grand narrative that is appealed to promises emancipation, freedom and progress through the institutionalization of the basic right of education (31–2). Lyotard linked philosophical legitimation to the spirit of the modern university as it was developed in nineteenth-century Prussia by Wilhelm von Humboldt. While Humboldt agreed that science is speculative, obeying its own rules and (ideally) unconstrained by external factors, he nonetheless insisted that it had the humanist end of aiding the spiritual and moral training of the nation (32). Again, science is wedded to a grand narrative which promises human progress. What both of the grand narratives have in common is that they work toward ethical-political ends like emancipation, freedom and world peace (xxiv).

What Lyotard underscored is that in the modern university there is a conflict between the language of science 'answerable only to the criterion of truth' and the metanarrative that legitimates it, governed by ethical, social, and political concerns. There is, then, a discord between science *as science* and 'utterances expected to be just rather than true' and which, strictly speaking 'lie outside scientific knowledge' (32–3). This leads Lyotard to make the following claim (the most quoted phrase from his book): 'I define *postmodern* as **incredulity toward metanarratives**'. This is the crisis mentioned above.

Incredulity toward metanarratives and the postmodern alternative

When a society develops its technologies to the point where information itself is the central commodity and it no longer believes in the ethical, philosophical, social, political narratives that were once thought of as providing the justification for education, learning and the production of knowledge then we have the postmodern condition. This incredulity is seen as a product of a crisis in the persuasive power of these legitimating narratives – and a crisis in the universities themselves, which are seen as becoming increasingly dominated by a skills approach to higher education, ruled by performance and efficiency (xxvi). This is what Lyotard calls '**performativity**' (47f.). Before I discuss the term more fully I want to reflect on the historical moment when Lyotard wrote *The Postmodern Condition* because this will help to contextualize his reading of the legitimizing narratives.

Like many left-leaning intellectuals after the Second World War, Lyotard was highly sceptical about the grand narratives of the dominant political ideologies of the time. Liberal politics, linked to colonialism and capitalism, had led to two major wars but the principal alternative, in the shape of the Soviet Union, had also led to the disillusionment of many on the left. This was because life in the Soviet Union was seen as repressive and as colonially motivated as in the capitalist West. Some intellectuals turned to Maoism for a brief time but that only led to further disillusion, and Marxism, while at the theoretical level considered a valuable intellectual tool, suffered the fate of the other 'grand narratives'. Reflecting many other intellectuals, Lyotard, like them, felt that Marxism had lost its credibility as 'a narrative of emancipation' (37).

For Lyotard, the alternative to the grand narrative was the proliferation of **little narratives**, which do not answer to universalizing principles. To elaborate his arguments Lyotard drew on Wittgenstein's notion of 'language games' (Wittgenstein, 1958: 5f.) to explain how the little narrative functioned. Lyotard claimed that each domain of thinking or knowledge is like a language game insofar as it functions according to the particular rules that are established for it. This has important political consequences because Lyotard argued that any attempt to silence someone who may challenge the universalizing terms of a grand narrative was actually an act of terrorism (1987: 63). Thus, Lyotard (like Derrida and Foucault) was deeply sceptical of the imposition of any overarching system of reason which, post-Auschwitz, he associated with Nazism and terrorism (Lyotard et al. 1985). This idea has helped to popularize the importance of alternative little narratives which function according to their own rules and are incommensurable: that is to say, their internal systems of logic are incompatible with one another (see Lyotard, 1985; Lyotard and Thébaud, 1988). To understand this better see the following Help File.

Help File: from metanarratives to little narratives

Lyotard's theory is very much dependent on the idea of incredulity toward metanarratives but it is possible to ask: up to what extent was this true? While it is possible to detect a slackening off of the humanist basis for knowledge and a weakening of beliefs in the kinds of projects Lyotard associates with the traditional grand narratives that legitimate the production of knowledge, this does not mean that the metanarrative dimension had (or has) disappeared.

An alternative to Lyotard's idea is to consider the possibility that new metanarratives can be constructed (or old ones can be adapted) to legitimate intellectual, economic or political practices. For example, during the 1970s, when Lyotard was developing these ideas, what is often referred to as 'neoliberalism', the free-market economics associated with Milton Friedman, was increasingly being used to legitimate the production of knowledge (within the sphere of economics). This economic, political ideology, with its emphasis on free trade, the breaking down of trade barriers and cuts in public spending, was linked to what was represented as a new way forward towards a global economy based on economic and cultural progress. However, the production of neoliberalist economic ideas (inside or outside the universities) was a perfect candidate for receiving research funds in the United States because it was easily perceived as optimizing the economic system's performance.

Thus, at least one important field of knowledge production (supported ideologically and pragmatically through organizations like the World Bank and the International Monetary Fund) had a metanarrative that could legitimate itself through the grand narrative of capitalism in its neoliberalist guise (for more on these issues, see the final chapters of the book).

The challenge of the little narrative

If you want to know how little narratives might function at the social-political level you might look at the activities of the World Social Forum (WSF), initiated in 2001, to debate alternatives to neoliberalism and reinvent democracy. What is interesting from the point of view of little narrative is that the WSF is a loose miscellany of all kinds of movements with no centralized power or political party to govern them (Klein, 2000: 454f.). The anti-corporate movement in general is characterized by all kinds of grass-roots organizations that refuse to be circumscribed by traditional political arrangements. Each group functions according to its own dynamic made coherent by its particular language game that justifies its actions (which may be peaceful or

(Continued)

(Continued)

violent). Therefore, when these decentralized groups unite to demonstrate against the G8, the World Bank, the International Monetary Fund or the World Trade Organization they demonstrate together but refuse to give up their autonomy, sometimes even contradicting one another (Klein, 2002: 14f.).

Lyotard's ideas might be modified to include the idea that grand narratives and little narratives are not incompatible and that they are locked in what Gramsci called hegemonic struggle, where the narratives compete with one another for ascendancy (Gramsci, 1973 – I will discuss these issues in greater depth in Chapter 14). Thus, there is the possibility that performativity *is* becoming more and more of a reality but this does not mean, as suggested above, that the metanarrative has been entirely abandoned. It may be present in some contexts and not in others. If we see culture like Raymond Williams did as dynamic (and characterized by dominant, emergent and residual cultures), then all these processes can be seen to be coexisting, where the trends can disappear, reappear, be reversed and intensified, etc. (Williams, 1981: 204f.).

Delegitimation and performativity

To return to the idea of performativity, Lyotard argues that the decline of the grand narratives is a result of transformations since the Second World War that have shifted the emphasis 'from the ends of action to its means' (1987: 37). Thus, in postmodernity the importance is not put on the emancipatory or speculative value of knowledge but on how efficient it is (performativity). Now science 'plays its own game' as such and no longer relies on grand narratives to legitimate it: 'the goal of emancipation has nothing to do with science' (41). This is what Lyotard calls the **'delegitimation'** of science and knowledge which (ironically) involves its (re)legitimation through performativity where each science establishes its own criteria for acceptance, through the consensus of experts, rather than through the traditional grand narratives (42–4).

Lyotard's basic argument is that in postmodern society 'the goal is no longer truth, but performativity' where input is minimized and output maximized and where the ultimate goal of the backers of research is power (46). This is achieved through technologies which help to master 'reality'. It is here that knowledge is able to divide itself from the grand narratives and become 'self-legitimating'. This brings us back to Bell and the post-industrial society because Lyotard stated that 'the growth of power, and its self-legitimation' were increasingly associated with data storage and accessibility and the 'operability' (or use-value) of information. What this means in postmodern society is that research funds are allotted by the state, or by other bodies like corporations, according to whether research is perceived as optimizing the system's performance (47). If not, it is threatened by obsolescence because the production of knowledge is not legitimated by the grand narratives of speculation or emancipation.

Lyotard also claimed that performativity would increasingly dominate higher education in postmodern societies so that, rather than train 'an elite capable of guiding the nation towards its emancipation', higher education is called upon to create skills, rather than ideals. Its role is no longer idealistic but practical, providing society with its needs, producing so many doctors, engineers, administrators, etc. (48). However, the performative side also includes the idea of the university increasingly being required to improve the efficiency of postmodern society by offering continuing education and retraining (49). Thus, the 'performativity principle' affects the autonomy of the universities and subordinates 'the institutions of higher learning to the existing powers' (50) (this resembles Bell's idea that attitudes towards science would be increasingly pragmatic and subordinated to 'state-directed goals'). With the collapse of the old grand narratives, the question in postmodern higher education is not 'Is it true?' but 'What use is it?' or even, 'Is it saleable?' Thus, this creates 'a vast market for competence in operational skills' (51).

In this context, Lyotard also envisaged the introduction of computer terminals into education which could replace the traditional teacher–student relationship. Here computer terminals would function as memory banks and students would be required to develop the necessary skills of choosing the appropriate memory bank while learning to use the terminals themselves. Thus, informatics and telematics (which deals with computer networks and wireless technologies for the transference of data) would become an indispensable requirement in universities (50–51). So it is that Lyotard did not argue that we are approaching 'the end of knowledge'; quite the opposite – he claimed that data banks are 'the Encyclopedia of tomorrow' and are 'nature' for the postmodern subject insofar as information (moving at ever faster speeds and constantly updated) is the primary matter upon which the student or researcher works (51–52).

These characteristics are augmented by a breakdown in the old disciplines of knowledge which, in the interests of efficiency and use, become increasingly interdisciplinary. This breakdown coincides with a greater emphasis on teamwork, which also facilitates greater efficiency and thus performativity (52). However, it would be wrong to impose this model of performativity on everything, Lyotard arguing that postmodern scientific knowledge, as it relates to fields like particle physics, mathematics, systems and catastrophe theory, 'has little affinity with the quest for performativity' (54) and is characterized and legitimated by discontinuities, unpredictability and paradox. This is what Lyotard refers to as 'paralogy' which, rather than reinforce the order of reason, disturbs or destabilizes it in order to generate alternative ways of thinking and new forms of knowledge (60–4).

Practice: performativity and higher education

If you are reading this and are in higher education, you will be in a good position to evaluate what Lyotard claimed would increasingly be the case of performativity in universities in postmodern societies. To decide if your education is postmodern-performative (or to what extent it has become so), you might ask yourself the following questions:

- Do you feel there is any emancipatory or speculative value to the education you are receiving?
- Do you think your educational experience is wholly skills based?
- Does your university offer continuing education and retraining? How many of the courses are dedicated to these ends?
- Are you required to understand informatics and telematics to successfully complete your course? Do you feel teachers are being replaced by computer terminals?
- Do you think that data banks have become the 'nature', or primary matter, upon which you are working?
- How much interdisciplinarity is there in your course? Does it work in the interests of performativity (or does it actually contribute to the speculative value of your studies)?
- How far do you think your studies actually lead towards the destabilization of the order of reason and emphasize discontinuities, unpredictability or paradox (parology)?
- In short, do you feel like a postmodern subject? Or, to what extent are you becoming one?

If you can answer yes to all (or most of) these questions, you would, from Lyotard's point of view, be receiving a higher education in key with postmodern society. You might ask friends or colleagues in other departments to see if different subject areas seem to have more or less performative goals. You might consider that while Lyotard uses the idea of 'paralogy' to define certain aspects of the sciences and mathematics it may be applied to many of the ideas being developed with relation to poststructuralism and postmodernism itself (which may suggest that many humanities courses challenge performative tendencies).

Lyotard and postmodern culture as eclectic

Appended to the English translation of Lyotard's *The Postmodern Condition* is a short essay entitled 'Answering the Question: What is Postmodernism?' This has also been very important in establishing how postmodernism has been understood in terms of the arts, but it also gives an idea of what it means to live the postmodern as eclectic experience. I will deal with this before discussing Lyotard's distinction between modernism and postmodernism. Lyotard defines postmodern culture as being dominated by the dictates of capitalism (something we will explore in much more detail when we look at Fredric Jameson). Here culture is defined by an eclectic mix-and-match approach to consumption where 'one listens to reggae, watches a western, eats McDonald's food for lunch and local cuisine for dinner, wears Paris perfume in Tokyo and "retro" clothes in Hong Kong'. Lyotard adds, with a touch of irony, that knowledge 'is a matter for TV games'. Postmodern culture is this 'anything goes' mentality which, in the absence of clear aesthetic criteria, is ruled by money and the value of different artistic works is decided by their popularity (that is, by 'the profits they yield' (76)). However, Lyotard answers the question of what postmodernism is by linking this eclecticism with a distinction between modernism and postmodernism (the latter being seen as an extension of the former rather than a new movement in itself).

Postmodernism and the arts

Lyotard associated modernism with the Kantian notion of the sublime which is an 'equivocal emotion' where pleasure is derived from pain (77). What he meant by this is that in avant-garde works aesthetic pleasure comes from the pain of making us see that the 'unpresentable exists'. The idea is to 'make visible that there is something which can be conceived and which can neither be seen nor made visible' (78).

This might be understood by trying to represent an abstract concept like 'the infinite' in a painting. We would soon realize that it could not be done. The only thing that could be done is to 'avoid figuration or representation' of the infinite – for example a canvas painted in a single colour like white entitled 'The Infinite' would introduce the concept but only enable us, paradoxically, to see 'by making it impossible to see'. It only pleases by causing pain in its failure to represent the unrepresentable (78). In narrative, Lyotard associates modernism with writers like Marcel Proust who, in works such as *In Search of Lost Time* (1913–27), conjures up the inner consciousness of time but in such a way as it is beyond representation (it is always somewhere else). Yet Proust does this 'by means of a language unaltered in its syntax and vocabulary' which conforms, albeit in a subverted way, to the classic novelistic tradition (80).

To distinguish modernism from postmodern Lyotard refers to James Joyce who also alludes to 'something which does not allow itself to be made present', but here the unpresentable is perceived in the writing itself. That is, in the signifiers that Joyce used. Lyotard did not offer a specific example, but if we take Joyce's *Ulysses* we find sentences like 'Bronze by gold heard the hoofirons, steelyringing Imperthnthn thnthnthn' (Joyce, 1922/1971: 254). Lyotard's point about writers like Joyce is that the 'grammar and vocabulary of literary language are no longer accepted as given'; they appear as 'academic forms' or 'rituals' which impede the 'unpresentable from being put forward' (1984: 80–1).

Lyotard's conclusion is that the postmodern artists or writers are in the position of philosophers insofar as they work without rules and have to formulate them for themselves. The rules 'are what the work of art itself is looking for'. In this Lyotard seems to align himself with the postmodern project because he writes 'it is our business not to supply reality but to invent allusions to the conceivable which cannot be presented' (81). One of the most effective ways of understanding Lyotard's approach to postmodern culture would be to present you with an alternative postmodern introduction to this chapter. What I shall do is to reflect some of the features Lyotard sees in Joyce's work and adapt them to an academic style, adding further layers of playfulness. The idea here is not to try to understand all the following paragraphs but to reflect on the following questions.

Practice: an alternative introduction

- Try to outline in what ways the alternative introduction challenges your expectations of an academic book.
- Can you list and analyse the writing techniques used in terms of their playfulness and the way they illustrate Lyotard's definition of postmodern style?

A Help File follows to offer some ways of navigating through this alternative introduction.

A postmodern academic style: an alternative intro-diction

All the characters in this chapter (including the author) are fictional. Any resemblance to real-life people is purely accidental. The author takes no responsibility for any resemblance to real people or events, and the ideas and opinions expressed in this work are entirely the responsibility of the reader.

FIRST PARAGRAPH: This first paragraph could have been – should have been – brilliant. I had all the ideas set out, the structure was perfect, it was suggestive, playful and full of wit, but it's all gone wrong and it's too late now to turn back. I had an impressive range of citations to impress you with – you know, like (Barth, 19something, Pynchon, 19something and Doctorow, 19something) but it's too much hassle to get all the references together and you'll have to make do with the names (they're well-known enough and you can Google them if you're interested). I had actually thought, at one time, to cite some 30,000 works – make a whole book out of the titles of my references but I ran out of steam. I was also going to pun on as many words as possible. The style was going to be a kind of 'thematics' (or 'theme-antics') a 'theo-heretical magnifying glass' – something like the following:

Dear, reader, who-air and where-air you be, a comment on my peculiar **id**iotsyncratic meth-odd – a prefatorial gust, a theoretical crumb … Rather than an abstract, I shall offer an abstruct or obstract: something which could be said to stand in the way rather than lighten it. Yet, I would have it retain something of the abstract:

an incorporeal substance (a hal[l]o)

floating above what lies below.

What is it that lies below? Any attempt to describe what happens there in a language which gestures towards an unambiguous style, clarity of argument, neat concision etc. would militate against my tendency to de-scribe and re-Joyce. I would say that this is not so much an article but an 'art-tickle'. Here, then, a ludic cycle, pedalgogical joy-ride into the uncommon, unorthodox terror-tory of CULTural theory: an attempt to Sir-jest (with a modicrumb of wit) an alter-native means of intro-juicing concepts.

Then there was going to be a series of phrases to impress you with my status as a species of 'foolosopher':

- The politico-religious vessel upon which male power *wood* have to be unlocked and based: PA-tree-Ark-key.
- Desire according to psychoanalysis may be iLUSTrated by sMothering it.
- The Fraudian sleep, I mean, Freudian slip: *it's not so much that we talk in our sleep but that we sleep in our talk.*

But I couldn't be arsed – I lifted all this, adapted it and mixed it up a bit – PLAYgiarizing myself (is that possible?) – from an article I once published. You don't have to make any effort to find it – it's online (Walton, 1998).

SECOND PARAGRAPH: What a load of preposterous, pretentious crap! And the first paragraph has already contradicted itself. Those quotations, are they properly a part of the first paragraph or do they stand separately? And, anyway, it's *not really* the first paragraph – there's stuff before it. Forget it. As a 'second paragraph' it's my job (although my ontological status has already been compromised) to move this chapter on a bit – get some development into the arguments or significantly amplify the exposition of aims, limits, etc. But, then, the problem with paragraphs like us is that they are like Laurence Sterne's *Tristram Shandy* – we spend so much time staring at our own navels that we never really get started. We love the seeming paradox, the mixed metaphors....

DAVOID WALTON: (shooing the paragraphs away) OK. Let's put a stop to these paragraphs before they overwhelm the book and alienate some readers. In terms of narrative fiction, the things I've done above are all fairly typical of what have been seen as postmodern styles of fiction (see McHale, 1987; Hutcheon, 1988) but adapted to the academic book. These are only a fraction of the conventions that have been seen to dominate postmodern narratives.

Help File: a postmodern academic style – an alternative introduction

The opening words appropriate a typical convention associated with films which may be associated with actual people or events, but wish to distance themselves from them (for legal reasons). While academic books focused on poststructuralism and postmodernism constantly emphasize the construction of identity, they rarely claim that all references to people are fictions and that it is the reader who bears responsibility for the ideas and opinions expressed (thus privileging the reader over the writer).

Most academic books do not name the paragraphs in this way and while you would expect a great deal of self-conscious discussion of the arguments, content and development of the material you would not normally find the paragraph or book announcing itself as a failure before it gets started. Of course, you expect many citations but not to be told that the author can not be bothered to give you many and then not give you the dates properly '19something' (you will notice that the three books are *not* featured in the References, which is considered by many academics to be an unpardonable crime – but, then, I did not actually quote from them).

Then there is the hypothetical book that never really got written, made up of book titles which, again, is abandoned and the works are not fully documented. Then you are told that the style was going to be a kind of 'thematics' (or 'theme-antics') a 'theo-heretical magnifying glass' but you *do* get a section which illustrates what the words seem to deny. Playful language and puns are by no means new to academic writing, but the density of the puns is unusual and often considered too distracting and ambiguous. What seems to be an original piece of writing only turns out to be a reworked piece published elsewhere – perfectly acceptable in academic circles but it is unusual to trick readers into acceptance and then reveal the trick.

Notice, too, the idiomatic turns of phrase (like 'I couldn't be arsed'), which, while not alien to academic writing, are uncommon in this form. The insults of the second paragraph are unusual in academic writing (although, in more refined form, not entirely absent) insofar that calling something 'crap' is not an argued response and academic writers do not normally set up their own writing to be knocked down or dismissed in such cursory fashion. The anthropomorphism of paragraphs (the attribution of human characteristics or behaviour to inanimate objects) and then having them driven away by the author is not part of the staple diet of your average academic essay (actually more in line with the style of Joyce's *Ulysses*, which is slyly alluded to in the word 're-Joyce').

The style is characterized by enormous playfulness, especially plays on the form of words and puns which constantly disrupt the flow of argumentation. Many sentences require the reader to pause and think out the possibilities of the play rather than move on. Many novels regarded as postmodern (although not all) require a similar reading strategy. There is much self-reflexivity (where the text recognizes itself as text) and this is another convention particularly associated with postmodern narratives (see McHale, 1987; Hutcheon, 1988). Notice, too, as in an earlier chapter, I play on my name which suggests that, as an author, I am an empty construct which (in line with Lacanian thinking) has a 'void' as its principal characteristic.

There is also the mixing of 'ontological levels' (where the 'actual' author intervenes in the fictional world) which breaks down the boundaries between an outside and inside of the fictional space. The deliberate highlighting of text as text (words distorted, capitals, italics and bold letters playfully IMPosed inside words which emphasize words *as* words), where the language itself overwhelms a sense of story, where the story cannot seem to get written (typical of what Lyotard regarded as distinguishing postmodern styles from modernist styles).

There is the self-conscious 'pseudo-plagiarism' of my own article (it is only pseudo-plagiarism because I actually cite it). There is much explicit and implicit inter-textuality which many critics regard as typical of postmodern narrative (for intertex-tuality see the Chapter 5 on Derrida). One implicit intertext is the style John Barth is famous for. If you look at his collection of short stories *Lost in the Funhouse* (1988) you will see I reflect his very self-conscious method of writing, ironically writing itself, and the hypothetical stories that do not get written. Many literary critics would probably recognize an implicit nod to J. D. Salinger's *Catcher in the Rye* (1969) in the sceptical, 'don't-care' tone of the paragraphs. For the word games and play it would be hard not to think of James Joyce's *Ulysses* and *Finnegan's Wake* or Christine Brooke-Rose's *Textermination*, which conjures up the idea of the text exterminating itself (1991). Other aspects that might be considered are the way the introduction is not only something which does not allow itself to be made present but that the failure is dramatized in the style of writing itself. Another factor is the effort of the writing to try to negotiate its own rules.

This section has indicated how modernism may be distinguished from postmodernism but the following chapters (and especially the one dedicated to Fredric Jameson) will develop this distinction further. Before, however, I go on to discuss the postmodern arts in more detail I shall outline an important conflict between the modernist and postmodernist conceptions embodied in the Lyotard versus Habermas debate.

Lyotard contra Habermas (and Marxisism)

By way of conclusion I shall outline Lyotard's criticisms of Jürgen Habermas. This will also help to explain why Marxist writers are often hostile to the idea of the postmodern. Lyotard's insistence on the failure of the grand narratives and on the importance of the 'language games' of little narratives meant that he was opposed to Marxist thinkers like Jürgen Habermas who defended moder-nity against postmodern thinkers. In his essay 'Modernity – An Incomplete

Project', Habermas argued that, while the dreams of the Enlightenment were over-inflated, they should not be abandoned.

In some ways he was in agreement with Lyotard because he believed that the twentieth century had shattered the optimism of the Enlightenment belief in the infinite progress of knowledge and in the limitless progress towards social and moral improvement (Habermas, 1981/1993: 103). Not only this, but 'aesthetic modernity' (associated with modernist (anti)art movements like Dadaism and Surrealism) had not only failed to destroy the traditional canons of art but they had ended up reinforcing them. However, Habermas was not prepared to declare the entire project of modernity a lost cause and argued that instead of giving up its projects society should learn from their mistakes.

For Habermas, one of the problems with 'cultural modernity' is the way knowledge has been splintered into highly specialized discourses, which become institutionalized and only understood by experts. The problem here for Habermas is that this distances these spheres of knowledge from the general public. Habermas argued that there was a real need to break down these forms of institutional control and return these debates to the public sphere (but without necessarily rejecting the idea of the specialist). For Habermas this was not just a question of the sciences: the difficulty of highly experimental modernist art had resulted in it being alienated from the public, thus, it lost its revolutionary potential and like the sciences had become confined to a coterie of experts. Therefore, Habermas argued for a revised and more modest continuation of the great ideals of the Enlightenment but one where the sciences, ethics and aesthetic criticism would be liberated from professional critics and returned to the 'life world' of everyday society (106). This would facilitate open public discussion of issues important to contemporary society.

Lyotard's problem with this thesis is centred on Habermas's reading of the way the totality of life is 'splintered into independent specialities which are left to the narrow competence of experts', while individual experience is seen in terms of a breakdown of structured meaning. Lyotard, rather than lamenting this splintering, saw possibilities for liberation from the grand narratives (including the Marxism that drives Habermas's thinking) that are no longer credible. Lyotard also objected to Habermas's notion of art which was to be freed from questions of taste and used to explore cognitive, ethical and political discourses in such a way that they could help to promote, in Lyotard's words, 'a unity of experience' (1987: 72). This is linked to his objections to Habermas's theory of **communicative rationality**.

In his essay on modernity as an incomplete project Habermas argued that thinkers like Derrida and Foucault were postmodern neoconservatives because their thought, in the last instance, supported the status quo (for more on this see Chapter 13 on Jameson). In place of the poststructuralist stance he put forward the idea of 'communicative rationality' which reflects Habermas's belief that individuals, with a will to communicate and understand, *can* make progress. That is, through constant dialogue with others in a reasoned way, individuals and society can hope to reach forms of consensus rather than be lost in endless discourses motivated by power and personal interests (Habermas, 1972/1996: 589).

Lyotard rejected these ideas because he was opposed to any attempt at totalizing experience which called for order, unity or singular identity (1987: 72). The search for consensus was only another way of reformulating the grand narratives and the old certainties that he would consign to history. He also feared that these kinds of projects, based on consensus, would 'liquidate the heritage of the avant-gardes' (whose role, as we saw above, was to (re)write the rules). So, whereas Habermas saw postmodern thought as conservative and his brand of Marxism as emancipatory, Lyotard saw postmodern thought as emancipatory and Habermas's Marxist project as oppressive and retroactive.

To conclude, Habermas's position is closer to that of the fellow Marxist thinker Fredric Jameson because both thinkers put the emphasis on the ability to understand the complex and highly structured contemporary world of late capitalism, rather than on the problematizing discourses of many of the poststructuralist (and with the introduction of Lyotard, postmodern) writers I have discussed up to now. However, before I move on to discuss Jameson and other objections to postmodernism I shall concentrate on the work of a key postmodern theorist, Jean Baudrillard, to look at how postmodern approaches work in practice and discuss their possible strategic strengths and weaknesses.

Summary of key points

This chapter began with some reflections on postmodernism as a problematic but indispensable concept and then went on to review Daniel Bell's definition of contemporary society as the post-industrial. Lyotard's classic diagnosis of the postmodern condition as incredulity towards metanarratives was outlined together with the assumption that the postmodern era no longer believes in rational human projects, as expressed in the grand narratives of scientific rationalism or the emancipatory socio-political projects like humanism and Marxism. Out of this crisis of legitimation, Lyotard's postmodern alternative has been explained in terms of his insistence on the importance of Wittgenstein's language games and the 'little narrative', reflecting his deep scepticism of the imposition of any overarching system of reason. The implications of Lyotard's belief that knowledge in the era of postmodernism is 'performative' has been explored as has his assertion that the institutions of education are now in the business of creating skills rather than ideals. Lyotard's distinctions between modernist and postmodern approaches to art have been explained as has his critique of Habermas's belief in 'communicative rationality' and the necessity of continuing the Enlightenment project.

Further reading

Lyotard's *The Differend: Phrases in Dispute* (1988) (written with Jean-Loup Thébaud) is a highly playful and creative book which can be seen as postmodern insofar as it is part of an effort to reformulate the rules of academic writing. David Harvey's *The Condition of Postmodernity* (1990b) considers different manifestations of postmodernity (including philosophy, architecture, art and cinema) from a Marxist perspective within social, economic and political contexts, and considers the postmodern as 'time–space compression'. Fredric Jameson's *Postmodernism, or, the Cultural Logic of Late Capitalism* (1991a) is essential reading and will be discussed in considerable detail in Chapters 14 and 15. To see how postmodern ideas have been applied to popular cultural forms see Angela McRobbie's *Postmodernism and Popular Culture* (1994) and John Dockers's *Postmodernism and Popular Culture: A Cultural History* (1994). Philip Hammond, in *Media, War and Postmodernity* (2007), uses a number of Lyotard's ideas (as well as those drawn from other postmodern thinkers) to argue that contemporary warfare can be understood as postmodern.

12

Identity and Consumption

Jean Baudrillard

Learning goals

- To understand how Baudrillard's theories are informed by structuralist ways of thinking and to see how his approach resembles deconstructive techniques.
- To appreciate how it is possible to link postmodern identity to consumption.
- To be aware of how Baudrillard represented contemporary culture as following the logic of the consumer society and leading to the breakdown of the high versus low culture distinction.
- To understand how concepts like simulation and hyperreality work in practice.
- To be able to assess Baudrillard's contribution to cultural critique and consider the wider implications of postmodern thinking with relation to feminist discourses.

Concepts

The key concepts introduced in this chapter are: the consumer society, postmodern identity, the breakdown of the high verses low culture distinction, simulation, simulacra and hyperreality.

Introduction

This chapter begins by showing how Jean Baudrillard's theories of consumption are indebted to semiotic ways of thinking and how the postmodern subject can be defined with relation to acts of consumption. It then reviews Baudrillard's reading of Pop art and shows how it illustrates the key postmodern idea of the breakdown of the distinction between high low culture. After this it explains the concepts of simulation and what Baudrillard called 'hyperreality' and illustrates how these concepts work with relation to Disneyland, the Watergate scandal and the first Gulf War. The final sections consider the value of, and objections to, Baudrillard's approach and uses feminist theory to consider the strengths and weaknesses of postmodern strategies.

A reluctant postmodernist?

The philosopher, social theorist (and photographer) Jean Baudrillard has, perhaps more than anyone else (apart from Lyotard), become emblematic of the postmodern cultural critic. Of course, a man whose writing career lasted almost fifty years can hardly be summed up by a single word. However, the aim here is to reflect how his ideas have been drawn into debates on the postmodern, rather than do justice to his entire academic output, and to show how his theories interact with others already introduced in this book. Once again, we will see that the terms (post)structuralism and postmodernism are not mutually exclusive but convenient labels. Interestingly, while Baudrillard has become one of *the* canonical 'postmodern' authors, he did not define himself in these terms or popularize the use of the term.

Baudrillard, (post)structuralism and consumption: postmodern identity

George Ritzer, in his introduction to Baudrillard's *The Consumer Society*, indicates that, while drawing on mainstream sociology and Marx, Baudrillard was very much influenced by a whole range of structuralist ideas, which he adapted to his own thinking. Baudrillard treated the world of consumption as a mode of discourse or language and thereby 'deployed the whole panoply of tools derived from structural linguistics including sign, signifier, signified and code' (Baudrillard, 1970/1998: 6). Furthermore, as I shall suggest below, there are moments when Baudrillard's way of reading contemporary society is highly reminiscent of Derridean deconstructive technique. Thus, the earlier chapters of this book should help you to understand Baudrillard's ideas.

Baudrillard's starting point for his analysis of **consumer society** is that, by the end of the 1960s, advanced capitalist societies were at the point where consumption was 'laying hold of the whole of life' (29). Baudrillard maintained that the act of consumption was not just about consuming commodities but messages (signs, brand icons, etc.) insofar that basic features of contemporary capitalist societies increasingly 'fall under a logic of significations' requiring 'an analysis of codes and symbolic systems' (33). What Baudrillard was indicating (which is so much more obvious in today's hyper-branded world) was that when we buy objects we are buying into what they are made to signify. That is to say, our identity, driven by the desires incited by these signs, is not something outside consumption but negotiated within it. Andy Warhol once summed this up very succinctly. When one of his interlocutors said, 'It's not the thing I want so much as the idea of the thing', Warhol replied, 'Then that's just advertising' (Warhol, 1975/2007: 195).

In more specific terms, what Baudrillard suggested is that consumption can be understood according to how these signs function with relation to what he argued was an underlying code, or 'social logic' – a general logic of signs and consumption (Baudrillard, 1970/1998: 115). This logic is not one of satisfaction, 'but of the production and manipulation of social signifiers' (60). Baudrillard argued, then, that consumption was not to be understood in the old sense of buying for use value but in terms of consuming signs: situating ourselves according to the way they function symbolically. Identity was becoming increasingly a question of not *who* we are but *what brands* we consume and the lifestyle associated with those brands – identity being rooted in sharing in these fictional constructions. Baudrillard's idea that there is a link between consumption and identity has led some cultural historians to define the shopper as a 'subject of consumption' (Bauman, 1988: 808) and this has been seen as a significant part of **postmodern identity**.

Baudrillard's 'social logic' was concerned with the 'process of status differentiation' which consumers, ever struggling to differentiate themselves from one another, experience as freedom, aspiration or choice. However, Baudrillard argued that consumers are actually unconsciously 'obeying a code', an underlying semiotic structure, which produces the desire for differentiation through aspiration and prestige but never allows their complete satisfaction – because it endlessly produces further differences which create further aspirations (1970/1998: 61–64). It is like consumers are on a treadmill to nowhere, competing with one another by trying to be different, richer, original, having better taste, greater social prestige, etc. This is how the system of consumption perpetuates itself. This opens up the possibility that freedom of choice is not a pleasurable act of liberty but a duty forced on people by the structural logic of consumer capitalism (72, 80) which necessitates a kind of 'enforced happiness and enjoyment' in a system which requires 'the *production* and continual innovation' of needs and well-being. It is as if people have 'no right not to be happy' (80). The structuralist basis of this way of thinking was made evident when Baudrillard claimed that:

> The circulation, purchase, sale, appropriation of differentiated goods and signs/objects today constitute our language, our code, the code by which the entire society *communicates* and converses. Such is the structure of consumption, its language [*langue*], by comparison with which individual needs and pleasures [*jouissances*] are merely speech effects. (79–80)

If we are looking for the motors that drive this we need to recognize that all this takes place within the 'language' of cities which is full of 'motives, desires, encounters, stimuli, the endless judgements of others, continual eroticization, information' and the 'appeals of advertising'. The production of goods is fused with this 'limitless promotion of needs' which serves the underlying code of consumption (65). There is much more of interest in Baudrillard's *Of Consumption* but this should give an idea of how the book is related to structuralist thinking and how the identity of the postmodern subject can be defined with relation to acts of consumption. Now it is time to look at a series of further Baudrillardian ideas which have become keys to understanding postmodernism.

Postmodernism and the breakdown of high versus low culture

Baudrillard saw consumption as so dominant that even art itself had become commodified and part of the logic of signs and consumption. Baudrillard saw the Pop art of the 1960s as reflecting this. In the work of Andy Warhol (with his serial prints of celebrities, Brillo Pad boxes and Campbell's soup tins, etc.) he discerned the logic of consumption eliminating 'the traditional sublime status of artistic representation'. What this means is that the traditional art object (as Walter Benjamin (1936/1973) had already noticed) was treated as if it were a sacred object with what Baudrillard regarded as a 'depth vision' of the world whereas Pop art (with its everyday objects that could be found in supermarkets) was analogous to the more one-dimensional world of advertising. Thus, these works reflected the 'manufactured character' of the system of industrial mass production that characterized the socio-economic world in which they were produced (Baudrillard, 1970/1998: 115).

Baudrillard develops from this a series of nuanced arguments, one of which is the possibility of considering Pop art as 'an American art', in the sense that products of Pop art have 'no other truth than that mythology which swamps them'. This is where consumer society is 'trapped in its own mythology' having 'no critical perspective on itself'. The factory-like production of Pop art reflects the assembly line of industrial production and the brand names of products *are* the art itself. This is a recognition of 'the obvious truth' of consumer society which is that 'the truth of objects and products is their brand name' (116). Art, using the same signs, speaks in the same register as commerce and the economic system in which it is produced. Just as Althusser argued that subjects are spoken by the system, here habits of consumption and art itself are products of a logic (a code) which could be said 'to speak' them (we will see this idea reappear in Fredric Jameson's reading of postmodernism).

In this we not only perceive the influence of structuralism but, as Ritzer has pointed out, the increasing commodification of culture which 'leads to one of the basic premises of postmodernism' – **the breakdown of the high verses low culture distinction**. This is where art becomes increasingly 'indistinguishable from any other commodity' (something seen in the Pop art movement's

tendency of mass producing and selling large quantities of numbered prints).
Thus, these mass-produced works of art 'become commodities like all others
and are therefore valued in the same way as other commodities' (Ritzer, in
Baudrillard, 1970/1998: 15). At this point you might turn back to Chapter 6
to review Hall's deconstruction of the 'popular' where I discussed the indeterminate hybrid forms associated with postmodern culture. So, Baudrillard's
The Consumer Society provides two ways in which to understand postmodernism: postmodern identity as something intimately linked to consumption,
and the breakdown of the high verses low culture distinction.

How to skive off school or avoid paying for the drinks in one easy lesson: dissimulation, simulation and simulacra

To continue my outline of Baudrillard's contribution to postmodern cultural
criticism I shall refer to his concepts of **dissimulation** and **simulation**, as
described in his book *Simulacra and Simulation*. The distinction between these
two words is fundamental to an understanding of Baudrillard's contribution to
postmodern theory. If you dissimulate you pretend *not to have something that
you have got* (in reality there is something behind appearance) (Baudrillard,
1981/1994: 3). If you go for drinks with friends and when the time comes to pay
you claim to have forgotten your money (and you are actually carrying some)
you are dissimulating because you are hiding something that actually exists.

If you simulate you pretend *to have something that you have not got* (there is
nothing behind the appearance). Children who trick their parents into believing they are suffering from fever (so they can have a day off school) by plac-
ing a hot-water bottle on their foreheads minutes before their parents take
their temperature have produced the perfect simulation: they have produced
the symptoms without a cause (there is nothing behind the appearance) (3f.).
However, Baudrillard brings out an important detail here because if you simulate an illness the difference between the true and the false is threatened
because you actually produce 'true symptoms' (even though they are of nothing). This ambiguity produces what Baudrillard calls an 'undiscoverable truth'.
If any symptom can be faked in this way all illness can be questioned – there is
no way of knowing the difference between the 'true' and 'false' symptom. This
idea of producing the signs without any reference to a cause and where signs
are beyond truth and falsity is fundamental to Baudrillard's notions of what
he calls **simulacra** (related to the 'hyperreality' – see below) where objective
cause, truth, knowledge and reference 'have ceased to exist' (3).

Here we see that Baudrillard is in the (post)structuralist tradition not only
because of the terms he uses (his interest was in signs and how they function) but also because his model assumes that simulacra are cut off from

the referential world in which they move. However, Baudrillard, unlike many (post)structuralists, rather than find the loss of meaning in the *condition* of the sign, argued that the loss of the referent was dependent on changes in late capitalist societies and it is to these that I shall now turn.

Substituting signs of the real for the real: contemporary society and hyperreality

By the early 1980s Baudrillard had announced that in advanced capitalist countries people no longer lived connected with the real (referential world), but were lost in what he called the 'hyperreal'. His basic argument is that before the era of advanced capitalism (the latter part of the twentieth century) people had different relations to the symbolic world. For example, a pre-capitalist model of representation is where language, or symbols in general, are conceived of as being transparent reflections of the real (a referential world outside language). The Industrial Revolution and capitalism (which define modernity) began to challenge this one-to-one relation between the sign and the referential world, with mass-produced images (prints and photography) and cinematic images becoming increasingly dominant. Baudrillard's basic thesis is that by the late twentieth century this tendency reached its climax where any one-to-one relation between the sign and the referential world was rendered impossible in such a way that individuals were hopelessly lost in the infinite proliferation of media images, information and advertising. This getting lost in a mass of circulating images with nothing to ground them in a real world is the vertiginous experience of **hyperreality**. We might note that 'hyper' means 'excess', so it is a state where people live with simulated reality in excess. As Baudrillard wrote: 'It is a question of substituting the signs of the real for the real [...] A hyperreal henceforth [is] sheltered from the imaginary, and from any distinction between the real and the imaginary' (2).

What Baudrillard seemed to be saying by asserting that the hyperreal is 'sheltered from the imaginary, and from any distinction between the real and the imaginary' is that in a world dominated by proliferating images there is no way of distinguishing between a referential world outside the images and the images themselves. In fact, according to Baudrillard, it is not just that simulation (the imaginary) and reality are no longer distinguishable but that simulation gives the effect of being more real than reality itself (hence it is hyper). In hyperreality images proliferate endlessly without reference to any clearly definable origin: reality is now confused with its simulation – it *is* simulation.

The hyperreal is where 'cinema plagiarizes itself' and 'remakes its classics' and where films endlessly refer to one another (47). Here you might think of films like *Scary Movie* (2000) and all its sequels and derivatives. They are entirely intertextual (or 'interfilmic') depending for their effects on the audience's recognition of their parodic reworkings of (mainly) horror genres. However, Baudrillard goes further, because he claims that the conventions of film reality are the only reality possible: art totally penetrates reality. In a world dominated by filmic conventions of representation, advertising, media overload, information and communication networks (that is, of simulation and the hyperreal) images no longer refer back to an original; they only refer to each other and reproduce themselves endlessly. This is a world where, to refer to the film *Lucky Number Slevin* (2006), Charlie Chaplin can enter a Charlie Chaplin lookalike competition – and come third. What lies behind the tinsel is only more tinsel.

Baudrillard summed up these ideas by claiming that:

> Simulation is no longer that of a territory, a referential being, or a substance. It is the generation by models of a real without origin or reality: a hyperreal. The territory no longer precedes the map, nor does it survive it. (Baudrillard, 1981/1994: 1)

Notice the territory (the real) has disappeared from view. Systems of the real can be anything from scientific theory (which gets lost in its own symbolism) to the image-dominated world of simulation (where models, the conventionalized ways of seeing precede understanding – something I will return to later). The following sections will explore how a theory based on simulation and the hyperreal can generate interpretations of contemporary culture.

Practice: simulation as the real

You might start to look out for films, games, series (or even gossip programmes) that constantly refer to one another. You might also try to become more aware of how reality (the real) and the imaginary (the forms of simulation) are constantly collapsing into one another. An example (although a little trivial) of how the real and simulations may have become indistinguishable from one another would be where viewers write letters to *characters* in soap operas, sympathizing with them or even offering themselves in marriage (Storey, 2009a: 187).

Another useful exercise is to think about how filmic representations impact upon *how* we see reality and what we regard as a realistic depiction. What looks most realistic: an explosion filmed at a distance, or one which resembles the expanding ball of fire with flying debris reminiscent of film and console games?

You might also ask yourself how far simulations are really encroaching on the real and in what ways it might be possible to distinguish between the two (for more ideas see the sections on Disneyland, Watergate and the first Gulf War below).

A trip to Disneyland (USA): Baudrillard in action

One of the most provocative interpretations Baudrillard put forward has to do with Disneyland. Baudrillard's theoretical framework enabled him make a surprising interpretive turn. The situation that Baudrillard outlined is one where customers queue up to enter Disneyland, California. This detail might seem trivial, but the opposition between outside and inside is going to be important. On paying the entry fee visitors leave what they may feel is the reality outside to enter a fantasy space of Mickey Mouse, Donald Duck and Pocahontas, etc. and prepare themselves for fun-fair rides and hi-tech gadgetry. They may think they go from the adult world into that of childhood imagination and play. But Baudrillard reverses the expected reading of Disneyland:

> Disneyland is presented as imaginary in order to make us believe that the rest is real, whereas all of Los Angeles and the America that surrounds it are no longer real, but belong to the hyperreal order and to the order of simulation. It is no longer a question of a false representation of reality (ideology) but of concealing the fact that the real is no longer real, and thus of saving the reality principle. (1981/1994: 12)

The upshot of this is that there is no difference between Disneyland and the rest of the United States, all these fantasy spaces (including Enchanted Village, Magic Mountain, Marine World and MGM Studios) *are* what the USA had become (and for Baudrillard all the other advanced capitalist countries were following the same trajectory). Baudrillard could be said to practise a kind of deconstruction (even though he does not mention Derrida). His reading is dependent on questioning and undermining the following oppositions: general US culture is opposed to Disneyland; the outside versus the inside; reality versus fantasy; and the adult world opposed to childhood innocence. His conclusions collapse these oppositions so that:

> General US culture is Disneyland
> Outside is inside
> Reality is fantasy
> The adult world is childhood.

For Baudrillard, Disneyland and all theme parks function in this way and are like recycling plants where dreams and fantasies are regenerated. Thus, rather than accepting that theme parks are fantasy spaces within the world of reality which encloses them, *they* are the reality which expose that late capitalist America is one giant simulated space of the hyperreal.

Revealing the truth by devious means: Watergate

Once you start playing around with these ideas all kinds of reversals are possible, and this has made Baudrillard both interesting to cultural critics, and controversial. For example, Baudrillard interprets the Watergate scandal in the same kind of way as he did Disneyland.

Help File: the Watergate scandal

Watergate is the name given to an infamous political scandal that rocked the political world in the United States between 1972 and 1974. The Republican President, Richard Nixon, and members of his administration were shown to be implicated in deliberate efforts to discredit members of the opposing Democratic Party by way of stolen documents and illegal phone tapping. Evidence was produced to prove that President Nixon was directly involved in phone bugging: a system for these purposes was discovered in his office together with recorded tapes. Not only this, but sizeable unlawful payments had been made from an illegal fund, and Nixon was shown to have lied under oath to protect himself and others implicated in the affair. To avoid impeachment, Nixon resigned his presidency.

The scandal became an important media event fuelled by journalists of *Time*, the *Washington Post* and the *New York Times*. Important to Baudrillard's interpretation of the events is that two reporters from the *Washington Post*, in order to get information that implicated the secret services as well as the White House, had to resort to secretive tactics themselves. This involved a high-ranking FBI source they nicknamed 'Deep Throat' (information based on Woodward, 2005; Kutler, 2009).

Baudrillard read the Watergate scandal as a repetition of the Disneyland scenario, only here there was what he called 'the scandal effect' that hides that there was no real difference 'between the facts and their denunciation'. That is to say, the *Washington Post* journalists used the same underhand methods of secrecy in order to indict the President as Nixon and his cohorts had used to smear the Democrats (Baudrillard, 1981/1994: 14). In short, it was a question of 'proving truth through scandal' (19). From the methodological point of view, once again, we see the collapsing of the outside and the inside and where the moral and immoral are interchangeable.

We might improvise a Baudrillardian conclusion that states: Watergate only exists to persuade us that political corruption is only a sporadic scandal that needs to be rooted out to preserve the integrity of the democratic system. It only functions as a disguise to cover the fact that corruption is everywhere. The scandalous exception is not an exception to the norm but is *itself* the norm. To experiment with this Baudrillardian way of thinking you might try to create this kind of reading around other political controversies to see how illuminating they may be. For more ideas on this, see the next practice section.

The Gulf War never happened: the strategic value of Baudrillard's thought

To sum up for a moment: for Baudrillard, in the world of simulacra and the hyperreal, history is dead. This is because the real has disappeared and there is no sense in which history (as a series of real events) can make sense anymore. There *is* life, there are human beings, but all is engulfed in the incessant exchange of signs mistaken for the real. This led Baudrillard to make a series of controversial assertions based around the idea that 'it is *now impossible to isolate the process of the real*, or to prove the real'. From this he argued that hold-ups, airplane hijackings, etc. are simulations 'in that they are already inscribed in the decoding and orchestration rituals of the media, anticipated in their presentation and their possible consequences' (21).

What Baudrillard was emphasizing here is that the contemporary world is mediated by the media services which encode 'events' according to their own conventions. These conventions are what dominate: so-called history is pre-packaged within dominant media practices (associated with the instant news of media giants like CNN). For Baudrillard the domination of these codes is so complete that the actual events are merely secondary, something upon which the media services (and government agencies) work in order to construct the kind of stories or fictions that suit their purposes. This idea can help us to think about up to what point 'events' are lost in media spectacles that conform to dominant narrative expectations like good (us) versus bad (them), played out against drama and suspense with elements of human interest, etc.

To give one of Baudrillard's most controversial examples I will refer to a book he wrote called *The Gulf War Did Not Take Place* (1991/1995). The question is: how is it possible to argue that a conflict, which resulted in suffering, widespread destruction and death could be said not to have taken place?

Help File: the Persian Gulf War

The Persian Gulf War ensued when the President of Iraq, Saddam Hussein, decided to invade Kuwait in 1990, justifying his actions by stating (among other things) that Kuwait was, historically, a part of Iraq (and therefore should be reunited with the mother country) and that Kuwait had caused Iraq economic problems by driving down oil prices. Even though the USA had supported Hussein with armaments (against Iran) and, together with the international community in general, had conveniently turned a blind eye to the suppression of Kurdish minorities (and other atrocities) in Iraq, it mobilized international condemnation of the invasion. This led to economic sanctions and an American-led United Nations military coalition to oust Iraq from Kuwait, something that was achieved in what is commonly known as the Gulf War of 1991, and which left Saddam Hussein still in power (see Atkinson, 1993; Finlan, 2003).

So, in what way did the Gulf War fail to take place? This is partly to do with Baudrillard's theories outlined above where he asserted that media practices order the world according to their imperatives (which is part of simulation and the hyperreal). This is particularly important given that Baudrillard argued that this was the first war that was largely stage-managed by and through the media. For Baudrillard news is not about direct contact with the world but a media construction of events: again, simulation is mistaken for the real. The 'real' of the news *is* the spectacle, the simulation. There is no sense in which the spectacle of war is based on one-to-one representation of events – the media operates with relation to its own codes, interests and conventions (or those of other parties like governments and the military) rather than a be-true-to-life model. As Baudrillard had already forewarned in *Simulacra and Simulation*, the media with its incessant flow of images and information, actually *erases* memory and meaning through information overload. In late capitalism people live, Baudrillard asserted, 'in a world where there is more and more information, and less and less meaning' (1981/1994: 79).

A similar idea was developed in *The Gulf War Did Not Take Place* when Baudrillard observed that when war has been turned into information, it 'ceases to be a realist war' becoming a purely virtual one that he calls 'symptomatic'. You may recall Althusser here but Baudrillard's use of the concept is different. Baudrillard saw the images of the war as they appeared in the media as a collection of bits of information which became objects for 'interminable speculation'. For example, he pointed out that one important part of reporting on the war was the endless conjecture about where it was going: a land offensive seemed forever imminent and in one week the destruction of Iraqi military potential oscillated wildly – the figures fluctuating 'like the fortunes of the stock market' (1991/1995: 41).

War as information speculated upon in this way meant that it was hard to know who to believe, the TV becoming 'the hysterical symptom of a war' with no substance (41). The war as an endless relay of simulacra created this atmosphere of 'irreality' and doubt. As Paul Patton observed in his Introduction to *The Gulf War Did Not Take Place* there were moments when the 'absurdity of the media's self-representation as purveyor of reality and immediacy broke through'. At one point CNN cameras filmed a group of reporters in the Gulf who confessed that they were 'sitting around watching CNN in order to find out what was happening'. In this way TV news coverage 'appeared to have finally caught up with the logic of simulation' (2) – the real of the news was, in reality, another news channel. Coming back to *Simulacra and Simulation*, Baudrillard had already (repeating a rhetorical strategy we saw with relation to Disneyland and Watergate) asserted that the media (and the official news services) 'are only there to maintain the illusion of an actuality, of the reality of the stakes, of the objectivity of the facts' (1981/1994: 38). This approach informed Baudrillard's reading of the Gulf War when he claimed that 'the direct transmission by CNN of real time information' was 'not sufficient to authenticate a war' (1991/1995: 61).

Yet there were further ways the Gulf War could be said to have been a simulation. In the first place Baudrillard saw the war as being won in advance in such a way that we would never have known 'what it would have been like had it existed'. This was because Baudrillard believed that Iraq never had a chance of winning. The fact that more than 10,000 tonnes of bombs were being dropped a day was not 'sufficient to make a war' (61). This was the giant simulation where the rules of the game were set in advance; where suitable images could be conveyed on TV (with the right spin put on them via the military and the White House), and where the US won with minimal losses and Hussein, having sacrificed part of his army, conveniently managed to escape back to Iraq and remain a hero to various parts of the Islamic world.

Not only this but the US fought this deceptively 'soft war' with its intelligent missiles and collateral damage (euphemisms which underplayed actual devastation, maiming and death), safely fought behind computer screens so that 'the enemy appears as a computerized target' (62) and the war appears (to extend Baudrillard's imagery) more like a relatively harmless video game (for the USA). However, all this is not to say that this 'non-war' had no consequences, as we shall see below.

The media and simulated reality

Naomi Klein recounts an incident (when she worked as a media editor) that helps to show how the media (even without direct government intervention) tailor the reality of suffering to their own agendas. The newspaper where she worked closed at 11 p.m., but two people were required to remain until one in the morning, just in case something happened that was so significant that it would require a change in the front-page story. On her first late night a tornado killed three people in a southern US state, which was enough to change the headline on the front page. However, on her second night she discovered that 114 people had been killed in Afghanistan and, feeling this was significant news, she called the Senior Editor to change the front page but was told 'Don't worry, those people kill each other all the time' (2002: 163–4).

Klein goes on to discuss 9/11 and the second Gulf War and the huge disparities between the reporting and relative (de)valuation of lives. As an on-the-spot journalist she also echoes Baudrillard's concern that the American public did not get to see 'real buildings exploding', people fleeing, the effects of the sanctions on children or the bombing of non-military targets like pharmaceutical factories.

The Gulf between Baudrillard and his critics: uncritical theory?

Many critics have been less than happy with a notion of the present where wars do not really take place and there is no way of distinguishing simulation from fact, truth, or the real, and where individuals are disarmed into passive acceptance. For example, Christopher Norris (1992: 6f.) has made the point that the problem with Baudrillard's ideas (and poststructuralist thought in general) is that it has accepted, without sufficient reason, that reality is a question of discourse, signs, codes or conventions. For Norris this has led to a situation where it is impossible to distinguish between truth and falsehood, something which makes reasoned ethical debate impossible. Thus, he accuses Baudrillard and other poststructuralists of ethical and political nihilism.

However, in his book on the Gulf War Baudrillard was at pains to stress that 'the consequences of what did not take place may be as substantial as those of an historical event' (1991/1995: 70), something he had already emphasized in another context in *Simulacra and Simulation* where war 'is no less atrocious for only being a simulacrum' (1981/1994: 37). This suggests that despite simulation and the hyperreal events *do* have consequences: 10,000 tonnes of bombs a day do have devastating repercussions but Baudrillard fixes his gaze on what gets represented and what gets ignored and the political sleights of hand surrounding the events:

> Saddam liquidates the communists, Moscow flirts even more with him; he gasses the Kurds, it is not held against him: he eliminates the religious cadres, the whole of Islam makes peace with him. Whence this impunity? Why are we content to inflict a perfect semblance of military defeat upon him in exchange for a perfect semblance of victory for the Americans? This ignominious remounting of Saddam, replacing him in the saddle after his clown act at the head of the holy war, clearly shows that on all sides the war is considered not to have taken place. (1991/1995: 71)

Thus, an argument can be put forward that Baudrillard very effectively draws out how deception and simulation work hand in hand and how the point of the first Gulf War was that it did not really have consequences for those managing world politics. The brutal results were suffered by those who got left out of the real-time news coverage and the machinations of the political spin-doctors. A sense of the tragedy is conveyed when Baudrillard points out that 100,000 Iraqi dead are the 'blood money' Saddam paid to save his regime, serving to prove that 'the war was indeed a war and not a shameful and pointless hoax' (72).

It may seem ironic, then, that Baudrillard denies any access to reality, insisting on the surface play of images and the meaningless flow of information and, at the same time, offers a critique of something which he says is, in the age of hyperreality, beyond critique. Baudrillard's rhetorical strategy is one that seems to assert that the war did not take place only because, in a certain sense, it actually did. It is as though (as in Althusser) everyone is blinded by the obfuscations of the contemporary world and it is only possible to see if one is Baudrillard (or if one immerses oneself in his particular privileged way of seeing). This actually contradicts another dominant way of seeing the postmodern condition found in Lyotard's assertion that it is characterized by 'incredulity towards metanarratives'. Baudrillard constructs a narrative with a special claim to seeing the truth that lies behind the simulations of hyperreality. This might give us pause to think and question whether the term 'postmodern' is adequate to sum up his thought.

However, there is another way of reading Baudrillard. One aspect of Baudrillard's thought is to see it as the art of provocation. This is because at times he appeared to delight in reversing what seemed obvious and at others he made statements that give the impression of being absurd but containing a grain of truth. Here is a section from his book *Symbolic Exchange and Death* where he piles up a series of seemingly absurd ideas:

> But we know what these hidden places signify: the factory no longer exists because labour is everywhere; the prison no longer exists because arrests and confinements pervade social space–time; the asylum no longer exists because psychological control and therapy have been generalised and become banal; the school no longer exists because every strand of social progress is shot through with discipline and pedagogical training [...] The cemetery no longer exists because modern cities have entirely taken over their function: they are ghost towns, cities of death. (1976/1993: 126–7)

Practice: Baudrillard and the art of provocation

It may seem odd to recommend a form of practice that insists on the value of provocation over statements which gesture towards some kind of truth. However, what looks like the art of flippancy may result in profound and 'serious' critique. This opens up the possibility of deliberately stating what seems, on the surface, to be untrue in order to provoke thought that may bring out some hidden dimension of what it is you want to understand. By writing that the Gulf War did not take place or by asserting that cemeteries no longer exist may shock the literalist but can help to question *in what ways* might a war be said not to have taken place or *in what sense* might death be thought to be everywhere. You might experiment with this rhetorical strategy and ask yourself whether or not it may help you to develop a critical sense of the world around you.

Despite the theoretical problems with Baudrillard's writing many critics feel that he does offer some valuable insights into what it means to live during the latter part of the twentieth century and into the twenty-first. Stuart Sim offers a useful summary of Baudrillard's strengths and weaknesses when he writes:

> Despite his perceived weaknesses as a theorist – he is neither a particularly systematic nor rigorous thinker in the main, as even his supporters quite readily admit ('patience and immersion in the

particular' not being amongst his virtues, as Douglas Kellner has quite rightly observed) – Baudrillard is nevertheless an important source of perceptive insights into the postmodern condition, with its radically altered relationship between the individual and technology. He may well overstate the power of simulation and simulacra in determining our perception of the world, but there is no denying that these entities are playing an increasingly important role in the construction of social reality. (Sim, 1995: 33)

Postmodernism and (some of) its discontents: the case of feminism

In this chapter we have seen how one form of postmodernism may work in practice but, as stated above, not all critics have been convinced by it – some feeling, like Docker (1994: 104f.), that Baudrillard reflects a kind of fatalism where there is no way out of the hyperreal. Docker's concerns reflect those who see postmodern critique as limiting rather than liberating; a debate which has been dramatized within feminism(s). To conclude this chapter I shall review the way feminism has engaged with debates within post-modernism; something designed to help you to develop your own thinking about the issues at stake and prepare you for the following chapter on Fredric Jameson. The arguments outlined here could just as easily be applied to questions of class, race/ethnicity or sexuality. A starting point for an understanding of how forms of feminism have engaged with postmodern discourses is to look at an essay by Nancy Fraser and Linda Nicholson entitled 'Social Criticism without Philosophy: An Encounter between Feminism and Postmodernism'.

Fraser and Nicholson begin by outlining a number of connections between postmodernism and feminism emphasizing that both domains have sought 'to rethink the relation between philosophy and social criticism so as to develop paradigms of criticism without philosophy' (in Nicholson, 1990: 19). Furthermore, different forms of feminism, along with postmodernism, have developed ways of reading/challenging history and culture with relation to gender issues to produce a politically effective social criticism that reflects the way women have been (mis)represented, marginalised or excluded.

Jilting the God's eye view of philosophy

However, Fraser and Nicholson put forward the idea of developing a paradigm of criticism without philosophy. They do not mean by this that feminist or any other kind of criticism should abandon the traditional norms of argumentation and thereby fall into nihilism or anarchy. It is not reasoned debate that is rejected but the way philosophers have tended to represent what they do. Their rejection is in line with Lyotard's rejection of philosophy as grand narrative, the 'God's eye view' of philosophy that puts it above all other forms of discourse by turning it into a *'founding* discourse'. This requires the post-modern solution where 'criticism floats free of any universalist theoretical ground', thereby becoming more 'pragmatic, *ad hoc*, contextual, and local' (21). However, Lyotard's work, although exemplary, is seen as too restricted insofar that it completely rejects large historical narratives and therefore ignores 'macrostructures' (34). For Fraser and Nicholson this does not allow for a satisfactory understanding of gender dominance and subordination (macrostructures), and this is where postmodernist approaches can learn from feminism (if you go back to Chapter 6 on deconstruction and practice you will see that this resembles the criticisms that Chris Weedon made of poststructuralism).

However, feminism, while not abandoning large historical narratives (the macrostructures of society), can learn from postmodernism by attuning itself to 'the cultural specificity of different societies and periods and to dis-tinct groups within societies and periods'. So as not to fall into oversimplify-ing the category of 'woman' (or 'man'), postmodern feminism would have to treat concepts like gender 'as one relevant strand among others, attend-ing also to class, race, ethnicity, age, and sexual orientation'. The image of postmodern feminism is 'a tapestry composed of threads of many different colours'. Thus, it would be more appropriate to speak of 'feminisms' – many discourses interconnecting with one another where possible. All this has important (postmodern) implications for feminist politics because it would be defined by alliances which resist 'unity around a universally shared interest or identity' (34–35).

A postmodern approach would have to recognize that woman is plural and that 'no single solution' (based on issues like child care, social security, etc.) could be 'adequate for all'. This fits in with postmodern approaches to politics in general where some women (or people) may share certain common interests and be up against some common enemies but 'such com-monalities are by no means universal' being 'interlaced with differences' or even conflicts (35) – something that defines the new social movements described in the following chapters. Following critics like Wittig and Butler, postmodernist feminism would be against a one-size-fits-all definition of gender.

Feminist postmodernism and its discontents: the incredible shrinking woman

However, not all feminists are in agreement about the ability of a postmod-ern perspective, however modified, to meet the demands of a method which would be theoretically and politically effective. Christine Di Stefano, following Nancy Hartsock, asks:

> Why is it, just at the moment in Western history when previously silenced populations have begun to speak for themselves and on behalf of their subjectivities, that the concept of the subject and the possibility of discovering/creating a liberating 'truth' become suspect? (Christine Di Stefano, in Nicholson, 1990: 75)

So, one of the objections to a postmodern feminism is that it is easier for men to question the intellectual tradition of the Enlightenment (having gained the fruits of its libertarian demands). They can attack the metanarrative, decentre the self and fragment themselves and the world but this might not be very effective for an incomplete feminist cause (we might think of Habermas here). The problem for Di Stefano is that the discourses of postmodernism tend to lead to post-feminism (see Bordo in Chapter 10). This problematizes the dominant concepts upon which many feminist challenges are based to such an extent that feminist politics would lose its radical power – the categories would all be deconstructed and feminists would resemble 'the incredible shrinking woman' (77).

Di Stefano's conclusion offers an alternative which considers postmodern critiques but ultimately rests on preserving the all-important category of gender (which aligns her stance with the modernist project which enabled feminist critique in the first place). Gender functions as the 'difference that makes a difference' (78). Thus, the category of gender has become so important to feminist critiques in general that many feminists, even those sympathetic to postmodern forms of thinking, are reluctant to abandon it. However, as Di Stefano is aware, the preservation of this concept may not, in purely intellectual terms, be justifiable – she could be said to compromise theoretically for the sake of political efficacy.

This sums up the dilemma for any radical criticism that seeks to transform the social and political world and these are the questions that you will need to consider when positioning yourself in relation to the debates within post-structuralism and postmodernism. Is there any way out of this dilemma? As a parting shot it is worth considering Sandra Harding's 'both-and' strategy which insists that:

> At this moment in history, our feminisms need both Enlightenment and postmodernist agendas – but we don't need the same ones for the same purposes or in the same forms as do white, bourgeois, androcentric Westerners. (Sandra Harding, in Nicholson, 1990: 101)

Curiously, this 'both–and' strategy is one that has been seen as particularly postmodern in its refusal to come down on one side or the other. However, this will be explained in more detail in the next chapter.

Summary of key points

This chapter began by showing how Jean Baudrillard's theories of consumption are indebted to semiotic ways of thinking and how the postmodern subject can be defined with relation to acts of consumption (as a mode of discourse). It went on to review how Baudrillard's reading of Pop art reflects the postmodern breakdown of the high versus low culture distinction. It has also explained the key concepts of simulation and hyperreality and has illustrated how these concepts work in practice with relation to Disneyland, the Watergate scandal and the first Gulf War. The final sections have discussed the value of, and objections to, Baudrillard's approach and, through references to feminist theory, considered the strengths and weaknesses of postmodern ways of thinking for radical political agendas.

Further reading

Baudrillard's *America* (1989) would make a good starting point to see how his provocative and impressionistic ideas construct various parts of North America as a kind of ambiguous post-ideological 'utopia achieved' which is actually an a-historical country lost in the simulations of the hyperreal. *Fragments: Interviews with Jean Baudrillard* (Baudrillard, 2003) is a useful source for readers who are coming to Baudrillard for the first time. Arthur Kroker and David Cook's *The Postmodern Scene: Excremental Culture and Hyper-Aesthetics* (1986) uses Baudrillard to explore contemporary culture from intellectual and artistic points of view. The book also engages with other thinkers explored in this book like Barthes, Derrida and Foucault and draws them into postmodern discourses. Richard Smith's *The Baudrillard Dictionary* (2010) offers comprehensive definitions of Baudrillard's key terms. To follow up the theme of postmodernism and consumer culture see Mike Featherstone's *Consumer Culture and Postmodernism* (1991) and Falk and Campbell's *The Shopping Experience* (1997). On the politics of postmodernism Andrew Ross's *Universal Abandon? The Politics of Postmodernism* (1988) brings together an important collection of essays (including the Fraser and Nicholson introduction mentioned above). It also includes an essay with Cornel West that focuses on black postmodernist practices which will be touched on in Chapter 14. Paul Virilio's work, whose theoretical approach is quite distinct from Baudrillard's, often touches on similar questions of the dissolution of the 'real' in an age dominated by speed, digital technology and information overload. See his *The Information Bomb* (2005), *Speed and Politics* (2006) and *The Aesthetics of Disappearance* (2009).

13

Postmodernism Unplugged

Fredric Jameson

Learning goals

- To understand the historical context of Jameson's ideas and how he historicizes postmodernism.
- To appreciate how Jameson's systematic privileging of high modernism over what he understands as postmodernism enables his critiques but also limits them.
- To develop an appreciative but critical awareness of how key ideas function with relation to the 'cultural logic' of postmodernism.
- To see how Jameson's ideas provide a way of interpreting a range of contemporary cultural forms and evaluating contemporary theories.
- To understand why Jameson believed that his idea of cognitive mapping, linked to a socialist political programme, may help to counter the worst effects of late capitalism.

Concepts

The key concepts introduced in this chapter are: postmodernism, late capitalism, postmodernism and 'the end of this or that', high modernism, the cultural logic of late capitalism, depthlessness, commodity fetishism, the waning of affect, the death of the subject, parody and pastiche, 'pastness', cultural schizophrenia and high-tech paranoia.

Introduction

This chapter focuses on Fredric Jameson's influential readings of what he understands as postmodern forms of culture. It begins by situating his ideas historically in terms of the collapse of the Soviet Union and with relation to transformations in late capitalism. Jameson's key notions of postmodernism are discussed and illustrated with relation to his idea of postmodernism as an extension of the logic of late capitalism. The final sections discuss the importance of cognitive mapping as a tool for countering what Jameson sees as the negative effects of postmodern thought and culture.

Situating Fredric Jameson historically

One of the aims of this chapter is, through a discussion of Jameson's approach to postmodernism, to introduce a fairly wide range of ideas and cultural products and processes which have been used to characterize the twentieth century (in late capitalist societies). I will discuss Jameson's approach to postmodernism in considerable detail because he has set out many of the key terms of the debate within (and outside) cultural studies. Jameson's range of intellectual and cultural experience is exceptionally wide and, I would argue, his interpretations are always stimulating and suggestive (even if his arguments are not always convincing). While this chapter is detailed, it by no means exhausts all Jameson's arguments but attempts to introduce some of the most suggestive, influential and controversial aspects of his understanding of postmodernism. Jameson developed his ideas on postmodernism over a period of years right through the 1980s but consolidated them in his key work *Postmodernism, or, The Cultural Logic of Late Capitalism* (1991a).

The historical context in which Jameson developed his ideas is enormously important to an understanding of his reading of postmodernism. As will be seen below, the years following the Second World War are associated with the rise of multinational capitalism and (at the end of the century) the announcement of 'the end' of all kinds of ideas and cultural forms. For Jameson, as a Marxist critic, the declarations of 'the end of ideology' were particularly worrying. By the end of the mid-1980s it was clear that the old Soviet Union was in crisis and by the time Jameson's *Postmodernism, or, The Cultural Logic of Late Capitalism* appeared it had collapsed. Much of the (Marxist) Left outside the Soviet Union had long been disheartened by the Soviet Union with its betrayal of the revolution, gulags and colonialist tendencies. Now they had to live with the triple deception of a failed Marxist revolution, the collapse of its biggest (totalitarian and inadmissible) manifestation and the seeming disappearance of the only ideological and political collective force felt to be capable of challenging the excesses of international capitalism. It is only by considering these circumstances that his ideas take on their full sense of urgency.

The third stage of capitalism, globalization and the multinationals

The first context for a definition of postmodernism for Jameson has to do with the particular circumstances of **late capitalism**. For this reason I will discuss very briefly how Jameson was influenced by Ernest Mandel's work *Late Capitalism* (1978). In this book Mandel distinguished various 'revolutions in power technology' within the history of capitalism leading up to late capitalism, or what Mandel called the Third Machine Age (Mandel, 1978: 118).

The first transformation is defined by free-market capitalism; this early stage is where capitalists were in free competition with one another at mainly national levels. Then comes the monopoly stage of capitalism where capitalists start to merge into huge cartels which attempt to take control of ever larger sections of the market. This corresponds to the stage of imperialism in capitalism because the few dominant capitalist countries (like Great Britain, France, Germany and the United States) significantly extended their already exploitative power over large parts of the world.

Out of this developed the third stage of capitalism where, with the help of a handful of the most powerful banks, the whole world is increasingly carved up according to the narrow interests of the ruling, capitalist classes. This is the stage that Daniel Bell called the 'postindustrial' stage (see Chapter 11) but which Jameson prefers to call the 'multinational' stage of capital (Jameson, 1991: 35). For Jameson this is postmodernism, the 'cultural dominant' of the later part of the twentieth century. Postmodernism, as late capitalism, is also defined by the rise of new forms of business organization (the multinationals or 'transnationals') that go beyond the monopoly stage because the activities of international capitalists transcend the nation state. This is in line with Marx's point in the *Grundrisse* that the 'world market' is the ultimate horizon of capitalism (xix). This is something associated with the debates around globalization.

Help File: globalization

This is a highly contested term and Jameson's position is not so much anti-globalization *per se* (which would deny any kind of internationalism) but anti-corporate globalization associated with multinational or transnational capitalism. For this reason many critics prefer the term 'counter-globalization' rather than 'anti-globalization' (Featherstone, 2008). Jameson's critique of globalization focuses on transnational capitalism; something which suggests there are forces and allegiances beyond national politics. Marxists have always been interested in the division of labour (which describes who

(Continued)

(Continued)

does what in the workplace) but with late capitalism it is now possible to talk of 'the new international division of labour' where multinationals seek out cheaper labour in different parts of the word. This is what Jameson calls 'the flight of production to advanced Third World areas' (xix). Here different areas of the world are exploited and abandoned according to the dictates of the multinationals (see the next chapter). Of course, it is also necessary to be aware of the social consequences of these movements in terms of (the lack or denial of) labour rights, child labour, dangerous working conditions, anti-unionism and pollution, etc. (for this see Klein, 2000, 2007).

As a politically motivated theory, Jameson preferred Mandel's historical model because, unlike Bell's, it did not deny 'the primacy of industrial production and the omnipresence of class struggle' which implies that the Marxist project was not redundant or outdated. (3). In terms of method, the multinational capitalism that Jameson associates with postmodernism brings about new situations for analysis and critique. Now it is no longer just a question (for the socially aware critic) of looking at what is happening within national boarders but analysing what the effects of capital are *across* boarders. This means that the cultural critic needs to take account of the extension and intensification of monopoly capitalism, or its imperialist stage. We might say that for globalized capitalism 'all the world's a stage'. This global context means that Jameson uses terms like 'late capitalism', or 'multinational capitalism' as synonyms for 'postmodernism' (1991: xviii).

Postmodernism and the end of this or that

Another way Jameson defines postmodernism has to do with the prediction of the **the end of this or that** meaning that since the Second World War all kinds of 'ends' have been announced: the end of ideology, social democracy, social class, the welfare state, art, communism, etc. For example, in Chapter 11 we saw that by the 1950s Daniel Bell had announced the end of ideology. Another conservative critic, Francis Fukuyama, announced the end of history and the 'last man' (1991). However, these writers did not consider the end of history in the same way as Foucault or Baudrillard (as a discursive construct or the effects of the hyperreal). With the fall of the Berlin Wall in 1989 and the subsequent dissolution of Soviet Russia many apologists for capitalism were repeating the 'end of ideology' claim in the interests of defending or recommending capitalism as the only viable socio-economic system. For Marxist critics like Jameson the fact that other critics on the Left could write of the end of class and of Marxism itself (Laclau and Mouffe, 1987; Gorz, 1988) has been particularly disturbing.

Another important 'end' was the one declared by philosophers like Gianni Vattimo (1985/1988) and architects like Robert Venturi (1966) and Charles Jencks (1984) who announced the end of modernity, and championing the postmodern in its place. This was another preoccupying trend for Jameson because these announcements are related to the questioning, weakening, rejection, or even extinction, of the ideas and dominant aesthetic values of modernism, or what Jameson thought of as **high modernism**.

Help File: Jameson and high modernism

By high modernism Jameson refers to movements like abstract expressionism in painting, existentialism in philosophy, T. S. Eliot or Wallace Stevens in poetry, novelists such as Joyce, Woolf, Kafka or Faulkner, or the great *auteur* directors in cinema like Ingmar Bergman, Akira Kurosawa, Alfred Hitchcock and Federico Fellini. Jameson generally laments how these examples of radical 'high modernism' have been challenged by movements associated with the Pop art of Andy Warhol (see below), the music of John Cage (and punk styles), the films of Godard or the novels of William Burroughs, Thomas Pynchon, Ismael Reed and those of the French *nouveau roman* (for example, Robert Grillet and Claude Simon).

From the breakdown of the high versus mass or commercial culture to the logic of late capitalism

In the chapter on Baudrillard we saw that an important definition of the postmodern is the breakdown between the high/low culture distinction (something Jameson also finds in the work of postmodern architects like Jencks and Venturi). However, Jameson rejected what he saw as the 'populist rhetoric' of supporters of postmodernism. What Jameson laments is the way the 'schlock' and 'kitsch' of things like the TV series, the *Reader's Digest* and the Hollywood B film are not just quoted negatively (as in Joyce and other modernists) but have become part of the very substance of postmodern forms. This links to another important theme – Jameson's claim that the high modernists had a critical edge which he believes the postmodernists have lost.

What Jameson argues (very reminiscent of Baudrillard) is that postmodern forms of aesthetic production are generally 'integrated into commodity production' (1991: 4). This means that while the great high modernists like Eliot and Joyce (in literature) and Corbusier and Frank Lloyd Wright (in architecture) placed themselves *outside* the dominant system to critique it, postmodern cultural production (with its populism) is fully integrated into the capitalism system: its forms of expression represent the purest form of capitalism.

In postmodernism there is the constant economic imperative to produce 'ever more novel-seeming goods (from clothing to airplanes), at ever greater rates of turnover'. This has a 'structural function' which demands constant 'innovation and experimentation' (4–5). In the postmodern age, 'culture' is just another commercial product. For Jameson, modernism was 'minimally and tendentially' the critique of the commodity and the effort to make it transcend itself. Postmodernism is the consumption of sheer commodification as a process' (x). And along side this, what has happened is that the 'solitary rebels and existential antiheroes' of high modernism, who struck imaginative blows against the system, have now vanished (321). One way of explaining this would be to refer to a poet like T. S. Eliot who quoted popular cultural forms in *The Wasteland* (1922) as a way of showing how popular songs, etc. were a debased and debasing form of culture which reflected the miserable, empty lives of those who consumed it. This is something mirrored in Eliot's own essays on culture which reflected the Arnoldian cum Leavisite critique of popular culture – and also has a tangential relation to Adorno's conception of the 'culture industry (see Chapter 1).

At this point it is possible to see why the subtitle of Jameson's book is '**the cultural logic of late capitalism**'. The cultural 'logic' is related to what we saw in Baudrillard: art–culture is fully complicit with the capitalist system. It has become completely incorporated within it. Jameson's account is shaped by his Marxist way of thinking where (postmodern) culture is the logical outcome of (late) capitalism. Implicitly, Jameson works with a couple of traditional Marxist concepts to describe culture: the base and the superstructure. The base, the dominant relations of production, determine the superstructure (the ideas, beliefs and culture) that the dominant classes create, police and share in order perpetuate their hegemonic control.

However, (to draw on a scene from the film *The Matrix*) in Jameson's work you can take the blue pill of postmodernism and remain where you are comfortably and complacently complicit with the system, or you can take the red pill (with its traditional left-wing associations) and critically transcend the capitalist matrix in which you are immersed. This political reading is intimately linked to the production of cultural forms mentioned above; I shall now illustrate them in more detail.

Postmodernism, 'depthlessness' and the role of commodity fetishism

One of Jameson's influential claims is that postmodernism is characterized by what he calls 'a new **depthlessness**'. In order to explain it, he interprets and compares a pair of images. The first he associates with one of the canonical works of high modernism, Van Gogh's painting 'A Pair of Boots' (1887), the other is what he thinks of as an illustrative example of the depthlessness of postmodernism: Andy Warhol's photo 'Diamond Dust Shoes' (1980). Jameson argues that the image of Van Gogh's peasant boots can be read as a reworking of the raw materials of the rural world. This emphasizes how the boots symbolize the 'whole object world of agricultural misery, of stark rural poverty, and the whole rudimentary human world of backbreaking peasant toil' (7). What Jameson argues is that Gogh's transformation of 'a drab peasant object world' is a 'utopian gesture' – a sensory compensation in painting for the misery which the primary objects represent.

Jameson goes on to argue, drawing on the philosopher Heidegger, that the painting of the peasant boots re-creates 'the whole missing object world which was once their lived context' (8). Here the painting is seen as a 'symptom for some vaster reality' (8) – where the content of the painting takes us back to all the features of the peasant world associated with peasant boots. Thus, Jameson's interpretation does not focus so much on the aesthetic qualities of the painting but uses it as a way of getting back to the circumstances of the world from which peasant boots come. This reading could not be more distant from Jameson's appraisal of Andy Warhol's 'Diamond Dust Shoes'.

What Jameson argues here is that, unlike Van Gogh's boots, these shoes are 'a random collection of dead objects' which do not evoke the 'life world' from which they come – they might as well be a 'pile of shoes left over from Auschwitz' (8). The idea is that Warhol's image does not allow the hermeneutic gesture that the peasant boots did: the image does not take the viewer back to that 'whole larger lived context of the dance hall or the ball, the world of jetset fashion of glamour magazines' from which the shoes may have come (8–9).

Jameson refers to Warhol's famous and provocative images like his billboard images of Coca-Cola bottles, his stack of Campbell's soup cans and his Brillo Pads, something which leads him to what he sees as one of the central issues of postmodernism and the politics behind it. Like Baudrillard, Jameson sees Warhol's work as turning 'centrally around commodification' (9), reflecting Warhol's beginnings as a commercial illustrator. This reinforces his belief that the whole Pop art movement, as a postmodern gesture, was complicit with the imperatives of the development of late capitalism, and thus fits into its determining logic. Hence, there seems to be no essential difference between commercial images and 'art': in postmodernism they are one and the same thing. In this way postmodern art lacks the political dimension of high modernism: Warhol's images 'ought to be powerful and critical political statements' concerning the '**commodity fetishism**' which is fundamental to late capitalism, rather than extensions of it.

Help File: commodity fetishism

Commodity fetishism is a concept used by Marx in *Das Kapital* (1867). Marx based the idea on the anthropological term 'fetish', which was used to describe how an ordinary object (like a totem) was understood to have magical (sacred) powers. For

(Continued)

(Continued)

a table to become a commodity it has to be fashioned into an object. If the carpenter keeps the table, instead of selling it, it would have use value, but would not be a commodity because in order to become one, it has to enter the market to be sold or exchanged for other goods. When it enters into a system of market exchange its value is no longer given by its use (although it still has it) but (in the first instance) by the amount of labour that has been invested in it (apart from the value given by the materials used to make it). According to Marx, it is through commodification that objects are given magical powers (like the totem). Once an object becomes a commodity it becomes 'transcendent' and is treated in such a way that the labour that went into producing it becomes invisible. In this way it is fetishized. Of course, (to bring the argument more up to date) it is obvious that media hyped goods are made out of various materials, but they are customarily treated within capitalism as if their value were not given by the workers who produced them. This loss of awareness about the circumstances of production opens up all kinds of questions about the circumstances of employment and exploitation ranging from child labour and sweat shops to union busting (see Chapter 4 on Althusser and the following chapter).

What Jameson suggests is that Warhol's use of Coke bottles, etc. are an extension of this fetishism. Following Jameson, it might be said that whereas the art of high modernism spoke a different language to that of the world of commerce and advertising, the language of Pop art is actually the same as that of the commodity and the bill board and locked into the vicious circle of commodity fetishism. Unlike in the high modernism of a Van Gogh, in postmodernism there is no critical distance and no radical politics. And this brings us back to the idea of depthlessness.

Postmodern culture, more 'depthlessness' and the waning of affect

We are now ready to see some further differences that Jameson sees between high modernism (as symbolized by Van Gogh's painting) and postmodernism (Warhol's shoes). If there is the possibility of seeing radical critique in the cultural productions of high modernism, in postmodernism there is 'a new kind of flatness or depthlessness, a new kind of superficiality'. For Jameson this is, perhaps, postmodernism's 'supreme formal feature' (1991: 9), meaning that postmodern art does not permit the reader or viewer to get back to some kind of reality behind the image – something that has preoccupied other important Marxist critics like Terry Eagleton (1986: 132f.).

For Jameson, Warhol's use of photography confers a 'deathly quality' to his work in such a way that Warhol's subjects are 'debased and contaminated' by their 'assimilation to glossy advertising images'. This notion of 'depthlessness' reveals the influence of Jean Baudrillard on Jameson's thought because it takes the emphasis off the content so that the images become 'simulacra' (1991: 9). This brings us onto another key feature of postmodernism for Jameson: '**the waning of affect** in postmodern culture' (10).

The basic idea here is that feeling, emotion, even subjectivity (consciousness) are ebbing away in postmodern culture. It is important to understand that it is a lessening, not a complete disappearance. For Jameson there is a certain 'decorative exhilaration' in 'Diamond Dust Shoes' but, unlike in the works of the high modernist writers like Rimbaud or a Rilke, there is no insistence that bourgeois subjects (who would be the expected readers of Rimbaud's or Rilke's poetry) should change their lives for the better. Here we only have 'gratuitous frivolity' (10). To explain this Jameson offers an interpretation of a canonical high modernist painting: Edward Munch's 'The Scream' (1893). This work is seen to express the great modernist themes of anomie, alienation, solitude, isolation and disintegration. Jameson argues that it does not just express these things but goes so far that it is a 'virtual deconstruction of the aesthetic of expression itself' (11). This is not a formal Derridean deconstruction but a suggestion that Munch's painting is such an extreme version of Expressionism that it seems to undermine or challenge the whole idea of it.

Help File: Expressionism

Put very simply Expressionism is a term used to refer to artistic tendencies which originated in Germany at the beginning of the twentieth century. Rather than explore the outside world, the artists associated with this movement sought to express the extremity of emotion through the use of what were often seen as exaggerated symbols. To get a better idea of this visual style see the work of the *Der Blaue Reiter* (The Blue Rider) and *Die Brücke* (The Bridge) groups.

The main point that Jameson makes is that postmodern forms of culture are so flat that we can hardly talk about inner feeling with relation to its images. Not so in Munch's painting, which functions with relation to ideas of the inside and outside: it assumes the externalization of feelings of alienation etc. From the point of view of interpretation (hermeneutics) Jameson calls this a 'depth model' which, in postmodernism, is replaced by the play of surfaces (12). This leads Jameson to a discussion of postmodern theoretical discourse, which he associates with poststructuralism (which includes the work of Michel Foucault).

What he argues is that postmodern theoretical discourses not only abandon the depth model outlined here but also reject other important distinctions which he finds valuable. For these theorists there is no essence – all collapses into appearance. This has meant that the old Freudian distinction between the latent (what is hidden) and the manifest (what is on the surface) is no longer seen as valid. Nor is the existential idea of the authentic and inauthentic. The depth model, then, is replaced by discourses, textual play and intertextuality (see Chapter 5). This brings us back to 'the waning of affect' where feeling, emotion, even subjectivity (consciousness), are ebbing away. However, Jameson's argument goes beyond this because he posits the disappearance of subjectivity itself with his notion of **the death of the subject** in contemporary theory (15).

The death of the subject and Marxist discourse

What Jameson means by the death of the subject is that contemporary post-modern theory signifies the 'end of the autonomous bourgeois monad, ego or individual'.

Help File: the monad

The term 'monad' is associated with philosophers like Gottfried Leibniz and Giordano Bruno and is used by Jameson to refer to the self as an indivisible unity that is wholly independent of other selves.

But why associate the monad with the bourgeoisie? This is because Jameson understands the idea of the autonomous, unified self as developing with the rise and gradual domination of capitalism and bourgeois forms of thought and egocentric individualism. Jameson uses Munch's 'The Scream' to exemplify this. The centred subject of high modernism had a price, as can be deduced from Munch's painting, which dramatizes the problems of individual subjectivity 'as a self-sufficient field' which is condemned to 'mindless solitude' (15). This is the suffering of angst that many critics have associated with the great high-modernist artists. For Jameson, postmodernism signals the end of the monadic bourgeois ego and the suffering that goes with it, but Jameson fears that it also represents the breakdown of all feeling (affect). His basic argument is that if the self is decentred (through Lacanian psychoanalysis or Derridian deconstruction etc.) there is, effectively, no self left to do the suffering (15). This is confirmed by Slavoj Žižek's Lacanian reading which posits that the postmodern is when we accept that the subject represented by 'The Scream' 'is *nothing but*' a 'dreaded "void"' (1992: 137).

For Jameson, the disappearance of the individual subject also threatens the notion of artists having a 'unique style' which marks out their works from others (15–16). In this context Jameson develops another important idea: the loss of the collective ideals of the artistic or political vanguard (1991: 15–16). Jameson's argument in this context can be seen as an implied answer to Jean-François Lyotard and his followers who, as we saw, claimed that the postmodern is characterized by a loss of faith in the traditional discourses which had legitimated knowledge (where knowledge is represented as serving the ends of human freedom or helps to perfect society). We saw that the consequence of this kind of thinking was that no form of knowledge can be privileged over any other form. They are all what Lyotard called Wittgensteinian 'language games' with equal rights to challenge one another. Anything else is a kind of discursive terrorism which attempts to exclude the other players from the game (Lyotard, 1984: 63f.).

For Jameson this way of understanding challenged and weakened political discourses like Marxism, which provide large explanatory systems with the end of changing the world through knowledge, critique, consciousness and struggle. This is a real problem for a committed Marxist – or anyone affiliated to political discourses that seek to transform the world with relation to a way of seeing which is regarded as superior to other ways. Much of what Jameson rejects as postmodern militates against explanatory systems which attempt to offer a more global view of the social, economic, political world. Part of the 'logic' of postmodernism is to be found in how thought and other forms of cultural production in late capitalism effectively fragment and delegitimate the discourses of collective struggle and change. If the 'logic' of late capitalism is understood in this way, it is possible to see why postmodern thought and art are exposed to such powerful critique in Jameson's work. Before continuing let us consider some crucial questions about these ideas.

Practice: reading visual culture with Jameson

First, can you see any reason why Warhol's 'Diamond Dust Shoes' should not be seen as a symptom for some 'vaster reality'? Do you agree that Warhol's image is complicit with commodity fetishism? Do you agree that a photographic image or negative denies the possibilities of opening up interpretation to 'depth' readings?

You might think about whether or not (or how far it might be said that) the reproduction of images of popular commodities like Coke bottles are an extension of this fetishism. How convincing do you find Jameson's suggestion that the art of high modernism spoke a different language to that of the world of commerce and advertising and that the language of Pop art is actually the same as that of the commodified world?

Do you feel that in the version of postmodernism illustrated here there is no critical distance and no radical politics to be found? How far do you think it is justified to privilege high modernism over the postmodern?

The following Help File will offer some answers to these questions.

Help File: reading visual culture with Jameson

In terms of considering if there is any reason why Warhol's 'Diamond Dust Shoes' should not be seen as a symptom for some 'vaster reality', it might be considered that nothing really stands in the way of using the shoes as a symptom of the life of the people who wear them. The title is not as clear as Van Gogh's but 'diamond dust' might suggest all kinds of social and historical contexts from entertainment and celebrity that relate to the lives of the super rich (or those who dream of such a life). In fact, you may notice that Jameson claims it is not possible to restore the shoes to their 'larger lived context' of the dance hall or the ball. Yet, that is precisely what Jameson *does* by immediately evoking the world of 'jet-set fashion' or glamour magazines.

There does not seem to be any reason why Gogh's painting *necessarily* evokes the *hardship* of peasant communities. It might be argued that interpretation can go in any direction. One possible response is not to see the boots as a 'utopian gesture' but an example of the ability to see beauty in the peasant world or even an idealization (or, ironically, a fetishization) of the rural world from which they come. Notice, too, *how* Jameson describes Warhol's image of shoes drawing (one might say arbitrarily) on the Nazi death camps to evoke a negative reading by association.

To consider Warhol's reproduction of commercial images as 'art' and as possible radical critique you might focus on the fact that Warhol called his studio 'The Factory'. While the name of his studio, in itself, does not prove that Warhol was creating radical critiques through his works, you may feel that this opens up the possibility for the 'depth' model of criticism that Jameson denies.

This means that 'depthlessness' may be more a question of *how* an image is read, that is, the critical strategy adopted, rather than something pre-existing in the image. This does not discount the possibility that some images seem to invite more political readings than others. For example, Barbara Krugar (ironically, often considered a key postmodern artist) took a photo of George Bush (senior) and added the phrase 'Pro-life for the unborn: Pro-death for the born'. This work brings out, in a very explicit way, her attitude to the Bush administration's posture on abortion and its belligerent militarism. What needs to be decided here is, while the addition of this kind of text makes political (or critical) readings readily available, does this exclude similar readings of works which provide no textual clues? For example, the title of Van Gogh's 'A Pair of Boots' is much less explicit than Kruger's title, yet this did not stop Jameson from applying his depth reading to the painting.

So it is that many artists thought of as postmodern actually directly invite criticism of commodity fetishism or capitalism. You might look at the work of Hans Haacke (see the next chapter). You might also explore artists like Hannah Wilke who photographed herself naked (and holding pistols) on top of a compressor with the slogan 'exchange value' (inviting the viewer to consider things like the connections between industry, armaments and the use of the erotic image).

In terms of Jameson's privileging of high modernism over the postmodern you might think of the way artists (prior to postmodernism) like Marcel Duchamp presented a urinal, a bottle rack or a bicycle wheel mounted on a stool as 'art'. These were found objects (*objets trouvés*) which challenged the whole idea of the artist as genius and the integrity of the work of art. These pieces can be seen as highly provocative attacks on the whole bourgeois notion of art (with its commodification through galleries and the art market). Duchamp, on being asked how his 'Bicycle Wheel' was to be interpreted, answered 'that machine has no intention except to get rid of the appearance of a work of art' and 'throw off the desire to create works of art' (in Harrison and Wood, 2002: 1024).

Yet Jameson, while recognizing the possibility of postmodernism as just an extension of modernism, constructs a notion of high modernism, which is very selective and bypasses these artistic gestures which already eat away at the idea of the older centred subject of the artist (with her or his creative originality) and the work of 'art' as having some special depth. It may have been for these reasons that Jameson found 'artists' like Duchamp difficult to place with relation to the modernist canon (1991: 302).

This last point may help you to question the canonizing labels that designate artistic or historical periods. You might ask to what extent it is useful to label and canonize. This is a difficult question which may resist an 'either/or' answer because artists have often identified themselves (however loosely) with one another against other artists, movements or periods. Also, while it is possible to question historical periodization, it is also possible to see how different forms of culture are made possible by, for example, technological changes (machine, book, photography, video, digital cultures, etc.).

Despite the possible problems of Jameson's arguments, the idea of reading visual culture as symptomatic of the wider world from which the objects are taken is a very suggestive idea. For further practice you might scrutinize products and their representations in ads to study the intensification of commodity fetishism which diverts attention away from production to create value in such a way that a commodity seems to have value *in itself*.

Parody versus pastiche, 'pastness' and crisis in contemporary history

I shall now turn to Jameson's distinction between **parody and pastiche** which are closely aligned with the ideas introduced in the last section. What pastiche and parody have in common is that they imitate a recognizable style, but Jameson values parody (associated with modernism) over pastiche (associated with the postmodern). For Jameson, parody imitates but with a 'satiric impulse' (17). The reason why this 'satiric impulse' is so important is because it has a critical edge where nonsense, hypocrisy, foolishness (and a host of other human follies) are criticized and laughed at through ridicule and irony, often with the end of correcting or changing things. But this is not the case with (postmodern) pastiche, which is a form of mimicry but without the ridicule.

The idea of the postmodern being dominated by pastiche is connected to his idea that everything in late capitalism is so fragmented that society has no guiding norms left – it has no sense of any 'great collective project'. With the collapse of the high modernist 'ideology of style' (a sense of stylistic original-ity and uniqueness) the producers of culture under postmodernism can only imitate or 'cannibalize' past styles – but not with any satiric purpose (17–18). This brings us back to history because, for Jameson (as for Baudrillard), the postmodern is an age in which the past (history) has become 'a vast collection of images, a multitudinous photographic simulacrum' or a mere collection of texts (18). Here films and books draw on the stereotypes of a past created by other films and books (simulacra) rather than regard history as a concrete referent (what Eagleton sees as dehistoricized forms of thought and culture (Eagleton, 1986: 131f.) – a common preoccupation in Left criticism).

One way to understand this is to look at what Jameson calls the 'nostalgia film' like George Lucas's *American Graffiti* (1973) (a teen film set in the early 1960s, full of drive-ins, drag racing and rock 'n' roll music). What Jameson argues is that these nostalgia films (others are Polanski's *Chinatown* and Bertolucci's *Il Conformista*) do not evoke the past as a 'referent' – some-thing real that happened with actual historical content. They only evoke the past through **pastness**, which means that the past is a question of 'stylistic connotation' – eliciting the right stylistic features to suggest '1930s-ness' or '1950s-ness', etc. (19). Jameson even links this stylistic nostalgia to futuristic science-fiction films like Lucas's *Star Wars* (1977), which are not nostalgic because they 'reinvent a picture of the past' but because they reinvent 'the feel and shape of characteristic art objects of an older period' (1985: 116).

Jameson links his assertions about the nostalgia film (and a similar discus-sion of the contemporary novel) to what he calls 'a crisis in historicity' (1991: 22). This is something that is reflected in the first sentence of the introduction to *Postmodernism, or, the Cultural Logic of Late Capitalism*, which presents the irony of trying 'to grasp the concept of the postmodern as an attempt to think the present historically in an age that has forgotten how to think historically in the first place' (ix).

Jameson demonstrates this point about this crisis in history by referring to E. L. Doctorow's novel *Ragtime* (1974), a work constructed around fictional and non-fictional characters. What Jameson finds both compelling and disqui-eting in this novel is that Doctorow deploys the 'strategies of pastiche' inso-far as he creates a sense of 'pastness' through his uses of well-known people and situations, but this 'pop history' can only represent ideas and stereotypes about the past. It is a history that is only the simulacra of history (25) – a his-tory of 'pseudoevents' (48). The consequences of this are that with the loss of history goes any sense of collective memory that might work for change. So, we might say that from Jameson's point of view in postmodernity 'history' has become a *faking disaster*.

> ## Practice: Jameson, pastness and pastiche and history as a *faking disaster*
>
> You might consider here Jameson's theory of pastiche as a historically empty strategy that only evokes history through images of the past. Do you think that novels, films, etc. can construct history in such a way that they can be regarded as reliable, factual accounts of the past? I have called contemporary history *a faking disaster*. Can you show how the pun might help to explain Jameson's attitude to how history is questioned or dissolved in contemporary writing?
>
> Do you think Jameson is asking too much of film to expect it to evoke the past as anything more than style? It is worth noting that Jameson does not actually give an example of a film which genuinely engages with history as a referent. You might think about the historical films or bio-pics you have seen to consider whether different approaches convey more or less historical authenticity.

Postmodernism and cultural schizophrenia

The crisis in history that Jameson perceives in postmodernism leads him to consider the question of 'temporal organization' and how this helps to fragment the world in such a way that it becomes increasingly meaningless. The idea is that if the postmodern subject has lost the capacity to organize the past and future into 'coherent experience' it is not easy to see how the cultural products stemming from such a subject could be anything other than 'heaps of fragments' (1991: 25) dominated by largely meaningless and random collections of things (like the pastiche described above). To describe this Jameson uses the idea of **cultural schizophrenia**, derived from the work of Jacques Lacan.

In Chapter 8 we saw that Lacan conceived schizophrenia in terms of, to quote Jameson's words, a 'breakdown in the signifying chain, that is, the interlocking syntagmatic series of signifiers which constitutes an utterance or a meaning' (26). For Lacan schizophrenia is the inability to unify the past, present and future because all experiences are a series of disconnected and unrelated 'presents in time'. For Lacan the signifying chain is like a sentence that has to be constructed in a particular order to make sense. To understand a sentence it is necessary to be able to relate all the parts together – if not, you just end up with a jumble of words (signifiers) that have to be experienced separately, which means you cannot make sense of anything.

This is one of the reasons Jameson calls postmodern cultural forms 'spatial' (rather than temporal): in them we find the loss of progressive temporality where the experience of 'existential time' and 'deep memory' (of high modernism) gives way to dislocation (154). This is the 'schizophrenic art' of postmodernity where the attention is focused in a very intense way on a series presents but where it is difficult to make sense of a greater whole. However, it should be added that there is one important change in Lacan's formulation. Jameson sees postmodern art not so much as isolated words but more like sentences 'in free-standing isolation' (28). There is some meaning there but everything seems discontinuous (but these isolated blocks of meaning may provide disjointed and intense moments).

Thus, postmodern cultural forms from poems like Bob Perelman's 'China' (with their free-standing sentences which make sense individually but do not seem to connect to one another) to the video installations of Nam June Paik (where multiple images and sounds happen simultaneously) defy higher levels of understanding (373). For Jameson, the same can be said of navigating postmodern 'hyperspace' (38), symbolized by huge postmodern architectural projects like the Westin Bonaventura Hotel in Los Angeles. Again we come back to Jameson's favourite distinction: in the international style of Corbusier's generation the high modernists, rather than blend in with the 'tawdry and commercial sign system of the surrounding city', inserted into it a different, more elevated 'Utopian language' (39). By creating a 'new Utopian space' the high modernists offered a challenge to the 'degraded and fallen city fabric' (41) rather than a reflection of it.

However, for Jameson postmodern architecture is closest to the imperatives of late capitalism because it is bound up with land values and receives patronage from the multinational businesses. Not only this but in navigating the vastness of interiors of structures like the Bonaventura Hotel the postmodern subject only gets confused, disorientated and suffers a loss of perspective. This brings us to a key idea in Jameson's writing: the importance of developing models which can help us grasp the complexity of late (multinational) capitalism.

Practice: (post)modernism and heaps of fragments

You might consider that heaps of fragments could be said to be a key idea within modernism (see, for example, T. S. Eliot's *The Wasteland* and James Joyce's *Ulysses*). Although these works are often seen to be held together by myth, many contemporary readers were struck by the fragmentation and lack of coherence as a symbol of an age dominated by anomie. Again, Jameson has to idealize a certain understanding of high modernism to make his arguments hang together.

Jameson's reading of Perelman's poem 'New China' (mentioned above) can help to show how his distinction between high modernism and the postmodern does not always hold up very well. He starts out by affirming a Lacanian 'schizophrenic fragmentation' only to admit that the poem does have some 'global meaning' which is precisely what he wants to deny the products of postmodern culture. Also, he finds ways of giving the poem depth by outlining *how* the poem came to be. Once we know this, its perceived disjointed character seems to be restored in the act of interpretation. However, what I want to suggest here is that Jameson's ways of distinguishing between the modern and the postmodern, while flawed, are very useful to an understanding of the tendencies that may define cultural production in the latter part of the twentieth century and into the twenty-first. In terms of practice you can test the ideas against the intellectual and artistic practices that you encounter to see how well they may explain not only aesthetic and analytic characteristics but the cultural-economic systems in which they are produced.

From high-tech paranoia to cognitive mapping

While Jameson offers a jaundiced account of postmodern thought and artistic production he does see something of great interest emerging in the 'most energetic postmodernist texts' (37), something he calls **'high-tech paranoia'** (38). Once again, what he tries to do is link his discussion of postmodern cultural production to the multi-national capitalism which provides its logic and in which it circulates. What he argues is that while technology should not be understood as determining either cultural production or social life it is of fundamental importance. The idea that Jameson puts forward is that certain science fiction genres can give us insights into the vast complexity of the world of multi-national capitalism. Jameson argues that contemporary technology (which is reflected in these narratives) can offer 'some privileged representational shorthand for grasping a network of power and control even more difficult for our minds and imaginations to grasp'. He is referring to the 'whole decentred global network of the third stage of capital itself' (38).

High-tech paranoia refers to those contemporary narratives in which the impossibly complex circuits of a global computer networks are linked to the labyrinthine machinations of rival information agencies. More particularly he refers to the genre of cyberpunk – the most popular manifestation of which is probably William Gibson's *Neuromancer* (1984), which helped to stimulate this kind of narrative. Ridley Scott's film *Blade Runner* (1982) can be seen as an extension or variation of this basic narrative pattern with its high-tech paranoia generated in and around advanced computer technology, cybernetics and corporate power. For Jameson these 'garish narrative manifestations' of conspiracy theory are a kind of 'degraded attempt' to 'think the impossible totality of the contemporary world system'. Cyberpunk, then, is 'fully as much an expression of transnational corporate realities as it is of global paranoia itself' (38).

This genre can help us to understand 'the impossible totality of the contemporary world system' and to grasp the practically incomprehensible character of the modern world, which can be grasped (albeit dimly) through these contemporary forms. Cyberpunk, then, is a suggestive cultural form to help us understand how the interests of the multinationals transcend the traditional nation state (the corporate globalization mentioned earlier). The importance of genres like cyberpunk, then, is that they can help us to cognitively map the complexity of the contemporary world as a means to changing it.

Jameson, popular culture, politics and new social movements

Jameson often adopts a disparaging tone when he describes examples of cyberpunk as 'garish narrative manifestations' or 'degraded' attempts to 'think the impossible totality of the contemporary world system'. He does not explain why these are garish or degraded – there is just the assumption that they are. This is out of step with much contemporary cultural studies which does not assume these negative value judgements as givens. This (de)valuation of popular forms is very much in line with other Marxist approaches to popular culture like the Frankfurt School (see Chapter 1).

If you read Jameson carefully you will see that he does have some positive things to say about postmodern architects, writers, painters, directors, etc. and admits that the postmodern embraces forms of oppositional culture like 'those of marginal groups, those of radically distinct residual or emergent cultural languages' (159). He also claims to be a 'relatively enthusiastic consumer of postmodern culture' (298) and commends the postmodern age as being more 'democratic', more literate and less prone to worshiping charisma and 'genius' (306). Yet, as this chapter has tended to show, Jameson consistently privileges high modernism over postmodernism and his political beliefs and radical politics largely prevent him from embracing what he regards as postmodernist thought or culture. Yet, as Terry Eagleton has written, oppositional culture *can* be expressed in what Jameson regards as postmodern forms (Eagleton, 2000: 86). Jameson is not fundamentally in disagreement with this but Eagleton, who is as sceptical of postmodern thought as Jameson is (Eagleton, 1996), does not tend to represent high modernism as a privileged site of resistance.

As we have seen, Jameson's rejection of postmodernism is wedded to his radical politics. As suggested above, the problem for Jameson is that depthlessness and the loss of history only intensifies a loss of understanding which works against any possible socialist transformation of society (a preoccupation also shared by Eagleton (1986: 131f.)). Jameson formulates questions like: how are we to understand the complex machinations of late capitalism if we have no sense of past time, or a past reduced to simulacra? How is it possible to effect changes in history if it has been deconstructed in the theoretical or artistic productions of the contemporary world?

To sum up, all this is part of the logic of late capitalism: any collective project, any ideological critique, is disarmed by the bourgeois culture that sustains it

(Jameson, 1991: 47). Late capitalism sucks everything into itself, and critical distance is erased by the colonization of formally independent spheres like art by commodifying processes (see the section on Warhol above) (405). For Jameson, given these cultural trends, there is a real need for theories, like Marxism, that can offer the possibility of stepping back and seeing all this at a distance, as more of a totality.

What is imperative for Jameson, then, is that the great collective project of socialism must not be abandoned. As indicated, this puts Jameson at odds with the kind of political movements associated with Lyotard's abandonment of grand narratives. Thus, Jameson is suspicious of the 'new social movements' (319–332), a postmodern politics (mentioned in the previous chapter) which is closely associated with writers like Laclau and Mouffe (1985). These movements challenge the older political system, dominated by party politics and dubious consensus and 'majorities', and replace them with smaller alliances between groups who support one another on particular issues rather than according to larger overarching ideologies. While Jameson is not against these groups *per se* he sees them as another product of the logic of late capitalism because politics, like everything else, is being fragmented to the point where we cannot deal with the larger issues (the menaces of late or multinational capitalism). This fits in with Jameson's belief that politics needs to be organized around class consciousness, if it is to be effective and durable (I shall go into more detail about the new social movements in Chapter 15).

The problem with micro politics without totalizing collective struggle is 'bad infinity' (Jameson, 1991: 330) – were you get struggle at the local level but no lasting change – groups just go on arguing forever. For Jameson there is a need for a more globalized form of politics to resist global capitalism linked to 'a new international proletariat' (417). This is linked to a need for a new political art, what he calls an 'aesthetic of cognitive mapping – a pedagogical political culture' that can devise 'radically new forms' to offer us, 'as individual and collective subjects', some special insight into our place within multinational capitalism.

Help File: cognitive mapping

The idea of cognitive mapping was first posited by the American psychologist Edward Tolman as a means to describe how environments are negotiated, perceived and understood (Tolman, 1948). Jameson has adapted this idea from psychology to apply it to understanding the vast economic and political complexities of late capitalism.

Here we see that the meaning and value of postmodernism is negotiated and fought over, something we saw reflected at the end of the last chapter. We also see that Jameson offers 'cognitive mapping' as a possible way to counter the bewilderment associated with the complexity of late capitalism and provide effective forms of critique. It is these two themes that will be discussed in depth in the following chapter.

Summary of key points

This chapter began by situating Jameson's ideas historically in terms of the collapse of the Soviet Union and with relation to transformations in late capitalism. Jameson's key notion of postmodernism, as the logic of late capitalism has been described, and critiqued with relation to ideas such as the end of history, the breakdown of distinctions between high versus mass culture and parody and pastiche. Other important themes like 'depthlessness', the loss of affect and the death of the subject, the crisis in history, and the idea of postmodernism as cultural schizophrenia have also been linked to Jameson's central thesis. The final sections have discussed the relation between what Jameson regards as high-tech paranoia and the importance of cognitive mapping as a tool for countering the negative effects of postmodern thought and culture.

Further reading

Jameson's *The Political Unconscious* (1981) gives an in-depth view of what Jameson considers proper historical criticism might look like from a Marxist perspective. Jameson's *Signatures of the Visible* (1990) and *The Geopolitical Aesthetic* (1992) usefully see cinema (and visual culture in general) as a window through which the social totality can be glimpsed and his *Archaeologies of the Future: The Desire Called Utopia and Other Science Fictions* (2005) while offering insightful readings of the genre also gives an idea of Jameson's vision of a new global federalism as the alternative to capitalism. *A Singular Modernity* (2002) explores the notions of modernity and modernism and helps to explain the ambiguities and weaknesses of the terms while stressing their importance. His later work, like *Valences of the Dialectic* (2009) and *The Hegel Variations* (2010), while philosophically oriented, offer many examples of the way Jameson reads contemporary culture. Dixon and Zonn's 'Confronting the Geopolitical Aesthetic: Fredric Jameson, *The Perfumed Nightmare* and the Perilous Place of Third Cinema' (2005) offers an overview of Jameson's project and critiques Jameson's cognitive mapping and general arguments. Brooker and Brooker's introduction to *Postmodern After-Images* (1997) questions Jameson's ways of reading postmodern cultures taking into account questions of active reception as does Jim Collins (in Collins et al. *Film Theory Goes to the Movies*, 1993). For more critiques of Jameson's ideas on the postmodern see the collection of essays in Douglas Kellner's *Postmodernism/Jameson/Critique*

(1989), Robert Young's 'The Jameson Raid' (Young, 1990) and Eagleton's 'Fredric Jameson: The Politics of Style' (Eagleton, 1986).

To follow up the idea of globalization see Jameson and Miyoshi *The Cultures of Globalization* (1998) which is a collection of essays on globalization that includes a very useful preface by Jameson. Other very useful studies are Zygmunt Bauman's *Globalization: The Human Consequences* (1998), Ulrich Beck's *What is Globalization?* (1999) and Michel Chossudovsky's *The Globalization of Poverty: Impacts of IMF and World Bank Reforms* (1997). Spivak, in Chapter 4 of *A Critique of Postcolonial* Reason (1999), subjects Jameson's concept of postmodernity to a thoroughgoing (and respectful) critique within the context of debates on subjectivity and post-colonialism.

14

Practising Cultural Studies

Hegemony and Cognitive Mapping

Learning goals

- To understand how concepts like postmodernism can be understood as sites of struggle.
- To appreciate how the idea of cognitive mapping can be used with relation to political art.
- To be aware of how novels like Susan Daitch's *L.C.* can be read to offer effective forms of cognitive mapping that resemble how cultural studies might read the corporate world.
- To understand how Gramsci's concept of hegemony may help to highlight how concepts are sites of struggle and how a key aspect of cultural studies is involved in politicized efforts to try to bring about positive change.

Concepts

The key concepts introduced in this chapter are: hegemony, cognitive mapping and the 'homeopathic strategy'.

Introduction

This chapter begins by considering how Gramsci's notion of hegemony can be applied to the meaning and valuation of terms like postmodernism as a means of showing how these concepts can be understood as sites of struggle within academic institutions. This is followed up by two in-depth analyses that show how Jameson's notion of cognitive mapping can be put into practice as a part of a 'homeopathic strategy' which exposes points of complicity between the corporate world and institutions of art. The final section comes back to the notion of hegemony to argue that a key feature of cultural studies is not only to raise consciousness but is linked to attempts to bring about positive changes in the world.

Theory wars: Gramsci, hegemony and the postmodern as a site of struggle

In the last chapter we saw that Fredric Jameson privileges high modernism over what he understands as the artistic cultures and intellectual currents he associates with postmodernism – all products of the cultural logic of late capitalism. At the end of the chapter I mentioned his notion of cognitive mapping, which attempts to devise radically new forms to offer special insight into our place within multinational capitalism. This chapter will explore this idea and recommend ways in which it can help to develop forms of practice. However, before I go on to explore cognitive mapping in more detail I want to take up another theme mentioned at the end of the last chapter concerned with the meaning and value of postmodernism.

In Jameson's work we see how notions of postmodernism and poststructuralism are negotiated and fought over. Struggles over the meaning and value of culture is often related to what Gramsci referred to as **hegemony** – a concept outlined in Chapter 1. We saw there that hegemony theory has become a very important reference point in cultural studies and I want to show how it can be applied to the different positions adopted with regard to postmodernism (including poststructuralism). In this way we will see hegemony at work in a specific context.

This hegemonic struggle over meaning reflects Jameson's observation (quoted in Chapter 11) that the postmodern as a concept is 'not merely contested', but also 'internally conflicted and contradictory' (Jameson, 1991: xxii). In part, this is because different critics disagree about how to define it but it is also because postmodernism (and all theories and methods) are marshalled in support of different political-institutional agendas. If you turn back to Chapter 1 you will see that the 'turn to', and theory of, hegemony within cultural studies has been used not only to describe the winning of consent in the wider political arena but can be adapted to the struggles for meaning in terms of the production of cultural forms (including popular culture). Here we see that the concept can help to throw light on the vicissitudes of cultural theory itself.

It is clear that Jameson is highly sceptical of anything he labels postmodern but, as we saw in the last chapter, he is just one critic, among many, who not only questions but tends to devalue or reject the cultures and forms of thought defined by the label. Other critics, like Spivak (1999) and Ziauddin Sardar (1998), have questioned the representativeness and often universalizing claims of postmodernism, forcing scholars to consider that postmodernism has its roots in colonialism and modernity and that, far from being emancipatory, actually represents a threat to non-Western identities and histories. On the other hand, other black American critics like Cornel West (1988) and bell hooks (1990) refuse to allow the postmodern to be disconnected from black Afro-American experience.

Within these different discourses different critics may adopt positive, negative or ambiguous attitudes towards the texts, forms and theories they associate with the postmodern. It is hardly surprising then that Ebbesen (2006: 1) has referred to postmodernism as a 'battlefield of contending ideas'. In this sense we can see postmodernism in hegemonic terms: as a site of struggle. This situation is made more complex still when critics like Linda Hutcheon claim postmodernism is characterized by radical ambiguity in such a way that it is 'a curious mixture of the complicitous and the critical' (Hutcheon, 1988: 201). Hutcheon's point is that postmodern artistic forms (seen in novels like John Fowles's *The French Lieutenant's Woman*, Salman Rushdie's *Midnight's Children* and E. L. Doctorow's *Ragtime*) both construct a sense of history but, at the same time, expose or undermine the conventions that are used to formulate it in the first place. Postmodern narrative – which not only includes literature but history and theory – is made complex, ambiguous and problematic by 'its theoretical self-awareness of history and fiction as human constructs' (7). This is what she calls 'historiographic metafiction' which, while exposing the conventions of novelistic worlds, 'both asserts and then undermines those worlds and their constructing' (202).

History, then, seems to exist and not exist at the same time. It is this indeterminacy 'that sets the postmodern up for the contradictory responses it has evoked from a vast range of political perspectives'. The problem here for Hutcheon is that one side of this ambiguity or paradox generally gets ignored so that postmodernism becomes either totally complicit or totally critical. For this reason 'it has been accused of everything from reactionary nostalgia to radical revolution' (201). The postmodern arts (and this is also true for theory), can, and have, been interpreted in opposite and 'mutually contradictory ways' as 'conservative and nostalgic' or 'revitalizing and revolutionary' (204) but Hutcheon insists that they should be seen as 'doubly encoded'.

Thus, for Hutcheon, postmodernism is 'unmarked' politically – its ambiguity can lead to it being considered Right, Left or Centre (205–6). Again, this tends to highlight the postmodern as a site of struggle, rather than something unambiguous or pre-given. At a practical level this means you have to make up your own mind about the cultural forms you consume or theories you read. Below I shall present two cases where works which could easily fall into Jameson's category of postmodernism (on stylistic and formal grounds) can actually be recuperated as politically engaged attempts at, ironically, providing the very thing that Jameson puts forward as a way of countering the debilitating effects of the logic of late capitalism: **cognitive mapping**.

I shall argue that, on one level, they may seem like products of the logic of late capitalism but, on the other, they provide very effective critiques of it (which, in the case of the artist Hans Haacke, Jameson agrees). In this I can be said to be involved in a hegemonic struggle over the meaning and value of the works I interpret, but I will also use these hegemonic interventions to propose other related strategies, which will be the subjects of the last chapter of this book.

Cognitive mapping, postmodern political art and the 'homeopathic strategy'

At the end of the last chapter we saw that Jameson argued that there is a need for a more globalized form of politics to resist global capitalism. This was wedded to a need for a new political art that he calls an 'aesthetic of cognitive mapping – a pedagogical political culture' that could formulate 'radically new forms' to offer special insight into our place within multinational capitalism. In this context Jameson mentions what he calls a '*homeopathic* **strategy**' (1991: 409) that he saw in the work of the artist Hans Haacke. This strategy is where an artist uses the very thing which is considered corrupt (like advertising images) to criticize the institutions in which they circulate (rather like a homoeopathist uses microscopic traces of potentially dangerous substances that, delivered in greater quantities, would produce the same symptoms as those of the disease being treated). It is interesting to note that Jameson regards Haacke as postmodern because of his deconstruction of 'perceptual categories', but what interests Jameson is that this deconstruction is redirected onto the art institutions themselves, thus producing a very effective form of political art (158).

This admission that a 'postmodern' artist can raise important political questions leads Jameson to reflect on the problems of defining postmodernism in totalizing terms. He realizes that this paints him into a corner where he is forced to acknowledge that the kind of cultural production associated with Haacke is 'clearly postmodern and equally clearly political and oppositional – something that does not compute within the paradigm and does not seem to have been theoretically foreseen by it' (159). This is what Derrida would call an *aporia* (see Chapters 5 and 6) that, to some extent, throws Jameson's theory into disarray (and reflects the ambiguities brought out by Hutcheon). Yet I want to insist on the value of Jameson's idea of cognitive mapping, which has a long history in cultural studies, which goes back at least to Raymond Williams who wrote about mapping changes in life and thought (1958/1987: xiii).

If Haacke is understood as a postmodern artist, then, he illustrates that postmodern artists *do* offer a way of negotiating different levels of reality within late capitalism. Jameson notices that Haacke's conceptual art links (and exposes) the institutional space of the museum (or art gallery) with the (often hidden or invisible) infrastructures around it – like the importance of its trustees and 'their affiliations with multinational corporations' and global capitalism (Jameson, 1991: 158).

Cognitive mapping in practice 1: Haacke's *MetroMobilitan*

To show how art can reflect on the institutional space of the art gallery and the hidden or invisible infrastructures around it I shall refer to Haacke's work *MetroMobilitan* (see Figure 14.1), which was shown at the John Weber Gallery in 1985. As Jameson does not go into great detail about Haacke's work I shall rely on an article by Travis English to show how Haacke's exhibits have 'focused on demystifying the relationship between museums and corporations' (English, 2007: 1). Haacke's *MetroMobilitan* featured the large banners that were beginning to be used to advertise exhibitions – a practice begun at the Metropolitan Museum of Art, New York, when it was run by Thomas Hoving (who has been cited as one of the first gallery directors to seek corporate funding). By choosing the title *MetroMobilitan* it is possible to see how Haacke cleverly puns on the names of the Metropolitan Museum and the Mobil Corporation (a major North American oil company which is now part of ExxonMobil), bringing out the relations between the two entities. What Haacke explores in his installation are the relations between the Mobil Corporation sponsorship of the Metropolitan and the latter's exhibition of ancient Nigerian art.

As English explains, at the time of Mobil's sponsorship of the Nigerian exhibition 'it was selling oil to South Africa's apartheid government, military and police, and was one of the largest U.S. corporations present in the nation'. Mobil's

Figure 14.1   Hans Haacke's MetroMobilitan shown at the John Weber Gallery (1985)

attitude to discontinuing sales was quoted by Haacke on one of his three exhibition banners: 'Mobil's management in New York believes that its South African subsidiaries' sales to the police and military are but a small part of its total sales' (English, 2007: 5). Haacke's central banner carried an image of a sculpture from the Nigeria exhibition and on the right of it another banner carried another official statement from Mobil: 'total denial of supplies to the police and military forces of a host country is hardly consistent with an image of responsible citizenship in that country' (6) and all three banners featured the Mobil corporate logo. At the rear of the banners was placed a large photomural of a funeral procession depicting black victims shot by South African police (see Figure 14.2).

Figure 14.2 Photomural of a funeral procession depicting victims shot by South African Police (detail)

Above the banners, and set into an entablature reflecting the Metropolitan Museum's architecture, was a plaque which quoted a pamphlet circulated by the Metropolitan entitled 'The Business Behind Art Knows the Art of Good

Business – Your Company and the Metropolitan Museum of Art'. This title already exposed the complicity between the Museum and the wider business community but the plaque hammered home the point:

> Many public relations opportunities are available through the sponsorship of programs, special exhibitions and services. These can often provide a creative and cost effective answer to a specific marketing objective, particularly where international, governmental or consumer relations may be a fundamental concern. (Quoted in English, 2007: 6)

As English avers, in this work Haacke exposes the processes of mystification that take place with relation to corporate backing and indicates how these seemingly dissimilar elements (an exhibition in New York and violence in South Africa) 'are related to one another vis-à-vis the financial ties of the corporation to the Apartheid government as well as the Metropolitan Museum' (6). This is very much in keeping with Jameson's reading of Haacke which emphasizes a critical dimension in his work that serves to unveil the affiliations between the gallery, multinational corporations and global capitalism.

This also opens up another line of thought connected to Pierre Bourdieu's notion of the distinction between economic and cultural capital. This is where it is possible to assess value not only on economic terms but in terms of how social reputation or kudos can be gained through contact with cultural forms (literature, opera, the fine arts, etc.) that confer higher status on the individual or group (Bourdieu, 1979/1986). In an interview with Bourdieu, Haacke specifically acknowledged how corporations attempt to gain symbolic (cultural) capital through their sponsorship of art exhibitions:

> I think it is important to distinguish between the traditional notion of patronage and the public relations manoeuvres parading as patronage today. [...] The American term *sponsoring* more accurately reflects that what we have here is really an exchange of capital: financial capital on the part of the sponsors and symbolic capital on the part of the sponsored. [...] Alain-Dominique Perrin, for example says quite bluntly that he spends Cartier's money for purposes that have nothing to do with the love of art. [...] In his own words 'Patronage [*le mécénat*] is not only a great tool for communication. It does much more: it is a tool for the seduction of public opinion'. (Haacke, in Grasskamp et al., 2004: 132)

Continuing in the spirit of cognitive mapping, Haacke goes on to reveal that it is taxpayers who end up sponsoring what the corporations save through the tax deductions that they are conceded through their 'generous' contributions (132).

MetroMobilitan has not been Haacke's only use of a form of cognitive mapping to attack ExxonMobil and other multinational corporations (or the links they have with the institutions of the art world) or the connections between big business and political regimes. It is a part of a long list of works that have dug up information including Daimler-Benz's role in Hitler's rise to power (and the way the corporation was rewarded by providing the majority of the engines used in the warplanes and military vehicles in the Second World War). He also uncovered Daimler-Benz's unethical employment activities under apartheid in South Africa – he revealed similar practices with regard to British Leyland. He has in 'Mobil: on the right track' shown how Mobil sponsored a coalition of conservative organizations in the United States which campaigned to stop the election of liberal politicians, thereby showing how politics may be made vulnerable by the interests of multinational companies.

For example, in 1990 Haacke turned Picasso's painting *Man with a Hat* (1912–13) into a cigarette advertisement (which he entitled *Cowboy with Cigarette*). In this, as in many of his works, we might say that he practises a kind of Althusserian symptomatic reading by revealing the gaps and (partial) silences that link the art world with capital. In the case of *Cowboy with Cigarette* it unearthed the Phillip Morris company's patronage of a Cubist exhibition at the New York Museum of Modern Art. These connections are becoming standard practice, something reflected by the recent petition signed by members of the art community against Tate Britain's continued sponsorship deals with British Petroleum which are seen as enabling the big oil companies 'to mask the environmentally destructive nature of their activities with the social legitimacy that is associated with such high-profile cultural associations' (*Guardian*, 2010).

It is no surprise, then, that Jameson is obliged to admit that postmodernism *does* include a 'space for various forms of oppositional culture' and that Haacke's work is 'clearly political' (1991: 159) – even if he has some reservations (409). Yet Jameson's (wise) admission that not all cultural production (from around the 1960s onwards) has been postmodern but is rather a 'force field' (a cultural norm which governs a particular historical time (6)) only serves to further complicate definitions of the 'postmodern'. Before moving on to consider another contemporary form of cognitive mapping (which also problematizes Jameson's definitions) here are a number of questions designed to help you to think through some of the issues explored above.

Practice: Haacke, cognitive mapping and the homeopathic strategy

- Why do you think Jameson uses the phrase *homeopathic strategy* to describe Haacke's art? In what ways might it be described as a form of cognitive mapping?
- In what ways do you think it makes sense to talk about Haacke's art as 'conceptual'?

You can check your responses against those in the following Help File.

Help File: Haacke, cognitive mapping and the homeopathic strategy

- Why do you think Jameson uses the phrase *homeopathic strategy* to describe Haacke's art? In what ways might it be described as a form of cognitive mapping?

Homeopathy treats a disease by using small amounts of substances that, delivered in greater quantities in healthy people, would produce symptoms similar to those of the disease being treated. What Haacke does in works like *MetroMobilitan* is to take examples of 'the disease' (the complicity between the galleries and the corporations) and introduce examples of it into the very space of the gallery. This opens up the possibility of an artistic strategy that 'diagnoses' the condition of the museum or gallery space and introduces into it a form of critical, corrective art that can be seen as a form of corrosive irony, which reflects very badly on the institutions that contain it. Haacke's strategy can be seen as cognitive mapping in the way that he links diverse spaces together. In terms of works like *MetroMobilitan* he starts with the institutional space of the art gallery and shows how its sponsorship strategies link it to a multinational company that has very questionable relations with the country that is featured in the exhibition. In this way he provides a map that links different cultural, political and economic spaces together.

- In what ways do you think it makes sense to talk about Haacke's art as 'conceptual'?

Works of art like Haacke's *MetroMobilitan* can be understood as 'conceptual' because he seems more interested in the political implications of the exhibition than in inviting sophisticated reflections on the aesthetic nature or significance of the work.

Notes on further practice

The implications for critical practice are that there is the possibility of doing a very similar kind of criticism which focuses less on the aesthetic dimension of the art exhibited and more on the relations that the galleries maintain with multinational corporations. This kind of criticism would tease out how the art world is both used by and complicit with the wider business world. Of course, this technique can be extended to include different forms of culture from the gallery, the arts centre, the opera house to the theatre, the cinema or the museum. You might begin by exploring a local gallery, arts centre or museum to see what its relations are with the world of business, and then investigate if the sponsors use their connections to the art world to garner cultural capital through patronage. With this material you might assemble a Haacke-like collage of texts, images and objects.

An analysis does not have to stop here. It is possible to look into who sponsors TV channels, film studios, sports events, etc. to trace similar lines of association. For example, at the time of writing a coalition of international artists are fighting to ensure that migrant worker rights are upheld during the construction and maintenance of the new Guggenheim museum being built in Abu Dhabi (*New York Times*, 17 March 2011).

Cognitive mapping in practice 2: Susan Daitch's *L.C.*

If we are interested in exploring how the art world and the business world are in collusion we might turn to a novel like Susan Daitch's *L.C.* (1986/2002). In the following practice section I shall use this novel to get you to consider its relations with Jameson's way of interpreting contemporary writing and how it may provide a model of 'conceptual mapping'. I shall give an outline of the novel's plot and themes as a way of showing how it resembles what Hutcheon called 'historiographic metafiction' (postmodern narrative forms which have an ambiguous relation to history) and yet provides what Jameson would regard as a piece of cognitive mapping. Thus, again, we see how the two are not necessarily incompatible.

Practice: cognitive mapping in practice 2: Susan Daitch's *L.C.*

Read my description of Daitch's novel and consider the following questions:

- Given what you know about Jameson's approach to postmodernism, which features of *L.C.* do you think he would appreciate and which would he read as negative symbols of postmodern culture?
- Can you see parallels between Haacke's critical strategies in *MetroMobilitan* and Daitch's in *L.C.*?
- In what ways might the novel challenge Jameson's strategy of representing postmodernism?

Here is the basic plot of *L.C.* In New York (in 1968) Dr Willa Rehnfield completes a translation of a (fictional) diary by the L.C. of the title, Lucienne Crozier (written between 1847 and 1848). She writes an introduction, which helps to show her credentials as a committed feminist and competent translator. However, after her death her translation of the diary is compromised by commentaries added by her literary executor, Jane Amme. Amme, now in New York, turns out to be an ex-student radical at Berkeley who is on the run from the police and the secret services for her (somewhat distant) participation in the student riots of the late 1960s. At one point, Jane Amme suggests that this is not her real name. She explains that Amme is 'Emma spelled backwards', for her grandmother, for the feminist anarchist, Emma Goldman, and for Emma Bovary, the protagonist of Flaubert's eponymous novel. She also points out that *l'âme* 'is the French word for soul and there is a pun on aim' but, as she informs us, at the time she adopted the name she had 'anything but definite aims' (1986/2002: 171).

When Amme begins to confess to the reader her own recent past it becomes evident that her life parallels, in some very important ways, the life of Lucienne Crozier: they both lived in periods of great upheaval and were, in an intelligent, critical and distanced way, part of radical movements led by men which left them, in distinct ways, fugitives. In this way, Crozier's diary is framed by Rehnfield's translation and this introduction is framed by Amme's further comments, observations, footnotes and alternative translation.

Daitch's novel is characterized by references to actual events, movements and people (both in revolutionary France and in the United States of the 1960s), which serve as a realistic backdrop to the fictional lives of the protagonists. However, the formal structure of the novel introduces doubt about the accuracy of the events depicted. For example, Rehnfield makes it clear that Crozier's diary is silent on crucial issues and that important things have been lost which might help to give a clearer idea of Crozier. For example, a portrait believed to have been done by the artist Eugene Delacroix has been lost and the original diary was destroyed in a bomb attack on the house of the man who took possession of it by devious means – apart from the last section of the diary, which was salvaged by Willa Rehnfield.

If these details begin to question the authenticity of the life depicted in the diary, Jane Amme further questions the value Rehnfield's translation going so far as to retranslate the final part of the diary, which Willa Rehnfield stole from the original manuscript when she realized that she would not have time to translate it before it was taken away from her. Jane Amme then claims that her translation of the last part of the diary is 'true to the original' (Daitch, 1968/2002: 262). Of course, this raises the question of whether Amme's translation is really absolutely true to the original, because, like 'history', we can never refer to the original to test out her claims. Thus, it is significant that Rehnfield warned the reader in her introduction that 'Diaries (especially translated ones) should be read with an element of mistrust' (5).

I want to argue that within this narrative structure Daitch performs some very illustrative cognitive mapping which uses fictional situations to reflect on actual corporate behaviour. In Daitch's novel Luc Ferrier, a corrupt American businessman, collector and art dealer (who asked Rehnfield to translate the diary to assess its worth), is killed in a fire bomb attack on his house. Jane Amme reveals that while two groups took responsibility for the attack, it was actually carried out by 'an anti-war group which had targeted Ferrier as the director of Carex, then building anti-personnel weapons used in Vietnam' (183). It turns out that he had also been on boards of corporations whose subsidiaries, a series of chemical companies, produced napalm and Agent Orange, both used in the Vietnam War; Agent Orange being a herbicidal chemical, which caused a huge number of deaths, disabilities and birth defects.

Towards the end of the narration of the diary, Jane Amme begins to interleave sections which tell the reader about the circumstances of her own involvement in the radical student politics of the late 1960s. She recounts how she got involved with a group which was a break-away movement of the Maoist Students for a Democratic Society which was interested in drawing attention to, targeting and attacking corporate support for the Vietnam war with relation to companies like IBM, Honeywell, Carex and Dow Chemical (233). Even the University of Berkeley turns out to have a '$70 million contract with the Defence Department' (241), which becomes a focal point for further campus riots in which Amme and other members of the group are involved. This fictional-cum-historical cognitive mapping (which reflects the actual relations between big business, education and the war effort) is assisted by the leader of the Maoist group, Winthrop Auersbach, who usually began meetings 'by discussing his research into a chain of connections, the links between institutions and the everyday, between our pedestrian actions – the quotidian behaviour rarely questioned – and the feeding of the war effort' (233). Auersbach explains that:

> 'Drugs, art theft, murder in Oakland, murder in Marseilles, and old American oil rig in Libya, a former governor of California's Indonesian correspondence [...] all fit into a long-armed acquaintance network, a sensational newspaper story [...] You take all your little stories and put them into one big story. Shave off a little here, add a bit there and it will all connect.' (242)

Later he reveals to Amme that:

> 'The President of the Board of Trustees of your favourite museum in San Francisco is also on the board of the Contel Corporation which owns diamond mines in South Africa, feldspar mines in Angola, Kennecot Copper in Chile, and Western Tin, to name three of his nine corporate affiliations. Each time you pay a dollar to see his art collection, you support apartheid, the war in South East Asia and the museum's anti-union policies towards its employees.' (244)

Luc Ferrier, the owner of the Crozier diary, turns out to be the President of the Board of Trustees of Amme's favourite museum (and the man selected by Auersbach to be the victim of a bomb attack on his home that would kill the corrupt businessman and destroy most of the original diary). Thus, we learn about how the diary came to be destroyed and what the connections were between Jane Amme and the death of the diary's owner and why she became a fugitive, eventually arriving in New York and becoming Dr Willa Rehnfield's assistant and, later, literary executor. Furthemore, Amme steals the diary (as Rehnfield had done), and has all references to it deleted from the library records where the rest of Rehnfield's papers were sent (164). By the end of the novel, we are completely in the dark about what has happened to the diary.

Help File: cognitive mapping in practice 2: Susan Daitch's *L.C.*

- Given what you know about Jameson's approach to postmodernism, which features of *L.C.* do you think he would appreciate and which would he read as negative symbols of postmodern culture?

From a Jamesonian point of view it is possible to see *L.C.* as containing within itself a demonstration of how 'cognitive mapping' may function in practice. This can be seen with relation to the circumstances surrounding the destruction of Lucienne Crozier's memoirs and the death of the corrupt American businessman, Luc Ferrier. Jane Amme's involvement in the radical student politics of the late 1960s and her involvement with the break-away movement help to reveal the corporate support for the Vietnam War with relation to companies like IBM, Honeywell, Carex and Dow Chemical. The leader of the group, Winthrop Auersbach, is constantly researching into the links between institutions and the war effort. The connections that Auersbach makes between things like drugs, art, theft, murder and apartheid, and how they may coalesce into a larger picture, provide an effective demonstration of the kind of criticism that Jameson recommends.

The radical student group represents the kind of critical edge Jameson associates with high modernism and, like Heidegger's reading of Van Gogh's 'A Pair of Boots', the group is involved in recreating 'a whole missing object world'. In this way the 'cognitive mapping' practised by the student radicals helps to counter the cultural logic of late capitalism which erases history and the complex connections between different spheres of life. Here, while the novel fits into Hutcheon's definition of postmodern 'historiographic metafiction', the narrative avoids another feature of what Jameson regards as typical of postmodernist narrative: cultural schizophrenia which fragments everything to the point where it is only possible to engage with the isolated blocks of meaning. The student group can be seen as utopian in the sense of using analysis to challenge and change society with relation to class consciousness and a collective project.

However, this novel in many ways reflects some of the key features of postmodern narrative as Jameson sees it. The novel mixes actual historical figures and situations with fiction, and questions the validity of the historical narrative that is constructed in its pages. It might be said that these features, coupled to other elements, like multiple framing, that problematize the integrity of the truth of the history help to suggest that stable, reliable history is open to all kinds mishaps and complications.

The narrative form of *L.C.* can be seen as typical of late (transnational) capitalism, which erases history and thus introduces a certain 'depthlessness'. History is in danger of becoming a play of surfaces, a series of simulacra with no stabilizing reality or historical referents to ground it. Crozier's history can be said to function as 'pastiche' because the past is a set of 'effects', which create history through the stylistic connotation of 'pastness'. This 'pastness' is achieved through juxtaposing actual names and historical events and well-known symbols with fictional characters that can be playfully 'deconstructed' by the self-conscious author.

When Jane Amme lets the reader know that her name is not the one she uses and that the one she has adopted is a reversal of Emma spelled backwards, these plays on words help to forge intertextual links with Emma Bovary and Emma Goldman and remind us that we are in an ambiguous universe. If 'history' is there it is one where the fictional Bovary and the historical Goldman exist on the same level, as do references to actual historical figures and situations in the diary. From a Jamesonian standpoint, this only introduces more 'depthlessness' into the so-called historical novel and into the contemporary situation of Amme. We do not even know her real name. If Amme suggests 'soul', how are we to understand this? Is she 'soul' in the sense of the essential or fundamental part of something or somebody, or does this indicate the immaterial part which is supposed to survive the body? And then there is the pun on Amme/ aims, which comes from a woman who seems to have had no real aims in life. These literary-historical references and the plays on Emma and Amme, can be connected to the idea of autoreferentiality where works tend to allude to themselves and emphasize their own constructedness. With relation to Lucienne Crozier's fate in the novel it is possible to offer a reading that emphasizes the waning of subjectivity in contemporary theory because the plays of textuality surrounding the 'truth' of the protagonist reflect the decentring or 'the death of the subject'. This is exemplified in things like the fact that the memoirs are partial, limited and questionable in themselves, the translation is doubtful and subject to multiple framing, and the original diary is lost. The problematizing of history also has negative consequences for Jameson because it challenges and weakens political discourses like Marxism which need history to provide large explanatory systems with the end of changing the world through knowledge, critique, consciousness and struggle.

- Can you see parallels between Haacke's critical strategies in *MetroMobilitan* and Daitch's in *L.C.*?

Both can be seen to incorporate a strategy of cognitive mapping that Jameson argues is so important in the age of multinational capitalism. It is possible to see *L. C.* as dramatizing a homeopathic strategy. Just as Haacke, in works like *MetroMobilitan*, took examples of 'the disease' (the complicity between the galleries and the corporations) and introduced examples of it into the very space of the gallery, so Daitch, through the radical student leader Auersbach, helps to show how the art world may be complicit with the interests of big business. This can be seen very clearly in the passage where Auersbach claims that the President of the Board of Trustees of Amme's

(Continued)

(Continued)

favourite museum in San Francisco was also on the board of the corporation which owned diamond mines in a variety of countries. This 'cognitive mapping' unmasks the fact that each time people pay to see a particular art collection, they are supporting 'apartheid, the war in South East Asia and the museum's anti-union policies towards its employees'. While I would not say that these examples fully illustrate Jameson's point that 'the underside of culture is blood, torture, death, and terror' (1991: 5), they do go some way to showing how the art world may be ethically compromised by its links to the social, economic and political world that helps to sustain it.

- In what ways might the novel challenge Jameson's strategy of representing postmodernism?

Daitch's *L.C.* can be seen to both play with the idea of history *and* introduce a very effective model of 'cognitive mapping'. It would probably be wrong to accuse Jameson of Manichaeism – of failing to appreciate that a single work might include both these facets. However, my representation of Jameson sees him as privileging a high modernist aesthetic over postmodern cultural forms, with their 'depthlessness', questioning of history and identity, etc. The answers offered here suggest that Jameson's way of thinking may be too biased to fully appreciate the more radical side of what he conceives as postmodernity.

These examples of how Haacke and Daitch practise a kind of cognitive mapping serve to prepare you for the final sections of this book where I will argue, through further exploration and illustration, that cognitive mapping as a critical practice may provide one way forward for cultural studies. Before I begin this, however, I want to review a number of comments that Lawrence Grossberg has made about Jameson's notion of cognitive mapping, and discuss cultural studies as a political project and link these to the notion of hegemony.

In the context of Jameson's argument that new maps are needed 'to enable us to understand the organisation of space in late capitalism', Grossberg is concerned that Jameson's model represents 'the masses' as mute, cultural dupes who are misled by dominant ideologies, and where cultural critics are depicted as the only ones 'capable of understanding ideology and constituting the proper site of resistance'. The problem is compounded by the fact that ordinary people seem to remain hopeless until 'someone provides them with the necessary maps of intelligibility and critical resistance' (Grossberg, 1988: 174).

Despite this telling criticism of Jameson's position, I want to show that different kinds of cognitive mapping are not only possible without this assumption but that these forms of resistance do not have to assume passivity on the part of 'ordinary' people. The last chapter will not only review how different groups have been involved in counter-hegemonic practices at a grass-roots level but suggest ways in which we, as interested students, citizens and cultural workers, can develop strategies to inform ourselves about how the multinationals (or businesses in general) function, the possible abuses that are perpetrated by them, and how they may seek to cover them up or rectify them.

'The philosophers have only interpreted the world [...] the point is to change it': Hall, Grossberg and the politics of change

As Stuart Hall (Hall, 1996a: 263) has asserted, cultural studies refuses to be 'a master discourse or a meta-discourse of any kind' and, while it should be conceived of as open-ended, it 'can't be just any old thing which chooses to march under a particular banner'. For Hall, cultural studies is a serious enterprise that is inscribed in what is sometimes referred to as its 'political' aspect. This is not to say that there is only one politics inscribed in it but 'there is something *at stake*'. It is significant that Hall is hesitant to define the political aspect in very clear terms so as not to restrict what 'politics' might mean. This creates a productive tension within the field: it should be a set of engaged projects but remain open-ended, subject to constant revision, but should not 'believe in the finality of a finished theoretical paradigm' (150).

This fits in with Lawrence Grossberg's contention that 'intellectual work matters, that it is a vital component of the struggle to change the world and to make the world more humane', and that cultural studies, as 'a particular sort of intellectual practice, has something valuable to contribute' (Grossberg, 2006: 2). If we look at the way Haacke and Daitch reflect on institutional life and relate it to interrelated social, political, economic and cultural contexts I think we get something of what constitutes 'committed political intellectual work' (3). (I shall sketch out how this may serve as a model and be extended in the following chapter.) What this commitment may be is mirrored in Henry Giroux's understanding of Hall's call for a cultural politics that implies 'a public pedagogy in which learning becomes indispensable to the process of social change'. This change is understood as a precondition for a politics that 'moves in the direction of a less hierarchical, more radical democratic social order' (Giroux, 2000: 145).

We can also see how this approach reflects what Grossberg (following others like Raymond Williams and Stuart Hall) feels is the cultural studies project of constructing 'a political history of the present', but this has to be done in 'a radically contextualist way'. What this means is that we must 'avoid reproducing the very sorts of universalisms (and essentialisms) that all too often characterize the dominant practices of knowledge production'. This is because these have contributed (consciously or unconsciously) to creating (through their reductionism) 'the relations of domination, inequality and suffering' that cultural studies seeks to change (2). If you think back over this book you can see that this is where we can learn from poststructuralist forms of thinking. However, for Hall and Grossberg, this would have to be without turning them into empty formalisms.

This committed political model also reflects Grossberg's increasing frustration with much cultural studies which, by the end of the 1980s, was, and to some extent still is, dominated by signifying practices narrowly focused on questions of ideology, identity politics and the politics of representation (1996a). These have often been articulated around the important themes of race/ethnicity, gender, sexuality, the post-colonial (with the subthemes of subjugation, marginality, otherness, etc.) and, as Hall (1996a: 274) has indicated, by the 1970s (referring to cultural studies in the US) there was hardly anything in cultural studies that *was not* theorized in these terms. Part of the problem is that while the theories commonly grouped under the term post-structuralism (including postmodernism) raise very important intellectual questions, and while identity politics (based in and around representations) is necessary and can be very revealing and empowering, there is the danger that certain forms of cultural studies end up by endlessly repeating themselves. Thus, for critics like Hall and Grossberg it is important to recognize that while these approaches are important they not sufficient (Hall, 1996b: 1f; Grossberg, 1992: 47) and that while it is necessary to push cultural studies in new directions, this has to be done without losing some kind of grounding in Left-inflected political projects.

These demands, which set out to intervene and transform the world through radical critique, show how cultural studies not only uses Gramscian hegemony theory as an intellectual tool but is itself, like all academic areas, constantly subject to hegemonic forces within itself. One very important force is related to Marx's oft-quoted statement in his 'Theses on Feuerbach' that 'The philosophers have only interpreted the world, in various ways; the point is to change it' (Marx, 1845/1976: 65). I would argue that this has remained one of the most important ethical tenets underpinning much cultural studies. As we saw in Chapter 1, for the early critics in cultural studies, like Thompson, Williams and those at the Birmingham Centre, the point of studying class, subcultures, race/ethnicity, gender, sexualities and the post-colonial situation was not just to produce new areas of interpretation and knowledge but to intervene in important debates with a view to becoming more conscious about inequalities, injustices and forms of marginalization as a means to contribute to what Williams called 'the long revolution' (Williams, 1961/1992).

I have tried to reflect something of this ethical concern (and utopian project) as a hegemonic force as it has moved through the various theories I have introduced, whether they be described as structuralist, post-structuralist or postmodern. The final chapter of this book will show how cognitive mapping can help cultural studies to continue in this vein. It will do this by demonstrating how, within (and outside) our educational environments, we can begin to foment, or be a part of, counter-hegemonic forces which not only analyse and understand the world around us but try to bring about what we feel are positive changes.

Summary of key points

This chapter began by considering how Gramsci's notion of hegemony can be applied to the meaning and valuation of terms like poststructuralism and postmodernism as a means of showing how these concepts can be understood as sites of struggle within academic institutions. This was followed by two in-depth analyses of the work of Hans Haacke and Susan Daitch to show how Jameson's notion of cognitive mapping can be put into practice via his 'homeopathic strategy'. The final section returned to the notion of hegemony to argue that a key feature of cultural studies is not only to raise consciousness but is linked to attempts to bring about positive changes in the world.

Further reading

The titles written by Jameson recommended in the previous chapter are also relevant to this one but Jameson's *Signatures of the Visible* (1991b) is particularly useful because it includes interpretations which Jameson regards as forms of cognitive mapping. Of particular interest is his defence of the Marxist notion of class and cognitive mapping of the social, economic, political world in the 1970s film *Dog Day Afternoon*. The journal *Transnational Cinema* publishes many essays which relate film to various forms of what can be considered cognitive mapping. To follow up the connections made by Haacke and Daitche between corporations and governments, Edwin Black's controversial studies like *IBM and the Holocaust* (2001) and *Nazi Nexus: America's Corporate Connections to Hitler's Holocaust* (2009) explore the relations between the Nazi regime and American corporations like IBM and General Motors.

15

Where to Go from Here

Cognitive Mapping and the Critical Project of Cultural Studies

Learning goals

- To understand how cognitive mapping can help to map the multinationals using journalism and activist webpages on the internet.
- To recognize how this approach may offer an alternative to the identity, subjectivity and politics of representation approach to cultural studies.
- To be aware of the possibilities and some of the pitfalls of using journalism and online resources.

Concepts

The key concepts introduced in this chapter are: cognitive mapping, oligopoly, military–industrial complex, the shock doctrine, disaster capitalism, empire, the organic intellectual, new social movements, culture jamming, the 'rhizome', 'arborescence', 'territorialization', 'reterritorialization' and 'destratification'.

Of begin(end)ings and the project of cultural studies

This is the final chapter of the book which, to repeat a useful cliché, should not be visualized as an ending but the end of a beginning – or an opening up or out. The hope here is that the previous chapters have helped to demonstrate something of the vibrancy and relevance of the theoretical legacy of cultural studies and show how the concepts and paradigms may work in practice. The aim, as I defined it in Chapter 1, was to provide an 'all-purpose toolbox' which would help readers to become members of a cultural studies 'interpretive community' (Fish, 1980). Each chapter has emphasized how many of what have become the dominant paradigms can be adapted to the analysis and understanding of many aspects of culture. However, despite this diversity, most of the chapters have been sutured by certain thematic threads which have emphasized the importance of not only *interpreting* the world but critiquing it in such a way that we become more conscious of the way groups or individuals have been marginalized, subordinated or subjected to dominant ways of thinking and organizing the world in the interests of dominant collectives (even if they are riven by complex hegemonic forces).

This is all part of what can be understood as the 'project' of cultural studies (mentioned in the last chapter) which includes the theoretically self-aware politicization of all aspects of culture wedded to the utopian gesture of altering the world to make it a more equitable and just place to live for all people (see below). Thus, this final chapter sets up possibilities for practice which emphasize this vital project of critical thinking linked to possible forms of agency (see Chapter 1). Yet, while it underscores the importance of applying concepts and theories to a critical understanding of modern capitalism (justifying the 'doing' of cultural theory of the book's title), it not only prepares readers to cognitively map the multinational corporate environment but returns the reader to what cultural studies is all about as a project or critical endeavour.

To (cognitively) map or not to map the corporate world?

At the beginning of the last chapter we saw that Jameson saw the need for a new political art that he called an 'aesthetic of **cognitive mapping** – a pedagogical political culture' that could formulate 'radically new forms' to offer special insight into our place within multinational capitalism. We saw how this functioned with relation to the '*homeopathic* strategy' that I demonstrated with relation to Hans Haacke and Susan Daitch. Jameson refers to the notion of cognitive mapping as 'aesthetic' because he prefers an approach which, through art or film, etc., 'addresses individual experience rather than something that conceptualizes the real in a more abstract way' (Jameson, 1998: 358). This puts the emphasis on artistic forms rather than the academic discourses of the human sciences. However, having illustrated the possibilities within the arts, what I propose below is to show how we might further use the idea of cognitive mapping as a form of possible practice within cultural studies. Before I begin, however, I shall discuss a number of possible objections to this project.

The idea of cognitive mapping has been resisted, especially by broadly poststructuralist critics because it seems to assume that there is an unproblematic totality that can be mapped in a reductive way (Jameson, 1988: 360f.). This is linked to Lawrence Grossberg's point that we cannot assume that our 'maps of meaning or the ways we interpret the world' constitute the 'essence of our "reality"'. The problem for Grossberg is that while these maps make our task easier and 'reassure us of the truth of our story and the sincerity of our politics' they reduce the complexity of the world we wish to understand (1992: 55). However, I would argue that we have to start somewhere and that these maps are justified if we see them as useful *starting points* which help to keep a sense of the political project of cultural studies very much in view (which is, after all, something that Grossberg insists upon). I want to suggest here, then, that cognitive mapping does not have to assume that there is a world (capitalist or otherwise) that can be caught within a simple theory. It is intended to reflect Grossberg's insistence that the maps that cultural studies fabricates do not claim to 'mimic' the real but to 'strategically open up its possibilities, to intervene into its present in order to remake its future' (64).

This might be seen within what Grossberg has termed 'spatial materialism', which may offer cultural studies a possible way forward. The starting point for spatial materialism is to be found in Grossberg's idea (reviewed in the last chapter) that cultural studies could theorize culture outside the dominant paradigms of (post)structuralism and postmodernism with their (over)emphasis on ideology, identity, subjectivity and difference within the politics of representation. To break with these approaches he turned to the challenging writings of writers like Gilles Deleuze and Félix Guattari (among others) to propose a politics of 'spatial becoming' or a 'pragmatics of the multiple' (Grossberg 1993, 1996a) in order to 'rethink the real' (1996b: 179). In a later section I will indicate how concepts adapted from Deleuze and Guattari might be adapted to the kinds of mapping suggested in this chapter.

The version of cognitive mapping cum spatial materialism I am putting forward here is akin to Giroux's idea of 'performative politics'. This is where cultural studies workers within and outside higher education not only recover education as a 'public good' but recognize that academic work is a 'social endeavour', and not just an end in itself. From this perspective education takes on meaning when it connects personal and public concerns to extend its 'critical, performative and utopian impulses' to tackle urgent social issues in the interests of promoting social change. Seeing cultural studies as 'performative act' involves employing theory as a resource to create the conditions for collective struggle and thus avoids the mere textualizing of everyday life to concentrate on revealing what Giroux calls the 'dominant machineries of power' (Giroux, 2001: 11–14). In this way cultural studies may align itself with Marx's dictum that 'the philosophers have only interpreted the world, in various ways; the point is to change it' (Marx, 1845/1976: 65).

A funny thing happened on the way to the fish fingers: cognitive mapping in the (super)market

To begin, I want to show how to develop a simple form of cognitive mapping. I could pick out many companies to illustrate the points I want to make but for the sake of concision I will limit my comments to a reduced number of them. From the early 2000s there have been scandals related to the Nestlé company (one of the world's largest food conglomerates) concerning its promotion of powdered milk in contravention of the World Health Organization's code which regulates the marketing of breast milk substitutes. According to Baby Milk Action (2010) Nestlé has been involved in promoting its powdered milk in Third World countries by suggesting that underfed mothers, those with twins, or those feeding premature babies are unable to feed these babies properly by breastfeeding them. Nestlé has been accused of things like handing out free milk and getting mothers used to it with the consequence that the mothers' breast milk dries up, creating a situation where they become dependent on commercially manufactured alternatives. There have been charges of milk dilution, which have led to malnutrition, and Nestlé and other companies have been accused of ignoring the question of unsafe local water supplies, which can cause severe diarrhoea and often death, which suggests that breast milk may have been much safer than the substitutes (see Everything2, 2010).

According to McSpotlight (2010) Nestlé has not only been guilty of the kind of irresponsible marketing already mentioned but has been accused of providing poor working conditions, discriminating against women and failing to provide proper protective clothing. It is alleged that this occurred in Brazil in 1989 and, as a result of a strike, forty workers (including most of the strike organizers) were dismissed. To add to this list of abuses the company has also been censured for supporting brutal or repressive regimes and testing products on animals. Unfortunately, these claims against Nestlé are not isolated incidents and if you follow the news and explore websites like the ones mentioned above you will see that according to many activists these practices are by no means limited to just one multinational corporation.

Another major corporation that has been criticized is Coca-Cola. According to War on Want (2010) the Coca-Cola Corporation has been at the centre of controversy in Colombia, where legal action has been brought against it for the alleged use of paramilitary services to deal with union action. The company has also been accused of questionable anti-union activities in countries like Nicaragua, Pakistan, Guatemala and Russia and it is also alleged that Coca-Cola has turned a blind eye to intimidation and even torture of trade unionists and their families in Turkey. There are also concerns about Coca-Cola's impact on community water resources, particularly in India, because their production plants are dependent on abundant water supplies. This has a potentially devastating impact on local communities because they are seen to be destroying the livelihoods of those whose lives depend on agriculture. This is all linked to charges of the contamination of water systems and the pollution of agricultural land through the dumping of toxic waste (see Gill, 2006, 2007; Higginbottom, 2007).

Thus, there is growing concern that multinational corporations like Nestlé, Coca-Cola and PepsiCo are buying up water supplies (sometimes at the expense of the local community) and selling it back – at a huge profit (see 'Global Water Sales' (2010)). All this is to ignore the possible environmental questions like the energy required to package and transport water, the disposal of waste plastics, and the possibility that bottled water may be no healthier than tap water. For example, in 1999 the Natural Resources Defence Council in the USA found that bottled water was no purer or safer than most tap water (for the report see the Natural Resources Defence Council, 2010).

If you are convinced that one or more of these kinds of claims are true, you may decide that you want to boycott the products of companies you feel infringe human rights or abuse the environment. However, a simple form of cognitive mapping would help to demonstrate that this is not as simple as it may seem. You may try to avoid all products marketed under the Nestlé or Coca-Cola name; however, this would not be enough. Nestlé and Coca-Cola make a bewildering number of products. If you have access to a computer type 'find Nestlé brands' or 'find Coca-Cola products' into your browser and look at the products sold worldwide under their names. This exercise will reveal that under the Nestlé logo you will find everything from milk, coffee, sweets, breakfast cereals, ready meals, sauces, frozen foods to low-fat foods, yogurts and dog and cat food (all sold under different brands from Findus, Cross & Blackwell to Toffee Crisp, Chambourcy and Friskies – and this only scratches the surface of the variety of brands in the Nestlé portfolio).

You may avoid all these products and feel that your cognitive mapping has saved you from being caught out but you may buy cosmetic products like L'Oreal, Lancome or Claudel only to find they are all owned or part-owned by Nestlé (or were at the time of writing). An added problem for any cognitive mapper is that massive corporations like Nestlé constantly buy and sell off companies, and it is not always easy to predict or keep up with all their mergers, divisions, sell-offs and investments.

Again, if you wanted to boycott Coke's products it would be hard because, according to Coca-Cola's own website (which will help you to do your own cognitive mapping – see Coca-Cola, 2010) the Coca-Cola Company offers more than 450 brands and 3,300 products including fruit drinks, waters, sports and energy drinks, teas, coffees, and milk- and soy-based beverages. A little cognitive mapping reveals that all these are distributed in more than 200 countries. All these brand names, united under one corporation, reveal the oligopoly that underlies the multinationals.

Help File: oligopoly

This term is related to monopoly. It describes a tendency where large corporations and conglomerates get increasingly greater control over markets by buying up the competition. Under oligopoly markets are dominated by huge companies, which gain greater control over the manufacture and supply of particular products. Thus, when we think we are choosing between different products, as demonstrated above, we are often only choosing between brand names, which may well be part of a limited number of larger conglomerates. Part of the effect of this is that these dominant manufacturers and suppliers can have greater control over things like wages, work conditions, distribution and, ultimately, prices. This can be seen as part of the globalizing tendencies that characterize the contemporary economic situation.

Practice: mapping the corporations for yourself

Here is some advice to help you develop your mapping skills:

- To begin with, you should choose a corporation (you can find lists of the largest in webpages like *Fortune* magazine, Wikipedia, CNN Money, Forbes and Doughroller, etc.). If you want to begin with major corporations that have been subject to criminal investigation because of corruption and scandals you might choose those mentioned by Giroux in this context (2003: 182): Enron, WorldCom, Tyco International, Qwest Communications, Computer Associates and ImClone Systems.
- You can continue your mapping by looking at the webpages of organizations like greenpeace.org, corporatewatch.org, or looking at others recommended by thecorporation.org like multinationalmonitor.org, corpwatch.org, corporate-crimereporter.com, business-ethics.org or ethicalconsumer.org. These sites will often have links to other useful forums that help to keep track of a corporation's activities and will help you evaluate a corporation's record.
- Make a list of the major claims and then check out the corporation's own official website (hoping that it is not a bogus one commandeered by The Yes Men!). Corporations will often deny criticisms or even try to silence them – like Trafigura that tried to silence claims that it was dumping toxic waste in the Ivory Coast – a practice that resulted in serious illness and deaths (see the BBC, and *Guardian* websites).
- Sometimes a corporation will acknowledge (or be forced to recognize) its guilt and often be obliged to compensate in some way. Of course, corporations may, to win public favour and/or revise their public image, start up valuable social

(Continued)

(Continued)

and environmental programmes (see below). This means that, while maintaining a critical stance, our cognitive mapping requires us to try to be aware of the *whole* picture and be aware of changes and not necessarily tar all corporations with the same brush.

Cognitive mapping: From sweatshirt to sweatshop

Some very effective forms of cognitive mapping have been done with relation to corporations like Disney and the manufacturers of clothing and sportswear (particularly Nike). Investigative journalism (which may appear in the mainstream or alternative press – printed or online) has been instrumental in not only exposing human rights abuses with relation to the setting up of special trade zones but in helping to map the connections between international capitalism and these practices. In the mid-1990s journalists began to intensify their interest in these practices to such an extent that Andrew Ross named 1995–1996 'The Year of the Sweatshop'. See below for websites that can help you to cognitively map these companies. Chapter 14 of Naomi Klein's *No Logo!* (2000) is dedicated to this theme.

Official websites, change and public image

You might check on the development of a corporation's business principles on the company's official website. For example, Nestlé, on its website, claims to be cooperating with some of the United Nation's Global Compact Principles. Thus, Nestlé, like many corporations, are interested in their public image and have a strong interest in countering negative press – you will see that they have dedicated a webpage to 'the community and the UN Millennium development goals' where they outline their objectives in terms of helping to eradicate poverty and hunger, combat HIV/AIDS, assist in bringing about primary education for all, working towards the empowerment of women, the reduction of child mortality, and bringing about improvements in maternal health and environmental sustainability.

You will also find that Pepsi, Coca-Cola and other companies that sell bottled water have also supported public water projects in the developing world (see 'Bottled Water: No Longer Cool?', 2000). This may be seen as vindicating activism but, of course, not everyone is convinced of their levels of commitment or achievement, but this does tend to reflect that while corporations are often seen to ignore, or even abuse, the environment, workers rights, etc. they may respond to criticisms when the company's negative image is in danger of affecting sales. It is equally important, of course, to try to recognize how much of a corporation's commitment is a mere public relations exercise. Many consumer organizations concerned about human rights, business abuses, etc., like The Ethical Consumer (see below) and War on Want, contrast the rhetoric of corporate social responsibility with the reality of companies' business practices.

There are many other ethical consumer associations that disseminate information, both positive and negative, which can be used to explore business structures, practices and abuses. In the Further Reading/Resources section (in 'Practice and further resources') there is a list of some that I have found very useful. You may think that reading company annual or seasonal report pages may be of limited use. Of course, you cannot expect them to criticize themselves in any significant way but you can use them to see how much profit they have made and where they are heading in terms of marketing strategies, buyouts, expansion, sales and sponsorship of environmental programmes, etc.

Brothers in arms: the military–industrial complex

I have shown how even products in the supermarket need a certain amount of cognitive mapping (which can be done via the internet) to understand the complex relations between multinational companies, brands, oligopoly, human rights, employment conditions and environmental effects. However, if we return to the cases that Haacke and Daitch explored in the last chapter we can begin to extend this cognitive mapping in more complex ways. For example, we saw that Haacke exposed Daimler-Benz's role in the rise of fascism, its manufacture of warplanes and military vehicles and its employment activities under apartheid in South Africa. He also showed how Mobil's sponsoring of a coalition of conservative organizations attempted to influence the course of politics in the United States. This suggests that to map the multinationals also requires us to make ourselves conscious of the relations between them and their relations with politics and war. This was something that was also apparent in Daitch's drawing attention to the connections between corporate profits and the Vietnam War.

Although, as in the materials above, I can only scratch the surface, I want to indicate the complexity and necessity of tracing out these kinds of connections, especially if we want to continue practising a form of cultural studies which unites cognitive mapping with projects that may help to challenge what we understand are abusive business practices. One particularly difficult task is to try to tease out how companies and corporations are implicated in what is known as the **military–industrial complex** where industry, the military and political interests converge. Concerns over the military–industrial complex focus on how government contracts for armaments (and all related products) make up a significant part of national economies.

If national economies are dependent on the production and sale of armaments and this employs significant numbers of people this means that any winding down of the production of weapons threatens to dent both local and national economic interests. This situation may encourage governments (aided and abetted by the arms industry) to perpetuate conflict for economic reasons. In this context a television address by the outgoing US president, Dwight Eisenhower (in 1961), is often quoted. Eisenhower warned against the 'undue influence' of the 'military–industrial complex' (a word coined by him and his speech makers). What concerned him was that the maintenance of a permanent armaments industry of 'vast proportions' and a huge military establishment was creating the risk of 'unwarranted influence' and 'misplaced power' being exercised by the military–industrial complex over liberties and democratic processes. He emphasized the role of ordinary people to make sure that security and liberty went hand in hand (thus justifying the role of pressure groups and activists). Eisenhower also diagnosed other threats from the military–industrial complex like the government funding of universities, where the intellectual liberty of the university was threatened by the domination of the nation's scholars by federal employment and the power of money. Eisenhower perceived the added threat that public policy could become 'captive to a scientific, technological elite' (Eisenhower, 1961).

Earlier we saw how Daitch's novel reflected the links between the Vietnam War effort, the corporations and the financing of universities. If we continue to be concerned about these links and their effects on public policy we need to cognitively map the global environment and be constantly vigilant to see whether the interests of the military–industrial complex, through its importance and use of lobby groups, is not put above the interests of ordinary citizens. This is even more urgent today if we consider that the situation that Eisenhower described has only become more intensified since the early 1960s. For example, by 2006 it has been estimated that the United States was spending 599 billion dollars on its annual defence budget (which might be considerably higher – up to a trillion dollars – if it included things like homeland security and anti-terrorist programmes (Higgs, 2007)). As Chomsky has commented, the military–industrial complex is more than just a question of the military: it can be seen as 'the core of the modern economy'. Computers, the internet, telecommunications, lasers, satellites and the aeronautical industry all grew out of publicly funded military projects (Chomsky, 2004). Mapping the relations between the corporations (including those who have investments or secondary links to the production of armaments) and government are not easy but a series of studies can serve as starting points (see Pursell, 1973; Lesley, 1994; Caldicott, 2002; Winer, 2007; Pavelec, 2010; Hartung, 2011; Ledbetter, 2011).

Homo economicus

Eisenhower's diagnosis, that the intellectual liberty of the university was compromised by the domination of the nation's scholars by federal employment and the power of money, can also be cognitively mapped in various ways. Daitch's reference to the $70 million contract that the University of Berkeley had with the Defense Department can be cognitively mapped not only in terms of the ways in which military or corporate interests are increasingly encroaching on higher education but how the freedom, scope and content of higher education is being threatened. For example, Chris Lorenz, within the context of the homogenizing of higher education within the Bologna Process in Europe, argues that '*homo academicus* is being modelled after *homo economicus*' (2006: 124). His concern is that economic imperatives are (and will) increasingly hold sway over all other considerations within the space of higher education.

Lorenz bases his assertions on the various Bologna Declarations in Paris and Lisbon (of 1988 and 2000 respectively), which manifested serious concerns about the competitiveness of European higher education. The fear in Europe was that Australia and especially North America were particularly adept at attracting valuable revenues from students from Asia. Thus, in Lisbon, the EC pronounced its intention to become 'the most dynamic and competitive economic bloc in the world' (127–120) – which explains the rush for European universities to hurry through reforms in higher education by 2010. In this the Bologna Process can be said to be postmodern, if we understand this with reference to Lyotard's idea that by the late 1970s universities and the institutions of higher learning were being required to create skills, rather than ideals. As we saw in Chapter 11, what Lyotard called the 'performativity principle' affects the autonomy of the universities and subordinates 'the institutions of higher learning to the existing powers' (1984: 50). From this point of view knowledge is increasingly becoming commodified in order to be sold for profit (4) and its production and distribution will increasingly fall outside state control (5). These kinds of preoccupations, together with funding cuts and a proliferation of profitable vocational courses in Britain, have led to what Bailey and Freedman deem an assault on the university (2011).

Given these observations it would seem to be appropriate to adopt what Henry Giroux has called 'radical pedagogy' (1986). This entails 'the possibility for counterhegemonic struggle and ideological battle' (49) within schools and universities, and this is what I am proposing here by adapting Jameson's idea of cognitive mapping. Radical pedagogy involves, then, the preservation of a public educational space for reflection beyond the direct interests of commerce – a theme taken up by Derrida who argued that critical thought could 'limit the private forces of appropriation, the concentrations of economic power' and impede 'a violent depoliticisation that acts in the name of the "market"' (Derrida, 2000). Derrida insisted that the university must be capable of providing a critical public space where discourses can be developed to resist 'the powers that limit a democracy to come'. That is, not democracy as it is practised but what it may evolve into (Derrida, 2001: 253–4).

If the autonomy of the university is seriously compromised by corporate interests this may jeopardize its power to protect a space where the future of democracy may be argued out. In this way radical pedagogy could help counter the forces which Lorenz sees as threatening higher education within the European Union (and Giroux in the United States). This is why Giroux (1999) has warned against the dangers of the free market and the selling out of higher education in the US, where corporations are very enthusiastic about providing valuable resources – but, as Giroux warns, the costs 'come with strings attached'. This leads to situations where corporations 'increasingly dictate the very research they sponsor, and in some universities, such as the University of California at Berkeley, business representatives are actually appointed to sit on faculty committees that determine how research funds are to be spent and allocated' (Giroux, 1986: 184).

There are many sources, including websites, which have attempted to manifest how corporations, or business interests in general, have affected education (see the Further Reading/Resources section at the end of the chapter). Here I shall only outline a few approaches as starting points for further research, which I shall take from investigative journalism.

The business of higher education

Naomi Klein, in her book *No Logo!*, has shown how corporations have stepped in with much needed resources for many schools and universities in the United States. This usually takes the shape of fast food, drinks, computer and sports wear companies sponsoring various aspects of the curriculum. This, as Giroux suggested, comes 'with strings attached' because these companies invariably insist on making their logos as ubiquitous as possible. This opens up the question of how far big business should be able to use academic spaces as opportunities to advertise; something particularly controversial in the case of younger students who may be more vulnerable to the drip-feed of constant advertising (where everything from exercise books, bike racks and campus billboards to libraries and bathrooms are marked with sponsors' logos (Klein: 2000: 91). In the context of Australian education, Sharon Beder has written of the 'corporate capture' of childhood by advertisers which may undermine a child's analytical skills (Beder, 2009: 66; related problems in Australia are discussed by Newlands and Frith, 1996).

Klein reports the case of the North American Channel One (and its Canadian counterpart), which negotiated a deal with many schools where, in exchange for equipment, students have to watch two minutes of TV advertising per day. It is significant that teachers cannot either change channel or turn down the volume on the TVs (89). According to Klein's research, by the end of the 1990s these sponsorship deals had risen to some 12,000 schools (90). However, Klein also makes the point that in many parts of the world universities are offering their research facilities and academic credibility for the brands to use at their will. These corporate university research partnerships have been involved in everything from 'designing new Nike skates, developing more efficient oil extraction techniques for Shell, [and] assessing the Asian market's stability for Disney' to 'testing the consumer demand for higher bandwidth for Bell' (99). These partnerships have helped the university to forge links with the business community but Klein argues that sponsorship is in danger of becoming a form of censorship.

The case of Dr Betty Dong helps to map out the potential dangers of what may seem to be mutually beneficial relations between big business and academe. As Klein explains, Dong, a researcher at the University of California, San Francisco, carried out research sponsored by the British pharmaceutical company Boots on their thyroid drug named Synthroid. The results of her research showed that the cheaper generic version of this drug was every bit as efficient as the original. This meant that the generic version could save $365 million a year (resulting in a possible $600 million loss for Boots). However, sponsorship soon turned into censorship when Dong tried to publish her findings (in the *Journal of the American Medical Association*, in 1995). This was because Boots used a clause in its partnership contract, which gave it veto rights over what could be published. Fearing a lawsuit, Dong's university decided to support the drug company and it was only when the *Wall Street Journal* got hold of the story that it was eventually published some two years later (99). I would argue that this not only highlights the dangers of the links between big business and the universities but emphasizes the importance of the free press and investigative journalism.

Klein reports other cases where universities have failed to support researchers whose findings have been censored by companies involved in sponsorship deals. Thus, the integrity of academic research may be made vulnerable where the interests of the researchers and the profit motives of the sponsors are in conflict. In a study focused on industry research partnerships at US universities it was revealed that in 35 per cent of all cases companies had the right to stop the publication of findings (Klein, 2000: 101; Cohen et al., 1994). If this is put into the context of the tripling of university research funding by private industry in the US between 1970 and 2000 this may give some idea of the possible threats to the freedom of academic research – although it should be kept in mind that these numbers, according to Bronwyn Hall, are actually lower than they were in the 1950s and 1960s (2004: 6, 28).

A similar picture can be painted with relation to higher education in Britain where there have been comparable efforts to link academic research with the interests of industry. George Monbiot, in his book *Captive State*, notes that between 1983 and 1999 research funds in Britain declined by 20 per cent and that these cuts have meant that universities have increasingly had to turn to private funds to sponsor research (Monbiot, 2000: 286). This helps to explain the setting up of professorial Chairs sponsored by corporations in universities like Oxford and Cambridge. For example, the latter university boasts professorships financed by Shell, BP, ICI, Glaxo, Unilever, Price Waterhouse and Marks & Spencer (to name only a few) (287).

Monbiot shows how recent government policy in Britain has been to make universities more dependent on business in efforts to finance research and capitalize on the economic potential of possible collaborations. As in the US, the dangers of these relations are to be found in the way the sponsors not only dominate what gets researched in the sciences but how they can distort or censor findings, which may be in conflict with a sponsor's interests. Monbiot draws on the research of Muttitt and Grimshaw who studied oil and gas firms that sponsored British universities – unsurprisingly, they found five times more research money was invested in gas and oil than in renewable sources of energy (288).

Like Klein, Monbiot claims to have found cases of censorship and the falsification of data to suit a sponsor's aims. For example, Monbiot mentions David Whyte, of the Centre for Criminal Justice Research at Liverpool John Moores University, who reported that a health and safety researcher discovered that one of the oil company sponsors had falsified its own accident figures. When he asked the sponsor of the research project why this was he was silenced. Monbiot suggests that this censorship goes deeper because Whyte himself, having exposed how the findings of projects funded (or partially funded) by the oil industry had been adapted to their particular needs, was called up before a senior manager at the Health and Safety Executive. The implication here is that an official government body that was responsible for funding university research into things like safety on oil rigs was itself party to censorship and distortion, and biased by the £6 million pounds invested by the oil companies in the Merseyside region (289–90).

Monbiot's mapping suggests that even the acceptance of *public* money may bring restrictions because members of the awarding bodies may also be representatives of important corporations. For example, the Office of Science and Technology's 16 Foresight Panels were largely controlled by representatives of big business, rather than scientists (295). According to Monbiot this has led to situations where government research bodies have issued, in some cases, 'misleading political statements' (and been involved in censorship), which appear to favour the interests of, for example, oil and biotechnology companies that invest in research, rather than in other projects like non-genetically modified crops or alternative sources of energy (292f.).

Thus, among the general consequences of the 'corporate takeover of science' are that research tends to become limited to the narrow economic interests of sponsors, where expensive cures for non-life threatening diseases in the First World are privileged over more pressing problems like developing less profitable vaccines for diseases like malaria (299). All this can be seen as a part of the 'dangerous turn' that Giroux sees in higher education where the critical power of higher education is weakened, especially 'in its ability to make corporate power accountable'. This is something that threatens the understanding of democracy as fundamental to basic rights and freedoms, 'and the ways in which we can rethink and reappropriate the meaning and purpose of higher education' (1986: 185).

> ## Practice: the business of higher education in your institution
>
> In Chapter 11 I got you to think about how far you thought your education could be described as postmodern (in Lyotard's terms). It is possible to explore your institution of higher education to see up to what extent its research is sponsored by big business. Questions you might ask are:
>
> - Are there any visible signs of corporate sponsorship in terms of things like computers and other forms of equipment, sports facilities, cafés, bars, etc.?
> - Are any departments financed, or partially financed, by private money?
> - If one of the above is the case, is there any evidence of corporate interests being represented in the content of courses or research? Have there been any reports of interference with research findings?

Shocking doctrines: the rise of disaster capitalism

It is possible to take this cognitive mapping to a higher level to explore how economic models are imposed on many parts of the world that represent the political and economic interests of the 'first world'. Naomi Klein's book *The Shock Doctrine: The Rise of Disaster Capitalism* (2007) is an audacious attempt at this kind of mapping. Again, I can only scratch the surface of the issues involved but I hope to convey something of the possibilities for analysis and research that this book suggests. Klein's basic thesis is that the narrow interests of powerful capitalists are, and have been, imposed all over the world through shock tactics, or **the shock doctrine**. These tactics are applied to all kinds of crises whether they be 'natural', like hurricanes and volcanoes, or provoked by wars, upheavals or economic meltdowns. Of course, it is possible to question Klein's thesis as being too reductive (and it certainly should not be accepted uncritically) but I want to stress its value as an example of cognitive mapping and its possible role in critical pedagogy.

Restricting my overview to Klein's discussion of the United States, part of Klein's thesis is that politicians use the shock caused by disasters to push through privatization agendas. Thus, the shock caused by Hurricane Katrina (in 2005) was used to push through the privatization of schooling and public housing; 9/11 was used to launch a new economy of privatized homeland security; and the war on Iraq was used to establish the Blackwater economy, a process which privatizes war and makes it into a vast opportunity for speculators. Klein's concern is that governing in the United States is increasingly becoming a question of redistributing public money into corporate hands in exchange for campaign contributions (something Monbiot fears in Britain). This perpetuates a corrupt system where the interests of powerful capitalists dominate the policies and decisions of central government so there is very little distinction between the interests of either party. All this is at the expense of civil liberties and the wider interests of the country. This is all part of what Klein refers to as **disaster capitalism** or corporativism.

Klein traces the economic philosophy behind this to the economist she sees as the architect of free-market capitalism, Milton Friedman, who had recommended that part of the billions of dollars allocated to the reconstruction of New Orleans after Hurricane Katrina should be dedicated to the reform of the education system. This involved setting up private schools, partially funded by the state, many of which would be run at a profit. She then describes how a network of right-wing think-tanks, aided and abetted by George W. Bush's administration, helped to make this a reality. This was something seen, especially by African-American parents, as divisive because it reversed 'the gains of the civil rights movement, which guaranteed all children the same standard of education' (2007: 4).

This use of catastrophe as 'exciting market opportunities', linked to the orchestrated pillage of the public sphere, is all part of disaster capitalism. The key to all this is the shock tactic that is employed at moments when the public is severely disoriented by events. According to Klein, this is a strategy that Friedman and his influential Chicago School followers have been perfecting for more than 30 years. It consists in waiting for (or provoking) a major crisis then 'selling off pieces of the state to private players' while citizens are still 'reeling from the shock', then rapidly making the reforms permanent (6).

Klein might be accused of free-market paranoia were it not for the fact that she quotes Friedman's own words to back up her argument. For it was Friedman who wrote that 'only a crisis – actual or perceived – produces real change. When that crisis occurs, the actions that are taken depend on the ideas that are lying around.' Friedman believed that his role (and that of his followers) was to 'develop alternatives to existing policies, to keep them alive and available until the politically impossible becomes politically inevitable' (Klein, 2007: 6; and Friedman, 1962: ix). Klein goes on to develop an argument where Friedman's shock doctrine is seen to have been used to modify or transform not only the economies of North America and Britain but those of countries as diverse as Chile, Argentina, Brazil, Indonesia, South Africa, Poland, China and Russia (to name only a few). Her argument is that in all these countries, combined with deregulation, the breaking down of trade barriers and the radical reduction of public spending, there has been a massive sell-off of national assets which have favoured global capitalists and the multinationals at the expense of national interests (one might see the same kind of strategies employed in the wake of the catastrophic collapse of the banking system in 2008 which has resulted in similar privatization measures and wholesale attacks on the public sphere in the most affected countries).

Klein isolates Chile as the forerunner of the shock doctrine when, acting as advisor to the Chilean dictator (General Augusto Pinochet), Friedman helped to engineer a set of changes which would act as the template for economic reforms in other parts of the world. Chile, in a state of shock after Pinochet's US-backed military coup in 1973, and suffering catastrophic hyperinflation, was subjected to the key notions of Friedman's free-market economics (otherwise known as the neoliberalism of the Chicago School – see above). Following Friedman, Pinochet created a free trade zone, which included deregulation, the cutting back of social spending, linked to the privatization of services and the imposition of tax cuts.

Friedman believed that these wide-reaching changes imposed over a short period would create the psychological conditions necessary to bring about the adjustments that he called economic 'shock treatment' (in Klein, 2007: 7). Of course, as Klein points out, Pinochet facilitated the necessary changes with his own brand of brutal shock tactics performed in the regime's torture cells. This is something that Klein brings out in many different contexts: when economic shock therapy is the chosen method for change it is all too often accompanied by an oppressive state apparatus and violent, bloody and ruthless repression. She goes as far as saying that the shock doctrine attempts to achieve on a mass scale 'what torture does one on one in the interrogation cell' (16).

Before I go on to examine forms of resistance against repression and the role of journalists I want to bring out another way in which I think Klein effectively maps economic policy and change: in her exploration of the relations between the World Bank, global capital and multinational corporations.

The IMF and World Bank, and the cultural *economic* logic of late capitalism

Milton Friedman was against the International Monetary Fund (IMF) and World Bank (on the grounds that the market should be left to find its own levels) but the Department of Economics at Chicago University (where Friedman was based) trained many American and foreign economics graduates who would end up in key positions in both their own countries and in these financial institutions. The irony, then, is that both these institutions would play a key role from around the 1980s in establishing Friedman's particular brand of free-market economics (backed by successive US administrations). The basic problem as Klein sees it is that when different countries' economies spiralled out of control they had no option but to turn to the World Bank and the IMF (162).

However, Klein maintains that these organizations, contradicting their founding principles to prevent future economic shocks and meltdowns, are dominated by Friedmanite free-market dogmas, which use these crises as excuses to lever open and exploit ailing economies. (At the time of writing, within the eurozone, Greece, Iceland, Ireland, Portugal, Italy and Spain are all in the firing line.) This is not only a question of the dominant Chicago School ideology but something made possible by the fact that the power structures that underlie the two institutions do not allow 'a one country, one vote' system; voting being carried out according to the relative size of each country's economy. This gives the United States a controlling hand over all decisions, followed by Europe and Japan. By 1989 the 'Washington Consensus' was fully in place, which demanded that all 'state enterprises should be privatized' and 'barriers impeding the entry of foreign firms should be abolished'. This effectively established the chief tenets of free trade with its privatization, drastic cuts in government spending and the deregulation of markets 163).

The problem for governments seeking aid is that these structural adjustments were (and still are) laid down as preconditions to receiving loans or any financial help. Klein quotes the IMF senior economist Davison Budhoo, who admitted that everything the IMF did between 1983 and 1988 was based on its mission 'to have the south "privatised" or die'. He went on to state that 'towards this end we ignominiously created economic bedlam in Latin America and Africa in 1983–1988' (164; also see Budhoo, 1990: 102). Furthermore, the structural adjustments insisted upon, according to the renowned Columbia University economist Dani Rodrik (who has worked closely with the World Bank), have had no direct link to creating economic stability (Klein, 2007: 165; and Rodrik, 1992: 95). If this is true it exposes how both the IMF and the World Bank were dominated by policies of questionable efficacy that tended to represent the interests of a narrow elite of capitalists. Adapting Althusser, it is possible to understand this Friedmanite ideology as rooted in not so much an ideological state apparatus but an ideological cross or multi-state apparatus, linked to (to tinker with the terms of Jameson's arguments) a cultural *economic* logic of late capitalism.

Klein's way of cognitively mapping the world is indirectly related to Michael Hardt and Antonio Negri's notion of **Empire**. Empire assumes that the world economy is dominated by the global capitalism of the multinationals (linked to the interests of the US and its allies) and bolstered by organizations like the G8, NATO the World Trade Organization and the IMF. This is the monolith, the all-encompassing late capitalist (Roman-like) 'Empire', that dominates and saturates not only politics and the economy but the law itself – and which guarantees the economic inequalities that maintain, on the one hand, huge accumulations of capital and, on the other, the perpetuation of poverty. The counterbalances to this overarching Empire are the various democratic forces, the NGOs, activist and religious groups and the United Nations General Assembly (Hardt and Negri, 2000, 2005). The next practice section suggests how this 'Empire' may function to the detriment of poorer countries.

Practice: *Life and Debt*

In order to see how you might cognitively map the relations between the policies of the IMF and the World Bank and a specific country you might start with Stephanie Black's documentary film *Life and Debt* (2001). The film focuses on the economic predicaments suffered by Jamaica since the mid-1970s and outlines how the IMF and

World Bank (and the Inter-American Development Bank) insisted on the adoption of structural adjustments like deregulation, cuts in government spending, privatization and the opening of its markets to outsiders if Jamaica was to take advantage of loans to help it out of crisis. As Dani Rodrik emphasized (see above), these Friedmanite measures were a failure, something which threw Jamaica into even deeper crisis. The film is partially structured around interviews with former Jamaican President Michael Manley, who claims that the structural adjustments demanded of countries in crisis are another form of imperialism where economies are opened up (and softened up) for exploitation by international capital.

The film shows how the Jamaican economy has been subjected to measures that have effectively resulted in an ever-downward spiral of repeated loans (under ever-more restrictive conditions) and increasing public debt. The demanded cuts in public spending and other structural adjustments can be seen in higher prices, lower wages (with the gap between rich and poor increasing), unemployment and other conse-quences like underinvestment in hospitals and education, resulting in poorer health, greater illiteracy and the rise of poverty, corruption, violence and crime. The film shows the impact that these policies have on ordinary people. In this way it is possible to map out the relations between international organizations, dominated by free-trade agendas, and the effects these have on everyday life.

We see the consequences of the regime put into place by the IMF and World Bank in a section of the film dedicated to Free Trade Zones, which gives a practical example of how countries are opened up for exploitation. The factories in the port of Kingston are fortressed behind high-security fences and are run by foreign garment companies. The way this is run is fairly typical of countries that have to negotiate loans to try to solve their economic problems. First, foreign companies pay low rents and pay little or no tax on materials they import. Secondly, they can take advantage of low wages and poor work conditions and are further attracted by a government ban on unions within the Free Trade Zones (Klein also emphasizes this and shows how these practices are quite widespread outside the first world (2000: 195f.)).

The film makes the connection between the Free Trade Zones and the US governments that have promoted them through the US Agency for International Development, which has invested millions of dollars of public money in encouraging American companies to relocate to take advantage of lower manufacturing costs in Jamaica. However, given the North American Free Trade Alliance, other countries like Mexico, the Dominican Republic and Costa Rica are now in competition with Jamaica for Free Trade Zones. (Klein (2000) also outlines how this divisive system works.)

Other themes brought out by *Life and Debt* concern how the opening up of Jamaican markets in the name of 'free trade' helped to undermine home-based banana and milk production and debilitate other businesses (for example, the US has allegedly dumped poor-quality chicken on Jamaica and insisted on removing subsidies while closely protecting its own food production by exercising rigorous import controls).

(Continued)

(Continued)

The film also helps to map the international situation when it explores how some 25,000 rival banana workers in Columbia went on strike for better wages, which resulted in ruthless repression and forty workers being killed. This shows how different parts of the world are subjected to a similar 'cultural-economic logic' and are pitted against one another. This helps to explain why so many pressure groups around the world have called for the radical reduction or cancellation of foreign debt.

Just as Haacke's installations or Daitche's novel can be seen as effective devices for cognitive mapping, so can film which is not in the documentary tradition. For example, Jameson, in his *The Geopolitical Aesthetic* (1992), demonstrates how films can function in terms of cognitive mapping. Jameson takes the Philippine director Kidlat Tahimik's *The Perfumed Nightmare* (1977) to show that, while reflecting the local (Third World) situation, it can be seen to reflect on the global economics of the First World. As Dixon and Zonn have remarked, what makes Tahimik's film so interesting for Jameson is that

> while Third World films tend to focus on the social disjunctures created by colonialism and neocolonialism, or work unconsciously to invoke a 'geopolitical Aesthetic' through their portrayal of 'archaic' categories such as nationality and myth, *The Perfumed Nightmare* is very much a self-conscious exercise that seeks to make a connection between the localised experience of the *individual* and the globalised totality that is late capitalism.

This is made possible through the use of symbols, allegories and techniques 'that invoke a sense of the global' (2005: 290f.). This opens up the idea of interpreting any kind of film to see up to what point it can serve to help cognitively map the world.

Further practice

There are many documentaries and other films you might explore in an effort to cognitively map the world in distinct ways. You might start with *Isle of Flowers* (*Ilha das Flores*, 1989), an award-winning Brazilian (mainly) non-fiction film (it mixes fiction, animation and documentary) made by Jorge Furtado. It ostensibly relates (with shocking images and macabre humour) the fate of a tomato but offers a savage indictment of the inhuman treatment of the poor in Porto Alegre. It can be seen as a piece of cognitive mapping in the way it cleverly weaves together different social and economic groups and contexts to underscore the relations between excess and need and privilege and poverty, in a world where people are less important than pigs and profits. The film can be seen in English using the following link: http://video.google.com/videoplay?docid=5263978110274124891#

Many political documentaries can be seen (free) online at the following addresses (although you should check to make sure they do not infringe copyrights):

http://freedocumentaries.org/

www.documentary-log.com/dcategory/politics/

The Media Education Foundation offers many titles that can be bought and provides study guides, handouts and transcripts: www.mediaed.org

Cultural studies, critical journalism, Gramsci and the organic intellectual

The books I have mentioned above like Monbiot's *Captive State* and Naomi Klein's *No Logo!* and *The Shock Doctrine*, and films like *Life and Debt*, can be seen as ambitious examples of cognitive mapping. What I want to suggest in this section is that cultural studies can work along side investigative journalism (including that produced in webpages and documentary films). This means that we can supplement our more obviously theoretical training with sources that are not produced in academic contexts.

Through reference to Gramsci's work it is possible to see the importance of the connections between academic cultural studies and investigative journalism. Gramsci, while considering all people intellectuals, made the influential distinction between the 'traditional' and the **'organic' intellectual** that I mentioned in Chapter 1 with relation to Stuart Hall's attempt to create intellectuals who could not only theorize culture but cooperate with groups outside educational institutions. For Gramsci, the traditional intellectual (who starts out as an organic intellectual) basically serves the intellectual needs of society (these are engineers, technicians, administrators, teachers, lawyers, artists and 'men of letters', etc.). However, the organic intellectuals, rising out of and serving the needs of a new class, have special roles to play. It is not enough for them to have technical knowledge but they need to have practical skills as organizers and be what Gramsci called permanent persuaders and thus be part of the (counter)hegemonic forces which help to (re)direct society (Gramsci, 1971: 9–10) – which is what Hall proposed as one of his goals at the Birmingham Centre (Hall, 1996a: 267–8).

As Steve Jones has indicated, the Gramscian notion of the organic intellectual can be linked to what is known as the **new social movements** (like those activist websites mentioned above that keep constant vigilance on human rights abuses and the environment) and to issues of media representation.

Help File: new social movements

In Chapter 13 I referred to writers like Laclau and Mouffe (who Jameson associated with the politics of the new social movements) who put more faith in the alliances between protest groups (or networks) that support one another on particular issues involving human rights rather than relying on well-established political parties with their formal organization and overarching ideologies. Fairly typical of the new social movements is avaaz.com, which is a global movement that attempts to empower people from all walks of life and to encourage them to take action on pressing global, regional and national issues, ranging from gay and women's rights, political corruption

(Continued)

(Continued)

and poverty to conflict and climate change. Avaaz's model of internet activism can be seen as a new social movement because its end is to transform individual effort into a powerful collective force. These groups are often referred to as part of the global justice movement but also, according to Gilbert (2008: 131), associated with anti-capitalism (see also Buechler, 1999; Clawson, 2003). The value and efficacy of the new social movements is highly contested (see Colás, 2002; Pugh, 2009).

Jones points out that 'contemporary forms of subordination grant a very prominent role to activist-intellectuals' uses of the Internet'. Referring to Downey and Fenton (2003), Jones indicates that different campaigns like those associated with the Zapatistas (in Mexico), the movements against the settlements in Palestine, and opposition to multinational food corporations, have adopted a strategy of 'offline protest and online counter-publicity'. What I want to stress here is how, within these movements, 'web intellectuals target the general public and the more established media sphere simultaneously' (Jones, 2006: 85).

If we see activists of all kinds as organic intellectuals, there is no need to assume that there are the intellectuals, on the one hand, and some other class that has to be led by the nose, on the other. This suggests that those in education (students and teachers who serve or may serve the intellectual necessities of society) may be a part of (or work alongside) other 'intellectuals' whether they be journalists, artists, members of the new social movements or from any other sphere. This more open model of the organic intellectual would have to insist on the importance of communicating with the widest audience possible, which entails attempting to break down the old barriers between academic writing, professional and non-professional journalism (in print and featured in webpages) and blogs.

These counter-hegemonic struggles bring us back to the themes explored at the end of the last chapter where I reviewed Hall's and Giroux's call for a pedagogy in which learning is intimately related to efforts to bring about social change and Grossberg's plea for a committed political model which avoids approaches too dominated by signifying practices narrowly focused on questions of the subject, ideology, identity politics and the politics of representation (Grossberg, 1992: 122).

Cultural studies within/beyond academe: don't just theorize – do it! New social movements, subvertizing, culture jamming and DiY

Part of the counter-hegemonic forces of 'offline protest and online counter-publicity' can be seen in the activist movements known as 'subvertizing', adbusters, 'hacktivists', culture jamming and DiY. The adbusters and subvertizers who subvert ads and billboards are part of what is known as **culture jamming**, where the messages of advertisers are sabotaged. According to Marc Dery, the strategies that culture jammers use include everything from 'billboard bandits' and 'textual slashers' to hackers who expose government misconduct and politically motivated media hoaxers who hack into radio or TV to disrupt live newscasts (Dery, 1993). The Yes Men! can be put into this tradition. The miscellaneous character of culture jamming can be seen from the AdBusters manifesto which states:

> We are a global network of artists, activists, writers, pranksters, students, educators and entrepreneurs. We are downshifters, shit disturbers, rabble-rousers, incorrigibles and malcontents. We are anarchists, guerrilla tacticians, neo-Luddites, pranksters, poet, philosophers and punks. Our aim is to topple existing power structures and forge a major shift in the way we live in the 21st century. We will change the way information flows, the way institutions wield power, the way industries set their agendas. Above all, we will change the way we interact with the mass media and we will reclaim the way in which meaning is produced in our society. (Adbusters n/d)

An example of culture jamming is where a sign (Figure 15.1) advertising Esso petrol (owned by the Exxon-Mobil corporation) was altered at the entrance to a petrol station near the Germany–Luxembourg border in 1992 where the word ESSO was doctored to read 'E$$O' (Greenpeace, 2007). This

Figure 15.1   Culture jamming in action

© Greenpeace/Bas Beentjes

simple change invites alternative reactions to the ad (like profits transcend human rights and environmental considerations). This is typical of culture jamming which relies on creative delinquent acts in attempts to sabotage the public image of selected corporations. Thus, culture jamming can be related to cognitive mapping (and Althusser's symptomatic reading) because these practices often try to reveal the business practices behind the images that corporations create for themselves. For example, Billboard Liberation once lopped off the 'M' in a Max Factor ad so it read 'ax Factor', which gave a sinister twist to the slogan 'a pretty face isn't safe in this city'. Billboard Liberation Front's erasure of the words 'of Beauty' from Stella Artois's 'She's a Thing of Beauty' shows how culture jamming can 'improve' ads to create counter messages which reflect on the habitual objectification of women in advertising (www.billboardliberation.com).

The broadening out of the themes that culture jammers address can be seen in BUGA UP (Billboard Utilising Graffitists Against Unhealthy Promotions), an Australian group formed in 1979, which encourages people all over the world to deface or change the messages of ads found on billboards that are felt to be 'unhealthy'. BUGA UP not only challenges what it sees as the malicious injury to community health but the wilful defacement of the environment caused by billboard promotions. One cigarette ad which was supposed to read '... anyhow have a Winfield' was re-sprayed to read 'anyhow have a Wank, it is healthier' and on another letters were sprayed out on Benson & Hedges to read 'Be on Edge' (see www.bugaup.org). Its webpage includes a gallery, press clippings and has a do-it-yourself graffiti guide.

What unites culture jammers is that they try (like The Yes Men!) to expose corporate business practices that they see as unacceptable, unjust, inhumane, prejudicial, dishonest or environmentally damaging by 'retouching' and thereby subverting official representations. It can be seen as a kind of semiotic warfare because culture jamming intervenes in these processes of meaning by subverting them. The role of raising public awareness through pressure groups is undoubtedly very important but this is a particularly interesting social phenomenon because it links semiotic guerrilla warfare with 'direct action'. However, what have become known as do-it-yourself (DiY) direct action groups in Britain and many other parts of the world have taken these practices to a higher level.

According to George McKay, the DiY phenomenon in Britain is a loose miscellany of different groups that may or may not be in agreement with one another about the projects, or the strategies, they adopt to bring about change. These groups resort to everything from using video activism (to record police brutality or direct state repression) to the occupation of trees (tree dwelling) and roads (Reclaim the Streets) more often than not in order to counter what are seen as the negative effects of capitalism and, especially, to resist the destruction of the environment. These groups may be motivated by socialist, anarchist or even New Age thinking and are often linked to ecstasy-fuelled street parties (which have been conscientiously repressed through legislation) and rave culture which may or may not involve violence (McKay, 1998: 1–53).

Studying these groups helps to redirect cultural studies in new directions and also suggests ways in which the concerns of critics like Grossberg and Giroux are taken up by groups which seem a long way from the lecture halls and seminar rooms of the university (even though some teachers and students are, or have been, involved in these movements). The themes explored in this chapter, however lightly, not only require us to continue to read books but also to delve into the massive resources of the internet and may also inspire us to consider new theories or concepts to help us map out the social, economic and political trends that dominate the societies in which we live.

Before I go on to offer some advice on using journalism and (non-academic) webpages I shall offer a few remarks about how the new social movements mentioned in this chapter may be theorized outside the dominant paradigms of the politics of the subject, identity and representation. One line of theory that is becoming increasingly more influential in cultural studies is that associated with the ideas developed by Gilles Deleuze and Félix Guattari (Hall and Birchall, 2006: 107f.). Here I shall only offer a few pointers to show how we might think with a number of simplified concepts from their work. I shall not put the concepts I introduce into their philosophical context (which would require a chapter in itself) but suggest how they can be adapted to a description of some of the things that have been cognitively mapped in this chapter.

Thinking with Deleuze and Guattari

Deleuze and Guattari created a series of concepts that may help us to cognitively map the new social movements while cognitively mapping our own cognitive maps. What I mean by this is that theories may map the geographical-cultural domain but also reflect back on how these theories go about their mapping. One concept which may have considerable descriptive power is the idea of the '**rhizome**' (Deleuze and Guattari, 1980/1987: 1f.). This is generally used to describe the roots of plants that spread horizontally instead of growing into the ground. This idea can be used as a metaphor for the new social movements described above because while they may have important points where energy or influences are concentrated (computer terminals, forceful individuals), they have no clear *hierarchical* power centres. This does not mean that power is eradicated but suggests that it spreads in a more horizontal, rather than vertical, way (although, as Deleuze and Guattari were aware, the distinction cannot be considered absolute (6)).

Traditional politics can be seen within the vertical model where obvious power centres connected to hierarchies dominate the individual members of a party who are expected, more or less, to toe the party line (regardless of whether we are talking about right- or left-wing political groups). In Deleuze and Guattari's terms, this is **arborescence** – a tree-like structure that fixes order (7–8). This is the strength that comes from the tree-like growth of root, trunk, branch and leaf all connected to a dominant centre. The new social movements can be seen as the 'horizontal' alternative to this model, where organizational nodes, power structures and hierarchies are more dispersed.

For example, when the Conservative–Liberal coalition in Britain decided to impose harsh cuts in education in 2010 much student agitation took the form of a rhizome-like spread of activism that included networking and blogging (through the use of Facebook and Twitter, etc.). This social networking functioned at a more informal level (which does not exclude crossover points with more organized or consolidated groups). As Sean Coughlan, the BBC education correspondent, explained, the protests that took place 'weren't organized by any conventional political organisation, but they managed to mobilise youngsters in towns and cities from Bournemouth to Edinburgh'. They were coordinated through social networking websites, with little of the more orthodox centralised control associated with the mainstream political parties. Coughlan appropriately called this 'DIY radicalism' (BBC, 2010).

Another set of terms which can be adapted to the new social movements described here are **territorialization**, **reterritorialization** and **destratification** (Deleuze and Guattari, 1972/1983: 222f.). If we come back to Naomi Klein's theory that the world economy has gradually been taken over by Friedmanite free trade (and assume that it has some validity) it can be seen as a part of a process of economic-political deterritorialization and reterritorialization of existing conditions that re-stratify economies according to the interests of corporate capital – mediated through institutions like the IMF and the World Bank. The sweat shops set up offshore (to ignore exploitation at home) can be seen as a (re)territorialization of geographical space: a colonization without formal invasion which entails shifting the population from things like agriculture to the exploitative manufacturing protocols of the Free Trade Zones.

The activities of the new social movements, including the culture jammers and the large number of internet based alternative media and pressure groups, etc., can be seen as attempts at 'reterritorialization' and re-stratification, insofar as they try to reclaim the image, the billboard and the street, while countering the way capitalism and traditional politics commandeer power and function with relation to tree-like power structures. The new social movements (often driven by computer link-ups) spread like the rhizome interconnecting between each other in vast and complex networks of multiple points but where no single point seems to ground them into a fully hierarchical system. As McKay points out, each group functions in a semi-autonomous way and, following Colin Ward, emphasizes their anarchist affiliations. Thus, these are small functional groups that do not depend on membership cards, votes and special leadership but 'ebb and flow, group and regroup, according to the task in hand'; they are 'networks, not pyramids' (Ward's words in MacKay, 1998: 52).

Of course, it must be realized that the uses of these metaphor-concepts of rhizomes and arborescence, etc. are only tools to help us theorize – for example, Hardt and Negri use the idea of the rhizome to describe the constitution of the global market itself as 'organized along a disciplinary model' that is 'traversed by tensions that open mobility in every direction; it is a transversal mobility that is rhizomatic rather than arborescent' (Hardt and Negri, 2000: 253). This suggests that these concepts do not reflect a so-called objective world but are, like any concept, a tool for thinking with (and can be adapted to various ends – and may be used in contradictory ways). While these are highly simplified uses of some of Deleuze and Guattari's very complex ideas, and while the assumptions upon which 'territorialization' is based may be rather too simplistic to capture the circuitous character of modern politics and late capitalism, they do begin to show how we might begin to mobilize different paradigms to cognitively map the contemporary world. As mentioned above, these ideas also help us to reflect on what kind of mapping we are doing – that is, we territorialize and deterritorialize with relation to the metaphor-concepts we mobilize to try to understand the economic, cultural, political terrain. This brings a certain theoretical self-consciousness (which characterizes much cultural studies) to the mapping exercises we practice.

Cognitive mapping, evaluating sources and further research

This section is designed to help refine research strategies and give some guidance about the evaluation of sources. Having chosen your topic you will need to find background information by searching for books, periodicals and web sources. As far as academic books and journals are concerned, they are generally peer reviewed to ensure a high level of argumentative rigour and exacting standards in terms of citing sources. Of course, this helps to preserve scholarly protocols but you may feel that their arguments are not convincing and/or that their range of reference is not sufficiently broad. You may feel that those are precisely the sources that *do not* interest you. You may find academic articles on corporate power or culture jamming but feel you want to see how these function in terms of documentary films, webpages and personal viewpoints.

This forces us to consider the possibilities of unreliability. One problem, then, of giving so much importance to information and data collected from critical journalism, documentaries and websites is linked to their dependability. Of course, any source has to be treated with care and there is no guarantee that data taken from academic books and journals will be accurate or reliable. However, if you have spent any time surfing on the internet you will know that many pages are derived from others (sometimes without acknowledgement) and sometimes no references are available whatsoever. Documentary films may provide very full information about sources and even have detailed webpages dedicated to those who want to do further research (for example, see *The Corporation* website).

Before you begin your cognitive mapping you might check your library to see if it offers advice on how to develop your research strategies. You will save a lot of time if you keep a copy of all web addresses that you consult – they should, of course, be rigorously cited, like any other source. Many library webpages have hyperlinks that give advice on each step of the research process. For example, Cornell University's library webpage offers, under 'background information', a useful general booklist to help you begin, and under 'finding books and articles on your topic' you will get advice on narrowing down your search.

Of course, after choosing your topic and finding and using materials (whether in a library or on websites) you need to evaluate your sources carefully. For example, the books I have used in this chapter, like those written by Naomi Klein and George Monbiot, while not strictly academic books, do offer full references to their sources. Of course, this does not guarantee that the information is reliable or that the data is correct, but it does mean that the sources can be checked. In some cases I have cited Klein and Monbiot *and* the source they have used because some of their information is second-hand (however, as journalists they often produce valuable first-hand evidence). You should also be aware of second-hand versions of theories, ideas, historical contexts, etc. in academic sources which sometimes, rather than quote directly from a primary source, will quote someone else's version of it. Most of the webpages I have recommended also give sources for the information, although, like the books mentioned, may have their ultimate sources in first-person experiences (of activists and journalists) and/or in newspaper reports. Sometimes, as in the case of Wikileaks, the credibility of the information put forward will be controversial but based on official documents (which may or may not be reliable).

However, sometimes it is necessary to accept that it is difficult or impossible (at a particular time) to check the validity of statements. Yet this does not necessarily invalidate a general line of argument. For example, we may not know exactly how many Jews died in the concentration camps, but the lack of a precise number does not justify denials of the Holocaust. Earlier I mentioned the scandals surrounding Trafigura, the corporation that tried to silence those who accused them of causing serious injuries and death. At the time, the only evidence available was from journalists and activists, and those who wanted to analyse the possible abuses had to accept the limitations of the sources. Of course, we can always rely on our ability to assess the *arguments* being put forward, and analyse how much the piece of writing or presentation relies on rhetorical devices rather than evidence and consider whether one independent source serves to substantiate or contradict another. Yet sometimes we may not be primarily interested in how strong an argument is. In this chapter I have not critiqued Klein's theory that Friedmanite free-market capitalism is colonizing the world because my main aim has been to suggest ways that we may cognitively map late capitalism (assuming that the latter term makes complete sense).

However, despite these possible handicaps, we can ask a number of questions to help us decide on whether or not we want to rely on a source. First, what are an author's or a website's credentials? Has s/he or it a reputation for being rigorous? Does it actually matter to us that a source is 'objective' or an author has credentials? For example, I cited George McKay (1998) above whose (academic) book is full of testimonies from different people linked to direct action movements. The point here is not to provide a set of views beyond all question but to bring together varying perspectives that may well contradict one another because we may want to explore the problems of understanding our sources and/or reflect differences of strategy or point of view. If we start out expecting to be objective (which, as we have seen from previous chapters, is a highly questionable notion), we may be asking the wrong or unrealistic questions. A source may be felt to be compromised by the fact that it addresses an audience of supporters, yet even this, while possibly leading to assertion or opinion over argument, and assumption over evidence, may be part of what we want to research or take into account.

In the case of books (academic or otherwise), reading reviews can be a guide. Is there widespread agreement that, despite weaknesses, the source has something valuable, original or relevant to say? A book or article may be questioned according to one of these criteria; however, an original but controversial study may be just what you are looking for. As far as websites are concerned, some will be referred to in academic sources (as in this book) as of relevance or interest. For example, I have recommended you to listen to Dwight Eisenhower's speech on Wikipedia. This 'people's encyclopaedia' has raised many questions about its reliability and credibility but it is a rich source of information – some of it scrupulously referenced. Like many websites, it is very uneven in terms of rigour and reliability; however, what is of importance, as in all things, is to maintain an open but critical view.

Following the advice on the Cornell Library website mentioned earlier (see the Cornell Library Research address in the References), there are a number of things we should consider when using web resources. One basic strategy is to check if the information is up to date because much information becomes outdated very quickly (although older information or data may still be of interest), for this reason many scholars cite the date the page was accessed (although this may not be necessary if your use of the information does not rely on being up to the minute). Another thing you can do is to check if an author is identifiable (look for links like 'who we are', etc.) and check the domain that a site belongs to: is it edu, gov, com, etc.? These abbreviations will help to indicate if it is an official government site or not. If the website is obviously trying to sell you something or promote a cause this will not necessarily render it useless – you may actually be directly interested in these kinds of sites – but if you are looking for reliable data for a more factual study you will have to be wary of any unsubstantiated claims.

Then there is the question of the use of search engines and the production of academic knowledge. As José van Dijck has observed, search engines like Google Scholar (which, with reservations, I would recommend), have an increasingly decisive influence on the production of knowledge. Van Dijck argues that when using these devices we need to take into account that they do not just convey knowledge to the user in a neutral way but 'co-produce' it. This is because all information is subject to ranking and profiling systems, which remain largely hidden from the user in a 'technological unconscious' (van Dijck, 2010: 574f.). This is another aspect we need to consider when using web sources – the first 20 items only reflect popularity not necessarily quality or rigour.

Finally, we might ask ourselves how important hard 'facts' are to our research. Is it possible to arrive at them? Whose facts are they? What or whose ends do they serve? What is the role of rhetoric, assertion and opinion? Can we always separate argument from rhetoric, assertion and opinion? Is there such a thing as objectivity or an impartial view? In what would the differences reside? All these questions take us back to many of the themes developed in the earlier chapters of this book and force us to consider the questions related to poststructuralism and postmodernism.

Postscript: struggling with theory

These last chapters may have disconcerted some readers because they seem to suggest that the theories outlined and demonstrated in earlier chapters have been challenged or even undermined. However, we do not have to be trapped into the simple binary choice of either/or. Stuart Hall once created the metaphor of 'struggling with angels' for theoretical work. What this entailed was that the 'only theory worth having is that which you have to fight off, not that, which you speak with profound fluency' (Hall, 1996a: 265–6). Of course, this book has been written for those who need a way into some of the dominant theories that have concerned practitioners of cultural studies. The next stage is to struggle with the theoretical angels to find your own way forward.

Summary of key points

This chapter began by looking at multinational companies like Nestlé and Cola-Cola to review some of the alleged abuses attributed to them and as a means to cognitively map them in terms of forms of oligopoly. Mapping strategies have also been explored with relation to the links between corporations and the industrial–military complex and higher education. Naomi Klein's notion of 'the shock doctrine' has been explored as a form of cognitive mapping with relation to Milton Friedman's free-market capitalism and the structural adjustments (aided and abetted by institutions like the IMF and the World Bank) that help to soften up local economies to multinational

exploitation and governance. Guidance has been given on how to map the corporations with relation to resources like investigative journalism and activist websites.
Activist alternatives like culture jamming and subvertizing have been explored and
a number of concepts taken from the work of Deleuze and Guattari have been introduced as a way of re-theorizing new social movements as an alternative to what
critics like Grossberg have seen as an overemphasis on identity politics and representation within cultural studies. Finally, some advice has been offered on evaluating
sources and further research.

Further reading/resources

Joel Bakan's *The Corporation: The Pathological Pursuit of Profit and Power*
(2004), and the film (2003), use the audacious idea of the corporation as
akin to the psychopath as a way of explaining how corporations function to
the detriment of society. These (together with the official website) are useful sources for information and ideas. The official website for the documentary film *The Corporation* (www.tvo.org/thecorporation/teachers.html) has
a number of study sheets, which offer ideas on how to evaluate sources and
information on electronic resources. One useful idea is to create your own
corporate posters to map the corporate world – you might use Hans Haacke's
work for inspiration. At a more academic level, the power of accusation in
terms of challenging corporate law-braking is explored by Robert Faulkner in
Corporate Wrongdoing and the Art of the Accusation (2011).

Gina McColl's 'Caught in a Jam' (2006) focuses on the increasing number
of companies in Australia (like McDonald's) that use culture jamming to
counter activist campaigns and consumer cynicism. Vince Carducci's 'Culture
Jamming: A Sociological Perspective' (2006) argues that by providing producers with incentives to respond to consumer demands for an end to human
rights abuses and a cleaner environment culture jamming may, ironically,
actually help to perpetuate the system it is at pains to critique. Heath and
Potter's *The Rebel Sell: Why the Culture Can't Be Jammed* (2006) is a provocative study that challenges the idea of an effective counter-culture providing a genuine alternative to consumerism (and it is very critical of many of
Naomi Klein's ideas). Max Haiven's 'Privatized Resistance: AdBusters and the
Culture of Neoliberalism' (2007) discusses the ambivalence that AdBusters
form of culture jamming has inspired in cultural criticism. That is, on the one
hand, it has been accepted as counter-hegemonic but, on the other, it has
been rejected because of the tacitly sexist approach to gender, its tendency
to be simplistic, ignore questions of class and race, and ambivalent political
vacillation between representing itself as revolutionary or reformist. For a
book which discusses the antecedents and effects of neoliberalism see Peter
Gowan's *A Calculaus of Power* (2010).

Stephen Crofts Wiley's 'Spatial Materialism: Grossberg's Deleuzean Cultural Studies' (2005) gives an excellent overview of the way Grossberg has used Deleuze and Guattari's work and adapted it to cultural studies. It also evaluates Grossberg's contribution and clarifies a number of ambiguous concepts in Grossberg's approach, while identifying areas which deserve further critical consideration. Diana Coole and Samantha Frost's *New Materialisms* (2010) is a collection of politically engaged essays which push the idea of materialist criticism in new directions, often with a Deleuzean twist, and in ways that often complement the theories outlined in this book.

Manuel Castells's *End of Millennium* (1998, 2nd edn 2000) (like Castells, 1996, and 1997) can be used to further theorize the role of web-based activist groups in terms of information flows. Like Deleuze and Guatarri, Castells visualizes network organizations as challenging vertical hierarchies as the dominant form of social organization.

Phillips and Roth's *Censored 2009: The Top Censored Stories of 2007–08* (2008) comes out of Project Censored which is the US's longest running media research project. It examines the under-reporting of corruption and censorship in the US press. Its principal objective is the active support and protection of First Amendment rights and freedom of information. Project Censored has been regularly publishing books of controversial and censored stories (see its website).

Practice and further resources (the following references are only a fraction of the possibilities available and only serve as starting points).

McSpotlight can be used to check on the extent of companies' activities and to monitor complaints. There are references to external sources – although not always, which makes following up some of the claims difficult. McSpotlight and other concerned groups have often used *The Ethical Consumer Guide to Everyday Shopping* (published in 1998), which ranked brands and stores according to their ethical and ecological practices and was the brainchild of the Ethical Consumer Research Association – otherwise known as The Ethical Consumer (www.ethicalconsumer.org/AboutUs.aspx). At the time of writing this is one of the UK's leading alternative consumer associations and has very useful research services, comment and analysis (including blogs), and information on boycotts on products from all over the world. It also publishes its own bi-monthly *Ethical Consumer Magazine*, which includes these features. Although the website offers information and 'free buyer guides', it carries a charge so that for more detailed information a daily, monthly or annual fee has to be paid. Nevertheless, you can go quite a long way using the standard online resources.

Corporate Watch (www.corporatewatch.org/), which also offers a wide range of free resources, has prepared a useful document, 'How to Research Companies', which can be bought for a moderate sum or (if you cannot afford to buy it) can be downloaded (www.corporatewatch.org/download.php?id=31).

The Corporate Critic is a webpage allied to the Ethical Consumer Research Association (www.corporatecritic.org/). This webpage indexes and provides ratings for over 50,000 companies from small independents to huge multinationals. The information provided includes companies' relations to environmental issues, human relations (human and workers' rights, irresponsible marketing, supply-chain policies, relations to armaments), animal rights, company politics (company ethos including genetic engineering, political activities, antisocial finance) and product sustainability (organic products, fair trade, positive environmental relations). Again, while there are charges on a daily, monthly or yearly basis, there is a 'free search for companies', which provides more limited information.

Another influential organisation is The Ethical Company Organisation (www.ethical-company-organisation.org/), which provides information on ethical shopping in the UK, listing companies that comply with their ethical shopping accreditation scheme. They also publish good shopping guides and provide a free ethical shopping programme and ethical shopping guides.

War on Want (www.waronwant.org/) provide a lot of information and reports on the multinationals and is a forum for social action. They also offer free downloads of 'alternative company reports' which criticize multinationals on their business practices.

Oligopoly Watch (www.oligopolywatch.com/) is a very useful site dedicated to oligopoly. It is not always up to date but it is a good starting point.

Labour Start (www.labourstart.org/) is a source which reports abuses and lists union demands from all over the world and reports on their successes and failures.

Democracy Now! (www.democracynow.org/) is an independent US radio news programme with its own extensive website which constantly monitors political and corporate activity in the interests of disseminating information to improve democracy. Other organizations worth exploring are Everything2.com, Human Rights Watch, Index on Censorship, The Corner House, and Global Witness, Avaaz (mentioned in earlier chapters) and Campaign Against Arms Trade.

Glossary

A mini-dictionary of key cultural concepts and terms used in this book

Words printed in bold refer to other entries in the Glossary to allow cross-referencing.

Anchorage: A term used by Roland Barthes to describe how the **signifieds** of a linguistic message help to limit the possible meanings generated by images.

Anti-essentialism: A term commonly found in **poststructuralism** and **postmodernism** that indicates an approach to **knowledge** which questions the idea that the **discourses** of the sciences can discover and reflect objective, essential **truths** which are not products of those discourses.

Arbitrary closure: A notion recommended by Stuart Hall where the critic uses **deconstruction** but subordinates its more radical potential to strategic political ends (and avoids becoming a slave to it).

Arborescence: A concept used by Deleuze and Guattari which describes vertical tree-like structures that fix order and can be used to describe more traditional political structures that rely on a vertical model where power centres, connected to hierarchies, dominate the functioning of the party. See **rhizome**.

Big Other: A highly ambivalent concept found in Jacques Lacan's work which very generally refers to the place of the **Symbolic** (with all its rules and structures) or, more specifically, can be experienced as benign or malicious hidden agencies controlling things behind the scenes (like the Christian God or a horrifying paranoiac agency).

Binary oppositions: In **structuralism** cultures are seen to make sense of the world through distinguishing between foundational opposites like life/death, good/evil, freedom/repression, etc., where one term is often taken to have positive connotations and the other negative.

Breakdown of the high verses low culture distinction: Drawing on the work of Jean Baudrillard, critics like Fredric Jameson and George Ritzer argue that this is one of the fundamental premises of **postmodernism.**

Code: In **structuralism, signifiers** and **signifieds** can only produce meanings if they are organized by a code (like a system of grammar).

Coded iconic message: According to Roland Barthes this is where meanings are created for images through deliberate patterning and manipulation, as opposed to the **non-coded iconic message**.

Cognitive mapping: Given the deconstructive tendencies of postmodern thought and cultures, Fredric Jameson argues that there is a need for a more globalized form of politics to resist global capitalism and a new political art that is capable of formulating new forms and strategies that might offer special insights into our place within multinational capitalism. See **high-tech paranoia** and the **homeopathic strategy**.

Commodity fetishism: A concept drawn from the writings of Marx which Fredric Jameson argues is fundamental to **postmodernism**. For Marx, once an object becomes a commodity it becomes 'transcendent' and is treated in such a way that the labour that went into producing it becomes invisible. In this way it is fetishized. See **late capitalism**.

Communicative rationality: In his essay on modernity as an incomplete project Jürgen Habermas rejected the basic premises of **poststructuralism** preferring the idea of 'communicative rationality' which posits that individuals, with a will to communicate and understand, can reach consensus through reasoned debate. Jean-François Lyotard rejected these ideas because he believed they were only another way of reformulating the **grand narratives** and the old totalities and certainties that he rejected.

Connotation: This describes meanings produced through suggestion or association as opposed to the explicit literal meaning of **denotation**.

Consumer society: Jean Baudrillard argued that advanced capitalist societies were at the point where consumption was invading every aspect of life and that the act of consumption was not just about consuming commodities but messages (signs, brand icons, etc.) in such a way that **late capitalism** was becoming increasingly a question of not *who* we are but *what brands* we consume and what lifestyles we adopt. In this way **postmodern identity** is not something outside consumption but negotiated within it.

Crisis of (or incredulity towards) metanarratives: This is a phrase used by Jean-François Lyotard to describe a condition where society no longer believes in the ethical, philosophical, social, political metanarratives that were once thought of as providing the justification for education, learning and the production of knowledge. See the **postmodern condition, grand narrative** and **legitimation**.

Critique of reason: A common notion found in **poststructuralism** and **postmodernism** (but not exclusive to them) and given emphasis in the work of Michel Foucault who did not reject reason *per se* but posed thoroughgoing questions about its nature, limits, historical effects and dangers. See **knowledge**, **discourse**, **truth** and **power**.

Culturalism: A simplifying label that has been used to describe the work of Richard Hoggart, E. P. Thompson and Raymond Williams which emphasizes the lives, cultures, experiences and resistance of ordinary people and their capacity to be active agents of change, rather than dupes of history.

Cultural logic of late capitalism: Fredric Jameson sees this cultural 'logic' at work when art and culture are fully complicit with the values of late capitalism (unlike the products of **high modernism**). This is part of **postmodernism** as he understands it.

Cultural schizophrenia: Adapting ideas from the work of Jacques Lacan, Fredric Jameson argues that in postmodern cultural forms there is a loss of progressive temporality where the experience of 'existential time' and 'deep memory' (of **high modernism**) gives way to dislocation, fragmentation and the loss of 'coherent experience'. See **depthlessness**, **parody and pastiche** and **waning of affect**.

Cultural studies: This is a loose miscellany of self-reflexive, inter-disciplinary approaches (spread across many nations) which Grossberg et al. (1992) claim has no precise methodology – practitioners typically drawing on whatever discipline is necessary in order to produce the knowledge required for a given project. Cultural studies often politicizes the understanding of culture (understood in its widest sense) by exploring how cultural products and practices relate to concepts like class, race/ethnicity, gender, sexuality, ideology, representation and relations of power. All these features complicate the identity of cultural studies, even while they help to establish dominant ways of thinking about and understanding it.

Culture: A notoriously difficult word to define but which, according to Raymond Williams (1983), describes processes of human development with relation to the cultivation of the mind, behaviour or society. In the most general sense it describes language, art, knowledge and belief but also things like law, ethics and customs. Williams emphasized that (in its modern sense) it should be located in the social and political changes brought about by industrial capitalism and linked to 'a whole way of life' and include not only 'high' culture but the understanding of institutions, the organization of production, social practices, sport, entertainment and everyday behaviour. Many contemporary critics stress the importance of understanding of signifying practices, and things like consumption habits and relations of power as a means to understand culture. However, while these lists of possibilities are very useful at a more general and abstract level, any attempt to limit the definition at the level of particular objects of analysis is futile because as the world changes new possibilities (or domains of interest) for the understanding of cultures are constantly appearing.

Culture and civilization tradition: This sums up nineteenth- and twentieth-century writers like Matthew Arnold and F. R. and Queenie Leavis who tended to privilege high cultural forms (and especially literature as the best that had been thought and written) as the means by which civilization could be defined, preserved, propagated and assessed. See **minority culture**.

Culture industry: This is a term used by Theodor Adorno and other Frankfurt critics to refer to forms of mass culture produced for profit and associated with the rise of mass entertainment and mass communications within industrial capitalism. Adorno saw mass culture as depoliticizing and pacifying the exploited masses, while acclimatizing them to the degrading conditions of their lives, while impoverishing them materially, emotionally and intellectually.

Culture jamming: This is a strategy of semiotic warfare where activists or 'subvertizers' sabotage, alter or deface advertisements (or intercept radio and TV programmes) in the interests of questioning the messages they transmit, often as a way of challenging the abuses of the major corporations. See **new social movements**.

Death of the author: An idea taken from Roland Barthes' writings which challenges the idea of limiting a text's meaning to the author's intentions. For Barthes, once the text is written the author is effectively dead in the sense that s/he cannot serve as a basis for grounding or controlling interpretation.

Death of the subject: A notion used by Fredric Jameson to convey the idea that in contemporary postmodern theory there is a loss of the centred subject, a demise in the capacity to feel (once expressed in angst) and a breakdown of the unique style associated with the great writers and artists of **high modernism**. See the **waning of affect** and **depthlessness**.

Decoding: Within **semiology** decoding describes how messages are deciphered by receivers with relation to pre-established codes within a given medium. See **encoding**.

Deconstruction: A complex system of thought initiated by Jacques Derrida which questions and undermines the basis of Western forms of thought through a series of (anti)concepts, wordplay, stylistic inventiveness and tortuous argumentation. See **poststructuralism**, **intertextuality**, **différance**, **difference**, **deferral**, **trace**, **structure**, **transcendental signified**, **logocentrism** and **phonocentrism**.

Deferral: Together with **difference** this term forms part of Derrida's deconstructive (anti)concept of **différance** which undermines the possibilities of fixed meanings. See **poststructuralism**.

Delegitimation: Within the context of **performativity**, Jean-François Lyotard argued that the crisis of **grand narratives** results 'from the ends of action to its means' (1987: 37) in such a way that science no longer relies on these grand narratives to legitimate it – hence the term delegitimation. In the **postmodern condition** each science establishes its own criteria for acceptance, through the consensus of experts, rather than referring to criteria outside themselves. See the **crisis of (or incredulity towards) metanarratives**.

Denotation: This describes the literal meaning of words as opposed to the associative meaning associated with **connotation**.

Depthlessness: A term used by Fredric Jameson to define the **cultural logic of late capitalism**. See **postmodernism**.

Desire: A multifaceted term used by Jacques Lacan which is seen to be the product of the **subject**'s entry into the **Symbolic**, rather than something which pre-exists or stands outside inter-subjective relations. See **need**.

Destratification: A concept used by Deleuze and Guattari that can be used to describe how things or spaces can be de-colonized and transformed by new powers or forces. See **territorialization** and **reterritorialization**.

Difference: Along with **deferral** this term forms part of Derrida's deconstructive (anti-)concept of **différance** which challenges the possibilities of stable meanings. See **poststructuralism**.

Différance: This is a key (anti)concept within Derridean **deconstruction** which plays on the concepts of **difference** and **deferral** in such a way that meaning in discourse is constantly divided and indefinitely postponed. In this way no text has an intrinsic meaning.

Disaster capitalism: An idea put forward by Naomi Klein where governments (aided and abetted by free-market economists) push through emergency measures when the public is vulnerable and severely disoriented. It consists in waiting for (or provoking) a major crisis then deregulating the markets, breaking down trade barriers and radically reducing public spending as part of a massive effort to sell-off national assets which tend to favour global capitalists and the multinationals at the expense of national interests. See the **shock doctrine**.

Discourse: Michel Foucault emphasized that **knowledge** and **truth** cannot be understood outside the discourses (branches of knowledge) which produce them and which are, in turn, regulated by key institutions. It is in these discourses that society generates its regimes or general politics of truth which exercise **power** over subjects. See also **Panopticon** and **gender as performative**.

Double reading: In Althusserian Marxism a double reading takes account of, on the one hand, the gaps and silences that reveal the ideological limits of the discourse (the **problematic**) and, on the other, the way texts inadvertently answer questions they never pose. See **symptomatic reading**.

Empire: A notion found in the work of Michael Hardt and Antonio Negri which understands the world economy as dominated by global capitalism and the multinationals (linked to the interests of the US and its allies) and supported by organizations like the G8, NATO the World Trade Organization and the International Monetary Fund. This is the (Roman-like) 'Empire' in **late capitalism** that guarantees the economic inequalities that maintain huge accumulations of capital and the perpetuation of poverty.

Encoding: Within **semiology** encoding describes how messages are structured into a particular form with relation to a given medium. See **decoding**.

First- and second-order semiological systems: These describe Roland Barthes' approach to understanding how images are read in semiological terms. The first-order system (the simple recognition of the image) functions as the **signifier** of the second-order system, which describes the culturally loaded meaning(s) of the image (which corresponds to **connotation**). See **modern mythololgies**.

Frankfurt School: This is the name given to the Institute for Social Research at the University of Frankfurt to which important Marxist critics like Thoedor Adorno, Max Horkheimer and Walter Benjamin were affiliated. They helped to fuse Marxist thinking with other important approaches like, in the case of Adorno and Horkheimer, psychoanalysis to create trenchant criticisms of contemporary culture and society. See the **culture industry**.

Genealogy: A Nietzschean term used by Michel Foucault to construct an approach to the writing of history that challenges more traditional accounts which assume it pre-exists historical writing and can be reduced to more or less 'objective' narratives, origins and ends. Foucault's approach is **anti-essentialist** and questions the neutral disinterested view that seeks continuities, forces and universal laws.

Gender: A widespread term used in much cultural criticism, especially that focused on feminism and gender studies. More specifically, it is theorized in the work of Michel Foucault and Judith Butler, the latter defining it against concepts like **sex** and **sexuality**. For Butler gender describes the characteristics that a given culture understands as masculine or feminine, dependent on social interactions and the assimilation of social norms. However, gender is seen as a cultural construction, not in terms of something given by nature.

Gender as performative: When discussing gender, Judith Butler uses this term to argue that carefully selected features associated with femininity or masculinity within normative social discourses are used to signify some interior essence. However, this inner essence, which seems to be described by the discourses, is actually a product of them. The implication of this for Butler is that gender is conceived of as the repeated performance of the chosen traits which stand for being woman or man and are made to *perform* gender. See **gender**, **sex**, **sexuality** and **gender subversion**.

Gender subversion: Judith Butler argues that parodic and hyperbolic practices like drag can serve to 'denaturalize' the body in such a way that what are commonly taken as the 'natural' characteristics of **gender** are exposed as the performative cultural constructs they are. See **gender as performative**.

Grand narrative: Jean-François Lyotard argued that, traditionally, science legitimated itself with relation to philosophical or political metanarratives (or grand narratives). The production of knowledge was justified with reference to criteria outside itself: that it is a good in itself or in the best interests of the people or the nation. However, the **postmodern condition** marks a point of the **crisis of (or incredulity towards) metanarratives**. See **performativity** and **delegitimation**.

Hegemony: This term derives from the work of the Italian Marxist Antonio Gramsci who used it to describe how, in modern democracies, political power and leadership, while ultimately backed up by force, depend on alliances and the winning of consent through compromise and negotiation. This challenges more simplistic notions of **ideology** that assume that ideas and values can be linked in deterministic ways to particular classes. These ideas have been used to describe all kinds of power relations, including those which govern the (de)valuation of different forms of culture.

High culture: This concept is used by critics, like those of the **culture and civilization tradition**, to refer to the most worthy and valuable cultural forms in opposition to what are seen as trivial and debasing products of **popular** (or mass, industrial) **culture**.

High modernism: A term Fredric Jameson uses to distinguish what he regards as the generally inferior cultural products of **postmodernism** from those of the most distinguished modernists. For him high modernism refers to movements like abstract expressionism in painting, existentialism in philosophy, and writers like Eliot, Stevens, Joyce, Woolf, Kafka and Faulkner (in poetry and the novel), or the *auteur* directors like Bergman, Kurosawa, Hitchcock and Fellini (in cinema). See the **cultural logic of late capitalism**.

High-tech paranoia: Within the writings of Fredric Jameson this refers to contemporary narratives (like cyberpunk) in which the impossibly complex circuits of global computer networks are linked to the convoluted intrigues of rival information agencies. For Jameson, these narratives can help to understand 'the impossible totality of the contemporary world system'. See **cognitive mapping** and **homeopathic strategy**.

Historiography: This idea is often used to describe the writing of more traditional historians who assume that historical narratives can more or less reflect the past in objective ways with relation to periods and movements. See **poststructuralism**, **postmodernism** and **genealogy**.

History of sexuality: This refers to one of Michel Foucault's major projects where he showed how sexual practices had been gradually reduced to a set of social and scientific **discourses** that could produce **truths** and forms of **knowledge** and **power** which would enable the social control and regulation of the sexualized body (while opening up discursive spaces for non-normative sexualities).

Homeopathic strategy: Within his conception of **cognitive mapping** Fredric Jameson recommends this tactic where an artist uses the very thing which is considered corrupt (like advertising images) to criticize the institutions in which they circulate. Thus, the corrupt form is used as a means to critique it. See **cognitive mapping**.

Hyperreality: Jean Baudrillard used this concept, which is often seen as a key notion defining **postmodernism**, to describe the condition in **late capitalism** where one-to-one relations between signs and the referential world are lost and individuals find themselves adrift in the infinite proliferation of media images, information and advertising (**simulacra**). This is *hyper*reality because it indicates simulated reality in excess where reality is confused with its **simulation** – it *is* simulation.

Ideological state apparatuses: Louis Althusser associated these apparatuses with politics, education, religion, the law, family, trade unionism, communications and culture (in general) which were conceived of as having a secondary repressive function – that is, secondary to the **repressive state apparatuses**.

Ideology: A notoriously difficult concept fundamental to Marxist analyses that, at the simplest level, describes the dominant ideas, beliefs and values that govern individuals, groups, processes or political parties or economic policies. It is sometimes contrasted with Gramscian **hegemony** theory. Roland Barthes discussed the notion with relation to mass culture seeing collective representations as sign systems that transform (petit-bourgeois) culture into nature. See also **modern mythologies**, and Althusser's notions of **ideological** and **state apparatuses**, **material** and **imaginary aspect of ideology**, **overdetermination** and **interpellation**.

Imaginary: A concept used within Lacanian psychoanalysis which deals with how subjects construct and misrecognize themselves (and identify with others) through images (or fantasies) that give the illusion of a unified identity. From this point of view the self is structured on a series of illusions; however, the Imaginary also establishes the basic coordinates of the self that *enable* the **subject's** functioning in the world. See **master signifiers**.

Imaginary aspect of ideology: This refers to Louis Althusser's idea that in **ideology** subjects do not express their 'real' relation to their conditions of existence but the way they *live* that relation. See **material aspect of ideology**.

Interpellation: In Althusserian Marxism this describes how **ideology** functions to shape individuals into 'subjects' subject to capitalist society and culture.

Intertextuality: A complex term coined by Julia Kristeva and used by Roland Barthes and often associated with **poststructuralism**. At its simplest level it refers to how texts incorporate others into themselves (through quotations, references, etc.). At a more complex level *language itself* can be seen as radically intertextual and thus any utterance or text is already implicated in complex networks of linguistic usages, sayings, tags, etc. before anything is formally cited or referred to.

Knowledge: In the writings of Michel Foucault knowledge is linked to regimes of truth. From this point of view it is not divorced from the exercise of multiple networks of power. See **truth** and **discourse**.

Langue: In **structuralism** this refers to a pre-established (but negotiable) system of common rules and conventions (which make up a code) which, within a given community, can be used to produce meaningful utterances (or *paroles*).

Late capitalism: Fredric Jameson argued that this characterized the **post-industrial** 'multinational' stage of capitalism associating it with **postmodernism**. This is where the whole world is dominated by the narrow interests of the ruling, capitalist classes whose activities transcend the nation state. See the **cultural logic of late capitalism**.

Legitimation: Jean-François Lyotard, when discussing the **postmodern condition**, claimed that in modern societies science does not only seek the truth of things but is also under an obligation to legitimate 'the rules of its own game'. These justifications, which are political or philosophical, are what Lyotard thinks of as discourses of legitimation which contain **metanarratives**. See **crisis of (or incredulity towards) metanarratives**.

Little narratives: For Jean-François Lyotard the little narrative avoids the universalizing principles and overarching claims of **grand narratives** which he felt, within the **postmodern condition**, were bankrupt and could no longer be justified. See **crisis of (or incredulity toward) metanarratives** and **delegitimation**.

Logocentrism: A term Jacques Derrida used to define a characteristic of Western thinking where meaning is grounded in the metaphysics of presence, and where presence (and speech) are privileged over absence (and writing). See **deconstruction** and **phonocentrism**.

Mass culture: This term is normally used by those who regard mass-produced culture for commercial ends as trivial and dangerous to those without the appropriate intellectual training to see through their dubious allurements. See the **culture and civilization tradition** and the **culture industry**.

Master signifiers: A term used by Jacques Lacan to indicate those **signifiers** which function to provide the basic coordinates of identity (gender, nationality, religious belief, class, sexual preferences, etc.) but only give the illusion of meaning because they are all dispersed through other signifiers. However, if a person does not rely on the master signifiers and internalize the basic rules laid down in the **Symbolic** (the rules symbolized by the **Name-of-the-Father**) the result would be psychosis. See the **subject** and the **Imaginary**.

Material aspect of ideology: This refers to Louis Althusser's idea that **ideology** is not just a question of thoughts, values and beliefs but is manifested in the official practices of everyday behaviour governed by rituals. See **imaginary aspect of ideology**.

Message without a code: Roland Barthes referred to **non-coded iconic messages** in this way meaning that the simple, literal (iconic) recognition of objects is a form of communication although there is no underlying code – unlike in the case of **coded-iconic messages**.

Military–industrial complex: This describes the intricate relations between arms manufacture and central government. The concern is that if national economies are dependent on the production and sale of armaments (and the sector employs significant numbers of people) those representing the armament industries may have an unfair and inordinate influence on the decisions taken by politicians, thus compromising the democratic process.

Minority culture: this is associated with the **culture and civilization tradition** where writers argued that narrow cannons of 'high culture' (the great poets, novelists, dramatists, etc.) needed to be preserved by the few enlightened minds capable of assessing and deciding what counts as culture. See **mass culture**.

Mirror Stage: Within Lacanian psychoanalysis this describes how a child, at the pre-linguistic **Imaginary** stage, undergoes identification with 'itself' on the way to becoming a **subject** within the **Symbolic**.

Modern mythologies: Roland Barthes used this term when analysing the products of mass culture and treating 'collective representations' as sign systems in such a way that he was able to uncover the mystifications that transform 'petit-bourgeois culture into universal nature' (Barthes, 1957/1972:11). See **ideology** and **semioclasm**.

Motivation: From Roland Barthes' point of view the modern myth (or ideological message) is drawn from the common stock of pre-existing meanings. These meanings are what 'motivate' the meanings of **modern mythologies**. See also **first- and second-order semiological systems**.

Name-of-the-Father: A concept found in Lacanian psychoanalysis that does not refer to an actual father (or the particular image of him that individuals may have) but is purely symbolic of the laws that govern cultures that provide the necessary structures for the **Symbolic** order so necessary to the structure and stability of the psyche.

Need: In Lacanian psychoanalysis the origin of organic need is found in the **Real** but the expression of need in the **Symbolic** (as **desire**) leads to constant deferral, frustration and lack. This is because the satisfaction of need is constantly deferred by its transmission through **signifiers**.

Negotiated readings: When discussing television discourse Stuart Hall used this to describe how audiences, while influenced by dominant codes of interpretation established by the producers of the message, may resist (or fail to recognize) aspects of the hegemonic **preferred reading**. See **encoding, decoding**, and **oppositional readings**.

New social movements: This term describes activists who form alliances (or networks) to keep a constant eye on things like human rights abuses and the environment. Rather than rely on well-established political parties with their formal organization and overarching ideologies (and members) they prefer to be independent of the political structures they see as antiquated, bankrupt and corrupt. These are often thought of as a postmodern approach to politics. See **culture jamming** and **rhizome**.

Non-coded iconic message: In Roland Barthes' work this describes how objects are recognized as images before any secondary meanings are attributed to them, as opposed to **coded iconic messages**.

Objets petit a: A complex and ambiguous term coined by Jacques Lacan which is short for *objet petit autre* ('the little object of the other') that Lacan refused to define in any strict way. One way of understanding the idea is to associate it with the importance given to things that are experienced as parts of, or complements to, the self and not understood or experienced as separate from it.

Oligopoly: This term is related to monopoly and describes a tendency in **late capitalism** where large corporations and conglomerates progressively gain greater control over markets by buying up the competition and monopolizing the manufacture and supply of particular products.

Oppositional readings: With reference to television discourse Stuart Hall used this concept to describe how audiences, while recognizing the meanings produced by the dominant codes of interpretation established by the producers of the message, resist aspects of the hegemonic **preferred reading**. In this way the audiences deliberately interrupt the relations between **encoding** and **decoding**. See **encoding**, **decoding**, and **negotiated readings**.

Organic intellectuals: This idea derives from Antonio Gramsci's writings and describes a class of intellectuals who could theorize culture and communicate counter-hegemonic ideals to a new revolutionary class.

Overdetermination: When discussing **repressive** and **ideological state apparatuses**, Louis Althusser adapted this Freudian concept to explain the complexity and relative autonomy of **ideology** (rather than rely on a more simplistic notion where the material base determines the ideological superstructure).

Panopticon: An idea created by Jeremy Bentham that Michel Foucault adapted to argue that the modern state, through pervasive **surveillance** mechanisms, produces subjects characterized by **self-regulation**.

Parody and pastiche: Fredric Jameson makes a distinction between these two notions to emphasize the differences between modernism and postmodernism. While they both imitate a recognizable style, Jameson values parody (associated with modernism) over pastiche (associated with the postmodern) because the former contains a 'satiric impulse' which is lost in the latter, which merely evokes previous styles. See **pastness** and **depthlessness**.

Parole: in **structuralism** *paroles* are meaningful utterances which result from *langue* (systems of pre-given rules and conventions which make them possible).

Pastness: Fredric Jameson argues that postmodern cultures manifest a crisis in history in the way that they no longer evoke historical referents (something real that actually happened with actual historical content) but only construct the past through nostalgic references, which means that the past is merely a question of 'stylistic connotation'. See **depthlessness** and the **cultural logic of late capitalism**.

Patriarchy: A disputed term referring to power relations where women are subordinated (partially or wholly) by men in the interests of preserving male domination.

Penis envy: A controversial and contested term (especially in feminist discourses) which is found in Freud's theory of psychosexual development where girls, on discovering that they lacks a penis, envy it and all that it represents in terms of power and authority. This discovery brings with it self-loathing and rejection of the mother. See **Phallus** and the **Name-of-the-Father**.

Performativity: For Jean-François Lyotard this term describes the tendency in the **postmodern condition** for society to become increasingly dominated by a skills approach to knowledge, which is ruled by performance and efficiency without reference to its emancipatory or speculative values. This is where input is minimized and output maximized and where the ultimate goal of the backers of research is power. See **crisis of (or incredulity towards) metanarratives** and **deligitimation**.

Phallus: This is a controversial and ambiguous term found in Lacanian psychoanalysis which does not refer to the genital organ, as such, but symbolizes things like authority, power, security and wholeness of being. While the concept is rooted in patriarchal notions of male power, either sex can aspire to what the Phallus represents. See **penis envy** and the **Name-of-the-Father**.

Phonocentrism: Jacques Derrida used this term to indicate that in Western thinking there is a tendency to privilege speech (as closer to the origin of production) over writing (understood as being secondary). Thus, speech is given priority over the written word because it is seen as more authentic. See **deconstruction** and **logocentrism**.

Photogenia: A term coined by Roland Barthes to describe the way aesthetic factors like posing, placement, lighting and trick effects influence the interpretation of images. See **photographic message**, **anchorage** and **coded iconic messages**.

Photographic message: A term used by Roland Barthes to describe the relations between texts and images (especially in the press) where headlines, captions and the article influence the way an image is understood. See **anchorage**.

Popular culture: a term often linked to mass culture and the **culture industry** (see the **Frankfurt School**) which usually describes the entertainment, tastes and choices of ordinary people and is contrasted with **high culture**.

Post-colonialism: This refers to a complex set of discourses which focus on the historical, economic, political and other cultural legacies of imperialist expansion.

Post-industrial society: A term popularized by the sociologist Daniel Bell which is used to describe societies founded on computers and telecommunications where knowledge replaces material goods as the most important commodity for production and exchange, as opposed to industrial and pre-industrial societies. See the **postmodern condition**.

Postmodern condition: For Jean-François Lyotard, this term defines society when it has developed its technologies to the point where information itself is the central commodity and society no longer believes in the ethical, philosophical, social, political narratives that were once thought of as providing the justification for education, learning and the production of knowledge. Lyotard's basic approach was to position these transformations in the context of what he called the **crisis of (or incredulity towards) metanarratives**. See **legitimation**, **grand narrative**, **performativity** and **little narratives**.

Postmodern feminism: Susan Bordo argues that when **gender** is meticulously fragmented by things like class, race, 'historical particularity' and subjected to **difference** in such a way that its meaning is 'constantly deferred' then we are in the presence of postmodern feminism.

Postmodern identity: This is associated with Jean Baudrillard's idea that **identity** in **late capitalism** is not be understood as something outside consumption but negotiated within it. See **consumer society**, **simulation**, **simulacra** and **hyperreality**.

Postmodernism: A complex set of (sometimes contradictory) **discourses** which attempt to characterize the cultures, thought and experiences of late capitalist societies. See **post-industrial society**, **postmodern condition**, **postmodern feminism**, **postmodern identity**, **late capitalism**, **hyperreality**, **simulation**, **simulacra**, **crisis of (or incredulity towards) metanarratives**, **cultural logic of late capitalism**, **depthlessness**, **the waning of affect**, **death of the subject**, **parody and pastiche**, **pastness**, **cultural schizophrenia**, **new social movements** and **high-tech paranoia**.

Poststructuralism: Generally speaking the term refers to the work of writers who use concepts taken from Saussurean linguistics, but who subject them to radical questioning. However, sometimes writers, like Michel Foucault, who do not use structuralist concepts in a systematic way, are related to the concept because their work shares certain thematic concerns with those deemed poststructuralist. See **deconstruction**, **différance**, **difference**, **deferral**, **trace**, **structure**, **transcendental signified**, **logocentrism** and **phonocentrism**.

Power: In Michel Foucault's writings he constantly stressed the relations between **truth**, **knowledge** and power. Power is a complex notion not conceived of as exclusive to dominant groups but something exercised at every level, moving in complex ways with relation to multiple contexts. See **discourse**, **self-regulation** and **surveillance**.

Preferred reading: When discussing television discourse Stuart Hall used this to designate an interpretation that corresponds to the intentions of those who encode a message. See **encoding**, **decoding**, and **negotiated** and **oppositional readings**.

Problematic: Within Louis Althusser's work this describes the theoretical or ideological limits of a text. Another variation is the 'invisible problematic' which is a symptom manifested by (and repressed in) the original problematic which is revealed by **symptomatic reading**. See **double reading**.

Real: Very simply put, in Lacanian psychoanalysis the Real (to describe this in Althusserian terms) is an absent cause and that upon which the **Symbolic** works. It can be understood as defining a baby's being prior to its identifications in the **Imaginary** and its symbolization and stratification in the Symbolic. See **need** and **desire**.

Relay: A term used by Roland Barthes to describe how words like 'earlier', 'later', etc. can be attached to a series of images to convey a sense of temporal progression.

Repressive state apparatuses: By this phrase Louis Althusser referred to things like the legal system (linked to the police, the courts and the prisons) and the army; apparatuses which are understood as key instruments of direct social control backed up by the secondary **ideological state apparatuses**.

Reterritorialization: A concept used by Deleuze and Guattari that can be used to describe how things or spaces can be re-colonized and re-stratified after a process of **destratification**, thereby transforming existing powers or forces. See **territorialization**.

Rhizome: A concept used by Deleuze and Guattari which can be used as a metaphor to describe any process which spreads and disperses power horizontally rather than rely on the more traditional vertical power structures associated with what they call **arborescence**. See **new social movements**.

Self-regulation: A concept found in Michel Foucault's work where he associates the rise of the modern state with an increasing reliance on the internalization of values by **subjects** who are characterized by self-control. See **surveillance** and **Panopticon**.

Semioclasm: A neologism coined by Roland Barthes where he combined the terms semiotics and iconoclasm to describe his general method when discussing **modern mythologies**. Semioclasm exposes the bourgeois class interests camouflaged in the culture of everyday life where history or culture is constantly dressed up as nature. See **ideology**.

Semiology: In **structuralism** the study of the relations between the **signifier** and the **signified** with relation to a **code** (otherwise known as semiotics).

Sex: A pervasive term used in much cultural criticism, especially that focused on feminism and gender studies. More particularly, it features strongly in the work of Michel Foucault and Judith Butler, the latter defining it against concepts like **gender** and **sexuality**. For Butler it functions within **discourses** to create debatable distinctions between males and females by emphasizing things like biological differences, chromosomes, hormonal characteristics, internal and external reproductive/sex organs, etc.

Sexuality: An extensive term used in much cultural criticism, especially that found in feminism and gender studies. More specifically, it is theorized in the work of Michel Foucault and Judith Butler, the latter defining it against concepts like **sex** and **gender**. Butler emphasizes that sexuality concerns how individuals are categorised with relation to sexual attitudes, choices and behaviour, which are often used to define what is properly or intrinsically male of female.

Shock doctrine: An idea put forward by Naomi Klein that holds that the narrow interests of powerful capitalists are, and have been, imposed all over the world through shock tactics where economists, on behalf of governments, plan austere privatization measures which often attack civil liberties. These strategies are applied to all kinds of crises whether they be 'natural', provoked by wars, or by economic meltdowns. See **disaster capitalism**.

Sign: In Saussurean linguistics the sign is made up of the **signifier** and the **signified**. It is fundamental to an understanding of **structuralism**.

Signification: Within **structuralism** this refers to the study of the relations between **signifiers** and **signifieds** to show how they produce meaning with relation to codes.

Signified: In the structuralist theory of the **sign** the signified designates the concept or idea attached to a **signifier**.

Signifier: Within **structuralism** this is the form a sign takes – this can be a word or anything that that is capable of conveying meaning and is related to its counterpart the **signified**.

Simulacra: This term, often seen as a key to the definition of **postmodernism**, is used by Jean Baudrillard when theorizing his notion of **hyperreality**. Simulacra describe images which, in advanced capitalism, cannot be traced back to an origin or cause in such a way that truth, knowledge and reference to a primary reality are no longer possible. See **simulation**.

Simulation: Jean Baudrillard used this concept to explain a key idea with relation to his theory of **hyperreality**, an idea that has become important to some definitions of **postmodernism**. To simulate is to pretend to have something that you have not got, meaning there is *nothing* behind appearance (as opposed to dissimulation, which is where someone pretends not to have something they have, in fact, got and, thus, there *is* something behind mere appearance). See **simulacra**.

Structuralism: This is associated with the Swiss linguist Ferdinand de Saussure's theory of the **sign** as a combination of **signifiers** and **signifieds**. From this point of view meaning is not produced because words refer to things but because pre-established codes allow the organization of paradigmatic elements to generate meaningful statements. Thus, structuralism is not referential but relational. These ideas have helped to develop a general theory of the sign and have been applied beyond language to many aspects of culture. See **semiology**, **syntagmatic and paradigmatic relations**, **binary oppositions**, *langue*, *parole* and **poststructuralism**.

Structure: This term is used in a very particular way by Jacques Derrida who argued that within Western philosophical thinking it tends to provide a centre or a stabilizing point of reference within a discourse and thereby limit its ability to signify indefinitely. **Deconstruction** challenges this. See **différance**, **transcendental signified** and **logocentrism**.

Subject: Within **structuralism** and **poststructuralism** (particularly in the work of Jacques Lacan) the term is generally used to challenge the idea that the self is prior to the entry into symbolic and cultural networks. Here the subject-self is a product of these things. See **subjectivity** and **desire** as an inter-subjective phenomenon.

Subjectivity: Within **structuralism** and **poststructuralism** (and particularly in the work of Jacques Lacan) the term indicates that what is understood as the self is the product of language and it is through it that humans are constituted as a **subject**.

Subject supposed to know: A term used in Lacanian psychoanalysis which indicates a living person (or an imaginary figure) who provides the grounds for belief, thereby displacing the authority for faith or knowledge onto others. See the **Name-of-the-Father**.

Surveillance: Michel Foucault saw surveillance as a key part of the modern state where subjects exercise **self-regulation** and control because all kinds of apparatuses create an atmosphere of permanent visibility (a surveillance society) which ensures the automatic functioning of **power**. See **Panopticon**.

Symbolic: In Lacanian psychoanalysis this concept refers to language, culture or any system through which meanings can be produced. Once immersed in the Symbolic the subject comes into existence and is effectively cut off from the **Real** because it is now mediated through **signifiers** and subject to **signification.**

Symptomatic reading: This describes part of Louis Althusser's **double reading** which involves acknowledging the gaps and silences that underlie the structure of a text. See **problematic**.

Syntagmatic and paradigmatic relations: In **structuralism** this refers to how (syntagmatic) combinations of elements (paradigms) create meanings (*paroles*).

Territorialization: A concept used in the work of Deleuze and Guattari that can be used to describe how things or spaces are taken control of or colonized. See **reterritorialization** and **destratification**.

The end of this or that: Referring to this idea Fredric Jameson argues that it characterizes an important strand of thought within **postmodernism**. This is where, since the Second World War, all kinds of 'ends' have been announced, like end of ideology, social democracy, 'man', social class, the welfare state, art, communism, etc.

Trace: An important term used by Jacques Derrida which posits that **signs** always mark an absence of a presence and indicate the absence of an authorial origin. See **death of the author** and **deconstruction**.

Transcendental signified: A term coined by Jacques Derrida within **deconstruction** that refers to something outside a system that would suspend the indefinite play of signification. See **différance**, **logocentrism** and **phonocentrism**.

Truth: According to Michel Foucault truth is not something other worldly or beyond politics or above the complex workings of **power** but something produced by them in **discourses** which create the conditions for its production. See **critique of reason**.

Two interpretations of interpretation: This refers to Jacques Derrida's point that interpreters can be grouped into those who dream of recovering truths and origins to discover fixed meanings and those who affirm textual play and renounce full presence and fixed identities (like the practitioners of **deconstruction**).

Waning of affect: A concept used by Fredric Jameson to express the idea that feeling, emotion and subjectivity (consciousness) are ebbing away in postmodern culture. It is important to understand that it is a lessening, not a complete disappearance. See **cultural schizophrenia**, **depthlessness**, **death of the subject** and **logic of late capitalism**.

Youth subculture: An important area of study within cultural studies that focuses on things like the social background, groupings, practices, values, concerns, styles, behaviour and consumption patterns, and meaning-making activities of young people. Other key notions are the production of generational differences and rebellion.

References

Adbusters Organization (2005) Culture Jammers Network. Retrieved 23 July 2005 from http://adbusters.org/network

Adorno, Theodor W. (1966/1973) *Negative Dialectics*. New York: Continuum.

Adorno, Theodor W. (1990) *Prisms*. Cambridge, MA: MIT.

Adorno, Theodor W. (1991) *The Culture Industry: Selected Essays on Mass Culture*. London: Routledge.

Adorno, Theodor W. and Horkheimer, Max (1947/1972) *The Dialectic of Enlightenment*. New York: Herder & Herder.

Agard, John (1985) *Mangoes and Bullets: Selected and New Poems*. London: Pluto.

Allen, Graham (2003) *Roland Barthes*. London: Routledge.

Althusser, Louis (1965/2005) *For Marx*. London: Verso.

Althusser, Louis (1971) *Lenin and Philosophy and Other Essays*. New York: Monthly Review Press.

Althusser, Louis and Balibar, Étienne (1968/2006) *Reading Capital*. London: Verso.

Anderson, Benedict (2006, revised edn) *Imagined Communities*. London: Verso.

Atkinson, Rick (1993) *Crusade: The Untold Story of the Persian Gulf War*. New York: Mariner Books.

Attridge, Derek, Bennington, Geoff and Young, Robert (eds) (1987) *Post-Structuralism and the Question of History*. Cambridge: Cambridge University Press.

Baby Milk Action (2010) http://info.babymilkaction.org/

Bailey, Michael and Freedman, Des (2011) *The Assault on Univeristies: A Manifesto for Resistance*. London: Pluto.

Bakan, Joel (2004) *The Corporation: The Pathological Pursuit of Profit and Power*. London: Constable.

Bakhtin, Mikhail (1986) *Speech Genres and Other Late Essays*. Austin, TX: University of Texas Press.

Baldick, Chris (1983) *The Social Mission of English Criticism, 1848–1932*. Oxford: Clarendon Press.

Barker, Chris (2000) *Cultural Studies: Theory and Practice*. London: SAGE.

Barth, John (1988) *Lost in the Funhouse*. New York: Anchor Books.

Barthes, Roland (1957/1972) *Mythologies*. New York: Noonday Press.

Barthes, Roland (1961/1977) 'The Photographic Message', in Stephen Heath (ed.) *Image, Music, Text*. New York: Hill & Wang.

Barthes, Roland (1964/1977) 'Rhetoric of the Image', in Stephen Heath (ed.) *Image, Music, Text*. New York: Hill & Wang.

Barthes, Roland (1966/1972) 'To Write: An Intransitive Verb', in Philip Rice and Patricia Waugh (eds) *Modern Literary Theory: A Reader*. London: Edward Arnold.

Barthes, Roland (1967/1985) *The Fashion System*. London: Jonathan Cape.

Barthes, Roland (1968/1977) 'The Death of the Author', in Stephen Heath (ed.) *Image, Music, Text*. London: HarperCollins.

Barthes, Roland (1970/1975) *S/Z*. London: Jonathan Cape.

Barthes, Roland (1970/1983) *Empire of Signs*. New York: Hill & Wang.

Barthes, Roland (1971/1977) in Stephen Heath (ed). *Image, Music, Text*. New York: Hill & Wang, 1977.

Barthes, Roland (1975/1977) *Roland Barthes by Roland Barthes*. New York: Hill & Wang.

Barthes, Roland (1977/1979) *A Lover's Discourse: Fragments*. New York: Hill & Wang.

Barthes, Roland (1980/2000) *Camera Lucida*. London: Vintage.

Baudrillard, Jean (1970/1998) *The Consumer Society: Myths and Structures*. London: SAGE.

Baudrillard, Jean (1976/1993) *Symbolic Exchange and Death*. London: SAGE,

Baudrillard, Jean (1981/1994) *Simulacra and Simulation*. Ann Arbor, MI: University of Michigan Press.

Baudrillard, Jean (1989) *America*. London: Verso.

Baudrillard, Jean (1991/1995) *The Gulf War Did Not Take Place*. Sydney: Power Publications.

Baudrillard, Jean (2003) *Fragments: Interviews with Jean Baudrillard*. London: Routledge.

Bauman, Zygmunt (1988) 'Sociology and Postmodernity'. *Sociological Review*. 36(4).

Bauman, Zygmunt (1998) *Globalization: The Human Consequences*. Cambridge: Polity Press.

BBC (2010) 'What's it Like Inside a University Occupation?' www.bbc.co.uk/news/education-11874633

Beasley, Ron and Danesi, Marcel (2002) *Persuasive Signs: The Semiotics of Advertising*. The Hague: Mouton de Gruyter.

Beauvoir, Simone de (1949/1984) *The Second Sex*. Harmondsworth: Penguin.

Beck, Ulrich (1999) *What is Globalization?* Cambridge: Polity Press.

Beder, Sharon (2009) *This Little Kiddy Went to Market: The Corporate Capture of Childhood: The Corporate Assault on Children*. London: Pluto.

Bell, Daniel (1973) *The Coming of Post-Industrial Society: A Venture in Social Forecasting*. New York: Basic Books.

Benjamin, Walter (1936/1973) 'The Work of Art in the Age of Mechanical Reproduction', in *Illuminations*. London: Fontana.

Benjamin, Walter (1973) *Illuminations*. London: Fontana.

Bennett, Andrew (1995) *Readers and Reading*. London: Longman.

Bennett, Tony (1986) 'Popular Culture and the "Turn to Gramsci"', in Tony Bennett, Colin Mercer and Janet Woollacott (eds) *Popular Culture and Social Relations*. Milton Keynes: Open University Press.

Bennett, Tony (1992) 'Putting Policy into Cultural Studies', in Lawrence Grossberg, Cary Nelson and Paula Treichler (eds) (1992) *Cultural Studies*. London: Routledge.

Bennett, Tony, Grossberg, Lawrence and Morris, Meaghan (2005) *New Keywords: A Revised Vocabulary of Culture and Society*. Oxford: Blackwell.

Benton, Ted (1984) *The Rise and Fall of Structural Marxism: Althusser and His Influence*. New York: St. Martin's Press.

Benveniste, Émile (1971) *Problems in General Linguistics*. Miami, FL: University of Miami Press.

Bertens, Hans (1995) *The Idea of the Postmodern: A History*. London: Routledge.

Bhabha, Homi (ed) (1990) *Nation and Narration*. London: Routledge.

Black, Edwin (2001) *IBM and the Holocaust: The Strategic Alliance Between Nazi Germany and America's Most Powerful Corporation*. New York: Crown Publishers.

Black, Edwin (2009) *Nazi Nexus: America's Corporate Connections to Hitler's Holocaust*. Washington, DC: Dialogue Press.

Bordo, Susan (1993) *Unbearable Weight: Feminism, Western Culture, and the Body*. Berkeley: University of California.

Bourdieu, Pierre (1979/1986) *Distinction: A Social Critique of the Judgement of Taste*. London: Routledge.

Bourdieu, Pierre and Wacquant, Loïc (1992) *An Invitation to Reflexive Sociology*. Cambridge: Polity Press.

Brooke-Rose, Christine (1991) *Textermination*. Manchester: Carcanet.

Brooker, Peter and Brooker, William (eds) (1997) *Postmodern After-Images*. London: Hodder Arnold.

Bruner, Jerome (2005) 'Foreword', in Stanley Milgram (1974/2005) *Obedience to Authority*. London: Pinter & Martin.

Buck-Morss, Susan (1977) *The Origin of Negative Dialectics: Theodor W. Adorno, Walter Benjamin, and the Frankfurt Institute*. New York: The Free Press.

Budhoo, Davidson (1990) *Enough is Enough: Dear Mr Camdessus … Open Letter of Resignation to the Director of the International Monetary Fund*. New York: New Horizons.

Buechler, Steven M. (1999) *Social Movements in Advanced Capitalism*. Oxford: Oxford University Press.

Butler, Judith (1993) *Bodies that Matter: On the Discursive Limits of Sex*. London: Routledge.

Butler, Judith (1999) *Gender Trouble: Feminism and the Subversion of Identity*. London: Routledge.

Butler, Judith. (2004) *Undoing Gender*. New York: London: Routledge.

Butler, Judith (2005) *Giving an Account of Oneself*. New York: Fordham.

Butler, Judith, Laclau, Ernesto and Žižek, Slavoj (2000) *Contingency, Hegemony, Universality: Contemporary Dialogues on the Left*. London: Verso.

Butler, Rex (2005) *Slavoj Žižek: Live Theory*. London: Continuum.

Byrne, Eleanor and McQuillan, Martin (1999) *Deconstructing Disney*. London: Pluto.

Cahoone, Lawrence (1996) *From Modernism to Postmodernism: An Anthology*. Oxford: Blackwell.

Caldicott, Helen (2002) *The New Nuclear Danger: George W. Bush's Military-Industrial Complex*. New York: The New Press.

Carducci, Vince (2006) 'Culture Jamming: A Sociological Perspective'. *Journal of Consumer Culture*. 6(1).

Castells, Manuel (1996, 2nd edn 2000) *The Rise of The Network Society*. Oxford: Blackwell.

Castells, Manuel (1997, 2nd edn 2004) *The Power of Identity*. Oxford: Blackwell.

Castells, Manuel (1998, 2nd edn 2000) *End of Millennium*. Oxford: Blackwell.

Centre for Contemporary Cultural Studies (1982) *The Empire Strikes Back: Race and Racism in 70s Britain*. London: Hutchinson.

Chambers, Ian (1985) *Urban Rhythms: Pop Music and Popular Culture*. London: MacMillan.

Chambers, Ian (1986) *Popular Culture: The Metropolitan Experience*. London: Methuen.

Chomsky, Noam (2004) 'War Crimes and Imperial Fantasies: Noam Chomsky Interviewed by David Barsamian'. *International Socialist Review*, 37, September–October.

Chossudovsky, Michel (1997) *The Globalization of Poverty: Impacts of IMF and World Bank Reforms*. London: Zed Books.

Clawson, Dan (2003) *The Next Upsurge: Labour and the New Social Movements*. Ithaca, NY: Cornell University Press.

Coca-Cola (2010) www.thecoca-colacompany.com/ourcompany/index.html

Cohen, W., Florida, R. and Goe, W. R. (1994) 'University Industry Research Centers in the United States'. Pittsburgh, PA: Carnigie Mellon University Press.

Colás, Alejandro (2002) *Interntional Civil Society: Social Movements and World Politics*. London: Polity.

Collins, Jim, Radner, Hilary and Preacher Collins, Ava (eds) (1993) *Film Theory Goes to the Movies*. London: Routledge.

Coole, Diana and Frost, Samantha (2010) *New Mateiralisms: Ontology, Agency, and Politics*. Durham NC: Duke University Press.

Cornell Library Research: www.library.cornell.edu/olinuris/ref/anthro189.html

Critchley, Simon (1992) *The Ethics of Deconstruction: Derrida and Levinas*. Edinburgh: Edinburgh University Press.

Crofts Wiley, Stephen B. (2005) 'Spatial Materialism: Grossberg's Deleuzean Cultural Studies'. *Cultural Studies*. 19(1).

Curran, James and Seaton, Jane (2009, 7th edn) *Power Without Responsibility: Press Broadcasting and New Media in Britain*. London: Routledge.

Daitch, Susan (1986/2002) *L.C.* Illinois: Dalkey Archive Press.

de Certeau, Michel (1988) *The Practice of Everyday Life*. Berkeley, CA: University of California Press.

Deleuze, Gilles and Guattarri, Félix (1972/1983) *Anti-Oedipus: Capitalism and Schizophrenia*. Minneapolis, MN: University of Minnesota Press.

Deleuze, Gilles and Guattarri, Félix (1980/1987) *A Thousand Plateaus: Capitalism and Schizophrenia*. Minneapolis, MN: University of Minnesota Press.

Derrida, Jacques (1967/1973) *Speech and Phenomena and Other Essays on Husserl's Theory of Signs*. Evanston, IL: Northwestern University Press.

Derrida, Jacques (1967/1978) *Writing and Difference*. London: Routledge.

Derrida, Jacques (1967/1984) *Margins of Philosophy*. Chicago: University of Chicago Press.

Derrida, Jacques (1967/1997) *Of Grammatology*. Baltimore: Johns Hopkins University Press.

Derrida, Jacques (1972/1981) *Dissemination*. Chicago: University of Chicago Press.

Derrida, Jacques (1972/1982) *Margins of Philosophy*. Chicago: University of Chicago Press.

Derrida, Jacques (1972/1987) *Positions*. London: Athlone.

Derrida, Jacques (1975/1987) 'Le Facteur de la Vérité', in *The Postcard: From Socrates to Freud and Beyond*. Chicago: University of Chicago Press.

Derrida, Jacques (1988) *Limited Inc*. Evanston, IL: Northwestern University Press.

Derrida, Jacques (1994) *Aporias (Meridian: Crossing Aesthetics)*. Stanford, CA: Stanford University Press.

Derrida, Jacques (1996) *Deconstruction in a Nutshell: A Conversation with Jacques Derrida*, ed. John Caputo. New York: Fordham University Press.

Derrida, Jacques (2000) 'Intellectual Courage: An Interview'. *Culture Machine*, 2. Available online at http://culturemachine.tees.ac.uk/articles/art_derr.htm

Derrida, Jacques (2001) 'The Future of the Profession or the Unconditional University', in Laurence Simmons and Heather Worth (eds) *Derrida Downunder*. Palmerstone North, NZ: Dunmore Press.

Derrida, Jacques (2002) *Ethics, Institutions and the Right to Philosophy*. Lanham MD: Rowman & Littlefield.

Derrida, Jacques (2005) *The Politics of Friendship*. London: Verso.

Derrida, Jacques (2006) *Spectres of Marx: The State of the Debt, the Work of Mourning and the New International*. London: Routledge.

Derrida, Jacques and Stiegler, Bernard (2002) *Echographies of Television*. London: Polity.

Dery, Marc (1993) 'Culture Jamming: Hacking, Slashing and Sniping in the Empire of Signs'. *Open Magazine Pamphlet Series* (I quote from the free online version at www.markdery.com/archives/books/culture_jamming/#000005#more)

Di Stefano, Christine (1990) 'Dilemmas of Difference: Feminism, Modernity, and Postmodernism', in Linda, J. Nicholson (ed) *Feminism/Postmodernism*. London: Routledge.

Dixon, Deborah and Zonn, Leo (2005) 'Confronting the Geopolitical Aesthetic: Fredric Jameson, *The Perfumed Nightmare* and the Perilous Place of Third Cinema'. *Geopolitics* 10(2).

Docker, John (1994) *Postmodernism and Popular Culture: A Cultural History*. Cambridge: Cambridge University Press.

Doctorow, E. L (1974) *Ragtime. American Review*. 20 (April).

Donoghue, Denis (1976) *The Sovereign Ghost: Studies in Imagination*. Berkeley, CA: University of California Press.

Dosse, François (1997) *History of Structuralism: The Sign Sets, 1967–Present*. Minnesota, MN: University of Minnesota Press.

Downey, John and Fenton, Natalie (2003) 'New Media, Counter Publicity and the Public Sphere'. *New Media and Society*. 5(2).

E$$0 (2002) www.greenpeace.org/international/photosvideos/photos/culture-jamming-the-esso-logo

Eagleton, Terry (1983) *Literary Theory: An Introduction*. Oxford: Blackwell.

Eagleton, Terry (1984) *The Function of Criticism: From the Spectator to Post-Structuralism*. London: Verso.

Eagleton, Terry (1986) *Against the Grain: Essays 1975–1985*. London: Verso.

Eagleton, Terry (ed.) (1989) *Raymond Williams: Critical Perspectives*. Cambridge: Polity.

Eagleton, Terry (1996) *The Illusions of Postmodernism*. Oxford: Blackwell.

Eagleton, Terry (2000) *The Idea of Culture*. Oxford: Blackwell.

Ebbesen, Jeffrey (2006) *Postmodernism and its Others: The Fiction of Ishmael Reed, Kathy Acker, and Don DeLillo*. London: Routledge.

Eco, Umberto (1962/1989) *The Open Work*. Cambridge, MA: Harvard University Press.

Eco, Umberto (1966) 'Narrative Structure in Fleming', in Bernard Waites, Tony Bennett and Graham Martin (eds) (1982) *Popular Culture: Past and Present*. London: Croom Helm/Open University Press.

Eco, Umberto (1978) *Theory of Semiotics*. London: John Wiley.

Eco, Umberto (1979/1981) *The Role of the Reader: Explorations in the Semiotics of Texts*. Bloomington, IN: Indiana University Press.

Eisenhower, Dwight (1961) http://en.wikipedia.org/wiki/Military_industrial_complex

English, Travis (2007) 'Hans Haacke, or the Museum as Degenerate Utopia'. *Kriticos: An International and Interdisciplinary Journal of Postmodern Cultural Sound, Text and Image*. 4, March: http://intertheory.org/english.htm

Evans, Jessica and Hall, Stuart (2001) *Visual Culture: The Reader*. London: SAGE.

Everything2 (2010) http://everttgubg2.com

Falk, Pasi and Campbell, Colin (eds) (1997) *The Shopping Experience*. London: SAGE.

Faulkner, Robert (2011) *Corporate Wrongdoing and the Art of the Accusation*. London: Anthem Press.

Fausto-Sterling, Anne (2000) *Sexing the Body: Gender Politics and the Construction of Sexuality*. New York: Basic Books.

Featherstone, David (2008) *Resistance, Space and Political Identities: the Making of Counter-Global Networks*. Oxford: Wiley-Blackwell.

Featherstone, Mike (1991) *Consumer Culture and Postmodernism*. London: Sage.

Feder, Ellen K., Rawlinson Mary C. and Zakin, Emily (eds) (1996) *Derrida and Feminism: Recasting the Question of Woman*. London: Routledge.

Fiedler, Leslie, A. (1955/1972) 'The middle against both ends', in David Lodge (ed.) *20th Century Literary Criticism: A Reader*. London: Longman.

Finlan, Alistair (2003) *The Gulf War 1991*. New York: Routledge.

Fish, Stanley (1980) *Is There a Text in this Class? The Authority of Interpretive Communities*. Cambridge, MA: Harvard University Press.

Fiske, John (1987) *Television Culture*. London: Methuen.

Fiske, John (1992) 'The Culture of Everyday Life', in Lawrence Grossberg, Cary Nelson and Paula Treichler (eds) *Cultural Studies*. London: Routledge.

Floch, Jean-Marie (2000): *Visual Identities*. London: Continuum.

Foucault, Michel (1961/1967) *Madness and Civilization: A History of Insanity in the Age of Reason*. London: Tavistock.

Foucault, Michel (1966/1974) *The Order of Things: An Archaeology of the Human Sciences*. London: Routledge.

Foucault, Michel (1969/2002) *Archaeology of Knowledge*. London: Routledge.

Foucault, Michel (1975/1977) *Discipline and Punish: The Birth of the Prison*. Harmondsworth: Pelican.

Foucault, Michel (1976/1990) *The History of Sexuality: Volume One: An Introduction*. Harmondsworth: Penguin.

Foucault, Michel (1978) 'Politics and the Study of Discourse'. *Ideology and Consciousness*. 3.

Foucault, Michel (1980) *Michel Foucault: Power/Knowledge. Selected Interviews and Other Writings 1972–1977*. New York: Harvester Wheatsheaf.

Foucault, Michel (1984) *The Foucault Reader*: *An Introduction to Foucault's Thought*, ed. Paul Rabinow. Harmondsworth: Penguin.

Foucault, Michel (1984/1986) *The Care of the Self: The History of Sexuality (Volume 3)*. New York: Pantheon.

Foucault, Michel (1984/1990) *The Use of Pleasure: The History of Sexualtiy (Volume 2)*. New York: Vintage.

Fraser, Nancy and Nicholson, Linda (1990) 'Social Criticism without Philosophy: An Encounter between Feminism and Postmodernism', in , Linda J. Nicholson (ed.) *Feminism/Postmodernism*. London: Routledge.

French, Marilyn (1985) *Beyond Power: On Women, Men, and Morals*. London: Jonathan Cape.

Freud, Sigmund (1905/1953) 'The Differentiation between Men and Women', in *The Standard Edition of the Complete Psychological Works of Sigmund Freud. Vol. 7. A Case of Hysteria, Three Essays on Sexuality and Other Works*. London: Hogarth Press.

Freud, Sigmund (1933/1964) 'Femininity', in *The Standard Edition of the Complete Psychological Works of Sigmund Freud. Vol. 22. New Introductory Lectures on Psycho-Analysis and Other Works*. London: Hogarth Press.

Freud, Sigmund (1949/1989) *An Outline of Psycho-Analyis*. New York: Norton.

Freud, Sigmund (1955) *The Interpretation of Dreams*. New York: Basic Books.

Freud, Sigmund (1957) *Collected Papers vol. II*, ed. J. Strachey. London: Hogarth Press.

Freud, Sigmund (1923–1925/1961a) 'The Infantile Genital Organization', in *The Standard Edition of the Complete Psychological Works of Sigmund Freud. Vol. X1X. The Ego and the Id and Other Works*. London: Hogarth Press.

Freud, Sigmund (1923–1925/1961b) 'Some Psychical Consequences of the Anatomical Distinction between the Sexes' in *The Standard Edition of the Complete Psychological Works of Sigmund Freud. Vol. X1X. The Ego and the Id and Other Works*. London: Hogarth Press.

Freud, Sigmund (1923–1925/1961c) 'Some Psychical Consequences of the Anatomical Distinction between the Sexes'. *Sexuality and Psychology of Love*. London: Collier.

Friedman, Milton (1962) *Capitalism and Freedom*, Chicago: Chicago University Press.

Frow, John (1995) *Cultural Studies and Cultual Value*. Oxford: Clarendon.

Frow, John and Morris, Meaghan (eds) (1993) *Australian Cultural Studies: A Reader*. Champaign, IL: University of Illinois Press.

Fukuyama, Francis (1992) *The End of History and the Last Man*. Harmondsworth: Penguin.

Gallop, Jane (1982) *The Daughter's Seduction: Feminism and Psychoanalysis*. New York: Cornell University Press.

Geertz, Clifford (1973) *The Interpretation of Cultures*. New York: Basic Books.

Gendron, Bernard (1986) 'Theodor Adorno meets the Cadillacs', in Tania Modleski (ed.) *Studies in Entertainment: Critical Approaches to Mass Culture*. Bloomington, IN: Indiana University Press.

Gilbert, Jeremy (2008) *Anti-Capitalism and Culture: Radical Theory and Popular Politics*. Oxford: Berg.

Gill, Lesley (2006) 'Fighting for Justice. Dying for Hope. On the Protest Line in Colombia'. *North American Dialogue*. 9(2).

Gill, Lesley (2007) '"Right there with you": Coca-Cola, Labor Restructuring and Political Violence in Colombia'. *Critique of Anthropology*. 27(3).

Gilroy, Paul (1987) *There Ain't No Black in the Union Jack*. London: Hutchinson.

Giroux, Henry (1986) 'Radical Pedagogy and the Politics of Student Voice'. *Interchange*. 17 (1).

Giroux, Henry (1999) 'Schools for Sale: Public Education, Corporate Culture, and the Citizen-Consumer'. *Educational Forum*. 63(2), Winter.

Giroux, Henry (2000) 'Public Pedagogy as Cultural Politics', in *Without Guarantees: In Honour of Stuart Hall*, ed. Paul Gilroy, Lawrence Grossberg and Angela McRobbie. London: Verso.

Giroux, Henry (2002) *Schools for Sale: Public Education, Corporate Culture, and the Citizen-Consumer*, in Alfie Kohn and Patrick Shannon (eds) *Education, Inc.: Turning Education into a Business*. Portsmouth, NH: Heinemann.

Giroux, Henry (2003) 'Selling Out Higher Education'. *Policy Futures in Education*. 1(1).

'Global Water Sales' (2010) http://world-tradeorganization.suite101.com/article.cfm/global_water_sales

Gorz, André (1988) *Critique of Economic Reason*. London: Verso.

Gowan, Peter (2010) *A Calculus of Power: Grand Strategy in the Twnety-First Century*. London: Verso.

Graff, Gerald (1980) 'Deconstruction as Dogma, or, "come back to the raft ag'n Strether honey"'. *Georgia Review*, 34.

Gramsci, Antonio (1971) *Selection from the Prison Notebooks of Antonio Gramsci*. London: Lawrence & Wishart.

Grasskamp, Walter, Nesbit, Molly and Bird, John (2004) *Hans Haacke*. London: Phaidon.

Green, Keith and LeBihan, Jill (1996) *Critical Theory and Practice: A Coursebook*. London: Routledge.

Greenpeace (2007) 'Exxon Still Funding Climate Change Deniers'. www.greenpeace.org/international/en/news/features/exxon-still-funding-climate-ch/

Grossberg, Lawrence (1988) *It is a Sin: Essays on Postmodernism, Politics and Culture*. Sydney: Power Publications.

Grossberg, Lawrence (1992) *We Gotta Get Out of This Place: Popular Conservatism and Postmodern Culture*. London: Routledge.

Grossberg, Lawrence (1993) 'Cultural Studies and/in New Worlds'. *Critical Studies in Mass Communication*. 10. March.

Grossberg, Lawrence (1996a) 'Identity and Cultural Studies: Is That All There Is?', in Stuart Hall, and Paul du Gay (eds) *Questions of Cultural Identity*. London: SAGE.

Grossberg, Lawrence (1996b) 'The Space of Culture, the Power of Space', in Ian Chambers and Lydia Curti (eds) *The Post-Colonial Question: Common Skies, Divided Horizons*. London: Routledge.

Grossberg, Lawrence (2006) 'Does Cultural Studies Have Futures? Should It? (Or What's The Matter with New York?)'. *Cultural Studies*. 20(1).

Grossberg, Lawrece (2011) *Cultural Studies in the Future Tense*. Durham NC: Duke University Press.

Grossberg, Lawrence, Nelson, Cary and Treichler, Paula (eds) (1992) *Cultural Studies*. London: Routledge.

Guardian (2000) 'Nebraska and India slam Oscar Injustices'. www.guardian.co.uk/film/2000/mar/29/oscars2000.oscars

Guardian, (2010) 'Curators, Crude Oil and an Outdated Cultural Mix', www.guardian.co.uk/business/2010/jun/28/bp-tate-curator-oil

Habermas, Jürgen (1972/1996) 'An Alternative Way Out of the Philosophy of the Subject: Communicative Versus Subject-Centered Reason', in Lawrence Cahoone (ed.) *From Modernism to Postmodernism: An Anthology*. Oxford: Blackwell.

Habermas, Jürgen (1981/1993) 'Modernity – An Incomplete Project', in Thomas Docherty (ed.) (1993) *Postmodernism: A Reader*. Hemel Hempstead: Harvester Wheatsheaf.

Habermas, Jürgen (1985) 'Neoconservative Culture Criticism in the United States and West West Germany: An Intellectual Movement in Two Political Cultures', in Richard Bernstein (ed.) *Habermas and Modernity*. Cambridge, MA: MIT Press.

Habermas, Jürgen (1987) *The Philosophical Discourse of Modernity: Twelve Lectures*. Cambridge: Polity Press.

Haiven, Max (2007) 'Privatized Resistance: AdBusters and the Culture of Neoliberalism'. *Review of Education, Pedagogy & Cultural Studies*. 29 (1).

Hall, Bronwyn H. (2004) 'University–Industry Research Partnerships in the United States'. http://elsa.berkeley.edu/~bhhall/papers/BHH04_Kansai.pdf

Hall, Gary and Birchall, Clare (2006) *New Cultural Studies: Adventures in Theory*. Edinburgh: Edinburgh University Press.

Hall, Stuart (1981a) 'The Determination of News Photographs' in Stanley Cohen and Jock Young (eds) *The Manufacture of News*. London: SAGE.

Hall, Stuart (1981b) 'Notes on Deconstructing "The Popular"', in John Storey (ed.) (2009b) *Cultural Theory and Popular Culture: A Reader*. Harlow: Pearson.

Hall, Stuart (1982) 'The Rediscovery of "Ideology": the Return of the Repressed in Media Studies', in Michael Gurevitch, Tony Bennett, James Curran and Janet Woollacott (eds) *Culture, Society and the Media*. London: Routledge.

Hall, Stuart (1986/1996) 'On Postmodernism and Articulation: An Interview with Stuart Hall', in David Morley and Kuan-Hsing Chen (eds) *Stuart Hall: Critical Dialogues in Cultural Studies*. London: Routledge.

Hall, Stuart (1988) 'Only Connect: The Life of Raymond Williams'. *New Statesman and Society*. February, 5.

Hall, Stuart (1996a) 'Cultural Studies and its Theoretical Legacies', in David Morley and Kuan-Hsing Chen (eds) *Stuart Hall: Critical Dialogues in Cultural Studies*. London: Routledge.

Hall, Stuart (1996b) 'Who Needs "Identity?"', in Stuart Hall, and Paul du Gay *Questions of Cultural Identity*. London: SAGE.

Hall, Stuart, Hobson, Dorothy, Lowe, Andrew and Willis, Paul (1973/1980) *Culture, Media, Language*. London: Hutchinson.

Hall, Stuart and Jefferson, Tony (eds) (1976) *Resistance Through Rituals*. London: Hutchinson.

Hall, Stuart and Whannel, Paddy (1964) *The Popular Arts*. London: Hutchinson.

Hammond, Philip (2007) *Media, War and Postmodernity*. London: Routledge.

Hardt, Michael and Negri, Antonio (2000) *Empire*. Cambridge, MA: Harvard University Press.

Hardt, Michael and Negri, Antonio (2005) *Multitude: War and Democracy in the Age of Empire*. London: Penguin.

Harding, Sandra (1990) 'Feminism, Science, and the Anti-Enlightenment Critiques', in Linda, J. Nicholson (ed.) *Feminism/Postmodernism*. London: Routledge.

Harris, John (2011) Personal e-mail (John Harris/reportdigital.co.uk).

Harrison, Charles and Wood, Paul (2002) *Art in Theory 1900–2000*. Oxford: Blackwell.

Hartley, John and Pearson, Roberta (eds) (2000) *American Cultural Studies: A Reader*. Oxford: Oxford University Press.

Hartung, William (2011) *Prophets of War: Lockheed Martin and the Making of the Military–Industrial Complex*. New York: Nation Books.

Harvey, David (1990a) 'Critical Theory'. *Sociological Perspectives*. 33(1).

Harvey, David (1990b) *The Condition of Postmodernity*. Oxford: Wiley-Blackwell.

Hawkes, Terrence (1977) *Structuralism and Semiotics*. London: Methuen.

Heath, Andrew and Potter, Joseph (2006) *The Rebel Sell: Why the Culture Can't Be Jammed*. Chichester: Capstone.

Hebdige, Dick (1979) *Subculture: The Meaning of Style*. London: Methuen.

Heidegger, Martin (1964/1978) *Martin Heidegger: Basic Writings*. London: Routledge.

Hekman, Susan (1996) *Feminist Interpretations of Michel Foucault*. Philadelphia, PA: Pennsylvania University Press.

Higginbottom, Andy (2007) 'Killer Coke', in William Dinan and David Miller (eds) *Thinker, Faker, Spinner, Spy: Corporate PR and the Assault on Democracy*. London: Pluto.

Higgs, Robert (2007) 'The Trillion-Dollar Defense Budget is Already Here'. *Independent Institute*, 15 March. www.independent.org/newsroom/article.asp?id=1941, accessed 2010.

Hines, Susan and Sanger, Tam (eds) (2010) *Transgender Identities: Towards a Social Analysis of Gender Diversity*. London: Routledge.

Hoggart, Richard (1957/1958) *The Uses of Literacy*. Harmondsworth: Penguin.

hooks, bell (1990) 'Postmodern Blackness'. *Postmodern Culture*. 1(1).

Horkheimer, Max (1939/1982) 'Traditional and Critical Theory', in *Critical Theory: Selected Essays*. New York: Seabury Press.

Horney, Karen (1967) *Feminine Psychology*. New York: Norton.

Hutcheon, Linda (1988) *A Poetics of Postmodernism: History, Theory, Fiction*. London: Routledge.

Inglis, Fred (1993) *Cultural Studies*. Oxford: Blackwell.

Irigaray, Luce (1985) *Speculum of the Other Woman*. New York: Cornell University Press.

Jakobson, Roman (1957/1971) 'Shifters, Verbal Categories, and the Russian Verb', in *Selected Writings, Volume II: Word and Language*. The Hague: Mouton.

Jakobson, Roman (1960/1981) 'Linguistics and Poetics', in *Selected Writings, Volume III: Grammar of Poetry and Poetry of Grammar*. The Hague: Mouton.

Jameson, Fredric (1981) *The Political Unconscious: Narrative as a Socially Symbolic Act*. London: Methuen.

Jameson, Fredric (1984) 'Postmodernism, or, the Cultural Logic of Late Capitalism'. *New Left Review*. 146.

Jameson, Fredric (1985) 'Postmodernism and Consumer Society', in Hal Foster (ed.) *Postmodern Culture*. London: Pluto.

Jameson, Fredric (1988) 'Cognitive Mapping', in Cary Nelson and Lawrence Grossberg (eds) *Marxism and the Interpretation of Culture*. Champaign, IL: University of Illinois Press.

Jameson, Fredric (1990) *Signatures of the Visible*. London: Routledge.

Jameson, Fredric (1991a) *Postmodernism, or, the Cultural Logic of Late Capitalism*. London: Verso.

Jameson, Fredric (1991b) *Signatures of the Visible*. London: Routledge.

Jameson, Fredric (1992) *The Geopolitical Aesthetic: Cinema and Space in the World System*. London: British Film Institute.

Jameson, Fredric (2002) *A Singular Modernity*. London: Verso.

Jameson, Fredric (2005) *Archaeologies of the Future: The Desire Called Utopia and Other Science Fictions*. London: Verso.

Jameson, Fredric (2009) *Valences of the Dialectic*. London: Verso.

Jameson, Fredric (2010) *The Hegel Variations*. London: Verso.

Jameson, Fredric and Miyoshi, Masao (eds) (1998) *The Cultures of Globalization*. Durham: Duke University Press.

Jefferson, Ann and Robey, David (eds) (1982) *Modern Literary Theory: A Comparative Introduction*. London: Batsford Academic.

Jencks, Charles (1984) *The Language of Post-Modern Architecture*. New York: Rizzoli.

Jenkins, Keith (1991) *Re-thinking History: New Thoughts on an Old Discipline*. London: Routledge.

Jenkins, Keith (ed.) (1997) *The Postmodern History Reader*. London: Routledge.

Jenkins, Keith (2003) *Refiguring History*. London: Routledge.

Jenks, Chris (1993) *Culture*. London: Routledge.

Johnson, Barbara (1977) 'The Frame of Reference: Poe, Lacan, Derrida'. *Yale French Studies*. 55–56 on *Literature and Psychoanalysis. The Question of Reading: Otherwise.*

Jones, Steve (2006) *Antonio Gramsci*. London: Routledge.

Jordan, Glenn (2002) 'Whose Story is it? On the Multiple Births of Cultural Studies', in David Walton and Dagmar Scheu (eds) *Ac(unofficial)knowledging Cultural Studies in Spain*. Bern: Peter Lang.

Joyce, James (1922/1972) *Ulysses*. Harmondsworth: Penguin.

Kaplan, Anne (1983) *Women and Film: Both Sides of the Camera*. London: Routledge.

Kaye, Harvey J. and McClelland, Keith (eds) (1990) *E. P. Thompson: Critical Perspectives*. London: Palgrave.

Kellner, Douglas (ed.) (1989) *Postmodernism/Jameson/Critique*. Washington, DC: Maisonneuve Press.

Kelly, Michael (1994) *Critique and Power: Recasting the Foucault/Habermas Debate*. Cambriidge, MA: Massachusetts Institute of Technology.

Kitses, Jim (1970) *Horizons West: The Western from John Ford to Clint Eastwood*. London: BFI Publishing.

Klein, Naomi (2000) *No Logo: No Space No Choice No Jobs*. London: Flamingo.

Klein, Naomi (2002) *Fences and Windows: Dispatches from the Front Lines of the Globalization Debate*. London: Flamingo.

Klein, Naomi (2007) *The Shock Doctrine: The Rise of Disaster Capitalism*. London: Penguin.

Krieger, Murray (1979) *Poetic Presence and Illusion*. Baltimore, MD: Baltimore University Press.

Kristeva, Julia (1980). *Desire in Language: A Semiotic Approach to Literature and Art.* New York: Columbia University Press.

Kroker, Arthur and Cook, David (1986) *The Postmodern Scene: Excremental Culture and Hyper-Aesthetics*. New York: St. Martin's Press

Kroker, Arthur and Kroker, Marilouise (eds) (1988) *Body Invaders: Sexuality and the Postmodern Condition*. London: Macmillan.

Kutler, Stanley (ed.) (2009) *Watergate: A Brief History with Documents*. Oxford: Blackwell.

Lacan, Jacques (1966/1977) *Écrits: A Selection*. London: Tavistock.

Lacan, Jacques (1968) *The Language of the Self: The Function of Language in Psychoanalysis*. Baltimore, MD: Johns Hopkins University Press.

Lacan, Jacques (1973/1979) *Four Fundamental Concepts of Psychoanalysis*. London: Penguin.

Lacan, Jacques (1975/1988) *The Seminar of Jacques Lacan. Book 1: Freud's Papers on Technique 1953–1954*. New York: Norton.

Lacan, Jacques (1981/1993) *The Seminar of Jacques Lacan. Book III: The Psychoses, 1955–56*. London: Routledge.

Lacan, Jacques (1985) *Feminine Sexuality. Jacques Lacan and the École Freudienne*. New York: Norton.

Lacan, Jacques (1991/2007) *The Seminar of Jacques Lacan. Book XVII: The Other Side of Psychoanalysis*. New York: Norton.

Lacan, Jacques (2008) *Jacques Lacan: My Teaching*. London: Verso.

Laclau, Ernesto and Mouffe, Chantal (1985) *Hegemony and Socialist Strategy: Towards a Radical Democratic Politics*. London: Verso.

Laclau, Ernesto and Mouffe, Chantal (1987) *New Left Review*. I/166, November–December.

Laviosa, Sara (2005) 'Wordplay in Advertising: Form, Meaning and Function'. *Scripta Manent*. 1(1). www.sdutsj.edus.si/ScriptaManent/2005_1/Laviosa.pdf

Leavis, F. R. and Thompson, Denys (1933/1977) *Culture and Environment: The Training of Critical Awareness*. Westport, CT: Greenwood Press.

Leavis, Q. D. (1932/1974) *Fiction and the Reading Public*. New York: Folcroft.

Ledbetter, James (2011) *Unwarranted Influence: Dwight D. Eisenhower and the Military Industrial Complex*. New Haven, CT: Yale University Press.

Lesley, Stuart (1994) *The Cold War and American Science: The Military–Industria–Academic Complex at MIT and Stanford*. New York: Columbia University Press.

Lévi-Strauss, Claude (1963/1974) 'The Structural Study of Myth', in *Structural Anthropology*. London: Basic Books.

Lévi-Strauss, Claude (1970) *The Raw and the Cooked*. London: Jonathan Cape.

Lévi-Strauss, Claude and Jacobson, Roman (1962) 'Les Chats de Charles Baudelaire'. *L'Homme*, 2.

Lorenz, Chris (2006) 'Will the Universities Survive the European Integration? Higher Education Policies in the EU and in the Netherlands Before and After the Bologna Declaration'. *Sociologia Internationalis*. 44.

Lule, Jack (1995) 'Enduring Image of War: Myth and Ideology in a *Newsweek* Cover'. *Journal of Popular Culture*. Summer 95, 29(1).

Lyotard, Jean-François (1984) *The Postmodern Condition: A Report on Knowledge*. Minneapolis, MN: University of Minneapolis Press.

Lyotard, Jean-François (1985) *Just Gaming*. Minnesota, MN: University of Minnesota Press.

Lyotard, Jean-François and Thébaud, Jean-Loup (1988) *The Differend: Phrases in Dispute*. Minnesota, MN: University of Minnesota Press.

Lyotard, Jean-François et al. (1985) *Immaterialität und Postmoderne*. Berlin: Merve.

MacKinnon, Kenneth (ed.) (1992) *The Politics of Popular Representation: Reagan, Thatcher, AIDS, and the Movies*. London: Associated University Presses.

Macherey, Pierre (1978) *A Theory of Literary Production*. London: Routledge.

Mandel, Ernest (1978) *Late Capitalism*. London: Verso.

Marx, Karl (1845/1976) 'Theses on Feuerbach', in *Ludwig Feuerbach and the End of Classical German Philosophy*. Peking: Foreign Languages Press.

Marx, Karl and Engels, Friedrich (1846/1970) *The German Ideology*. London: Lawrence & Wishart.

McColl, Gina (2006) 'Caught in a Jam'. *Business Review Weekly*. 28(45).

McHale, Brian (1987) *Postmodernist Fiction*. London: Routledge.

McHale, Brian (1992) *Constructing Postmodernism*. London: Routledge.

McKay, George (ed.) (1998) *DiY Culture: Party and Protest in Nineties Britain*. London: Verso.

McRobbie, Angela (1978) in Women's Study Group, Centre for Contemporary Cultural Studies, University of Birmingham, *Women Take Issue: Aspects of Women's Subordination*. London: Hutchinson.

McRobbie, Angela (1994) *Postmodernism and Popular Culture*. London: Routledge.

McRobbie, Angela (2005) *The Uses of Cultural Studies*. London: SAGE.

McSpotlight (2010) http//:mcSpotlight.org

Merquior, José Guilherme (1985) *Foucault*. London: Fontana.

Mill, John Stuart and Bentham, Jeremy (1987) *Utilitarianism and Other Essays*. Harmondsworth: Penguin.

Millett, Kate (1970) *Sexual Politics*. New York: Doubleday.

Milne, Seumus (2004, 2nd edn) *The Enemy Within: The Secret War Against the Miners*. London: Routledge.

Monbiot, George (2000) *Captive State: The Corporate Takeover of Britain*. London: Pan Books.

Montag, Warren (2003) *Loius Althusser*. London: Palgrave Macmillan.

Mookerjea, Sourayan, Szeman, Imre and Faurschou, Gail (eds) (2009) *Canadian Cultural Studies*. Durham, NC: Duke University Press.

Moore, Robert, B. (2005) 'Racism in the English Language', in Jodi O'Brien and Peter Kollock (eds) *The Production of Reality: Essays and Readings on Social Interaction*. Newbury Park, CA: Pine Forge Press.

Moores, Shaun (1993): *Interpreting Audiences: The Ethnography of Media Consumption.* London: SAGE.

Morley, David (1992): *Television, Audiences and Cultural Studies.* London: Routledge.

Morley, David and Chen Kuan-Hsing (eds) (1996) *Stuart Hall: Critical Dialogues in Cultural Studies.* London: Routledge.

Mulhern, Francis (1979) *The Moment of Scrutiny.* London: New Left Books.

Mulvey, Laura (1975) 'Visual Pleasure and Narrative Cinema'. *Screen* 16(3)

Mulvey, Laura (1989) *Visual and Other Pleasures.* Bloomington, IN: Indiana University Press.

Munns, Jessica and Rajan, Gita (eds) (1995) *A Cultural Studies Reader: History, Theory, Practice.* London: Longman.

Murdock, Graham and Golding, Peter (1977) 'Capitalism, Communication and Class Relations', in James Curran, Michael Gurevitch and Janet Woollacott (eds) *Mass Communication and Society.* London: Edward Arnold.

Natural Resources Defence Council, The (2010) www.nrdc.org/water/drinking/nbw.asp

Newlands, Tracey and Frith, Stephen (eds) (1996) *Innocent Advertising? Corporate Sponsorship in Australian Schools.* Sydney: University of New South Wales.

Newton, Esther (1972) *Mother Camp: Female Impersonators in America.* Chicago: University of Chicago Press.

Nicholson, Linda, J. (ed.) (1990) *Feminism/Postmodernism.* London: Routledge.

Norris, Christopher (1992) *Uncritical Theory: Postmodern Intellectuals and the Gulf War.* London: Lawrence & Wishart.

Ortner, Sherry B. (1972/1995), 'Is Female to Male as Nature is to Culture?', in Jessica Munns and Gita Rajan (eds) *A Cultural Studies Reader: History, Theory, Practice.* London: Longman.

Owen, Sue (ed.) (2007) 'Richard Hoggart and the *International Journal of Cultural Studies* – 10 years on'. *International Journal of Cultural Studies.* 10(1).

Owen, Sue (ed.) (2008) *Richard Hoggart and Cultural Studies.* London: Palgrave.

Pavelec, Sterling Michael (2010) *The Military–Industrial Complex and American Society.* Santa Barbara, CA: ABC-CLIO.

Peirce, Charles (1894/1988) 'What is a Sign?', in *The Essential Peirce. Selected Philosophical Writings* (Vol. 2). Bloomington, IN: Indiana University Press.

Phillips, Peter and Roth, Andrew (2008) *Censored 2009: The Top Censored Stories of 2007–08.* New York: Seven Stories Press.

Plato (c. 370 BC/1973) *Phaedrus and Letters VII and VIII.* Harmondsworth: Penguin.

Popper, Karl (1963) *Conjectures and Refutations: The Growth of Scientific Knowledge.* London: Routledge.

Preciado, Beatriz (2002) *Manifiesto Contra-Sexual: Prácticas Subversivas de Identidad Sexual.* Madrid: Opera Prima.

Preciado, Beatriz (2008) *Testo Yonqui.* Madrid: Espasa.

Propp, Vladimir (1968) *Morphology of the Folk Tale.* Austin, TX: University of Texas.

Pugh, Jonathan (2009) *What is Radical Politics Today?* Palgrave Macmillan.

Pursell, Carroll (1973) *Military–Industrial Complex: A Reader.* London: Harper.

Ramsey, Danielle (1999) 'Feminism and Psychoanalyis', in Sarah Gamble (ed.) *The Routledge Companion to Feminism and Postfeminism.* London: Routledge.

Rancière, Jacques (1974) *La Leçon d'Althusser.* Paris: Gallimard.

Rice, Philip and Waugh, Patricia (eds) (1972) *Modern Literary Theory a Reader.* London: Edward Arnold.

Rodrik, Dani (1992) 'The Limits of Trade Policy Reform in the Developing Countries'. *Journal of Economic Perspectives.* 6(1).

Rose, Gillian (1978) *The Melancholy Silence: An Introduction to the Thought of Theodor Adorno*. London: Macmillan.

Ross, Andrew (1988) *Universal Abandon? The Politics of Postmodernism*. Minneapolis, MN: University of Minnesota Press.

Rubin, Gayle (1975) 'The Traffic in Women: Notes on the "Political Economy" of Sex', in Rayna R. Reiter (ed.) *Toward an Antropology of Women*. New York: Monthly Review Press.

Salinger, J. D. (1969) *The Catcher in the Rye*. Harmondsworth: Penguin.

Sapir, Edward (1929/1958) 'The Status of Linguistics as a Science', *Culture, Language and Personality*, ed. D. G. Mandelbaum. Berkeley, CA: University of California Press

Sardar, Ziauddin (1998) *Postmodernism and the Other: The New Imperialism of Western Culture*. London: Pluto.

Sarto, Ana del, Rios, Alicia and Trigo, Abril (eds) (2004) *The Latin American Cultural Studies Reader*. Durham, NC: Duke University Press.

Sarup, Madan (1993, 3rd edn) *An Introductory Guide to Poststructuralism and Postmodernism*. London: Harvester Wheatsheaf.

Saussure, Ferdinand de (1916/1959). *Course in General Linguistics*, ed. Charles Bally and Albert Sechehaye, in collaboration with Albert Reidlinger; trans. Wade Baskin. New York: McGraw-Hill.

Saussure, Ferdinand de (1916/1983) *Course in General Linguistics*, ed. Charles Bally and Albert Sechehaye, in collaboration with Albert Riedlinger; translated and annotated by Roy Harris. London: Duckworth.

Saussure, Ferdinand de (2006) *Writings in General Linguistics*. Oxford: Oxford University Press.

Schwarz, Bill (2005) 'Stuart Hall'. *Cultural Studies*. 19(2).

Scoop (2007) 'Exxon Proposes Burning Humanity for Fuel'. www.scoop.co.nz/stories/W00706/S00281.htm

Searle, John (1977) 'Reiterating the Differences: A Reply to Derrida'. *Glyph*. 1.

Silverman, Kaja (1983) *The Subject of Semiotics*. Oxford: Oxford University Press.

Sim, Stuart (ed.) (1995) *The AZ Guide to Modern Literary and Cultural Theorists*. London: Prentice Hall.

Slater, Phil (1977) *Origin and Significance of the Frankfurt School: A Marxist Perspective*. London: Routledge.

Smith, James (2005) *Jacques Derrida: Live Theory*. London: Continuum.

Smith, Richard (2010) *The Baudrillard Dictionary*. Edinburgh: Edinburgh University Press.

Spivak, Gayatri Chakravorty (1985/1996) 'Subaltern Studies: Deconstructing Historiography', in Donna Landry and Gerald MacLean (eds) *The Spivak Reader*. London: Routledge.

Spivak, Gayatri Chakravorty (1990) *Postcolonial Critic: Interviews, Strategies, Dialogues*. London: Routledge.

Spivak, Gayatri Chakravorty (1999) *A Critique of Postcolonial Reason: Toward a History of the Vanishing Present*. Cambridge, MA: Harvard University Press.

Stam, Robert (2000) *Film Theory*. Oxford: Blackwell.

Stavrakakis, Yannis (2007) *The Lacanian Left: Psychoanalysis, Theory, Politics*. Edinburgh: Edinburgh University Press.

Steiner, Peter (1984) *Russian Formalism: A Metapoetics*. Ithaca, NY: Cornell University Press.

Storey, John (2009a, 5th edn) *Cultural Theory and Popular Culture: An Introduction*. Harlow: Pearson Prentice Hall.

Storey, John (2009b, 4th edn) *Cultural Theory and Popular Culture: A Reader*. Harlow: Pearson Prentice Hall.

Strinati, Dominic (1995) *An Introduction to Theories of Popular Culture*. London: Routledge.

Stryker, Susan and Whittle, Stephen (eds) (2006) *The Transgender Studies Reader*. London: Routledge.

Thompson, E. P. (1963/1968) *The Making of the English Working Class*. London: Penguin.

Thompson, E. P. (1978/1995) *The Poverty of Theory*. London: Merlin.

Todorov, Tzvetan (1977) *The Poetics of Prose*. Oxford: Blackwell.

Tolman, Edward C. (1948) 'Cognitive Maps in Rats and Men'. *Psychological Review*. 55(4).

Tudor, Andrew (1999) *Decoding Culture*. London: SAGE.

Turner, Graeme (1992) 'It Works for Me: British Cultural Studies, Australian Cultural Studies, Australian Film', in Lawrence Grossberg, Cary Nelson and Paula Treichler (eds) *Cultural Studies*. London: Routledge.

Turner, Graeme (2003, 3rd edn) *British Cultural Studies: An Introduction*. London: Routledge.

Turner, Graeme (2011) *What's Become of Cultural Studies?* London: SAGE.

Tylor, Edward Burnett (1871/1958) *Primitive Culture: Researches into the Development of Mythology, Philosophy, Religion, Art and Custom*. Gloucester, MA: Smith.

van Dijck, José (2010) 'Search Engines and the Production of Academic Knowledge'. *International Journal of Cultural Studies*. November, 13.

Vattimo, Gianni (1985/1988) *The End of Modernity: Nihilism and Hermeneutics in Post-Modern Culture*. London: Polity Press.

Venturi, Robert (1966) *Complexity and Contradiction in Architecture*. New York: Museum of Modern Art.

Virilio, Paul (2005) *The Information Bomb*. London: Verso.

Virilio, Paul (2006, 2nd edn) *Speed and Politics*. Cambridge, MA: MIT Press.

Virilio, Paul (2009) *The Aesthetics of Disappearance*. Cambridge, MA: MIT Press.

Waites, Bernard, Bennett, Tony and Martin, Graham (eds) (1982) *Popular Culture: Past and Present*. London: Croom Helm/Open University Press.

Walton, Dav(o)id (1998) 'Theme-antics and the the-eerie Class: CrWitticism in wRap'. *Miscelánea: A Journal of English and American Studies*. 19. www.miscelaneajournal.net/images/stories/articulos/vol19/walton19.pdf

Walton, David (2008) *Introducing Cultural Studies: Learning Through Practice*. London: Sage.

War on Want (2010) *Coca-Cola: The Alternative Report*. www.waronwant.org/attachments/Coca-Cola%20-%20The%20Alternative%20Report.pdf

Warhol, Andy (1975/2007) *The Philosophy of Andy Warhol*. London: Penguin.

Webster, Richard (2005) *Why Freud Was Wrong: Sin, Science and Psychoanalysis*. London: The Orwell Press.

Weedon, Chris (1997) *Feminist Practice and Poststructuralist Theory*. Oxford: Blackwell.

Weeks, Jeffrey (1989) *Sex, Politics and Society: The Regulation of Sexuality since 1800*. London: Longman.

West, Cornel (1988) 'Black Postmodernist Practices', in John Storey (ed.) (2009) *Cultural Theory and Popular Culture: A Reader*. Harlow: Pearson.

White, Hayden (1973) *Metahistory: The Historical Imagination in Nineteenth-Century Europe*. Baltimore, MD: John Hopkins University Press.

White, Hayden (1978) *Tropics of Discourse: Essays in Cultural Criticism*. Baltimore, MD: Johns Hopkins University Press.

White, Hayden (1999) *Figural Realism: Studies in the Mimesis Effect*. Baltimore: Johns Hopkins UniversityPress.

Williams, Patrick and Chrisman, Laura (eds) (1993) *Colonial Discourse and Post-Colonial Theory: A Reader*. London: Harvester Wheatsheaf.

Williams, Raymond (1958/1987) *Culture and Society: Coleridge to Orwell*. London: Hogarth.

Williams, Raymond (1961/1992) *The Long Revolution*. London: Hogarth.

Williams, Raymond (1974) *Television: Technology and Cultural Form*. London: Fontana.

Williams, Raymond (1980) *Problems in Materialism and Culture*. London: Verso.

Williams, Raymond (1981) *Culture*. London: Fontana.

Williams, Raymond (1983a, rev. edn) *Keywords: A Vocabulary of Culture and Society*. London: Flamingo.

Williams, Raymond (1983b) *Writing in Society*. London: Verso.

Williamson, Judith (1978) *Decoding Advertisements: Ideology and Meaning in Advertising*. London: Marion Boyars.

Wimsatt, William and Beardsley, Monroe (1946) 'The Intentional Fallacy'. *Sewanee Review*. 54.

Winer, Stan (2007) *Between the Lies: Rise of the Media–Military–Industrial Complex*. Carbondale, IL: Southern Universities Press.

Wittgenstein, Ludwig (1958) *Philosophical Investigations*. Oxford: Blackwell.

Wittig, Monique (1981) 'One is Not Born a Woman'. *Feminist Issues*. 1(2).

Wolin, Richard (1991) *The Heidegger Controversy: A Critical Reader*. Cambridge, MA: MIT.

Woodward, Bob (2005) *The Secret Man: The Story of Watergate's Deep Throat*. London: Simon & Schuster.

Wright, Will (1975) *Six Guns and Society*. Berkeley, CA: University of California Press.

Yes Men, The (2004) *The True Story of the End of the World Trade Organization*. New York: Disinformation.

Young, Robert (1990) *White Mythologies: Writing History and the West*. London: Routledge.

Žižek, Slavoj (1991) *Looking Awry: An Introduction to Jacques Lacan Through Popular Culture*. Cambridge, MA MIT Press.

Žižek, Slavoj (1992) *Enjoy Your Symptom: Jacques Lacan in Hollywood and Out*. London: Routledge.

Žižek, Slavoj (1997) *The Plague of Fantasies*. Verso: London.

Žižek, Slavoj (1997/2005) 'With or Without Passion. What's Wrong with Fundamentalism, Part 1'. www.lacan.com/zizpassion.htm

Žižek, Slavoj (1998) 'The Interpassive Subject'. *Traverses*. www.lacan.com/zizek-pompidou.htm

Žižek, Slavoj (2002) *Welcome to the Desert of the Real*. London: Verso.

Žižek, Slavoj (2009a) *Violence: Six Sideways Reflections*. London: Profile.

Žižek, Slavoj (2009b) *First as Tragedy, Then as Farce*. London: Verso.

Žižek, Slavoj (2010) *Living in the End Times*. London: Verso.

Index